Introduction to Computers and Data Processing

Introduction to Computers and Data Processing

HARRY KATZAN, JR.
Pratt Institute

D. VAN NOSTRAND COMPANY
New York   Cincinnati   Toronto
London   Melbourne

D. Van Nostrand Company Regional Offices:
New York   Cincinnati

D. Van Nostrand Company International Offices:
London   Toronto   Melbourne

Published by D. Van Nostrand Company
135 West 50th Street, New York, N.Y. 10020

10   9   8   7   6   5   4   3   2   1

PREFACE

Data processing is no longer simply one among many varied and diverse computer applications. It is a discipline in its own right with concepts, techniques, and applications. As such it enables the boundaries of the field to be established and permits a greater degree of concentration by students, teachers, and computer professionals.

Computer people have learned that they cannot function in a vacuum. An effective data-processing professional must be responsive to the needs of users and society. Businesses and other organizations, both public and private, must also be responsive to social needs. The book, therefore, includes information on computers and society, privacy and confidentiality, and computer security.

The objective of *Introduction to Computers and Data Processing* is to survey the concepts, techniques, and applications of data processing. The subject matter is divided into six parts: Introduction, Hardware, Programming, Computer Software, Systems and Applications, and Topics in Data Processing. Essential aspects of data processing are covered—basic concepts, computer networks, micrographics and automated offices. Topics such as computer auditing and data-base concepts are also covered, not only because they are popular but also because they are important to those engaged in computer data processing.

The book is designed as a text for undergraduate Introductory Data Processing or Computer Science courses offered by Data Processing, Computer Science, Management, and General Business departments. An accompanying Instructor's Manual is available containing instructional objectives, suggestions for presentation of the material, and examination questions.

It is a pleasure to acknowledge the assistance of Mr. Robert J. Gargagliano and Mr. Thomas L. Gibson, and of Professors Donald Davidson, La Guardia Community College; Jack Harpool, the University of Akron; Charles Williams, Georgia State University; Edward Cross, Old Dominion University; Meyer Grumet, Baruch College; and Frank Rand, New York City Community College. I am also indebted to my wife, Margaret, who helped in the preparation of the manuscript and was a constant companion throughout the project.

CONTENTS

Part

1

Introduction

1

Introduction to Information Systems, Data Processing, and Computer Applications

ESSENTIAL CONCEPTS

A Look at Data
Not Just Data—Reality
The Concept of Information
Data Processing
Information Systems

CHARACTERISTICS OF COMPUTERS

Flexibility
Speed
Accuracy
Reliability
Capacity
Expandability
Cost Efficiency

INFORMATIONAL NEEDS OF MODERN ORGANIZATIONS

Accuracy
Timeliness
Completeness
Conciseness
Relevancy
Availability

GENERAL SURVEY OF MAJOR COMPUTER APPLICATION AREAS

Data Processing
Problem Solving
Models and Simulation
Feedback and Control Systems
On-Line and Real-Time Systems
Information Systems
Artificial Intelligence

ith the increased complexity of modern society, most organizations have had to go to computers to handle the large amount of information necessary to sustain everyday operations and to satisfy legal requirements. While individual views regarding computers may vary widely, one can be confident in knowing that the widespread use of computers is here to stay. In fact, the computer industry has enjoyed a high rate of growth, and this growth is predicted to continue into the foreseeable future. It is also true that the upward trend is not reversible in modern society as we now know it. Recent legislation, for example, states that in many areas of the chemical industry and in related fields, an employer is legally required to store, along with an employee's personnel information, that employee's exposure to various chemical agents. It is possible for legislators to pass such a law because they know that businesses are capable of maintaining this information by using established computerized data processing techniques. Thus, computers are currently part of the evolution of modern society and the growth of business enterprise.

This book is designed for those people who will be involved with the management, creation, or utilization of computer-based information systems.

ESSENTIAL CONCEPTS

Data processing and information systems go hand-in-hand—even though they are not the same thing. An understanding of both concepts requires a general familiarity with the notions of data and of information.

A Look at Data

When humans wish to record the occurrence of an event or recall a characteristic of something, they conveniently deal with symbolic representations of those entities. Similarly, when a scientist or analyst, for example, wishes to record values, such as a temperature or a sales volume, numbers are simply recorded. These numbers are *data*. Not all data are numeric. An accountant may record an important date and a salesperson may record an important customer's name or address. Data that are not numeric are said to be "descriptive." In general the recorded form of the symbolic representation of an entity is regarded as an item of data.

Normally when an item of data is inscribed on a computer input medium, such as a punched card or magnetic tape, it is not transformed in any way—simply recorded. If someone were to look at an item of

FIGURE 1.1   **An item of data that could mean different things to different people.**

data without knowing what it referred to, its meaning would not be readily available. Figure 1.1 gives an example of an item of data that could mean different things to different people. Clearly, data exists in many places and in many forms. Before it can be used by a computer, it must first have been placed on a medium that a computer can read, or it must have been entered into the computer system through a data entry device.

Not Just Data—Reality.   A well-known computer advertisement reads something like the following: "Not just data. Reality." The implication is powerful, indeed, because the prime objective of a computer system is not solely to replace routine clerical tasks—although this is certainly an important consideration in business. An equally important function of the computer is to provide insight into the processes of problem solving, decision making, and data analysis. Insight requires information, and this fact relates to another important aspect of computer utilization. The computer can be used to store large amounts of data and make it available to a user at a moment's notice. Most computer applications involve a combination of computational, data management, and information storage and retrieval operations.

The Concept of Information

In the computer field, ideas about the nature of information are numerous. One computer expert states, "Information is the communication or reception of knowledge or intelligence." Another writes, "Information is the content or meaning of a message." Still another specialist has stated that, "Information is organized knowledge recorded in accessible medium, such as the printed characters on a page." What is needed obviously, is an operational definition of information.

Figure 1.2 presents a basic model of an information system. The components of the basic model are the input, the processing, and the output. Collectively, the three components are intended to demonstrate that *information* is processed data, and it is the element of computer processing that gives meaning to data.

Data Processing

Based on the above definitions of data and information, data processing is the manipulation of data and its transformation into information. Data has to be manipulated to support the record-keeping activities of organizations. Some typical record-keeping activities are:

1. Creation, addition, deletion, updating, and storage of employee records
2. Maintenance of inventory data
3. Storage of payroll transactions and calculation of pay data
4. Storage and updating of sales figures

During data manipulation, input data are matched against previously stored data, and the stored data are updated accordingly. This process is depicted in Figure 1.3. The input data are known as *transactions;* the stored data are known as *files.* (The term file is analogous to the "file of records" in an office.) A sample transaction might involve the updating of an employee record in a personnel file to reflect a change in marital status or in the number of dependents.

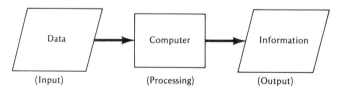

FIGURE 1.2   Basic model of an information system.

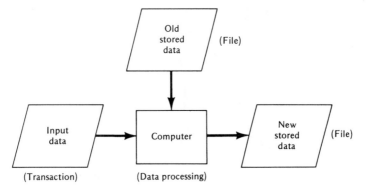

FIGURE 1.3   Conceptual model of data manipulation. (Input data—that is, transactions—are matched against previously stored data, which are updated accordingly.)

Data have to be transformed to support the reporting activities of an organization. Some typical reports would be:

1. Inventory reports
2. Sets of employee paychecks
3. Pay registers or government reports
4. Sales commission lists

During data transformation, stored data are organized into a required format and presented in a form accessible to people. This process is depicted in Figure 1.4. In some data processing applications, data manipulation and transformation are combined into one comprehensive process as suggested by Figure 1.5. In the combined case, input to the data processing application is a set of transactions and also the reporting requirements. This arrangement permits the desired report to be gener-

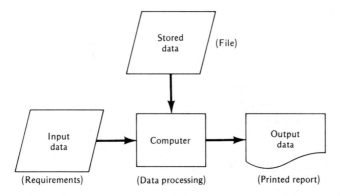

FIGURE 1.4   Conceptual model of data transformation. (Input data give the specifications of a printed report, which is generated as a result of computer processing.)

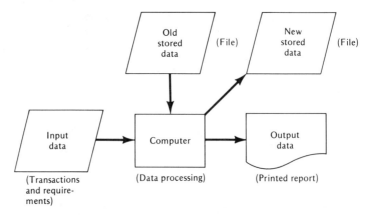

FIGURE 1.5   **Combined set of data processing operations. (Data processing and reporting are combined in a practice known as *process grouping*.)**

ated during the data manipulation process, thereby eliminating the need for running a special program and making a separate pass over the data file just to obtain the report. In data processing, the practice of combining two or more programs in this way is known as *process grouping*.

The computer is a tractable machine so that the methods of data processing are usually determined by the needs of a particular organization.

Information Systems

As computer systems became more widely used, it was soon obvious that they could be used to store large amounts of data, and through advanced techniques, the data could be made available to a person at a moment's notice. In addition to data processing, therefore, the computer could readily be used for management control, planning, and decision making.

In the modern view of data processing, the informational needs of an organization are satisfied with a computer-based information system. The traditional functions in data processing are provided by the information system, and the data processing techniques contained therein are used to provide other informational services. Data processing is important because it provides the needed technology for computer-based information systems.

CHARACTERISTICS OF COMPUTERS

Computers are now part of everyday life. In addition to their use in information systems, computers are utilized in sports, art, and poetry.

They can be found in automobiles, hospitals, and homes—to name only a few places. There are distinctive characteristics that enable computers to be used for such a variety of applications.

Flexibility

One of the most significant characteristics of modern computers is that they are flexible. In the context of data processing, this means that a general-purpose computer can be used to perform a wide range of jobs and is not limited to performing a specific organizational activity, such as credit card billing. Thus, if an analyst can define a task to be performed by a computer, then the computer can be programmed to perform that task. The concept of a computer program is covered later; for now, it is sufficient to know that a computer program is a set of instructions that controls the execution of a computer system during each step of a data processing application, such as payroll or inventory control. Programming a computer to perform a task is analogous to teaching a person to do something.

Speed

In a computer, an instruction commands the computer to perform a discrete function—such as to add two values or to move an item of information from one place in the computer to another. Modern computers can execute many thousands of instructions in a single second, and they are thus able to perform tasks that were beyond the scope of human imagination before the advent of computers. The high speed of computers permits jobs to be done that could not be done otherwise because of the time factor involved.

Accuracy

"One rotten apple spoils the barrel." If one incorrect calculation is detected in a series of computations, then there is good reason to suspect that the whole series of computations is possibly inaccurate. This was the problem facing computer designers before error detection and error correction features were invented. A modern computer contains special circuits that monitor its operation and the internal movement of data. Certain types of errors can be detected so that when malfunction of this type is recognized during normal processing, a "danger signal" is raised. Other types of errors can be automatically detected and corrected by the computer. Most modern computer systems contain extensive error detection and correction facilities making them very accurate and suitable for data processing operations.

Reliability

On the surface, it might seem that accuracy could be equated with reliability. Not so. Reliability refers to the capacity of a system to continue with normal data processing operations in spite of hardware malfunctions that cause individual components to fail. Through advanced methods of computer organization, the computer can continue to operate and produce needed information in spite of individual component failure.

Capacity

The capacity of a computer system is not only measured by its internal computing speed. Another measure of capacity is the amount of data that can be stored in an accessible form in a mass storage unit that is external to the computer and the speed required to transfer data between the computer and that mass storage unit. In modern computers, millions of characters of data can be stored off line—the term used to indicate that the storage unit is outside the computer. When necessary, this data can be transferred between the off-line mass storage device and the computer at speeds up to 2.5 million characters per second.

Expandability

Modern computer systems can and do grow. Hardware units are modularized so that when additional capability is required, an additional unit—such as a card reader, printer, or mass storage unit—can be acquired and integrated into the total computer system. Expandability is achieved through a "standard interface" that permits units from different manufacturers to be integrated in a single computer system.

Cost Efficiency

In conventional, manual record processing, the economics of the process is determined on a "cost per record" basis. As the number of records is increased, the cost per record processed increases due to worker fatigue, increased handling requirements based on the volume, and additional storage needs. In a computerized data processing environment, the cost per record processed decreases as the number of records is increased. The initial investment in computer equipment and programs is high relative to manual data processing, but the inherent capacity of computer equipment is normally much higher.

This phenomenon—increased workload causing decreased costs—also occurs when new data processing applications are added. With manual systems, the average cost per application increases as the number of data processing applications increases because of increased organizational requirements—that is, more workers must be hired or the present staff must spend more time on each record. With computer data processing, the initial overhead is high, but additional data processing applications can be added at a decreased rate per application.

The concept demonstrated by the two examples is "economics of scale" as depicted in Figure 1.6. This is one of the essential characteristics of computer data processing.

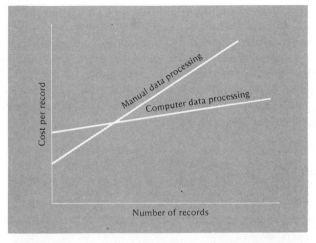

For one data processing application

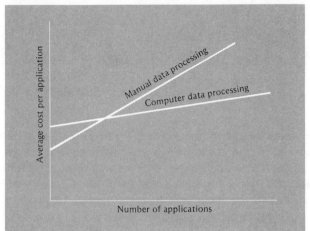

For many data processing applications

FIGURE 1.6   **Use of a computer for data processing allows an organization to benefit from "economies of scale."**

INFORMATIONAL NEEDS OF MODERN ORGANIZATIONS

In the not too distant past, the automobile replaced the horse as the primary means of transportation in modern society. Most economic analysts will agree that the shift has been economic and not functional, even though the automobile does supply a capability and a convenience far beyond that ever imagined with the horse. The initial expense of acquiring a horse and the maintenance costs of using one, and possibly the need for a spare horse, simply could not compete with the cost of a mass-produced automobile. As a result, people shifted to the automobile, so that in today's world the horse is not even considered a viable means of transportation in most countries. The decision to switch from manual record-keeping to computer data processing, on the other hand, is not as easy to make. Computer costs are high, and in most organizations several important factors are regarded as economic variables in the justification of a computer system. Six of the most important of these factors are accuracy, timeliness, completeness, conciseness, relevancy, and availability. Clearly, the factors correspond closely to the characteristics of computers, and it is obvious why the most widespread use of computers is for data processing. Data processing together with computer-based information systems also represent one of the fastest growing applications of computers.

Accuracy

Accuracy refers to the percentage of correct information in an information system. In systems or applications that handle financial information, such as:

Banking—for example, checking account statements
Payroll—a person's paycheck
Accounts receivable—credit card billings
Accounts payable—refund checks
General ledger—an organization's financial statement

an accuracy of 100% must be maintained so that the user will have confidence in the data. Briefly stated, most individuals simply will not tolerate any sort of an error in matters that relate to their personal finances, and most business people will not tolerate any sort of error that relates to the business's financial record keeping. In other areas, such as planning, forecasting, and inventory control, small errors may be tolerated, but significant errors often result in a loss of credibility.

Computer equipment malfunctions infrequently, and most computer errors are detected by the hardware itself. Therefore, more inaccuracies of data are the result of human errors, which can be eliminated through more careful attention to the interplay of the computer and human resources.

Timeliness

In journalism yesterday's events are usually without news value. The same philosophy holds true, to some extent, in computer-based systems. The value of information, as depicted in Figure 1.7, is a function of its age, so that a sales report, for example, is useful to a sale's manager only if it is available within a reasonable period of time. In manual data processing, many kinds of reports that can be developed through routine clerical procedures are not used because the reports cannot be prepared in time to be useful. Computerized data processing is extremely useful because the lead time to obtain information is considerably diminished.

Computer-based information systems also enable people to query the computer for specific items of information. A salesperson, for example, in quoting a delivery date to a sales prospect, may need to dial into the computer via telecommunications facilities to determine product availability. This kind of "quick response" information is routinely provided with modern data processing systems.

Completeness

Some managers prefer to have all the information available on a situation so they can make the best decision possible in light of the most recent data. Although this need relates to timeliness, covered above, it additionally refers to the concept of "completeness." A report is complete if it provides at one time all the information necessary for

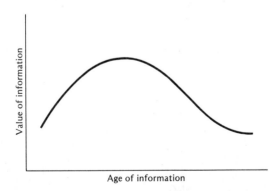

FIGURE 1.7   **The value of information is a function of its age. Before data is processed and reported it is less valuable than afterwards. After some time, processed information gradually loses its value.**

making a decision. With computer data processing, the notion of completeness is usually taken for granted. With manual data processing, completeness is a state that is usually strived for.

Conciseness

If an organization generally runs smoothly, managers and administrators take special action only under special circumstances. This action is frequently triggered by an exception report. Conciseness commonly refers to "reporting by exception," which is analogous to "management by exception."

One advantage of computer data processing is that large amounts of information can be examined for evidence of situations that require special notice, and that evidence is summarized in an exception report. Inventory systems that use computerized reports for reordering provide an example. When the inventory level of a particular item goes below a fixed amount, then that item is placed on the "reorder report." Subsequently, if shipment is not received within a specified time period, the same item may be placed on a "late shipment report." In the supplier's organization an inventory item that is not available for shipment may be placed on an exception report known as the "back order list."

Conciseness also refers to the computer's ability to perform data analysis and manipulation for planning, forecasting, and management control.

Relevancy

Relevancy refers to the ability of the computer to provide the information that is desired without making the user wade through a lot of irrelevant and unnecessary material. Through the use of the logical capabilities of modern digital computers, the computer can be programmed to select, summarize, and report only that information that is needed. The concept of relevancy also pertains to the kinds of information an organization needs to know, and it relates to the broader social issues of privacy and confidentiality.

Availability

One of the most urgent requirements of private and public organizations is to have necessary information available when it is needed. While this need seems to relate to timeliness, it is more basic than that. Simply stated, availability refers to the ratio of the time an information system is available for use to the total working time of an organization. An availability of .95, for example, means that the computer is up and performing productive work 95% of the time. Even though normal production delays occur in a computer facility just as in any other process, a high availability indicates that information is likely to be available when needed.

Except in rare circumstances due to organization and staffing problems, computer equipment is noteworthy for its high level of availability. Moreover, the high level of availability is fairly constant throughout the computer industry.

GENERAL SURVEY OF MAJOR COMPUTER APPLICATION AREAS*

Organizations such as businesses, governmental agencies, and schools are the primary users of computers. Most computers are fairly expensive, and computer people are reasonably well paid. The computer applications necessary to justify these expenses are varied and substantial. This section contains a general survey of the various computer applications grouped into the following categories: data processing, problem solving, modeling and simulation, feedback and control systems, on-line and real-time systems, information systems, and artificial intelligence. Some applications are presently more useful to society than others. Data processing, for example, is more useful to more organizations than is artificial intelligence. On the other hand, artificial intelligence is academically more productive than is data processing. In the following paragraphs no emphasis is placed on the relative importance of the various areas, which is a matter of individual judgment.

One final note is necessary. Complete comprehension of the following descriptions of the various computer applications is not required. Only a general familiarity is needed; however, this familiarity goes a long way in helping to make the study of data processing relevant and interesting. It is a good practice to constantly try to relate the methodology of data processing to the types of applications given here.

Data Processing

Data processing involves the storage, processing, and reporting of information. Although data processing is definitely related to the record-keeping activities of an organization, it is not restricted to those activities and usually encompasses many clerical and time-consuming functions.

One of the more useful applications of data processing is customer billing in firms like utility companies. Each customer has a customer file with a record of his or her name, address, billing rate, credit status, cumulative usage, previous meter reading, and service category. Each

* This section can be skipped without a loss of continuity.

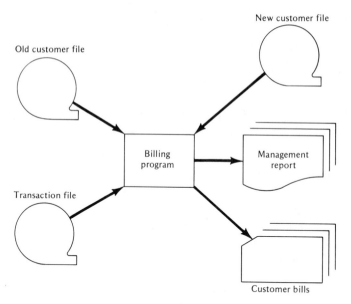

FIGURE 1.8   Typical data processing application—a billing program.

month the customer's meter is read by a meter reader, and the current use is recorded. Subsequently, each customer's reading is keypunched, and each customer's use of electricity is reflected on a single card. To the data processing program, each of these cards is referred to as a *transaction.* At the end of the billing period all transaction cards are placed on magnetic tape and sorted by customer's account number, since it would be inefficient to run the program separately for each customer. This is referred to as *batching.** The billing program can now be run using the "old" customer file and the transaction tape as input, as depicted in Figure 1.8. The program processes the customer file and the transaction tape sequentially, and a bill for each customer is computed. Output from the billing program is a "new" customer file containing "updated" records, a set of customer bills, and a report that summarizes the processing that was performed. The "old" customer file and the transaction tape are saved for emergency purposes. The "new" customer file will be used in the next month's run of the billing program.

Data processing often combines several operations—such as, transaction processing, record keeping, bill preparation, and management reporting—and almost always involves at least the following input and output files: old master file, transaction file, new master file, and

---

* The term *batch* is also used with operating systems technology, wherein a set of jobs to be run on the computer is collected on an input medium. This is covered later.

report file. Other common data processing applications are accounts receivable, accounts payable, inventory control, and payroll. In fact, any high-volume operation that must be performed on a periodic basis lends itself to data processing methods. The input operation may vary in data processing; for example, check processing in a bank involves a magnetic ink character reader, and inventory processing in many department stores requires special merchandise ticket readers.

Problem Solving

The earliest use of computers took place in the areas of scientific and engineering problem solving. This was a normal consequence of the fact that computers were invented and developed by scientifically trained people who were keenly interested in the computational processes of the computer. The concern for data management and the problems of business and government came later.

Currently, problem solving activities with the aid of the computer are not restricted to science and engineering and now encompass business, education, and many other disciplines, such as architecture, medicine, and the humanities. In some cases, applications that fall in this category do not actually involve solving a problem but rather performing a task that lends itself to computers, such as the calculation of a space trajectory or the statistical analysis of a set of data values.

A typical engineering problem would be the computation of design parameters for a bridge or a road. Important here is the time factor and the accuracy level. Obviously, engineers have designed and constructed bridges and roads for centuries without the use of computers. With the use of computers, however, the computations can be performed in a very short period of time, allowing different design alternatives to be evaluated. Contrary to the opinion held by some people, computers are extremely accurate. Most modern computers include error checking circuitry to detect errors that occur during computation. The need for an engineering aid to check calculations is not usually necessary after construction has begun. It is important to note that any inaccuracies that do occur are normally the result of human error.

A problem that falls into this category characteristically involves a small amount of input, a relatively large number of calculations during processing, and a small number of results in output. Problems range from simple calculations to complex iterative procedures. A simple problem might be the calculation of compound interest as described by the formula:

$$V = P\left(1 + \frac{r}{n}\right)^n$$

where

P is the principal
r is the interest rate per time period
n is the number of time periods
V is the value of P after n time periods

Similar calculations might be to compute the yield of a bond issue or the predicted size of a herd of cattle after a given number of years.

Another common example might be the calculation of the roots of a quadratic equation of the form:

$$ax^2 + bx + c = 0$$

The roots r of this equation can be computed using the quadratic formula:

$$r = \frac{-b \pm \sqrt{b^2 - 4ac}}{2a}$$

Although these examples may represent trivial applications of the computer, they demonstrate cases where the use of a mathematical concept can be made more practical with the aid of an appropriate computer program.

The quadratic formula was given in the preceding paragraph for computing the roots of a quadratic equation. Not all equations of which we wish to find the root have well-defined solutions. Figure 1.9 de-

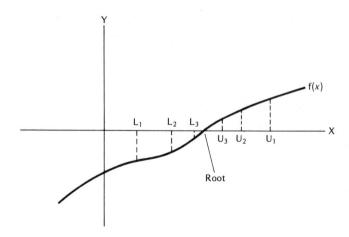

FIGURE 1.9   The iterative method of interval bisection can be used to calculate the root of an equation.

picts an equation that is assumed not to have a well-defined solution. The root of an equation of this type requires an iterative solution known as *interval bisection*. The root of the equation is given by the point at which the equation $f(x)$ intersects the x axis. The method of solution successively halves the interval while ensuring that $f(L_i)$ and $f(U_i)$ have different signs until a solution with the desired accuracy is reached.

Problems in this category vary in scope and magnitude. Computer programs are used to calculate the trajectory of a space vehicle from an earth orbit to a moon orbit; in this case there is considerable output for very little input. Data analysis programs, such as those used with the U.S. census, generate a relatively small amount of output in the form of summarized data in response to a tremendous amount of input. In fact, computer programs have been written for practically any type of problem for which a solution is known. Programs have been used to calculate the exact ingredients of sausage and to prepare an index for a book. Most of us have even received mail addressed by computer and letters written by computer.

The dividing line between data processing and problem solving is a fine one. Data processing is characterized by periodic computer runs involving large amounts of data. Problem solving is characterized by nonperiodic runs and a predominance of machine computation. As it turns out, there is no defining characteristic for either category.

Models and Simulation

A model is defined as an abstraction of a real-life situation that can be used to draw conclusions or make predictions about the future. In a sense, a model is a duplication of a system or subsystem, often with an emphasis on certain aspects that are of interest to those who create the model. Once a model is developed, it is usually more convenient to manipulate the model than to work with the actual system. Typical examples of models are road maps and aerodynamic models used in wind tunnels.

Models are classified as iconic, analog, and symbolic. An *iconic model* physically resembles the system it represents; examples are aerodynamic models, globes of the world, photographs, and blueprints. An *analog model* establishes a correspondence between a system, subsystem, or variable of a system and an analogous variable in the model; examples are bar charts in sales graphs, schematics, and electrical analogs. A *symbolic model* uses logic, mathematics, and empirical generalizations (that is, laws of nature) to establish a set of assumptions about a real-life phenomenon, from which conclusions can be deduced. Symbolic models are frequently referred to as *mathematical models*, which are the kind used in computer applications.

A familiar mathematical model describes the fall of an object in a vacuum. This law of nature, proposed by Galileo, gives the relationship between distance fallen d and time t as follows:

$$d = 16t^2$$

If an object is dropped from a height of 10 feet, it can be concluded from the model that after 0.5 second, the object will have fallen 4 feet, or be 6 feet from the ground.

When models are constructed, the determination of the element of the system that needs to be abstracted—or modeled—is of prime importance. Once a model is developed, its validity becomes of immediate concern. In short, it is necessary to know how well the model represents the system being studied.

Simulation is the use of models to attain the essence of a system without having to develop and test it. One of the most familiar forms of simulation is the "trainer" used to train pilots and astronauts. The objective of such devices is to give the participant experience in a realistic operational environment. A *computer simulation* is a computer model of a real situation; a computer model uses mathematical models, as discussed above, and computational procedures to achieve a realistic description of a system.

Typical computer simulations involve the description and flow of traffic in a major city, the number of check-out counters needed in a supermarket, and the design specifications of a digital computer. Computer simulation is widely used because many processes or systems cannot be described by mathematical equations. However, these same processes or systems can be described with flow diagrams, and a computer program can be written to simulate them. Running the program with various input values is analogous to the operation of the real system. Thus, a system can be analyzed without having to experiment with real-life situations. Traffic flow in a city is a reasonably good example. Before the possibility of computer simulation, traffic commissions would establish one-way streets on a trial basis. After a period of time, the change would be evaluated. In the event of a poor design, people have to suffer during the period in which it is being evaluated. With a computer the traffic flow can be simulated; when a good design is achieved, then the physical implementation can be made.

Feedback and Control Systems

The terms *feedback* and *control* are almost self-explanatory. The most common example of a feedback and control system is the combination of automobile and driver. The output of the system is the path of the automobile; the driver provides the objective of the system and receives "road information" as input. The driver provides control signals to the automobile as required. Another common example of a feedback and control system is the heating system found in most homes. The thermostat serves as the control mechanism. The output of the system is the heat produced by the furnace. The automobile-driver system is an *open system* because of the driver in the feedback loop. The heating system is a *closed system* because it can operate without human intervention.

In computer control systems, the computer serves as the control mechanism. A typical application might be the control of temperature, among other things, in a chemical process. The chemical processing equipment contains sensing devices that send signals to an analog-to-digital converter, which serves as an input device to the computer. The computer is programmed to sample the input signals on a periodic basis and compare the values against prescribed limits. If the temperature is too high or too low, the computer generates appropriate output signals to achieve the desired result. The output signal is converted to analog form and serves as input to a control mechanism that is part of the chemical process. The above process is shown in Figure 1.10. In actual applications, the monitoring of hundreds of input signals is not unusual. This application of computers is referred to as *process control;* the technology is widely used in applications that range from control of space vehicles to control of a sewage disposal plant.

Computers are also used in manufacturing processes through a concept known as *numerical control.* Using conventional machining techniques, the production of a precision part is a time-consuming and costly process. Moreover, successive pieces produced by the same machinist vary in precision, within given tolerance limits, due to human

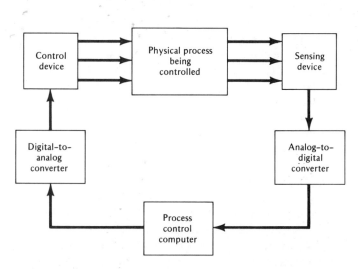

FIGURE 1.10   Feedback and control system using a digital computer as a control mechanism.

limitations. When using numerical control, a machinist/mathematician, known as a part programmer, describes the piece to be machined in a computer-oriented language. The description of the piece in that language is known as part program. The machine tool used to machine the part is directed by a control system that accepts signals from the computer and guides the machine tool accordingly. There are two modes of operation. In the on-line mode, the computer is connected directly to the control system. In the off-line mode, a punched tape is produced by the computer, and the tape is read by the control system to guide the machine tool.

On-Line and Real-Time Systems

An on-line system is one in which the computer communicates directly with a component external to the computer—regardless of whether that component is a person using a terminal device via telecommunications facilities or is a control system of an independent physical process. The term *real time* refers to two things. In simulation, there is the time of the problem (that is, the time in the system being modeled), and there is the clock time in which the computer executes the simulation program. The clock time is known as real time. The second kind of real time occurs in physical processes or on-line systems in which it is necessary for the computer to respond within time limits in order for the results to be useful in the real world.

Two common examples of on-line, real-time systems are the airline reservations system and the savings bank system. In an airline reservations system a central computer records passenger reservation information for scheduled flights. When a customer requests space accommodations, the central computer is queried via a specially built terminal device and telecommunications facilities to determine if the requested facilities are available. If the customer makes a reservation, the amount of remaining available space on the aircraft is reduced and the customer's data are recorded. In a system of this type, the requirements are such that the computer must respond within a specified period (for example, 10 seconds or less) in order to ensure customer satisfaction. Flight records, which change dynamically as reservations are made and cancelled, must be stored on mass storage devices in order to meet the real-time requirements of the application.

In a savings bank system, customer records are stored on main storage devices at a central computer. Teller stations (that is, input/output terminal devices) are located in each branch of the bank. As deposits, withdrawals, and other transactions are made, each transaction is recorded in the customer's records at the time of transaction. As a result, banking facilities are available at all times to all customers at all bank branches.

Information Systems

An information system is a set of hardware, software, and informational facilities that permits the accumulation, classification, storage, and retrieval of large amounts of information. An information system not only stores data but also provides facilities for assigning meaning to data and, hence, for providing information. The scope and complexity of information systems vary from a deck of punched cards to comprehensive library retrieval systems.

An information system consists of three major components:

1. A large repository for data—called a data base
2. A means of accessing data
3. A means of processing the data for analysis and reports

A *data base* is a collection of physical data that are related to each other in a prescribed manner. For example, a data base may be the total collection of data known to be in a business, or it may be a central record of all known criminals in a major city. The key point is that all pertinent data is available through a central facility and that access to the facility provides the latest up-to-date information.

The manner in which data are organized in an information system is dependent upon the needs of the computer applications that use the system. For example, an information system may contain documents that are retrieved by author, title, or key words; or it may contain customer data (for a data processing application) that are accessed sequentially or by account number.

Information systems are frequently accessed by people who are not computer professionals. Sometimes a query language is used so that an informational request of the form:

IN FILE ALPHA-3
IF AGE > 30 AND MALE AND MARRIED
LIST NAME, ADDRESS, EMPLOYEE-NO, YEARS-OF-SERVICE

is entered to retrieve information from the system. Usually, an input request with this general form is interpreted by a special computer program written for that purpose. The program scans the input lines, determines the information required, retrieves the information, and displays it for the user. This is an example of the current trend in information systems. An experienced group of systems analysts and programmers develops a system and a language that can be used by nonprofessional people. The language is frequently made up to suit the needs of a particular application. The implications, of course, are far-reaching: once a system is developed, practically anyone can use it with ease.

Artificial Intelligence

The question, "Can a machine think?" is one that has been debated for some time now and is not likely to be answered in this book. However, the subject is fruitful from the point of view of "what the computer can do."

There are various opinions on the subject. Some say that thinking is an activity that is peculiar to human beings; therefore, machines cannot think. Although thought as something unique to humans may have been in the minds of philosophers when they first considered the subject of thinking and intelligence, this definition does not really define the activity. Others maintain that a machine is thinking when it is performing activities that normally require thought when performed by human beings. Thus, adding 2 and 2 must be considered a form of thinking. To continue, some psychologists have defined intelligence in the following simple way: intelligence is what an intelligence test measures. In light of the preceding section on information systems, all that needs to be done is to feed enough information into an information system and to develop an appropriate query language, and the result is an intelligent machine. This line of reasoning also skirts a clear definition. Perhaps it is a waste of time to worry about precise definitions, but the fact remains that computers are doing some amazing things—such as playing chess, guiding robots, controlling space vehicles, recognizing patterns, proving theorems, and answering questions—and that these applications require much more than the conventional computer program. Richard Hamming,[1] developer of the Hamming code for error detection and correction in computers, gives a definition of intelligent behavior that may be useful here:

> The ability to act in suitable ways when presented with a class of situations that have not been exhaustively analyzed in advance, but which require rather different combinations of responses if the result in many specific cases is to be acceptable.

This is an important subject because it may indicate the direction in which society is moving. Currently, machines are used for two reasons: (1) the job cannot be done by a human being, and (2) the job can be done more economically by machine. To this list, another reason must be added: some jobs are simply too dull to be done by humans, and it is desirable from a social point of view to have such jobs done by machine. This requires a greater number of "intelligent" machines, since people seem to be finding more and more work they consider to be dull and routine.

1. R. W. Hamming, *Computers and Society* (New York: McGraw-Hill, 1972), p. 267.

Vocabulary   The student should be familiar with the following terms in the context in which they were used in the chapter.

accuracy	information system
artificial intelligence	input media
availability	intelligent behavior
capacity	model
completeness	on-line system
conciseness	problem solving
data	process grouping
data entry devices	real time system
data processing	relevancy
economies of scale	reliability
expandability	simulation
feedback and control system	speed
file	timeliness
flexibility	transaction
information	

Questions   1. Why is the current trend toward increased dependence on computers not reversible in modern society?

2. How is data normally distinguished from information?

3. In what way is the term *transaction* related to conventional business activity?

4. What is the probable origin of the term *file?*

5. In what way are computers being used to improve our "quality of life?" (Hint: review the section on artificial intelligence.)

Exercises   1. Name as many areas as you can in modern society for which extensive record keeping or government reporting are required.

2. Describe several data entry devices that you encounter in everyday life.

3. A number punched in an IBM card is data; a bank check is information. What is the difference and why is this so?

4. Discuss manual data processing and computerized data processing according to the following characteristics: flexibility, speed, accuracy, reliability, capacity, expandability, and economics.

5. Compare the automobile and horse according to the following characteristics: original cost, repair parts, maintenance, operating cost, and replacement. Apply the same method of analysis to manual and computerized data processing.

Related Reading

Cole, R. W. *Introduction to Computing.* New York: McGraw-Hill, 1969.

Dorf, R. C. *Introduction to Computers and Computer Science.* San Francisco: Boyd and Fraser, 1972.

Feigenbaum, E. A. and J. Feldman, eds. *Computers and Thought.* New York: McGraw-Hill, 1963.

Feldzamen, A. N. *The Intelligent Man's Easy Guide to Computers.* New York: David McKay, 1971.

Hamming, R. W. *Computers and Society.* New York: McGraw-Hill, 1972.

Katzan, H. *Information Technology: The Human Use of Computers.* New York: Petrocelli/Charter, 1974.

Sanders, D. H. *Computers in Society.* New York: McGraw-Hill, 1973.

Squire, E. *The Computer: An Everyday Machine.* Reading, Mass.: Addison-Wesley, 1972.

Evolutionary Development of Data Processing Systems—Past and Present

nderstanding computers is like understanding many aspects of the physical universe. On the surface an event or a physical entity may appear to be too complex to describe or understand. Once the event or entity is broken down into its component parts and basic laws or principles are applied, the complete system becomes understandable and is frequently manageable as well. The same kind of approach can be taken to understand computers and computer applications.

The following key point must be emphasized: *As in the case of the automobile and the airplane, a person need not be capable of designing and building a computer in order to realize and use its capabilities.* A working knowledge of the functional components of a computer is all that is needed to integrate a computer effectively as a component in an overall business or scientific information system or to utilize a computer in a problem solving activity.

One of the major difficulties in learning a new subject is determining what is going on in that area in today's world. Thus, a small dose of computer history is in order, followed by a brief survey of the evolutionary development of data processing. Some organizations are on the leading edge of technological developments in data processing, while others are just beginning. Most organizations are somewhere in between.

IN THE BEGINNING . . .

The processing of information is present in almost every activity of our lives and takes place whenever two or more persons or pieces of equipment interact. Throughout history, many devices have been developed to aid in this information (or data) processing. One of the first aids was the notched stick, which served as an aid to counting and remembering. The first machine was the abacus developed by the Romans in ancient times. A more popular version, the Chinese abacus, was developed in the 12th century and is still used in China today.

The next major advance in computing machines was the slide rule, invented in 1621 by William Oughtred, an Englishman. Since that date, many improvements have been made to the slide rule for both general and special-purpose applications. Credit for the invention of the first adding machine in 1642 is given to Pascal, the famous French mathematician. This gear-toothed machine was followed in 1673 by a machine that performed multiplication by repeated additions; it was developed by the mathematican Leibnitz. The machines of Pascal and Leibnitz are the forerunners of modern desk calculators.

The modern era in computing began in 1804 when Joseph Marie Jacquard invented a loom in which the weaving operations were controlled by punched cards. The first automatic computer was designed by Charles Babbage in 1822; it could perform numerical calculations. The machine, called the automatic difference engine, was originally proposed by J. H. Mueller in 1786 and finally built in Sweden by George Scheutz in 1853. Another of Babbage's machines, the analytical engine, was designed in 1833 but was never built. It is the forerunner of today's stored program computers.

The punched card and related processing equipment were developed in the 1880s for use in the U.S. census. As it turned out, the development of the punched card became one of the most significant events in the widespread acceptance and use of data processing equipment.

The first automatic computer was completed by Harvard College and IBM in 1944. This machine, called the Mark I, was constructed from mechanical components and handled 23 decimal digit words. The inherent slowness of the Mark I resulted in the design and development of the first electronic computer, the ENIAC, at the Moore School of Engineering at the University of Pennsylvania in 1946. Modern computers are an outgrowth of this pioneering research of the middle 1940s.

Every advance in computing machines was associated with an actual need. Ancient cavemen and shepherds, for example, needed the notched stick to count their flocks. Similarly, the adding machine resulted from the need for tax computations in France; Babbage's computers were a response to a need for difference tables; and the Mark I and ENIAC were built largely because of needs for technological advances triggered by World War II.

The computer explosion, which we are now witnessing, is not simply the result of a new invention or a new technique—although a multiplicity of technological innovations have been made in the last 25 years in the computer field. Other factors have contributed to this widespread growth.

In fields of scientific computation, computers have played a major role in many significant advances, and as a result of these advances, computer use has snowballed. Examples of areas where this interdependence has occurred include missile guidance, simulation studies, and computer control systems—in addition to traditional scientific problem solving.

Computers play an equally important role in business and government, although for various reasons advances in these areas are usually not as glamorous as those in the scientific community. The volume of business and governmental data processing has grown enormously along with the growth in size of businesses and the expanding scope of government. The use of computers for diverse operations, such as check processing, has given rise to a variety of advanced input, output, and mass-storage devices. Many management problems created by geographical locations and distances are presently relieved through the use of telecommunications facilities that permit information to be transmitted between remote locations at electronic speeds. Here again, reasonable success in using the computer to reduce the volume of clerical operations has caused the use of computers to snowball. Another important factor in the growth of computer utilization is that people are now more adept at identifying computer applications and at applying the computer to those applications.

With computers it seems as though success breeds success. To summarize, the computer era is the result of three major advances:

1. Development of the punched card and card processing equipment
2. Development of the automatic electronic digital computer
3. Development and understanding of computer software
4. Development of telecommunications facilities for transmitting computer data between remote locations.

Each of these major advances utilizes its own technology and has contributed in its own way to the vigorous growth, at home and abroad, in the use of computer technology.

BASIC COMPUTER CONCEPTS

A computer can be conveniently viewed as a "numerical transformation machine," as depicted in Figure 2.1, even though, as discussed previ-

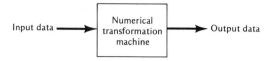

FIGURE 2.1   The computer can be viewed as a numerical transformation machine.

ously, data need not necessarily be numeric in computer data processing. The concept of computing, however, is presented through the use of numbers because most people are familiar with them. The process of computing involves three "basic" steps:

1. *Input,* whereby data on which the computer is to operate are entered into the machine
2. *Computing,* whereby the data are transformed to meet the needs of a given application
3. *Output,* whereby the results are made available for subsequent use

The notion of computing in this sense is certainly not new. For example, an ordinary mathematical operation, such as addition, uses a similar concept, shown as follows:

In general the computer can be viewed as a "black-box" type of device that performs a "well-defined" operation on the input data and that produces appropriate output data.

If the computer is to be viewed as a black box, then it must be capable of operating automatically without human intervention—at least between elementary operations such as addition or division. This is, in fact, the precise manner in which it does operate, and this serves to distinguish an automatic computer from a calculator.

A Useful Analogy

As a means of introducing computers, it is useful to outline the steps people follow when solving a computational problem with the aid of a pencil and paper, desk calculator, slide rule, or ordinary adding machine. Human calculators usually have a list of instructions they are to follow and a set of input data. The process by which the calculations are performed can be summarized as follows:

1. *Information is stored* by writing the list of instructions, as well as input data, on the piece of paper. During the course of performing the calculations, intermediate calculations are also written on the paper; however, people frequently keep some information in their heads while using charts and tables, and other information is held temporarily in the calculating device.
2. *Information is processed* by utilizing the computing device—that is, the slide rule, the desk calculator, or the adding machine—to perform the elementary calculations required by the computational process. Each operation is performed by taking data values from one place on the paper, performing the specified operation, and recording the result in a definite place elsewhere on the paper.
3. *The computational process is controlled* by the human calculator by referring to the list of instructions and by carrying each instruction out in a specified order. Each instruction is read, interpreted, and executed by the person performing the calculations, and the execution of an instruction is completed before the next is begun.

Although this is an oversimplified analogy to the functional structure of a computer, hardware components that correspond to the piece of paper and to human calculators and their computing devices actually exist; they are covered in the next section together with representative input and output devices.

Overview of a Computer System

The major hardware units in a computer system (see Figure 2.2) are main storage, the processing unit, and input/output devices. *Main storage*

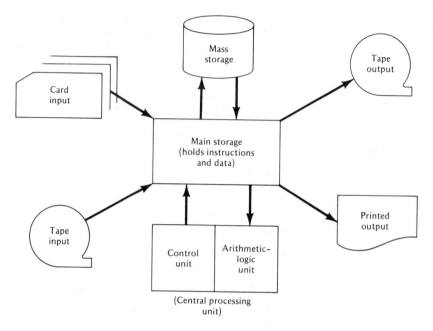

FIGURE 2.2   **Functional structure of a computer system (simplified).**

is analogous to the "piece of paper," mentioned in the previous section, and is used to hold computer instructions and data. The *central processing unit* is analogous to human calculators and their computing devices and consists of a control unit and an arithmetic/logic unit. The *control unit* is the means by which the computer can operate automatically. The control unit reads an instruction from main storage, decodes it, and sets up the circuitry necessary to have the instruction executed. When the execution of an instruction is completed, the control unit reads the next instruction and the preceding steps are repeated. The *arithmetic/logic unit* contains the circuitry necessary to perform the arithmetic and logical operations of the computer. The arithmetic/logic unit normally includes a limited amount of high-speed storage, called *registers,* for holding the values used during computer operations. Registers are analogous to the accumulator in a hand calculator or adding machine.

Input and output devices are necessarily related to a specific recording medium. The most frequently used input and output devices can be briefly summarized as follows:

1. *Card readers* and *card punches* are used to read punched cards and to punch cards, respectively.
2. *Magnetic* and *punched tape units* are used to read and write magnetic and punched tape, respectively. (Tape is used for both mass storage and conventional input and output.)

3. *Direct-access devices,* such as magnetic disk or drum, are used for mass storage and allow data to be accessed directly, without having to pass over preceding information as is the case with tape or card devices.

4. *Terminal devices* are used to communicate with the computer via telecommunications facilities. Terminal devices are usually similar to an ordinary typewriter or utilize a visual display along with a suitable keyboard.

To summarize briefly, computer systems contain: a processing unit for performing computer operations, a storage unit for holding instructions and data during computation, and input and output units for entering data into main storage so that it can be used by the processing unit and for taking data from main storage and placing it on a recording medium for future use. One of the most popular recording (output) media is the printed page, needed so that the output can be read by people. Two frequently used input media are the punched card and the computer terminal. Computer terminals are also used for low-volume computer output.

EVOLUTION OF DATA PROCESSING

Now that a few useful concepts and associated terminology have been established, it is possible to trace the evolution of data processing. Technologically, this evolution has taken place over time, with the more advanced topics obviously being developed later. A prospective user of data processing in today's world, however, may tap into the evolutionary cycle at any point. Thus, the history of data processing provides much more than a means of benefiting from past mistakes— as is frequently the case with history; it is a modern "snapshot" of available data processing technology.

Stage One—Unit Record Systems

As was mentioned previously, the modern era in data processing began with the invention of the punched card in the 1880s. The punched card serves as a convenient input and output medium. The printed page serves as an equally convenient output medium, since both the card and the page can be read by the human eye. Cards and the printed page are classed as *unit records*—a term that means that a unit of a particular media (such as punched cards) corresponds to a group of related data,—which is termed a record.

Punched Card Systems.   Punched card systems are characterized in two ways:

1. Punched cards serve as the storage medium.
2. There is manual intervention between the various steps in the processing cycle.

The characteristics of punched cards and printed output are covered later in a more general context. The manual intervention is suggested by Figure 2.3, which depicts a punched card billing system. Between each step in the process, represented in the diagram by a box with input and output arrows, a manual operation is required. Each operation is performed through the use of a card processing machine, hand wired to perform a specific function. Because of the inherent need for manual operations with punched card data processing systems, card processing machines are not generally regarded as computers. However, card processing machines were an important step in the evolution of computer technology.

There are several inefficiencies in punched card systems—even though they continue to be used in today's world in particular instances. First, the manual intervention between steps, such as to move cards from one machine to the next, is cumbersome and time consuming. Second, the cards are difficult to handle and store, especially in large volumes. Next, the wiring of a control panel to control the card machine is an ineffective means of implementing a data processing function. Finally, card-oriented machines are too slow to meet the needs of a modern society. Figure 2.4 gives drawings of some representative card processing machines.

Card processing machines were invented in the 1800s and gained widespread popularity in the 1930s. They are still used in many data processing departments. Their popularity has diminished considerably, however, because computer systems are more cost effective.

Card-Oriented Computers.   After the invention of the computer, as introduced earlier in this chapter, it became obvious that the various steps in a data processing cycle could be integrated into a computer program that would go from step-to-step without operator intervention. Moreover, instead of having to physically wire a control panel, methods were invented for conveniently programming a computer and subsequently loading the program into computer storage. The capability for storing data on magnetic tape also became available in this period, and it was no longer necessary to use cards as an intermediate storage medium between data processing steps. Data could be written to magnetic tape for both intermediate and long-term storage.

Card-oriented computers continue to be used in today's data pro-

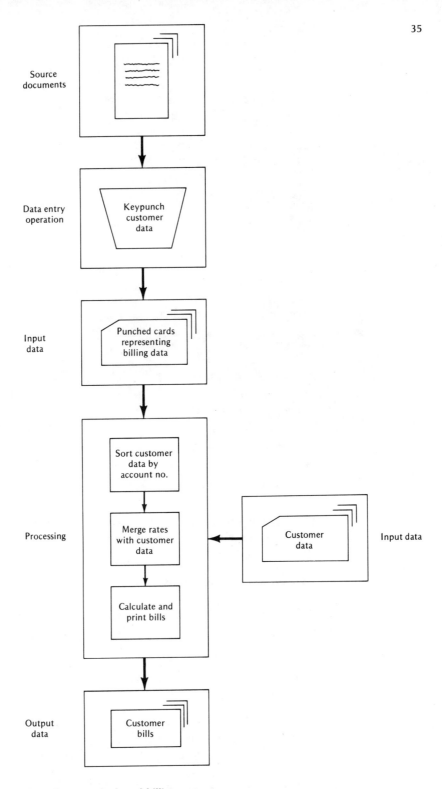

FIGURE 2.3   Steps in a punched card billing system.

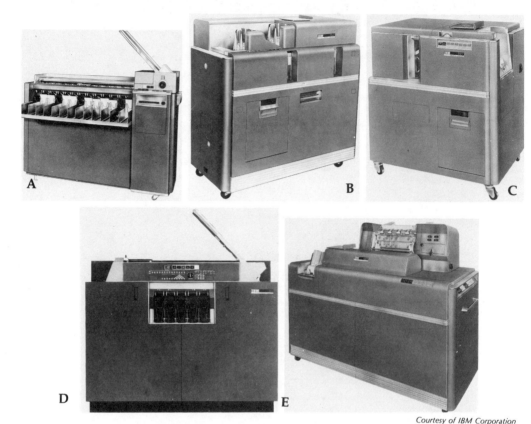

FIGURE 2.4   **Representative sample of card processing machines. A) sorter B) reproducer C) interpreter D) collator E) accounting machine.**

cessing world. The primary input of source documents is through cards, and the primary user output is the printed page.

Stage Two—Manual Operations

Through the use of a computer and an appropriate program, a complete application—such as accounts receivable or payroll—can be done in its entirety with a minimum of human intervention. The execution of a program of this type is normally referred to as a *job*. If a computer has executed 10 jobs, this usually means that 10 application programs were run on the computer.

Manual Setup.   Even though a job runs automatically and continuously on the computer until completion, a certain amount of manual activity is required between jobs, before and after the job is run:

1. Loading cards into the card reader
2. Mounting tape reels on the magnetic tape drive

3. Loading the program into the computer
4. Removing cards and tape reels
5. Gathering the printed output

These activities are referred to as *manual setup.*

In some organizations the end user actually runs the computer by performing manual setup and by using the dials, switches, and keyboard on the computer console. This method of operating a computer is used today by many small businesses with computers. In most organizations, however, full-time computer operators are employed.

Closed vs. Open Shop. In computer jargon an *open shop* means that any user can go in and operate the computer. A *closed shop* indicates that only computer operators employed by the data processing department can operate the computer. The concept of open vs. closed shop also applies, in some cases, to which personnel can program the computer. Practically all large computer installations use a closed shop; most users of small business computers use an open shop.

Time Scheduling. With manual setup and an open shop, computer time is scheduled through a sign-up procedure whereby a user group signs up for a block of time in advance. At the scheduled time, the personnel arrive on the scene with cards, tapes, and programs; however, because of normal delays, more often than not schedules are not accurate and a fair amount of inconvenience is frequently experienced. In general, this mode of operation is most appropriate with small business computers used for a specific set of applications.

With manual setup and a closed shop, a job is normally submitted by a user to the operations group that runs the totality of jobs submitted on a first-come-first-served or a priority basis.

Stage Three—Operating Systems

The disadvantages of manual setup are obvious. The manual intervention, or *setup time,* between jobs is extremely wasteful of computer time, since it involves loading the card reader, mounting tapes, setting switches, and readying programs for execution. The situation is depicted in Figure 2.5. For long-running jobs, the setup time is significant; however, the situation is worse for small jobs because the setup time and the execution time are not proportional. The obvious solution of increasing the speed of the computer does reduce "total elapsed time" but makes the idle time proportionally higher, since jobs are processed in a shorter time but setup time remains the same.

The Concept of an Operating System. The solution to the above problem is as obvious as the problem is. Have a computer program

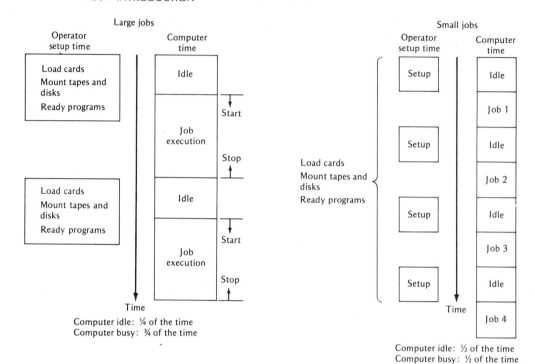

FIGURE 2.5   Relationship between idle and busy time for large and small jobs.

perform job scheduling and provide automatic job-to-job transition. A system of programs that schedules how the computer system is used and allows the computer to pass between the various jobs automatically without human intervention is known as an *operating system.* The end result is that the computer essentially runs itself; all the operators have to do is to get it started and tell it what they want done.

Batch Processing.   Devices that perform mechanical operations, such as reading cards or printing, operate at mechanical speeds that are much slower than computers that operate at electronic speeds. One method of speeding up the process is to use *batch processing,* which operates as follows:

1. A collection of jobs—called a *batch*—is assembled.
2. Using a small peripheral computer, the batch of jobs is put on magnetic tape. Magnetic tape input is faster than card input.
3. The main computer reads the input tape and places output on an output tape.
4. When the processing of the batch of jobs is completed, the output tape is printed using the same or another small peripheral computer.

Batch processing is depicted in Figure 2.6.

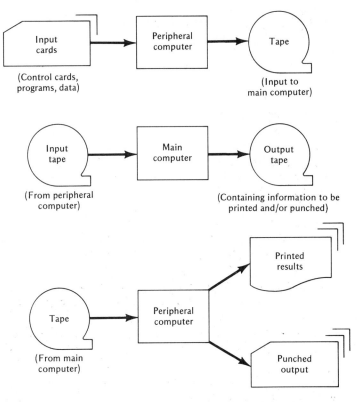

FIGURE 2.6   **The use of a peripheral computer in an early batch processing system.**

Multiprogramming.   Multiprogramming is a sophisticated name for a simple but very important concept to data processing. So far it has been established that in order to have the computer do something, there needs to be a program for that purpose. The program runs on the computer, and the work gets done. Computers are expensive, however, and computer people do not want to waste even a part of a second. When it is necessary to read information into the computer, the computer has to wait. That is where multiprogramming comes in.

Multiprogramming means that more than one job is in the computer at one time. When one job has to wait for some reason, another job is executed in the central processing unit so that valuable time is not wasted.

An example of the way a business could use multiprogramming might involve two applications—a payroll job and an on-line inventory system. The payroll program produces paychecks and reports in the usual fashion. The inventory system permits the user to interact with the computer via telecommunications facilities from a remote location. During normal operations, the data processing program would execute. However, if a user desired to interact with the inventory system, then the data processing program would be temporarily suspended until the remote user's query was satisfied. Through the use of multiprogramming, therefore, a data processing installation can provide various kinds of service to meet the diverse needs of an organization.

Stage Four—Advanced Systems

Through a variety of storage and terminal devices and advanced systems concepts, computers can presently communicate with each other and supply access to large amounts of data. Computer technology has evolved to the stage where it is relatively straightforward for an organization to synthesize complex systems of computers, information banks, and people.

Distributed Systems.   A distributed system is one in which the processing is parceled out to regional centers. A typical system is shown in Figure 2.7. Normal data processing is done at the regional centers during the day. Then in the evening, summary processing is performed,

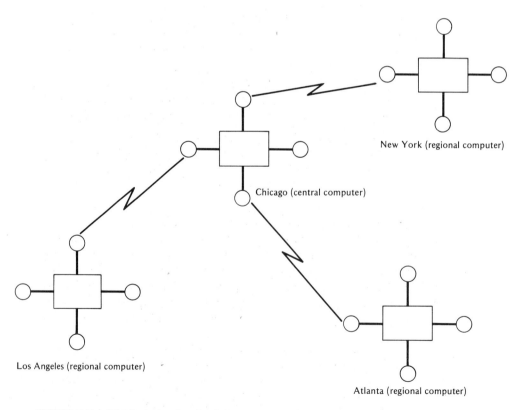

FIGURE 2.7   Distributed network of computers.

and the results are transmitted to the central computer. In this manner an organization has the advantage of both decentralized and centralized computer centers.

A related example is familiar to most people. In supermarkets and department stores there are relatively new cash registers that guide a

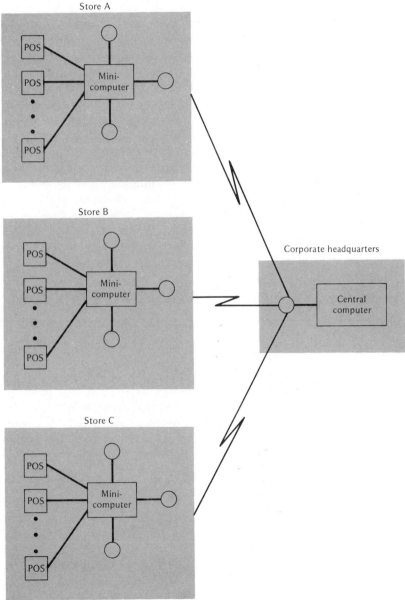

Legend: POS = Point of Sale Device

FIGURE 2.8   Distributed system for a retailing organization.

salesperson through a check-out and are called *point-of-sale devices,* or POS devices. A POS device contains a small computer that performs the sequencing of the check-out and records financial and inventory data. If it is a charge sale, the credit card data is also recorded. When the sale's check-out is complete, all information regarding that sale is sent to a minicomputer in the back of the store. Then, at the end of the day, all financial, inventory, and charge account data for the entire store are summarized and sent via telecommunications facilities to a central computer in a remote location. Thus, all ordering and billing is centralized for both management control and efficiency. This application is depicted in Figure 2.8.

Data Bases.   An integrated set of files for an organization is called a *data base.* The term *integrated* means simply that redundant data is eliminated. Consider, for example, two employee files: payroll and personnel. The common data include items such as name, address, and social security number. In a data base the payroll and personnel file would be combined in a logical manner so that the name, address, and social security number would be stored only once. An integrated set of files does not mean, however, that all information about an employee is automatically part of the output. Through advanced access techniques, confidential payroll data, for example, may be unavailable to personnel employees. In general, when data is integrated, an information system can provide access to a wide range of data and can find ways to relate various sets of data.

Data base technology is frequently combined with distributed processing systems and the use of telecommunications facilities. The end result is that managers and administrators have convenient access to complete organizational records for planning, forecasting, and making effective decisions.

The evolution of data processing is a direct result of new and advanced technology. This chapter has attempted to cover some of the technological advances—especially those directly related to data processing—but it definitely does not cover all of the advancing technology. Many other computer innovations that have led to advances in data processing are dealt with in subsequent chapters.

Vocabulary   The reader should be familiar with the following terms in the context in which they were used in the chapter.

arithmetic-logic unit	closed shop
batch processing	computing
card punch	control unit
card reader	data base
central processing unit	direct-access device

distributed system
input
job
magnetic tape unit
main storage
manual setup
multiprogramming
numerical transformation
open shop

operating system
output
point-of-sale device
punched tape unit
register
setup time
terminal device
unit record

Questions

1. What is the "defining characteristic" of a computer?
2. Where are instructions in a program held in a computer during the execution of the program?
3. What is the advantage of magnetic tape over punched cards as an input medium?
4. How and why do you imagine that operating procedures using manual setup time are tolerated for small business computers?
5. What is the connection, if any, between a computer application and a job?

Exercises

1. Choose a known computer application such as payroll or accounts receivable. List inputs, outputs, and processing steps.
2. List the ways that the execution of a program can go wrong when using manual operations.
3. Using the computer concepts presented in this chapter, develop a "human informations system," establishing a correspondence between electronic and biological components.
4. Develop a comprehensive list of everyday business activities that would not be possible without the use of a computer that can operate automatically.
5. With a large centralized computer facility, an organization can take advantage of economies of scale. Yet, there appears to be a movement toward smaller dispersed computers—termed *distributed systems.* Try to develop a list of reasons for this apparent "conflict of objectives."

Related Reading

Bernstein, J. *The Analytical Engine: Computers—Past, Present, and Future.* New York: Random House, 1963.

Brabb, G. J. *Computers and Information Systems in Business.* Boston: Houghton Mifflin, 1976.

Cotterman, W. W. *Computers in Perspective.* Belmont, Calif.: Wadsworth Publishing, 1974.

Haloren, M. O. *Computers and Their Societal Impact.* New York: John Wiley and Sons, 1977.

Katzan, H. *Operating Systems: A Pragmatic Approach.* New York: Van Nostrand Reinhold, 1973.

Sanderson, P. C. *Management Information Systems and the Computer.* London: Pan Books, 1975.

Data Processing, Computers, and Society

The most severe of data processing critics have said that the computer community exists in a vacuum without regard to or concern for people, organizational objectives, and management. Some people doubt that this situation ever existed, except perhaps in unique specialized organizations. Even so, the days of the "programming prima donna" or the "computer super person" are long gone. Nevertheless, it is important that data processing professionals as well as the business community are aware of the overall impact of data processing and computers on society. The objective of this chapter is to relate the computer to societal needs.

INTRODUCTION

In its broadest sense society is defined as the totality of social relationships among human beings. People participate in society as individuals and through organizations to which they belong. Organizations can accomplish tasks that are impossible for the individual to perform— in any time frame—and in an analogous fashion individuals can do things that are very cumbersome to accomplish in an organizational environment. Organizations depend upon people, and people depend upon organizations.

A similar situation exists with the computer. It can perform computational tasks that would be impossible for an individual or an organization to perform in a lifetime. As a simple example, it can compute the payroll more reliably, more accurately, and more economically than a multitude of payroll clerks. It has been said that information is power, but in spite of its power, the computer is dependent upon the organization and the individual for its very existence.

The fact that humans, as a society, have entered into a working relationship with the computer has serious implications. It means that the computer affects people's everyday lives, and if they are to benefit from this relationship, they must understand the partnership.

The Organization

This is a society dominated by organizations such as businesses, governmental agencies, schools, religious groups, hospitals, and various social organizations. Most people belong to more than one organization. An organization is a system; the resources of the system include people, capital, machines, and buildings. Thus, the resources of an organization are analogous to the components of a system. The various components of the system communicate through information.

Organizations are the primary users of computers. Historically, business has led the way in the use of computers because of the profit motive and because some businesses, such as banks and insurance companies, are essentially information processing organizations. Currently, most organizations, large or small, use computers. If an organization lacks qualified personnel or finances, it can now share common computing facilities with another organization or have its computing services performed by a computer service company. Many banks, for example, perform payroll services for their customers on a regular basis.

The advantages of computers to the organization are significant and are summarized as follows:

1. Additional information becomes available
2. Information can be made available more quickly
3. Information is more inclusive and accurate
4. Information can be presented in a form that is more useful to the decision maker or administrator

Other than problem-solving activities performed by scientists, engineers, and analysts and routine data processing, the greatest benefit of computers to organizations occurs in three areas: planning, decision making, and controlling. The precise techniques tend to vary between organizations but generally involve optimization, simulation, prediction, scheduling, and measurement of organizational performance.

When computers are used extensively in organizations, there seems to be a tendency toward centralization of authority. Centralization or decentralization is a matter of degree rather than an absolute concept. In organizations that employ decentralization as an operating technique, decisions are made by lower-level administrative or management personnel because of time, distance, and familiarity with the factors affecting the decision. Through the effective use of computer facilities, higher administrative and management personnel can participate in local decision making to a greater extent because they can be supplied with appropriate information in a shorter period of time.

The use of computers does not imply centralization, and the absence of computers does not imply decentralization. Other factors affecting the situation are the size of the organization, management philosophy, physical facilities, organization growth, and type of business the company is in. To sum up, the use of computers provides the practical means for centralization, regardless of whether or not an organization decides to go in that direction. However, the use of computers does require organizational changes in both structure and everyday operation. Changes normally occur in the following areas:

1. Departments engaged in data processing
2. Departments engaged in informational services
3. Service departments using computer services

4. Organization and training departments
5. The computer department itself
6. Higher administrative levels that support the computer function

The data processing department is and will continue to be a problem to most organizations, since operators, programmers, analysts, and capable managers are presently in short supply. On the other side of the coin, the data processing department is a good source of quality personnel for the organization. The perseverance necessary to become a good programmer is a valuable trait that is applied well to other organizational occupations. The typical systems analyst knows a great deal about an organization and is always a prime candidate for promotion into administrative or management positions. Data processing managers, because of their managerial and technical background, are frequently tapped for executive positions.

Another benefit of computers to organizations is standardization. In many cases the interface between departments is ill-defined, and the organization essentially operates through informal organizational procedures. Before a computer can be used in a system, that system is usually described in detail and subsequently formalized. Many organizations have benefited considerably from the process of studying how they actually operate. The standardization of reports and time schedules has also helped organizations realize the scope of information that is and can be made available to them.

The Individual

The use of computers has changed organizations to the extent that the lives of individuals, both in and out of those organizations, have been markedly influenced. The subject has been treated as an emotional issue by social scientists and journalists and has aroused the fears of society in general. The following quotations from William Rodgers' celebrated book about the founders of IBM, *Think: A biography of the Watsons and IBM,* demonstrate some modern points of view:

E. B. White, a serious humorist and essayist, wrote that he did not believe in computers very much, since the convenience they afforded some people was regarded as more important than the inconvenience they caused to all. 'In short,' he wrote in *The New York Times,* 'I don't think computers should wear the pants or make the decisions. They are deficient in humor . . . The men who feed them seem to believe that everything is made out of ponderables, which isn't the case. I read a poem once that a computer had written, but didn't care much for it. It seemed to me I could write a better one myself, if I put my mind to it.'

Tom Watson at IBM, like Howard Aiken, the designer of the original Mark I, has assured the world that the computer is no more than a tool, a view held by most people who profit by, or in, this field of technology. Others are certain that it is already something of a monster, corrupting values and causing distortion of viewpoints. Some fear it is an instrument that, by compiling a lifetime accumulation of details about each person's life, will doom human beings to a loss of privacy.[1]

Generally, fear of computers is diminished through knowledge of the subject matter. A certain amount of apprehension always accompanies a new technology: for example, the automobile was disliked because engines were noisy and dirty, and the telephone was initially regarded as an invasion of privacy. However, there are some valid concerns over the computer revolution, which many people feel they are now experiencing. Some of the key issues are:

1. *Automation and jobs:* Does automation eliminate job opportunities? What kind of jobs exist in a computerized society? Will organizational structure change with an increase in the use of computers? Will this become a society of specialists?
2. *Personal issues:* Are information systems destroying privacy? Is dehumanization a fact or a myth? Are people victims of computers or are computers victims of people? Can the confidentiality of information be ensured?
3. *The future:* What does the future hold in a computerized society? Will books still be used in the year 2000? What about leisure time? Specialization? Changing careers? Personal computers?

The computer is here to stay. Let there be no doubt about that. It has changed the way people look at the world to such an extent that they could never retreat back to an earlier way of life. Moreover, people have adapted to the pace of change so that they continually expect new and better products, increased productivity, more leisure time—items that the computer has helped to bring about. Like practically everything else in society, it is necessary to take the bad with the good. Perhaps the lack of privacy or depersonalized education systems, for example, are the price that must be paid for the benefits of computers. This and other topics are explored in this chapter.

BUSINESS

The biggest use of computers in business is in the areas of problem solving and data processing. Analysts, scientists, and engineers are able to use the computer for numerical calculations and have expanded

1. William Rodgers, *Think: A Biography of the Watsons and IBM* (New York: Stein and Day, 1969), pp. 291 and 294.

its functional capabilities to a considerable degree. Data processing is used for operations that involve routine logic and mathematics but require the same processing to be applied to a great many similar transactions. Utility billing, payroll, dividend checks, and inventory records are examples of areas that utilize data processing methods. In addition, many information-service companies use computers to provide immediate service to their customers. Service companies now exist, for example, that will verify the validity of a credit card. To verify a credit card, a business person makes a toll-free call to the service company, which verifies that the card is neither lost, stolen, nor expired. If the card turns out to be "bad," then the service company is held responsible for the charges. Without verification, the acceptance of a bad credit card becomes the responsibility of the business. Other services, called "information banks," store large amounts of information for use by customers on a demand basis via telecommunications facilities. Computer sevice companies are regarded as special cases, since their product is essentially the computer.

Management Information Systems

Businesses that limit their use of the computer to problem solving and data processing, however, tend to gain less from their computer than those that attempt to integrate the computer into the total business system. In other words, information systems should not be justified solely on the basis of cost-reduction grounds but also on the basis of how management can benefit from the increased information a computer system can provide.

Essentially, what is being described is a *management information system,* frequently referred to as an MIS. The objective of an MIS is to provide a means for the information of a business to be integrated and dynamically updated so that it can be used for planning, decision making, and control purposes. Conceptually, an MIS is an on-line, real-time information system consisting of the following components, facilities, or resources:

1. Centralized data base consisting of an integrated set (or subset) of company files
2. Comprehensive set of data on the company, its operating structure, and the competitive environment
3. Capability for retrieving data from the data base for analysis and reporting
4. Set of planning models for use in prediction and planning activities
5. Set of control models that can be used to monitor performance of the company

6. Set of decision models to be used for decision making, using the information in the data base

No one attribute or collection of attributes defines a management information system, which seems to be more a commitment to the concept of an integrated business system than a set of physical facilities.

Planning is the most widely developed area in which management information systems are used. Planning is known to exist at three organizational levels:

1. *Long-range planning* to develop organizational objectives, establish corporate goals, and set corporate policies
2. *Tactical planning* to make efficient use of resources such as money, machines, and personnel
3. *Operational planning* to develop alternatives for specific functions or products

The information necessary for planning is derived from competitive analysis, market research, and internal statistics, and from known operational characteristics of the company.

Long-range planning frequently involves the financial status of the organization and its relationship to the business environment. National economic forecasts and political information are frequently used at this level to establish a sound basis for decisions. Information is usually made available to executives in the form of reports.

Tactical planning is analogous to what is generally known as management control and utilizes feedback and control systems to determine how resources are acquired, organized, and employed. Exception reporting is frequently used.

Operational planning usually involves optimization and data analysis techniques to organize daily activities. Delivery schedules, trucking routes, and purchase orders are frequently developed by computer because of the number of independent variables involved.

Operational planning is closely related to *decision making,* which uses the computer to develop and evaluate alternatives. Statistics and simulation are frequently used for selecting courses of action for the business to follow at each of the above levels of planning.

Computers serve control purposes in businesses in two principal ways: (1) as a means of controlling how the company operates, such as in savings bank, credit, and inventory systems; and (2) as a means of measuring performance and alerting appropriate people to unusual conditions that need attention. Operation of an organization has been discussed previously. Performance measurement is usually achieved through periodic reports and specific informational requests. This is an area in which a management information system is invaluable. When information is needed for a decision at one of the planning levels, an analysis can be made from the central data base, often within hours when an on-line, real-time system is used.

Business Information and Control System

Systems that alert people to unusual conditions are still in their infancy but offer great potential for the future. The basic idea is this: a *business information and control system* is used, into which all planning, operational, environmental, and competitive data are entered and maintained on a continual basis, day-to-day or hour-to-hour. Routine decisions, such as when to reorder supplies or raw materials, are made by the computer and the departments involved are informed automatically. The computer essentially operates the business by keeping track of *all* information and by making routine decisions. Since the computer serves only a control function, the outward appearance of the business is the same. Many routine clerical jobs, such as ordering pencils, are eliminated, and the people are moved into information-gathering positions. Top management has more time to allocate to planning and less time is needed for day-to-day operations. Thus, humans are doing what they can do best—planning—and the computer is employed in its best capacity—routine operations. The use of this type of control system may be accompanied by a gradual shift in middle management from managing people to managing products and resources.

One of the key features in a business information and control system is that at any point in time, any item of information worth knowing about business is stored in the computer, and it can be accessed by authorized people.

GOVERNMENT AND LAW

One of the major functions of government is to meet the needs of society, whatever they are. Most governmental officials can attest to the fact, however, that it is impossible to please everyone. Problems are usually complex and require compromises. First, it is difficult to determine what programs are needed and to assess appropriate priorities. Second, it is difficult to determine what has been done. Third, frequently it is impossible to tell if a program is successful until it is past "the point of no return" in terms of finances and time. And last, it is difficult to manage a governmental agency that is characteristically understaffed and underfinanced. In the past, governmental officials frequently used the method of "incremental change" for decision making.

The *method of incremental change* involves making a small change in a given direction. If the reaction to it is favorable, then another small change in the same direction is made, and so forth. If the reaction to the incremental change is not favorable or if funds for the project "dry up," then it is relatively easy to back up and make an effort in a different direction. This description is overly simplified, but it illustrates an important point. Significant changes often extend over unreasonably long periods of time, which is frustrating to the populus and to the administrators themselves. The use of the computer in government has helped alleviate this problem somewhat.

Federal Government—Executive Branch

The single biggest user of computers in the United States is the federal government. The objective of most computers installed in the government is increased productivity through information systems. Information systems allow government planners to make better plans and decisions, to improve operating efficiency, and to better serve society. There are also some fringe benefits of computers in government. Computers are often regarded as capital expenditures by the government and are not charged to the budget of a particular agency. Thus, the administrator of that agency is given the capability of doing a better job without additional expenditures if he or she decides to utilize computers. The computer has also helped many administrators with their human relations. This is a socially conscious society, similar in concept to the economically conscious society that existed after the depression of the 1930s. A variety of economic indicators, such as the gross national product, give people an idea of the health of the economy. Although social indicators are not in widespread use among the citizenry, statistical data, available through information systems, have aided many governmental agencies in assessing how well they are serving the needs of society.

It is practically impossible and certainly impractical to list all of the uses of computers in the federal government. Moreover, many of the applications are either classified for national security or not available to the general public. A sampling of computer applications is given in the following paragraphs.

Internal Revenue Service.   The agency best known to the average citizen for its computer capability is the IRS. Through the years the use of computers has reduced the occurrences of "tax cheating" and has substantially increased revenues. The IRS has a network of regional centers and a national center that employ computers. Computers are used to verify the arithmetic on returns and to cross-check reports from employers and banks on income, withholdings, interest, and dividends with actual declarations. Estimated tax as well as name changes, moves from one region to another, and other items of information are also processed. Most IRS regional centers use keyboard devices for data entry from returns and reports, and information is normally available to auditing personnel through television-like terminal devices. Regional centers submit tax records to the national center, where a record is kept for each taxpayer. (There are 80 million taxpayers and tax-paying entities in the United States.) Tax refunds, delinquent notices, and bills are made through the national center. The computer is also used for auditing purposes. Through the years IRS personnel have developed criteria to indicate when an audit may be necessary. For example, if medical deductions were greater than 70 percent of a taxpayer's income, the computer might signal that the return should be checked. It has been conjectured, but by no means substantiated, that one of the benefits of tax preparation firms is that they supposedly know the limits on the size of deductions in each category. (It has also been conjectured that these same companies use their customers as guinea pigs to determine what these limits are.)

Census Bureau.   In the most recent census (1970), the U.S. Census Bureau collected and processed information on 205 million people living in the United States. Although the 1970 census resulted in minor criticism because of the personal questions involved, the facts are used to allocate Federal funds and to realign the boundaries of congressional districts. The Census Bureau has elaborate procedures to ensure the privacy of individual data. The number of people involved in a sample, for example, is large enough to guarantee individual privacy. Census data is available to researchers, but only after it is processed to remove any personal information.

Military.   The military is a relatively large user of computers in five general areas: the Defense Supply Agency, space observations (that is, satellites), weapon systems, command and control systems, and strategic decision making. The Defense Supply Agency, which is a consolidated source of supplies for all of the services, maintains centralized records on 1.5 million different items; it has been called the world's biggest supermarket. The Air Force Space Detection and Tracking System (SPADATA) keeps track of all man-made objects in space. It uses a network of observation stations to detect new objects and verify the existence of old ones. Computers are used in most weapon systems for guidance and trajectory computations. Moreover, once a ballistic missile is launched, a computer keeps track of its location. Command and control systems use a vast network of radars and computers to detect the invasion of the airspace over the United States. Radar data from observed aircraft are entered directly into computers for comparison against flight patterns. Unusual events are detected and strategic forces are alerted. In the area of decision making, computers are used to keep track of ships, planes, and men, and to perform complex statistical analyses regarding military actions. Mobile computers are used in the field, on board ships, and in planes, whenever computational power is needed. Push-button war, however, is largely fiction, for local commanders are incorporated into the decision-making loop whenever possible. Simulation techniques are widely used in the military for gaining analytical and decision-making experience through the use of war games, which include both tactical and logistical aspects of military conflict.

Other Agencies.   Computers are also used in other governmental agencies. The Veterans Administration processes the paperwork associated with hospital, educational, and insurance benefits. The Treasury Department issues government checks. The Food and Drug Administration processes new drug applications. The Labor Department assists in job placement. The Weather Bureau forecasts weather for periods up to 30 days. The U.S. Postal Service speeds up postal service with automatic scanners and sorters. The Social Security Administration processes earning records and deductions, routine monthly payments, and Medicare and Medicaid systems. The Social Security Administration uses at least 27 computers and is the largest single computer installation in the world.

Congress

One of the areas of the government that is suffering most from "information overload" is the legislative branch. The computer is needed by legislators to keep track of pending legislation and to assess the needs of their constituents. For example, the 89th Congress considered over 26,000 bills, and in the 90th Congress over 29,000 pieces of legislation were introduced. Legislation has been introduced in the U.S. Congress for an information system for Congress. Other proposals include an electronic voting system and an on-line, real-time system that would have access to all federal data bases. At this time, at least five state legislatures (Florida, Hawaii, New York, North Carolina, and Pennsylvania) provide their members with computerized reports on pending bills and other legislative data.

Courts and Law

A major problem that has accompanied the increasing crime rate in the country is the backlog of pending court cases. Persons accused of crimes often have to wait in jail for years, when bail is not available, and in addition to the personal injustices involved, these cases cause overcrowding of jails and a burden to the taxpayers. In both criminal and civil cases, details of the cases are often forgotten by witnesses before the cases come to court. Several states and cities use computers for court administration to keep track of backlogged cases, prepare trial calendars, generate subpoenas and notices to prisoners, and prepare status reports so that lawyers can plan their own schedules accordingly. Another area in which computers have been successfully used is in the area of jury selection.

Although lawyers have been relatively slow to use the computer, many law firms now use computer services for billing; for account, tax and estate computations; and for legal information retrieval. In the latter case the computer is used to search for legal precedents. Lawyers, using a terminal device, enter data on their own case. The computer then searches through voluminous information and generates referrals to specific cases that can be used as legal precedents.

Local Government

The computer has been a boon to state and local governments that are forced by their very nature to deal with messy social problems. Typical state and local problems include: transportation planning, real estate assessment and taxation, water and air pollution control, urban and land-use planning, social welfare management, and a variety of other "headaches" such as pest control, pet licenses, and road repair. Some of these problems, such as transportation and urban and land-use planning, are handled through computer simulation. Computers are also used to prepare land assessments and tax bills and to generate reminders and daily work lists for a variety of other state and local government functions.

Computers have helped several welfare programs considerably, especially in large municipalities where a welfare recipient can register at more than one regional center. In New York City, for example, one welfare recipient was eventually caught after receiving welfare checks for several years from different welfare centers in three of New York's five boroughs.

With the current concern over pollution control, computers have been used to improve on the efficiency of various facilities. Recent applications involve the monitoring of a power generating station, controlling a sewage treatment plant, and controlling traffic lights. Traffic control by computer has great potential for the years to come. By controlling traffic lights to meet the needs of the traffic at any point in time, congestion, travel times, and air pollutants are reduced.

Police and Criminal Systems

Through the use of automobiles, airplanes, trains, and buses, this has become an extremely mobile society. Criminals can benefit from this fact; in the past all they had to do was "blow town," and they were relatively free. The Federal Bureau of Investigation, however, has reduced criminal's mobility considerably with its National Crime Information Center (NCIC), which is an on-line, real-time computerized information network. The NCIC system stores the arrest records of people and information on wanted persons and stolen property. Local and state law enforcement personnel can query the NCIC system to obtain information on a subject that warrants further investigation.

The Justice Department is also making use of computer technology through its Law Enforcement Assistance Administration (LEAA). LEAA has a $7 million research project, System for Electronic Analysis and Retrieval of Criminal Histories (project SEARCH) to produce a nationwide on-line information network for exchanging criminal histories. Eventually, local, state, and federal agencies are expected to use the SEARCH system.

Many states have now computerized their motor vehicle registration and driver's license facilities so that they can be accessed by state agencies and local police to obtain the name of the owner of an automobile and verify the validity of a registration or a driver's license.

In addition to being connected to the NCIC information system, many state, county, and local law enforcement agencies have information systems of their own. Notable examples of systems that have achieved some degree of success are the Law Enforcement Information Network (LEIN) at Michigan state headquarters in East Lansing, the California Law Enforcement Telecommunications System (CLETS), the Chicago "hot-desk" system, the New York State Identification and Intelligence System, and the County Law Enforcement Applied Regionally (CLEAR) system developed in Cincinnati and Hamilton counties in Ohio and adopted elsewhere. Law enforcement systems of this type are accessed via telecommunications facilities in the station house, the patrol car, or both. From a patrol car, requests are normally radioed to an operator manning a terminal device. The operator, who is experienced at querying the information system, can normally respond in less than a minute to the police officer. Terminals in patrol cars have been implemented for some systems, but it is difficult to tell at this point whether they were installed after a thorough systems analysis or as the result of an aggressive equipment salesperson.

Politics

Computers have even been used in political campaigns, vote counting, and election-night broadcasting. The first major political figure who used computers was John F. Kennedy, prior to the 1960 presidential election. The Kennedy campaign staff built a model of the voting public from sample data obtained from a public opinion polling company. The model was used to evaluate strategies for dealing with campaign issues—one of which was the fact that Kennedy, if elected, would be the country's first Catholic president. The eventual strategy worked out with the aid of the model was to approach the problem "head-on" rather than to sidestep the issue.

In general, computers are used in political campaigning in two principal ways: (1) as a means of doing routine clerical operations and (2) as a means of analyzing voter characteristics. In the first category, typical operations include the following:

1. Compilation and maintenance of voter names, addresses, and voting preferences
2. Preparation of address labels for mailing campaign literature
3. Preparation of special appearance letters—generated by computer
4. Selection of voters from the mailing list (operation 1) that are sensitive to a particular campaign issue so that they can be sent special campaign literature or so that they can be omitted from the lists for mailings of literature with which they may disagree
5. Management of contributors—potential and actual—of campaign funds

Typical operations in the second category include the following:

1. Analysis of voters by geographical area—taking into consideration income level, ethnic group, past voting habits, race, religion, and a variety of other political factors
2. Correlations of political issues with geographical areas identified in operation 1
3. Assessment and prediction of voter behavior through simulation and other modeling techniques

These and similar techniques were used in Winthrop Rockefeller's campaign for governor of Arkansas in 1966 and in Robert Griffin's campaign for senator from Michigan in the same year.

Vote counting is an area in which computers have fared rather poorly. The basic objective, of course, is to have complete election results shortly after the polls close in a voting district. In fact, IBM formerly marketed a vote-counting machine that accepted specially punched cards as input. However, late and controversial tabulations in several localities have caused computerized vote counting to be viewed with distrust, and at least 11 states have outlawed the concept completely.

Most people are familiar with election-night reporting on television, wherein a candidate is declared the winner by the computer after only a small percentage of the vote is in. Almost without exception, the eventual vote count proves the computer to be correct. How is it done? Primarily, predictions are made with statistical techniques and historical voting patterns of that district. The basic thinking behind the methods goes somewhat as follows: if a certain percentage of the voters vote a certain way, there is a given probability that the remaining voters will vote that way also, the prediction is made by putting the two percentages together.

Medicine

This society is entering, or perhaps is already in, a crisis period as far as medical and health care are concerned. Services are becoming increasingly expensive, and people are demanding more and better care. In addition, the medical sciences have become exceedingly complex to the extent that available knowledge doubles every five to ten years. Thus, medical people must know more, patients expect more, and services in general cost more. Increased medical costs are not limited to increased needs for medical treatment, but are also the result of expanded administrative services, such as hospital drug control, blood-bank inventory control, and the control of laboratory tests. It is expected that the effective use of computers in medicine will help reduce or at least help control rising costs and aid medical people in providing better medical and health care.

The primary applications of computers in the field of medicine and health services include:

1. Monitoring a patient's condition
2. Storing a patient's medical records
3. Assisting in the diagnosis of diseases
4. Maintaining central information systems

It is important to add to this list the widespread use of computers in medical education and research and in hospital administration.

Patient Monitoring.   The most dramatic use of computers in medicine is in the area of patient monitoring. Control computers are frequently used in intensive care units to monitor the condition of patients after a severe operation, such as open-heart surgery. The computer monitors and records the patient's heart rate, blood pressure, temperature, and fluid drainage. Obviously, the computer does not perform the monitoring itself but rather controls a variety of sensing and recording equipment that perform the required services. A single computer can monitor hundreds of post-operative patients. The computer is programmed to detect unusual conditions and to administer medications and blood infusions.

Control computers are also used to screen electrocardiograms so that a patient can receive an electrocardiogram and have it analyzed in less than a minute. Normally, the computer can screen several electrocardiograms at one time.

Medical Records.   Physicians are often notoriously good at doctoring and notoriously bad at paperwork (and writing). The fact that people move frequently and change doctors only compounds the problem. The information about a patient is recorded, either from written records or with a terminal device, in a centralized medical information system. Medical personnel with the proper authority can retrieve specific facts about a patient or the patient's entire medical profile. In today's age of specialization, a patient's records could be scattered among several doctors' offices. With the centralized system, a complete medical history of a patient is available to allow doctors to provide more effective medical treatment.

A recent innovation in medical recording is referred to as *automated medical recording.* The method uses computer-administered questioning so that an examination can be tailored to the characteristics of the patient. The physician uses a television-like (that is, cathoderay tube or CRT-type) terminal device. Questions are presented on the screen; depending upon the question, either the physician, the nurse, or the patient can respond.

Some of the advantages of a centralized medical information system are that records can be analyzed to discover diseases without outward symptoms that might go unrecognized by doctor or patient and to detect the possibility of epidemics.

Clinical Decision Making and Treatment.   In a book on statistical decision analysis, Howard Raiffa gives a "simple" decision that must be made by a doctor. The doctor does not know whether a patient's sore throat is caused by strep or a virus. If it were strep, the doctor would prescribe penicillin; if it were caused by a virus, rest, gargling, and aspirin would be prescribed. Failure to treat a strep throat with medication might result in a serious disease, such as rheumatic heart disease. On the other hand, penicillin should not be prescribed indiscriminately because of a possible reaction or the development of penicillin-resistant bacteria. The doctor should take a throat culture; however, the bacteria could die before the analysis is complete, and the presence of strep does not guarantee that it is causing the sore throat. The doctor has several possibilities:

1. Take no culture; treat sore throat as viral
2. Take no culture; treat sore throat as strep
3. Take no culture; prescribe penicillin for 10 days

4. Take culture; prescribe penicillin if positive
5. Take culture and prescribe penicillin; continue penicillin if positive and discontinue pills if negative

And a sore throat is regarded as a simple problem.

The three basic steps in diagnosis are listed by Richard Dorf[2] as:

1. Obtain patient's condition through examination and history.
2. Evaluate the relative importance of the various symptoms.
3. Consider all diseases with similar symptoms and systematically eliminate diseases until an appropriate disease category is found.

The computer is used to store all diseases and their symptoms, thereby eliminating one of the sources of possible error. In a *clinical decision support system,* the physician interacts with the computer through a type-writer-like device in his office. The computer contains information on known diseases. In response to a set of symptoms entered by the physician, one computer produces a list of likely causes and can produce upon request, the optimum treatment plan.

Clinical support systems are not in widespread use, but it is difficult to determine if the situation is a result of the fact that few systems exist or because physicians do not want to use them.

Medical Information Systems.   Medical information systems encompass two functions: medical record keeping, mentioned previously, and hospital accounting and control systems. It is estimated that approximately 25 percent of all hospital costs are for accounting, billing, medicare and medicaid systems, and a variety of other clerical and administrative functions. Conventional data processing facilities are usually sufficient for patient accounting; however, many hospitals have gone to on-line, real-time systems. Small hospitals frequently share a common hospital accounting system.

Computers have helped enormously in the administration of hospitals and medical centers. Problems of these institutions are unique in the sense that advanced technology is applied whenever possible. Within a given operational budget, administrators usually prefer to minimize clerical expenditures and maximize expenditures on staff and equipment to provide the best possible medical care. The use of computers has reduced the "per patient" cost of clerical services and has generally improved medical care.

2. Richard Dorf, *Introduction to Computers and Computer Science* (San Francisco: Boyd and Fraser, 1972), p. 507.

Other Medical Applications. Other uses of the computer in medicine by hospitals and physicians are:

1. Patient billing by physicians, usually through a computer service bureau
2. Menu planning in hospitals
3. Scheduling in clinics and wards
4. Inventory and drug control
5. Blood bank management
6. Control of laboratory tests

In medical research, computers are used to model the brain, the circulatory system, and the side effects of various drug treatments; computers are used for physiological simulation in medical training. In fact, the University of Southern California medical school has a computer-controlled mannequin complete with heartbeat, blood pressure, breathing action, jaws, eyes, and muscles for the training of resident doctors. The computer-controlled mannequin can suffer from a variety of diseases and even die. However, this patient prepares a printed report on how well the attending physician performed.

EDUCATION

The use of computers in education has not been as successful as their use in other areas, perhaps because original expectations were too great. A good economic rule of thumb is that "increased productivity accompanies increased costs." This has been true in manufacturing, government, marketing, banking, and even medicine. It has not, however, generally been true in education. The cost of education has skyrocketed, but the educational system continues to be constrained by the traditional teacher-student relationship. It was hoped by many that computers would help in this regard, but substantial results have been slow to arrive. From a performance point of view, most computer-based educational systems and techniques have been successful. The costs of computerized systems, however, are high, perhaps as high as 10 to 1 over conventional methods.

The uses of computers in education can logically be placed into three categories:

1. For clerical operations in educational administration
2. As a technique and/or tool for use in the educational process
3. As a field of study—computer science and data processing

This section is concerned with items 1 and 2.

Administration

One area in which computers *have* reduced educational costs is in the area of administration and control. Many school systems have replaced manual record keeping with a computerized version using conventional data processing methods. Computerized systems are more reliable and accurate and can be programmed to produce a variety of reports useful for school administration. Many systems also include medical records so that the data can be used for a variety of analyses. Centralized record keeping is useful when students frequently are moved from school to school, as is the case with the children of migrant farm workers. When students in this category enter a new school, their complete records can be received in hours, and they can be placed immediately. Most school systems currently require medical examinations and inoculations for the various communicable diseases. Students who are transferred are frequently given the same shots over and over again. With a computerized system, the whole process of changing schools can be made less traumatic to the child involved.

Computers are commonly used for class scheduling, for curriculum planning, and for the grading of examinations. Class scheduling is a cumbersome and time-consuming process. Scheduling can now be handled by computer programs that optimize the use of classrooms and institutional personnel. Curriculum planning is a recent concept that has great potential in the areas of staffing and physical facilities. It has been shown that future needs of a school can be reliably predicted on the basis of current class enrollments, student aptitudes, and student interests. Because of the newness of this area, sufficient time has not elapsed for results to be achieved and reported. Computer facilities for grading examinations are a welcome resource to teachers at all levels of instruction. The key point is that it frees them for more productive activities.

Instruction

Computers are used in instruction in three principal ways:

1. As a means of testing skills, such as in the area of arithmetic and language
2. As part of a programmed learning situation
3. As an analysis and problem-solving tool

As a means of testing skills, a computer system is programmed to present the student with exercises. The student is seated at a terminal device. (The specific type of device is not important.) If the student responds correctly, he or she is presented with another exercise. If the response is incorrect, the student is given the answer, and the session continues with another exercise. The length of the session is usually dependent upon achieving a prespecified number of correct answers. (One student pointed out a danger in this method: playing with the computer terminal is so much fun that students may make mistakes to prolong the session.)

Programmed instruction (frequently called computer-aided instruction or CAI) is more complicated and requires that a course be synthesized as a set of programmed steps. CAI systems are available for assisting the teacher in "course writing." The student sits at a CAI terminal (usually a CRT-type device) and is presented textual material, which the student reads. The student is then asked questions. If the response is correct, the CAI system goes on to the next topic. If the response is incorrect, the student is given the answer and a brief review of the subject matter. This process allows a subject to be treated in greater or lesser depth, depending upon the course author and the CAI system.

CAI systems are primarily on-line systems that can usually service hundreds of students. The CAI programs take care of sequencing and terminal control. The course author takes care of the course content, which may vary among students using the system at any one time.

The advantage of CAI is that it allows students to proceed at their own pace and gives them individual attention (note that the word *personal* was not used) that is not available in many classroom situations. CAI costs are very high, ranging from $200 to $2,000 per instructional hour.

The use of the computer as a problem-solving and an analysis tool in mathematics, science, engineering, and business has been well demonstrated. It has also been used successfully in the social sciences, the humanities, and the arts. Applications range from a simple computer program to generate random poetry to an extensive system for language translation. A few sample uses of the computer in these areas are listed below:

Study of linguistics
Language translation
Concordance generation
Literary analysis
Poetry writing
Attribution study (authorship problem)
Music analysis
Programs that solve porblems
Symbolic mathematics
Simulation of a neurotic person (behavioral science)
Analysis of census data
Political simulation
Simulation of a cell (biology)
Game plan analysis (football)

Computer-generated art forms
Music composition
Creation of motion pictures
Choreographic description
Fiction writing

Computers have even been used to generate horoscopes and parapsychological experiments.

The potential for the use of computers in education is well summarized by Donald Sanders:

> A primary purpose of using computers as an instructional tool in the classroom would be to *provide insight* and not merely compute numbers or process documents.[3]

The educational community has hardly begun to use computers in this way, but in the application of systematic thinking and problem-solving methods, computer training provides a valuable learning experience.

AUTOMATION AND JOBS

It is true that the computer has displaced some people. Automation always does. It is difficult to generalize about automation because each situation is different, and research data is often conflicting. Displaced persons are often absorbed into other units or leave the labor force through retirement, pregnancy, or for other reasons. In spite of the negative aspects of automation, economists agree that the concept is beneficial to society in the long run and that displacement should not be prevented. It is difficult for the employee being displaced to be philosophical about the matter, and reeducation and retraining are frequently necessary. This should be part of the planning process.

Management and Organization

The effects of automation on management and organization can be summarized as follows:

1. Planning and control is centralized at a higher level of the organization.

---

3. Donald Sanders, *Computers in Society: An Introduction to Information Processing* (New York: McGraw-Hill, 1973), p. 334.

2. It has made the middle manager's job more complex. (It was predicted that automation would reduce the number and status of middle-management jobs. This prediction never materialized.)
3. It has increased the middle manager's and supervisor's needs for human relations skills.
4. It has reduced the span of supervision—that is, the number of employees a supervisor can effectively manage.

Item 4 is particularly significant in the computer field, where a typical first-line manager may have five to eight programmers or systems analysts reporting to him or her.

As computers are assigned to routine tasks, more of the energy of the organization is devoted to the solution of nonroutine problems. This requires a certain amount of imagination and creativity that the typical bureaucratic organization, with its rigid structure and personnel pigeonholing, is not designed to cope with. Therefore, a decline of bureaucratic organizational characteristics tends to accompany a computerized organization. It could be that the Peter Principle, which claims that "in a hierarchy every employee tends to rise to his level of incompetence,"[4] will finally be refuted.

Overall, information systems and decision-making models have enabled executives to reassume many of the decision-making functions that were subordinated to middle management in the previous generation of decentralized organizations. More time can be spent on policy matters and less time on "fighting fires." Middle management has more time for planning and control, and lower-level management can devote needed time to the human relations problems associated with a changing society.

Education, Specialization, and the Professions

Automation requires more professional and scientific employees to manage and control the complex systems involved. Clerical workers are moved into more responsible positions; blue-collar workers are upgraded to white-collar jobs. The people who suffer most from automation are the ones lacking in basic education, intelligence, or aptitude for retraining, because it is difficult to place them in other jobs in the organization. Large organizations tend to be better in this regard for the simple reason that they possess the resources and the job opportunities to do it. In smaller organizations, displaced employees are more likely to be laid off.

The computer revolution has brought about a special breed of "pro-

4. Lawrence J. Peter and Raymond Hall, *The Peter Principle* (New York: William Morrow, 1969), p. 25.

fessional specialist," uncommitted to an organization. This modern technocrat is described by Alvin Toffler in *Future Shock* as follows:

> He is willing to employ his skills and creative energies to solve problems with equipment provided by the organization, and within temporary groups established by it. But he does so only so long as the problems interest *him*. He is committed to his own career, his own self-fulfillment.[5]

Thus, it can be said that the loyalty of the professional person in the new technology is to his or her profession and not to the organization that is employing him or her at any point in time. Specialization increases the number of different occupations and dissolves the traditional boundaries of the bureaucratic organization.

Planning and Implementation

The problems that automation causes for people can be partially solved through effective planning and careful implementation. People resist change for many reasons, including:

1. Possible loss of job
2. Uneasiness about working environment (for example, the need to make new friends)
3. Fear of not being able to learn the new skill required
4. Possible loss of status in the community

People faced with the above fears, however, usually do not simply say, "I resist." The resistance is manifested in other ways—such as forgetting to enter data, withholding output, low morale, and ignoring computer facilities. Many organizations solve the problem by keeping employees informed of anticipated changes, by allowing employees to participate in the development of the new system, and by careful timing of the implementation of the system. Some organizations have even gone so far as to guarantee in writing that the employee will not be displaced when the new equipment or facilities are installed.

PERSONAL ISSUES

There seems to be a popular attitude toward computers and information gathering that is expressed by McLuhan and Watson in *From Cliché to Archetype* as follows:

5. Alvin Toffler, *Future Shock* (New York: Random House, 1970), p. 134.

As information itself becomes the largest business in the world, data banks know more about individual people than the people do themselves. The more the data banks record about each one of us, the less we exist.[6]

Many writers in the social arena have expressed similar concerns. Lewis Mumford is concerned with the dehumanizing aspect of computers when he writes:

The process of automation has produced imprisoned minds that have no capacity for appraising the results of their process except by the archaic criteria of power and prestige, property, productivity and profit, segregated from any more vital human goals.[7]

There are, of course, differing opinions. For example, Alvin Toffler in *Future Shock* believes that the new technology has provided people with too many options at too great a rate. He attributes much of what is bad in the society to this rate of change and not to the change itself.

The Number Game

One of the biggest complaints heard from students, customers of a public utility, credit card holders, and others who deal with large bureaucracies is, "I'm just a number to them. They don't know who I am." The problem is created out of necessity rather than a disregard for human dignity. If it is necessary to record information on thousands of persons, it is simply more efficient to code them by number than by name. Names are frequently misspelled and abbreviated, and sometimes initials and nicknames are used; therefore, it is not altogether unreasonable to use numbers inside of the computer. The use of identification numbers is also an outgrowth of traditional batch processing systems in which the respondent has no means of interacting with the computer. With the widespread use of modern on-line interactive systems, the situation will probably change somewhat, since the computer can communicate with the respondent to remove any ambiguities.

Computer Victims

Most Americans have either a credit card, a utility account, a checking account, or a magazine subscription, and the average citizen has at

---

6. Marshall McLuhan and Wilfred Watson, *From Cliché to Archetype* (New York: Viking, 1970), p. 13.
7. Lewis Mumford, *The Myth of the Machine: The Pentagon of Power* (New York: Harcourt, Brace, Jovanovich, 1970), p. 192.

least one of each. Many people have experienced the helpless feeling associated with the following sequence of events:

1. The person receives a bill for $0.00 and ignores it.
2. Next month a dunning letter (that is, a demand for payment) arrives.
3. The person consults with friends and finally sends a check for $0.00.
4. The computer responds by stating it does not accept checks for $0.00.

Another recurring case goes somewhat as follows: A person has dinner at a restaurant and uses a credit card. He is never billed. He inquires of the company and is informed, "Be patient, the bill will arrive," so he does nothing. Subsequently, he tries to use the same credit card. The validity of the card is verified with one of the service companies (mentioned earlier in this chapter), and he is told that a bill is outstanding and credit will not be accepted.

The person's credit rating may be ruined. (Credit ratings are also computerized.) However, this is not known until credit is refused and the person investigates the reason why. There are numerous documented cases of persons who have even been turned down for jobs because of poor credit ratings that they did not even know about.

Individuals are practically helpless. They may have a dispute, for example, with a department store for an erroneous charge. They are given a poor credit rating. The dispute is finally resolved, and the erroneous charge is cancelled, but the store never bothers to inform the credit company, which acts as an information handling company and takes no responsibility for the accuracy of the data. The individual could consult a lawyer, but that could eventually cost thousands of dollars. It is no wonder that many people wish computers would go away.

Things are even worse than meet the eye at first glance. Credit card companies, department stores, and other businesses are profit-making organizations, and they do make a profit regardless of who suffers. Consider the problem of straightening out a customer's account, and suppose the customer is right. There are two options open to the company:

1. Investigate the situation, answer the customer's letters, and seriously attempt to straighten out the matter.
2. Ignore the customer's letters. The customer will either pay the bill or get angry and cancel the account.

From a business point of view, the most profitable course of action might very well be the second one. Many customers will pay their bill, however erroneous, in order to preserve a good credit rating. If the customer does cancel the account, the cost of the advertising to get a new customer is usually far less than the cost of resolving the original problem.

The same reasoning holds true for the correcting of "programming bugs," such as the bill for $0.00 mentioned previously. The programming, check-out, and computer time necessary to correct a simple "bug" may cost thousands of dollars. In light of the situation, it is a wonder that most systems operate as well as they do.

These problems obviously are not the fault of the computer. They are problems caused by people because of poor systems design, poor programming, or sloppy input. Not only are people victimized by the computer, but the computer is also victimized by people.

Privacy and Confidential Information

Another area of concern to most people is privacy. Alan F. Westin defines privacy as "the claim of individuals, groups, or institutions to determine for themselves when, how, and to what extent information about them is communicated to others."[8] The concern for privacy is nothing new, and organizations have always collected information of various kinds. However, the problem has been brought to the public's eye in recent years with the widespread use of computers, information systems, and telecommunications facilities. The use of computers has not created the privacy problem but has enlarged the scope of information gathering. Privacy involves organizations, individuals, and society as a whole. There is a tendency for individuals and organizations to invade the privacy of others for reasons ranging from curiosity to criminal blackmail. Within societies, surveillance techniques are generally accepted when used by authorized agencies against enemies of that society. Privacy, then, can be both desirable and undesirable, depending upon the factors involved.

From the individual's point of view, privacy is exceedingly important because it provides basic psychological and legal needs. Some of the more obvious of these needs are:

1. *Personal autonomy*—a person's hopes, fears, shame, and aspirations are protected against public scrutiny
2. *Emotional release*—a person can "unwind," "let it all out," or show intimate feelings without fear of events being misinterpreted
3. *Self-evaluation*—a person can employ introspection, observation, and other means to improve himself or herself
4. *Limited and protected communications*—a person can seek and utilize counsel (legal, clerical, or other) without fear of incrimination

8. Alan F. Westin, *Privacy and Freedom* (New York: Atheneum, 1967), p. 7.

There are other reasons why privacy is important to the individual. First, it has become increasingly difficult to determine exactly what information is known about a person and under what circumstances that information will be released. For example, several federal agencies—including the IRS, the FBI, the Social Security Administration, the Veterans Administration, the Department of Justice—keep files on individuals. Each agency generally has its own procedures for collecting data and ensuring its accuracy, value, and appropriateness. Usually, an agency's regulations for the release of information are developed in light of its collection procedures, which is also the case with credit companies. What happens, however, when information is shared, as in a data bank? Since it is less expensive to obtain information from a data bank or another agency than for an agency to collect the information itself, it seems reasonable that agencies will increasingly use data bank facilities. Once information systems are integrated, the regulations of a particular collecting agency do not necessarily apply to the agency that is using the information. Consequently, information that an individual has given to a particular agency may now be information available to many agencies, and the individual may not know who has access to the information.

Another concern about information systems is that the past can very easily get in the way of the future. Suppose a first grade teacher subjectively remarks in a child's record that the child is "hyperactive" or has a "short attention span." It is unlikely that anyone who might see the child's record could accurately interpret the significance of the remark. Twenty years later, however, when that person is seeking employment, who knows how a prospective employer might respond to a subjective remark? In addition, the terms *hyperactive* and *short attention span* might have entirely different meanings in 20 years. Arthur R. Miller has this to say about the situation:

> In the past, there was a limited risk that subjective appraisals by individual teachers would be widely circulated. Now, with missionary zeal our well-intentioned information handlers are ready to offer their files 'to anyone who had access to individual school records' as well as to 'prospective employers.'[9]

In short, we do not have control over information that can and is released about ourselves. There has been extensive legal consideration of the subject, and Miller's book is recommended to the reader for an introduction to what has been accomplished in this regard. Personal factors, however, are just as important, for as Miller points out, "The objective of protecting the individual privacy is to safeguard emotional and psychological tranquility by remedying an injurious dissemination of personal information. . . ."[10]

9. Arthur R. Miller, *The Assault on Privacy* (Ann Arbor: University of Michigan Press, 1971) p. 21.
10. Ibid., p. 227.

To complicate the situation, there is even some debate over exactly what constitutes "private" information. In a research study performed by E. V. Comber,[11] the following factors were given that may apply in determining when an item of information is private:

1. Context within which the specific information is embedded
2. Amount of information assembled and accessible
3. Intrinsic nature of the information
4. Sophistication of the social values held by the individuals concerned
5. Character and scope of the subculture
6. Significance of personal attributes such as age, ancestry, social status, race, and so forth.

The discussion of privacy must necessarily conclude with the fact that the problem does not lie with computers but rather with the discipline and conduct of people, who are the designers and users of information systems.

THE FUTURE

In attempting to assess the immediate future of computer technology, it is always wise to look at other technological innovations to determine how they were absorbed into society. Neither telephone nor electric power, for example, would be in widespread use today if national and international networks did not exist, allowing people and organizations to "tie in" to satisfy their particular needs. Fortunately, the same telephone networks used for telephone calls can be used for the computer networks of tomorrow.

John Kemeny, President of Dartmouth College and coinventor of the Beginner's All-purpose Symbolic Instruction Code (or BASIC language), predicts the development of huge computer networks in the next decade, similar to airline reservation systems and the time-sharing networks operated by several service companies.

In his "Man and Nature" lectures given at the Museum of Natural History in New York City in the fall of 1971, Dr. Kemeny outlined a network of nine regional centers that would service the 80 cities in the United States with populations of 150,000 or over. The nine centers are depicted in Figure 3.1. None of the 80 cities would be more than 500 miles from a regional center, and many suburbs and small cities would also be picked up by the system. In addition to providing service to their respective regions, the centers would be connected together

11. E. V. Comber, "Management of Confidential Information," *Proceedings of the 1969 Fall Joint Computer Conference, 139,* pp. 135–143.

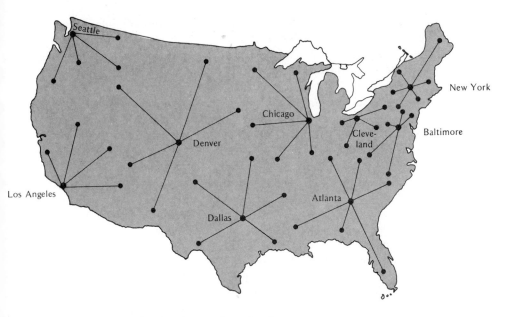

FIGURE 3.1   **Proposed national computer network.**

via microwave or high-speed lines to balance the workload and provide emergency service in case of system failure. The regional centers would be used to provide time-sharing service, on-line information systems, and remote job entry facilities.

It is likely that each regional center will utilize a set of central processing units (a multiprocessing system) sharing the same main storage, direct-access storage, and peripheral input/output units. Systems of this type are in existence today, and network computer service is currently available at many colleges and universities.

In the next decade it is likely that the home terminal will come into widespread use. Home terminals will be used for computation service and for computer-aided instruction (CAI) on a large-scale basis. Kemeny further describes the future "library" system that will allow people to access a large information system from their own homes. With many persons vying for computer service, scheduling will be a problem. Complex operating systems will be used to control computer processing, terminal service, and the running of background jobs.

Kemeny's library of the future will be a complete library stored in the computer. It will be federally funded and maintained on a national basis. Although the costs would be staggering, there are many advantages. The growth rate of libraries in number of volumes doubles approximately every thirty years, and a high percentage of the books are never consulted. By providing access to heavily used information through the computer from the national library system, local library facilities (such as those in colleges and universities) could be reduced considerably. Storage large enough to hold this voluminous amount of information is viewed as a problem, and Kemeny sees books and journals stored as photographic images, similar to microfilm storage. Instead of publishing books publishers will prepare photographable material suitable for entry in the computer. Royalties would be paid on usage, and seldom-used publications would be removed from the system to provide faster access to the other information in the system. An added benefit of the concept is that the lead time for publication would be decreased so that information available to researchers and students would be more relevant and up-to-date.

Kemeny also foresees the day of the *personalized newspaper,* available through the home terminal. Instead of publishing thousands of copies, a newspaper such as *The New York Times* would store information in a computer memory tied to a national computer network. Reporters could type their stories directly into the computer, through the network, and the newspaper's staff could perform routine editing and make policy decisions on its contents. Each reader of the newspaper would have a profile, stored in the computer, of topics of interest to him or her. For example, the reader might be interested in business, sports, and the society section. The computer would display a list of the available news in each topic, and the reader would choose stories he or she wants to read—in much the same manner that a person scans the headlines while reading the paper in the conventional manner. The computer would then type the story at normal reading or display it on a CRT-type device. At any point in time, the reader could discontinue reading and go on to the next topic. The advantages are that readers would be provided up-to-date news on topics of interest to them. What about advertising? Kemeny give two possibilities: (1) displaying ads between pages of text or (2) paying an extra fee for the option of eliminating advertisements.

If all this sounds far-fetched, the following paragraphs will surprise you. Alvin Toffler reports in *Future Shock* that

> . . . in the mid sixties, Joseph Naughton, a mathematician and computer specialist at the University of Pittsburgh, suggested a system that would store a consumer's profile—data about his occupation and interests—in a central computer. Machines would then scan newspapers, magazines, video tapes, films and other material, match them against the individual's interest profile, and instantaneously notify him when something appears that concerns him. The system could be hitched to facsimile machines and TV transmitters that would actually display or print out the material in his own living room.[12]

The subject of personal or home computers continues to fascinate people. Scientists at the Massachusetts Institute of Technology (MIT) are experimenting with a personal computer concept, called OLIVER,

---

12. Toffler, *Future Shock,* p. 249.

for helping to deal with the decision and information overload. OLI-VER, which is an acronym for On-Line Interactive Vicarious Expediter and Responder and which is named for Oliver Selfridge, is a computer programmed to store information for individuals—information such as the date of an anniversary, a husband's shirt size or wife's dress size, stock prices, and weather forecasts—and to perform routine tasks such as paying bills and ordering food. OLIVER could store a multitude of professional details and serve as a handbook or question-answering device. Moreover, OLIVER could be programmed to identify with its owner to the extent that as its owner's attitudes, likes, and dislikes changed, OLIVER could modify itself accordingly. The MIT people even foresee groups of OLIVERs communicating among themselves to handle routine matters for their masters.

CONCLUSIONS

It is only fair to admit that it *is* difficult to put the impact of computers on society in perspective. Knowledge of the subject matter is ostensibly the solution to the dilemma, but once a person learns about the field, it is difficult to remain objective. One solution is to consider outside authorities. First, a pessimistic judgment from Charles Reich in *The Greening of America:*

> The American Corporate State today can be thought of as a single vast corporation, with every person as an involuntary member and employee. It consists primarily of large industrial organizations, plus nonprofit institutions such as foundations and the educational system, all related to the whole as divisions to a business corporation. Government is only a part of the state, but government coordinates it and provides a variety of needed services. The Corporate State is a complete reversal of the original American ideal and plan. The State, and not the market or the people or any abstract economic laws, determines what shall be produced, what shall be consumed, and how it shall be allocated. It determines, for example, that railroads shall decay while highways flourish; that coal miners shall be poor and advertising executives rich. Jobs and occupations in the society are rigidly defined and controlled, and arranged in a hierarchy of rewards, status, and authority. An individual can move from one position to another, but he gains little freedom thereby, for in each position he is subject to conditions imposed upon it; individuals have no protected area of liberty, privacy, or individual sovereignty beyond the reach of the State.[13]

A contrary opinion from someone familiar with the potentials of computers can be found in *Computers in Society:*

> . . . the optimists believe that the sophisticated computer systems of the future will permit a more human and personalized society that will further

13. Charles Reich, *The Greening of America* (New York: Bantam, 1970), p. 93.

reduce the need for individual conformity. They argue that the complexity of our present society, the millions of people crowded into it, and the inadequacy of our present information systems act to encourage conformity and thus to restrict personalization and human freedom of choice. However, when sophisticated information systems are developed and widely used to handle routine transactions, it will then be possible to focus greater personal attention on exceptional transactions. Therefore, more humanistic attitudes will emerge.[14]

Vocabulary The student should be familiar with the following terms in the context in which they were used in the chapter.

business information and control system
CAI
centralization
decentralization
incremental change
LEAA

management information system
NCIC
planning
privacy
society
standardization

Questions 1. Who are the primary users of computers?
2. Is there a relationship between computers and centralization?
3. What is the supposed role of the individual in a computerized society? Has this role actually materialized?
4. In what way can the computer be used to "provide insight"?
5. In modern society as we know it, is the concern over privacy really justified?

Exercises 1. List as many computer applications as you can that are not covered in this chapter.
2. Give examples of consumer problems that have been classified as so called computer problems.
3. Write a short essay containing your opinion of the numbers game. (Alternative topic: libraries of the future.)
4. List types of information that may not be relevant to personal privacy. List types of information that probably would be relevant to personal privacy. What factors seem to determine whether information is of a private nature or not?
5. Discuss the subject of computers and politics. Some people think that it is unfair to assess voter attitudes by computers and utilize

14. Sanders, *Computers in Society*, p. 252.

the resulting information for campaign purposes. Do you agree or disagree? Why?

Related Reading

Comber, E. V. "Management of Confidential Information." *Proceedings of the 1969 Fall Joint Computer Conference.* AFIPS Volume 34.

Davis, K. *Human Relations at Work.* New York: McGraw-Hill, 1967.

Dorf, R. C. *Introduction to Computers and Computer Science.* San Francisco: Boyd and Fraser, 1972.

Hamming, R. W. *Computers and Society.* New York: McGraw-Hill, 1972.

Katzan, H. *Computer Data Security.* New York: Van Nostrand Reinhold Company, 1973.

Kemeny, J. G. *Man and the Computer.* New York: Scribner, 1972.

Martin, J., and Norman, A. R. D. *The Computerized Society.* Englewood Cliffs, N.J.: Prentice-Hall, 1970.

McLuhan, M., and Watson, W. *From Cliche to Archetype.* New York: Viking, 1970.

Miller, A. R. *The Assault on Privacy.* Ann Arbor: Univ. of Michigan Press, 1971.

Mumford, L. *The Myth of the Machine: The Pentagon of Power.* New York: Harcourt, Brace, Jovanovich, 1970.

Peter, L. J., and Hull, R. *The Peter Principle.* New York: William Morrow, 1969.

Raiffa, H. *Design Analysis: Introductory Lectures on Choices under Uncertainty.* Reading, Mass.: Addison-Wesley, 1968.

Reich, C. A. *The Greening of America.* New York: Bantam, 1970.

Rodgers, W. *Think: A Biography of the Watsons and IBM.* New York: Stein and Day, 1969.

Rothman, S., and Mosmann, C. *Computers and Society.* Chicago: Science Research Associates, 1972.

Sanders, D. H. *Computers in Society: An Introduction to Information Processing.* New York: McGraw-Hill, 1973.

Toffler, A. *Future Shock.* New York: Random House, 1970.

Westin, A. F. *Privacy and Freedom.* New York: Atheneum, 1967.

Part

2

Hardware

Operation and Structure of a Computer

ne of the defining characteristics of a computer is the fact that it can operate automatically without human intervention. The computer is able to do this through an ingenius assemblage of storage and operational structures in the computer hardware. The term *hardware* refers to the computer itself and all of the mechanical, magnetic, electrical, and electronic parts of computers. In contrast, the term *software* refers to the programs, or stored sets of instructions, that tell the computer what to do and make the hardware run. The overall concept of computer operation is relatively straightforward and is covered here. This chapter is intended to be an introduction, however, and the reader should not expect full comprehension of the subject matter.

STORAGE STRUCTURES

As discussed earlier, the purpose of the main storage unit of a computer is to hold instructions, data, and computed results while a set of computations is being performed. Main storage is *not* used for long-term storage of instructions and data for several reasons:

1. Main storage is relatively expensive.
2. Only a limited amount of main storage can be attached to a computer.
3. Main storage is not portable.
4. Main storage is volatile—which means that when electric power is turned off, the information contained in main storage is lost.

For long-term storage of instructions and data, mass-storage devices such as tape or disk are used. Information is also stored on punched cards, although the use of cards for storing large amounts of information is declining because of the sheer bulk involved.

Main Storage

Conceptually, main storage is organized somewhat like a group of numbered mail boxes in a post office. In the post office each box is identified and located by its number, which is the box's address. In the computer main storage is organized in much the same manner into a set of locations. Each location can be used to hold a specific unit of data—such as a character, a digit, a series of characters, or a number, depending on the system. To insert or remove data at a location, the address must be known.

When data enters a location, it replaces the previous contents of that location. When data is taken from a location, however, the contents of the location remain unchanged so that the same data may be used many times.

Registers

A high-speed storage location that is used by the central processing unit is called a *register.* Different computers have different registers. For example, some computers have several accumulator registers, and others have a single accumulator (see below). The question of how many registers a computer has is one of basic design philosophy and is governed, to some extent, by the applications for which the computer is intended. Three registers are usually found in every computer and can be briefly described as follows:

1. The *accumulator register* is used for performing arithmetic. Temporary results are frequently left in the accumulator for the next arithmetic operation. When more than one accumulator is used, they are usually identified by number.
2. The *current address register* contains the address in main storage of the instruction currently being executed. (The significance of this register will become obvious later.)
3. The *instruction register* holds the current instruction during execution.

Of the three registers, the only register that is used explicitly is the accumulator. The current address and instruction registers are used internally by the computer and are not normally of concern to the data processing person.

INFORMATION STRUCTURES

One of the reasons that modern computers utilize the concept of a stored program is that the processing unit has access to instructions and data at electronic speeds, rather than having to retrieve each instruction and data item individually for processing from an electromechanical input/output device. This design methodology is one of the contributing factors to the extremely high speeds that are achieved by modern computer systems. Both instructions and data are held in main storage and it is important that care be taken not to interchange the two. Instructions and data are usually coded in the same form— which is usually *binary,* meaning a numbering system that has only the two symbols 0 and 1. Instructions and data are both regarded as a series of bits. (The term *bit* is an abbreviation for binary digit.) However, it is important to note that instructions and data differ because of the interpretation placed on their format and content, even though each is a sequence of bits.

Instructions

The format of a computer instruction varies between computers; however, all formats require, as a bare minimum, three items:

1. An *operation field* that denotes what operation the computer is to perform
2. At least one *operand field* that denotes the data on which the computer should execute the operation (specified in the operation field)
3. *Modifier fields* that augment the operation field or the operand field

A typical computer instruction might be:

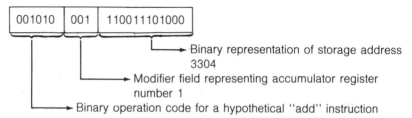

All computers require instructions of this type to sustain continued and automatic operation, and this is one of the defining characteristics of computers. Instructions of the above type, represented in binary form, are normally of concern only to specialists or technologists concerned with internal computer operations.

Data

The form of computer data is governed by the type of application to be run, the nature of the information to be stored, and the computer to be used. As an example, a numeric value of +37 might be stored as:

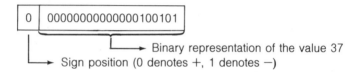

Descriptive data, on the other hand, is stored in a coded form, wherein a sequence of binary digits represents a specific character. (This code is covered later in the chapter.) One of the most significant aspects of modern computer technology is the fact that people who use a computer do not have to deal with information in binary form, for a serious attempt has been made by computer scientists to adjust data processing to meet the needs of people.

OPERATION OF THE COMPUTER

The preceding discussion is leading up to a brief discussion of how the computer operates. All computer instructions are executed in precise units of time that are governed by pulses emitted from an electronic clock, which is a part of the computer's control circuitry. A fixed number of these pulses is termed a *machine cycle.* The computer can execute one or more microsteps that are combined to form conventional computer instructions, such as ADD or MULTIPLY. The exact number of microsteps that constitutes a given computer instruction is governed by the nature of the instruction itself and the data involved.

Instruction Cycle

The central processing unit operates in a prescribed sequence when executing instructions. Two cycles are involved: the "instruction" cycle and the "execution" cycle. The *instruction cycle* (referred to as the I-cycle) comes first and involves the fetching of the next instruction from main storage and the decoding of it to determine the operation to be executed. The following functions are performed during the I-cycle:

1. The address of the current instruction in main storage is obtained from the current address register.
2. The instruction is fetched from main storage and held in the instruction register of the central processing unit.
3. The instruction is decoded.
4. The current address register is updated to point to the next instruction.
5. Control signals are sent to the processing unit to have the specified operation executed.

The current address register is usually set initially to the first instruction in a prescribed set of instructions. Normally, instructions are executed sequentially so that the current address register is updated with the address of the next instruction during the I-cycle. Most computers incorporate a "branch" instruction that discontinues sequential execution and permits execution to continue from a specified location. Usually, a branch instruction simply alters the contents of the current address register.

Execution Cycle

The *execution cycle* (referred to as the E-cycle) follows the I-cycle and involves the execution of the prescribed operation. If an arithmetic operation is involved, the operand is fetched from main storage using the address portion of the current instruction and the operation is performed using the specified operands. The length of the E-cycle depends upon the instruction to be executed. Other computer instructions include input and output, loading, storing, branching, shifting, testing— to name only a few.

Function and Use of Computer Instructions

As an example of the function and use of computer instructions, consider the familiar data processing computation of adding overtime pay to regular pay to obtain gross pay, represented in a programming language as:

ADD OVERTIME TO REGPAY GIVING GROSSPAY

A computer cannot directly execute statements in this form so the specified computation must first be translated into computer instructions. A symbolic form of the above computation is:

```
L    1,REGPAY          (1)
A    1,OVERTIME        (2)
ST   1,GROSSPAY        (3)
```

Symbolic instruction numbered (1) says: "Load the regular pay into accumulator register number one." Symbolic instruction numbered (2) says: "add the overtime pay to the contents of accumulator register number one." Symbolic instruction numbered (3) says: "store the contents of accumulator register number one in main storage as the gross pay." Thus, if the instructions were executed in sequence, the desired computation would be performed.

Instead of stringing out the instructions in binary, suppose they were represented in main storage as follows:

Instruction	Representation			Location in Main Storage
L 1,REGPAY	LOAD	1	7384	4050
A 1,OVERTIME	ADD	1	9123	4051
ST 1,GROSSPAY	STORE	1	7386	4052

The instructions indicate that the data are stored in the following locations:

Data Item	Location in Main Storage	Initial Value
REGPAY	7384	+123
OVERTIME	9123	+14
GROSSPAY	7386	0

Figure 4.1 depicts the execution of the three computer instructions in a hypothetical computer. The *first instruction* is located at main storage address 4050. This fact is denoted by the contents of the "before" current address register. The instruction in storage location 4050 appears as follows:

```
LOAD   1   7384
```

It tells the computer to load the "contents" of storage location 7384 into accumulator register number 1. (The previous contents of accumulator register 1 are simply replaced.) The current address register is updated to contain the address of the next sequential instruction (that is, 4051). The *second instruction* is located at main storage address 4051 and is as follows:

```
ADD   1   9123
```

It tells the computer to add the "contents" of storage location 9123 to the "contents" of accumulator register number 1. Accumulator register number 1 contained +123 and storage location 9123 contains +14; the result is placed in accumulator register number 1, so that it now contains +137. The contents of storage location 9123 remain unchanged. The contents of the current address register are updated to contain 4052. The *third instruction* is located in the main storage location numbered 4052 and is:

```
STORE   1   7386
```

It says that the current "contents" of accumulator register number 1 should be placed (that is, should be "stored") in the main storage location numbered 7386. The contents of the accumulator remain unchanged, and the current address register is updated to contain 4053.

Even though the above example is oversimplified, it effectively demonstrates three important points: (1) The computer executes discrete instructions; (2) both instructions and data are held in main storage; and (3) everything the computer does must be broken down into individual steps.

INTERNAL REPRESENTATION

Like the human brain, the computer is a symbol processor. When people think about a house or a train, they do not have a house or train in

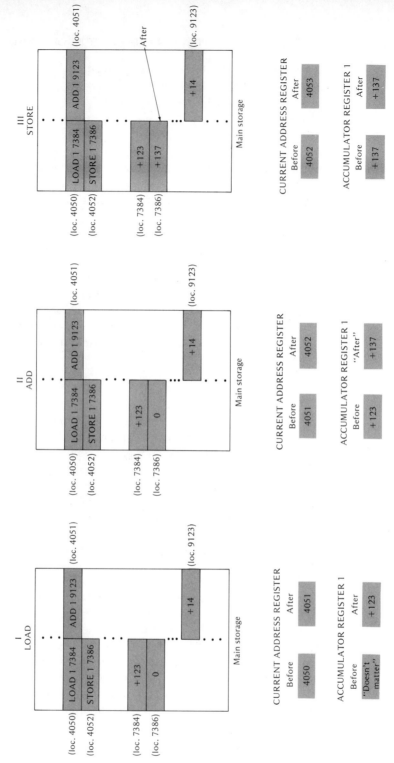

FIGURE 4.1 Execution of three instructions—LOAD, ADD, and STORE—in a hypothetical computer.

their brains; they have a mental image of a house or a train stored in the brain, and the thinking process uses that mental image. A mental image, therefore, is a symbolic representation of an object. (The human brain, however, goes further and frequently deals with abstract concepts that do not represent any particular object in the physical world.)

Binary System

The computer operates in a similar manner and is designed to process symbols. However, a computer is not a natural phenomenon; it is a physical machine made by human beings, and the symbols processed must be something physical that a computer designer can work with. Modern computers use binary symbols, representing "on" and "off" conditions, for two reasons:

1. Binary symbols can easily be represented physically, as depicted in Figure 4.2.
2. Binary symbols are a relatively efficient means of recording an amount of information.

Each binary device must be in either of the two states. It is convenient to ignore the type of device and to represent the two states by the symbols 1 and 0. (Note that any two other symbols, such as $+$ and $-$, would be equally useful.) The symbols 1 and 0, used in this manner, are not to be regarded as numerals but as marks representing the two states of a binary system.

A single binary device is capable of representing only two symbols and is insufficient for building or describing a computer. Thus, binary devices are used in combination to represent a larger number of symbols. For example, two binary devices can be used to represent four distinct symbols as follows:

Device

1	2	
0	0	Symbol represented by 00
0	1	Symbol represented by 01
1	0	Symbol represented by 10
1	1	Symbol represented by 11

A single 1 or 0 is referred to as *bit,* so two bits can be used to represent four symbols. Similarly, three bits can be used to represent eight symbols, that is, 000, 001, 010, 011, 100, 101, 110, 111. It follows that n bits can be used to represent 2^n symbols, that is, $2 \times 2 \times 2 \ldots \times 2$, where 2 appears as a factor n times. One of the major differences

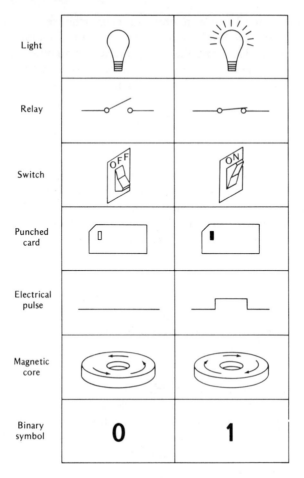

Light		
Relay		
Switch		
Punched card		
Electrical pulse		
Magnetic core		
Binary symbol	0	1

FIGURE 4.2   **Representation of binary symbols.**

between computers is the manner in which bits are combined for the storage of information.

Words vs. Bytes

It was mentioned earlier that main storage consists of "locations" used to hold information and that each location is identified by and referenced with an address, usually taken to be numeric in nature. One question considered in computer design is, "How much information should a location hold?" Two basic philosophies, or schools of thought, are widely used. The first school says that a location should be capable of storing a relatively large number of bits—say 36. A computer that employs this philosophy is referred to as a *word-oriented computer,* and each group of 36 bits is referred to as a *word.* We will see in the next section that a word can represent a number, a computer instruction, or several characters of information. The second school says that a location should be capable of storing a relatively small number of bits—say 8. A computer that employs this philosophy is referred to as a *byte-oriented computer,* and each group of eight bits is referred to as a *byte.* A byte can represent a single character of information; successive bytes are used to represent numbers and computer instructions.

It is important to note that in a word-oriented computer, a word in main storage is directly addressable and in a byte-oriented computer, a byte in main storage is directly addressable.

Characters and Numbers

Information in the computer is stored and interpreted according to conventions established by computer designers and users. In other words, a series of bits, such as 010001, has an agreed upon meaning. (In a 6-bit code, 010001 is a representation for the letter A.) It is important to note, however, that a series of bits may have a different meaning, depending upon how they are used. Thus, more than one convention exists, depending upon how the information is used. Table 4.1 gives commonly used 6-bit and 8-bit character representations. Using the 6-bit representations, the characters UNITED STATES OF AMERICA would be stored in a word-oriented computer, with 36-bit words, as depicted in Figure 4.3. Using the 8-bit representation, the characters OMAR KHAYYAM would be stored in a byte-oriented computer, with 8-bit bytes, as depicted in Figure 4.4. There are advantages to both the word- and byte-oriented methods that are discussed after the representation of numbers is presented.

Numbers are stored as computer words using the binary number system, as presented in the preceding section. The 1 bits in a binary number correspond to "on" conditions of a binary device, and the 0 bits in a binary number correspond to an "off" condition. In a word-oriented computer, the bits of the word correspond to the bits in a binary number. For example, the binary word

0	00000 000000 000000 000000 000101 010001

represents the number*

$$0 \times 2^{34} \ldots + 0 \times 2^{11} + 0 \times 2^{10} + 0 \times 2^9 + 1 \times 2^8 + 0 \times 2^7 + 1 \times 2^6$$
$$+ 0 \times 2^5 + 1 \times 2^4 + 0 \times 2^3 + 0 \times 2^2 + 0 \times 2^1 + 1 \times 2^0$$

which is evaluated as

$$0 + \ldots + 0 + 0 + 0 + 256 + 0 + 64 + 0 + 16 + 0 + 0 + 0 + 1 = 337$$

* The first bit represents the sign: 0 for plus and 1 for minus.

TABLE 4.1   REPRESENTATIVE 6-BIT AND 8-BIT CODES

Character	6-bit code	8-bit code
0	000000	11110000
1	000001	11110001
2	000010	11110010
3	000011	11110011
4	000100	11110100
5	000101	11110101
6	000110	11110110
7	000111	11110111
8	001000	11111000
9	001001	11111001
A	010001	11000001
B	010010	11000010
C	010011	11000011
D	010100	11000100
E	010101	11000101
F	010110	11000110
G	010111	11000111
H	011000	11001000
I	011001	11001001
J	100001	11010001
K	100010	11010010
L	100011	11010011
M	100100	11010100
N	100101	11010101
O	100110	11010110
P	100111	11010111
Q	101000	11011000
R	101001	11011001
S	110010	11100010
T	110011	11100011
U	110100	11100100
V	110101	11100101
W	110110	11100110
X	110111	11100111
Y	111000	11101000
Z	111001	11101001
blank character	110000	01000000
=	001011	01111110
+	010000	01001110
−	100000	01100000
*	101100	01011100
/	110001	01100001
(	111100	01001101
)	011100	01011101
, (comma)	111011	01101011
. (period or dec. pt.)	011011	01001011
$	101011	01011011
' (quote)	001100	01111101

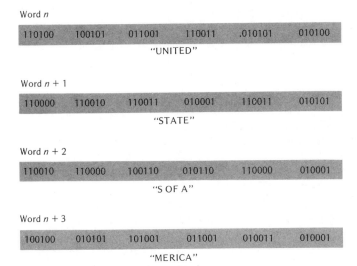

FIGURE 4.3 Storage of the characters UNITED STATES OF AMERICA using 6-bit representation with 36-bit computer words.

It is also important to note that the same word can represent the characters "00005A" using the 6-bit codes in Table 4.1.

In a byte-oriented computer, words are comprised of two or more bytes, depending upon the precision desired by a particular computer application. Standard word sizes are established by the computer manufacturer. For example, one well-known computer allows 2-byte, 4-byte, and 8-byte words. For example, the 2-byte word

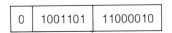

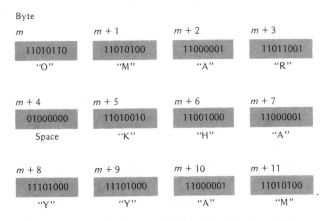

Figure 4.4   Storage of the characters OMAR KHAYYAM using 8-bit representation in a byte-oriented computer with 8-bit bytes.

represents the number

$$1 \times 2^{14} + 0 \times 2^{13} + 0 \times 2^{12} + 1 \times 2^{11} + 1 \times 2^{10} + 0 \times 2^9 + 1 \times 2^8 + 1 \times 2^7 + 1 \times 2^6 + 0 \times 2^5 + 0 \times 2^4 + 0 \times 2^3 + 0 \times 2^2 + 1 \times 2^1 + 0 \times 2^0$$

which is evaluated as

$$16384 + 0 + 0 + 2048 + 1024 + 0 + 256 + 128 + 64 + 0 + 0 + 0 + 0 + 2 = 19906.$$

The same two bytes can also represent the characters "(B" using the 8-bit codes in Table 4.1.

In both of the above examples, the information stored as words or bytes could be interpreted as character data or as numeric data. (The precise meaning is dependent upon the instructions that process the data.) If an instruction designed for character data references the data, then it is interpreted as character data. Similarly, if an instruction designed for numeric data references the data, then it is interpreted as numeric data. The computer is a precise instrument that does not allow any ambiguity.

The relative merits of 6-bit characters and 8-bit bytes are discussed later. As far as this section is concerned, it is important to note that a 6-bit character allows 2^6 (or 64) possible different characters and an 8-bit byte allows 2^8 (or 256) possible different characters; 8-bit bytes are characteristic of some modern computers, and one of the reasons why they were adopted is that a range of 64 different characters is insufficient for some applications.

Computer Instructions

The basic parts of a computer instruction are the operation code, the modifier, and the instruction operands. In a word-oriented computer, the length of a computer instruction is usually fixed and takes the following general form:

Operation Code	Modifiers	Operand Address

Each of the three fields exists as a series of bits that represents a specific computer instruction. The instruction is composed of an operation code that specifies the operation to be performed, a modifier that augments the instruction in some fashion, and an operand address. The operand address is the address of the location in main storage of data to be used in the instruction. The bits comprising the address field are interpreted as a positive number that denotes the relative location of the data word used as an operand. Thus, the number of bits in the operand field implicitly specifies the number of locations there can be in main storage. As an example, if the operand address field comprised 4 bits, then main storage could contain 2^4 (or 16) locations, numbered 0000, 0001, 0010, 0011, 0100, 0101, 0110, 0111, 1000, 1001, 1010, 1011, 1100, 1101, 1110, and 1111. If the operand address field contained 15 bits, then main storage could have 2^{15} (or 32,768) locations. Similarly, if the operation code field contained 5 bits, then 2^5 (or 32) different computer instructions could be possible.

In a byte-oriented computer, different sized instructions are permitted. Thus, some instructions can utilize registers only, as in the following 2-byte instruction:

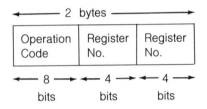

The instructions given are hypothetical but representative of several modern computers. A sample instruction might be: Add the contents of register 1 to the contents of register 2. A typical 4-byte instruction, including a modifier, might be:

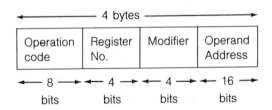

A sample instruction might be: Subtract the contents of the specified main storage location from the contents of the specified register. A typical 6-byte instruction would be:

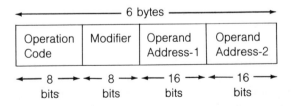

A sample instruction might be: Move the bytes starting at operand address 2 to byte locations beginning in operand address 1; the length of the move is specified in the modifier field. In all cases, the *length in bytes of the instruction* is implied in the operation code.

Although this discussion of computer instructions has been simplified, it demonstrates two important points:

1. The format of the instructions for a particular computer determines the range of main storage addresses that can be addressed and the number of different operation codes that can be used.
2. The word- vs. byte-oriented storage question does make a difference in the types of instructions (for example, one operand vs. two operands) that can be used.

Clearly, the difference between word- and byte-oriented computers does not matter for some computer applications, such as those that deal primarily with numerical calculations. When a substantial amount of character handling is involved, however, then there seems to be some advantage to a byte-oriented computer over a word-oriented computer. Basic computer design, however, can be misleading, since most users do not deal with the computer itself. They use computer software to communicate with the computer, so that the effectiveness of the computer system is ultimately related to the software and is not completely dependent upon hardware. Good software can compensate for poor hardware, and vice versa. The current trend is to integrate the design of the hardware and the software.

MAIN STORAGE TECHNOLOGY

Main storage is one of the critical components in a computer system because large amounts of it are costly. Two technologies for implementing main storage are generally used: passive and active. *Passive* memory devices possess two states, and energy (that is, electricity) is not needed to maintain a given state. Energy is only needed to change the state. Passive devices are also *nonvolatile,* meaning that the information is not destroyed when the power is turned off. *Active* memory devices require energy to maintain the state of the device.

Magnetic Cores

The most frequently used main storage technology uses ferro-magnetic cores, a passive device, referred to as core storage. A magnetic core is an "iron doughnut" about $\frac{1}{16}$ of an inch in diameter with wires strung through it, as depicted in Figure 4.5(a). The presence of a bit (that is, a 0 or a 1) is represented by the fact that a core can be magnetized in either of two directions, as shown in Figure 4.5 (b). Cores are organized into planes and into stacks, as shown in Figures 4.5 (c) and 4.5 (d), to represent bytes or words.

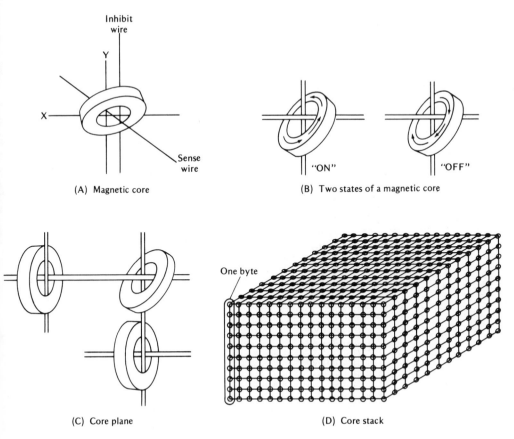

(A) Magnetic core

(B) Two states of a magnetic core

"ON"   "OFF"

One byte

(C) Core plane

(D) Core stack

FIGURE 4.5   Magnetic core storage.

A core is selected for reading by sending half the current necessary for "sensing it" through the X and Y wires, as depicted in Figure 4.6. Note that only the core at the intersection of the two wires receives the full current; other cores receive only half the current. The presence of a 1 bit is detected by the fact that the presence of current in the X and Y wires causes the state of the core to "flip" so that current flows in the sense wire. This process is referred to as *destructive read-out*, since a 1 bit is cleared to a 0 bit. The core must be reset by sending current through the X and Y wires in the opposite direction. This is where the *inhibit wire* is used (see Figure 4.5); current is sent through the inhibit wire to prevent the core from being reset if it was originally 0. The process of writing a magnetic core is essentially the same as the procedure for resetting a core after a destructive read-out. The primary advantage of core storage is that it is relatively inexpensive to manufacture. One of the main disadvantages of core storage is that as the size of main storage is increased, its physical size becomes a limiting factor on its speed, remembering that modern computers operate at speeds measured in billionths of seconds.

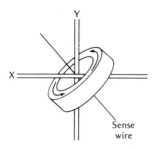

(A) Representation of "1" bit

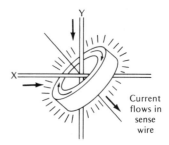

(B) Current is applied to X and Y to
     "select" the core. The core is
     flipped (magnetism is reversed)
     causing current to flow in sense
     wire denoting presence of bit.

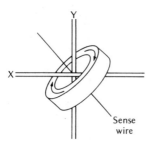

(C) Representation of "0" bit

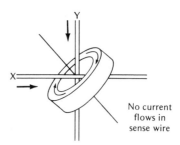

(D) Current is applied to X and Y to
     "select" the core. The core is not
     flipped and no current flows in
     the sense wire.

FIGURE 4.6   Operation of core storage.

Transistors

One means of implementing main storage with very high speeds is
to use electronic components, such as transistors. Figure 4.7 depicts a
schematic of a basic storage cell that utilizes two transistors to collectively represent the on and off states. The storage cell, referred to as
a "flip-flop," is read by raising the word-line voltage, causing the flip-
flop current to transfer to one of the bit lines and be detected by a
current-sensing amplifier. Writing is accomplished by varying the voltage on the bit lines and thereby forcing the flip-flop into the specified
state. This is an example of an "active" memory device. The primary
advantage of using circuitry for main storage is that many memory
circuits can be etched into chips, frequently made of silicon, so that
physical size becomes less of a limiting factor. (In the IBM System/
370 Model 145, for example, a silicon chip approximately $\frac{1}{8}$ inch square
has 1,434 circuit elements etched in it. These circuit elements form
128 bits of main storage.) Also, the cost of circuitry of this type has
been reduced by modern manufacturing methods.

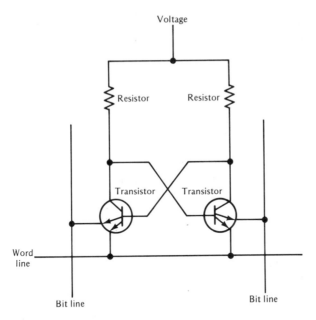

FIGURE 4.7   Schematic of a basic memory cell using electronic components.

Clearly, the design of high-speed main storage is in the domain of the electrical engineer, and it is only fair to mention that other methods of storing information exist. Most users of computers need not be concerned with how main storage is constructed. All they have to do is use it with the techniques given previously. In fact, many computer programmers and systems analysts actually know very little about the computer hardware. Although at first this seems to be a bit unusual, one quickly realizes that the same philosophy also applies to a wide variety of other modern machines.

SUMMARY

The next step will be to put the pieces together to form a computer system. This topic is covered in the next chapter, but the following list summarizes what we already know about computers and their operation:

1. The computer is constructed from electronic components that are synthesized in a logical fashion.
2. The computer operates under control of instructions that perform well-defined operations; the instructions along with data are held in main storage.
3. The central processing unit controls the operation of the computer.

4. Before a computer can be used, a computer program must be written.
5. Computer languages and other descriptive techniques are used in program preparation.
6. Computer programs, called language processors, are used to translate programs written in a computer language into internal machine language.

Vocabulary   The student should be familiar with the following terms in the context in which they were used in the chapter.

accumulator	instruction register
binary device	magnetic core
binary number system	main storage
bit	modified fields
byte	number
byte-oriented computer	operand field
character	operation field
computer instruction	register
current address register	6-bit code
8-bit code	transistor storage
execution cycle	word
instruction length	word-oriented

Exercises   1. Describe five devices (other than those given in Figure 4.2) that are binary in nature.

2. Decipher the following quotation using the 6-bit codes in Table 4.1:

```
010001  110000  100011  100110  010001  010110  110000  100110
010110  110000  010010  101001  010101  010001  010100  110011
110000  010001  110000  100001  110100  010111  110000  100110
010110  110000  110110  011001  100101  010101  111011  110000
010001  100101  010100  110000  110011  011000  100110  110100
110000  010010  010101  110010  011001  010100  010101  110000
100100  010101  110000  011001  100101  110000  110011  011000
010101  110000  110110  011001  100011  010100  010101  101001
100101  010101  110010  110010  011011
```

3. Convert the following numbers from the binary positional number system to the decimal positional number system:

10	1	1000000	1010
110	10101	1000	10100
10111	1111	100	11110

4. Given a computer with the following instruction format:

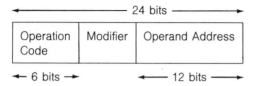

Compute the maximum size of main storage and the total number of operation codes permitted.

5. Try to develop a rationale for determining how many arithmetic registers a computer should have.

6. The chapter mentions that many machines (or devices) exist in our everyday lives about which the user knows very little. Other than the automobile and the kitchen can opener, try to name 12 others.

Related Reading

Abrams, M. D., and Stein, P. G. *Computer Hardware and Software: An Interdisciplinary Introduction.* Reading, Mass.: Addison–Wesley, 1973.

Crowley, T. H. *Understanding Computers.* New York: McGraw-Hill, 1967.

Davis, G. B. *Introduction to Electronic Computers.* 2nd ed. New York: McGraw-Hill, 1971.

Katzan, H. *Computer Organization and the System/370.* New York: Van Nostrand Reinhold, 1971.

The Computer as a System

STRUCTURE OF A COMPUTER SYSTEM

Central Processing Unit
Main Storage
The Concept of a Data Channel
Input/Output Control Unit
Input/Output Device

OPERATION OF THE CENTRAL PROCESSING UNIT

Operating Control
Supervisor and Problem States
External Events
Computer Instructions

MAIN STORAGE

Organization, Addressing, and Access Width
Access Time
Main Storage Interleaving

DATA CHANNELS

Channel Operation
Standard Input/Output Interface and Access Width
Channel Design Factors
Subchannel Concept
Input/Output Completion and Interruption

MULTIPLE COMPUTER SYSTEMS

Peripheral Computers
Satellite Computers
Attached Support Processors
Multiprocessing Systems

system is commonly regarded as a set of components with a relationship between the components. The relationship can be a physical connection, a logical similarity, a causal rule, or any one of a large number of ways of forming a relationship. Moreover, all systems possess a structure, and operational rules govern how the system responds to input conditions. A computer is a particular kind of system that is controlled by a program. The components of a computer system communicate through the transfer of control information and data.

STRUCTURE OF A COMPUTER SYSTEM

A schematic diagram of a computer system is given in Figure 5.1. The following components (or units, as they are usually called) are shown:

> Main storage
> Central processing unit
> Data channels
> Input/output control units and devices

Main storage and the central processing unit have been mentioned previously and are covered in more detail in this chapter.

Central Processing Unit

The *central processing unit* is composed of a control unit and an arithmetic/logic unit. The *control unit* maintains the current instruction address, fetches instructions from main storage, decodes the instructions, and sends control signals to the arithmetic/logic unit to have the instructions executed. The *arithmetic/logic unit* contains the arithmetic registers and electronic circuitry for executing computer instructions. The central processing unit provides a variety of other control functions that are necessary for continuous operation.

Main Storage

Modern computers use the stored program concept, which means that both computer instructions and data are available to the central processing unit at electronic speeds from a component referred to as *main storage,* as introduced earlier. Main storage is not used for the permanent storage of programs and data, and a program is placed in main storage only when it is being executed. Usually, computer instructions and constant data values are placed in main storage by a loader program.

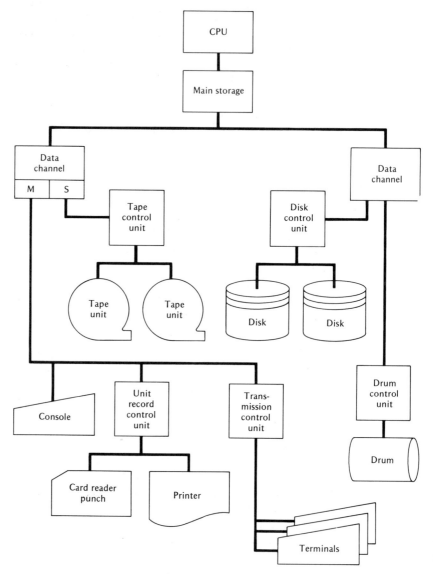

FIGURE 5.1   Schematic diagram of a typical computer system.

Program data are read into main storage with input instructions; data are recorded on a storage medium, such as magnetic tape or punched cards, with output instructions. Main storage is organized and used in a variety of ways, as discussed later in this chapter.

The schematic of a typical computer system given in Figure 5.1 is a static representation of the structure of a computer. Figure 5.2 gives a description of a computer system that is more functionally oriented. It is referred to in subsequent paragraphs.

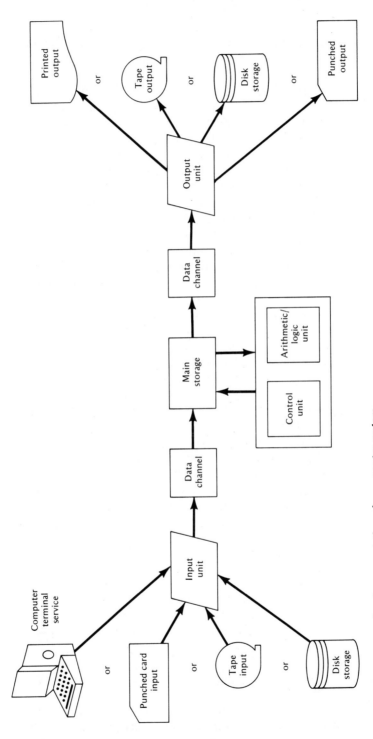

FIGURE 5.2   Functional representation of a computer system.

The Concept of a Data Channel

The central processing unit and main storage are electronic devices. Input and output devices are both electronic and mechanical, and since electronic devices are inherently faster than mechanical devices, the central processing unit is faster than input and output devices. For example, it takes approximately 100 milliseconds for a card reader to read one punched card. In that time, an average computer can execute approximately 50,000 instructions. Therefore, the central processing unit, which is an expensive component, should not be kept waiting for input and output. This is where the data channel comes in. A *data channel* is essentially a small computer connected to main storage; it receives control from the central processing unit. The central processing unit, under control of a computer program, tells a data channel to transfer data between main storage and an external device (and also gives the amount and location of the data). Then while the central processing unit continues to operate, the data channel signals to the input/output device and manages the data-transfer operation concurrently. A read operation is taken as an example. The data channel accepts information from an input device (perhaps a card reader) one character at a time at a relatively low speed. The characters are put into a buffer. (A *buffer* is a storage area or register used to compensate for the difference in the speed of two devices.) When enough characters are accumulated, the operation of the central processing unit is temporarily interrupted, and the information is placed in main storage by the data channel. The central processing unit and data channels are designed to operate concurrently, and this fact contributes to the input/output and processing overlap that exists with most computer systems. The concept of overlapped processing as compared to serial processing is shown in Figures 5.3 and 5.4. The effective use of data channels is directly related to computer system efficiency. This topic is covered later in this chapter.

Input/Output Control Unit

An *input/output control unit* monitors and controls the operation of one or more input/output devices. The input/output control unit manages the data flow to and from an input/output device and performs other nondata-transfer operations such as a tape rewind or a disk seek (discussed in Chapter 6).

Input/Output Device

An *input/output device* serves to transfer data between the computer and the external world. Input/output devices can be grouped into four

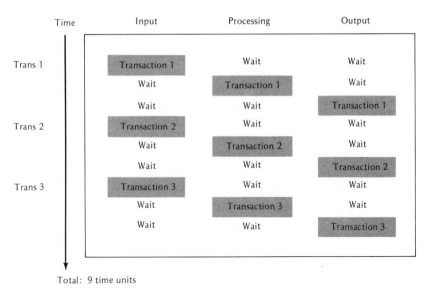

FIGURE 5.3   Conceptual view of serial processing without overlap for three data processing transactions.

classes: (1) unit record devices, (2) serial devices, (3) direct-access devices, and (4) miscellaneous devices. *Unit record devices* include the card reader, the line printer, and the card punch; a "block" of information transmitted between main storage and the device normally corresponds to a physical unit, such as a card or a line. *Serial devices* include magnetic tape and paper tape; these devices are characterized by the fact that information is stored serially and that access to the *n*th block requires that the unit pass over the (*n*-1)st block. *Direct-access devices* include disk storage and drum storage; these devices, frequently referred to as rotating devices, are characterized by the fact that a block of information

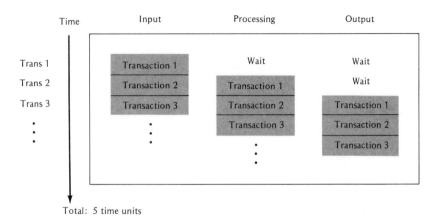

FIGURE 5.4   Conceptual view of overlapped processing for three data processing transactions.

can be located directly on the medium prior to input or output operation. *Miscellaneous devices* include data terminals, cathode-ray-tube (CRT) devices, audio-response units, and so on. Each device has characteristics of its own. The *terminal device* is frequently used in programming and has the general characteristics of a unit record device. More specifically, a terminal is a keyboard-driven unit used to transmit information between a computer and the terminal unit via telecommunications facilities. Input and output devices and their respective storage media are considered in the next chapter.

OPERATION OF THE CENTRAL PROCESSING UNIT

The central processing unit controls the operation of the entire computer system by fetching instructions from main storage, decoding them, and setting up control signals to have the instructions executed. The central processing unit processes *all* instructions and initiates all input and output operations. This section covers the function organization that permits the central processing unit to control the operation of the computer system in a complex operating environment. The material presented here is representative of the many computers in existence today.

Operating Control

In previous chapters, it was mentioned that the location in main storage of the next instruction to be executed is contained in a current address register, and when the control unit of the central processing unit is ready for the next instruction, it uses the current address register to determine its location. (The current address register usually is not addressed directly by a computer program.) This is only part of the story. There are other indicators besides the current program address that determine the current state of the computer system. Some of the most frequently encountered indicators are a storage key used for referencing main storage (covered later), mask bits that determine the kinds of events that can take place in the system, and a condition code that is set as the result of a comparison operation. Collectively, these state indicators, along with the current address, are contained in a word termed the *status word.* At any point, the state of the computer system is reflected in the status word, and changing the contents of the status word is tantamount to altering the state of the computer.

Supervisor and Problem States

When introducing the data channel earlier in this chapter, the difference in the relative speeds of the central processing unit and input/output devices was mentioned. Although the use of a data channel alleviated the situation somewhat, delays of the central processing unit are inevitable. Modern computer systems are designed to accommodate several programs, for an equal number of users, in main storage at one time. When one program experiences an unavoidable delay, control of the central processing unit is given to another program. The technique is referred to as *multiprogramming* and is intended to keep the costly central processing unit busy. (A set of programs that manages the resources of the computer system is referred to as an *operating system*.)

Because several programs can share main storage and mass storage media, it is necessary that the various users be protected from each other by limiting the functions they can perform. Two states of the central processing unit are defined in most modern computer systems: the supervisor state and the problem state. A program operating in the *supervisor state* has access to all of the facilities of the computer system, including the ability to reference all of main storage, to change the status word, and to perform input and output operations. Operating system programs normally operate in the supervisor state. A program operating in the *problem state* is limited in the sense that it can execute only instructions that cannot affect other programs. Instructions that can be executed in the problem state (and also in the supervisor state) are referred to as *nonprivileged instructions*. Typical nonprivileged instructions are the arithmetic/logic instructions, the branching and control instructions, and shifting, comparison, and character manipulation instructions. Instructions that can be executed only in the supervisor state are referred to as *privileged instructions*. Instructions that perform input and output functions, modify the status word, and deal with storage protection (covered later) are classified as privileged instructions.

A program being executed is dependent upon the operating system for critical operations, such as input and output. When a program executing in the problem state needs to have an input or output operation performed, it makes an appropriate request to the operating system to have that function performed. Thus, the operating system is able to manage critical resources on a system-wide basis.

In an operating system environment, user programs, such as a payroll program, operate in the problem state. The central processing unit enters the problem state when an appropriate bit is set in the status word. That bit can be set only when the central processing unit is in the supervisor state. When an operating system program executing in the supervisor state decides to give control of the computer to a user program, it loads a new status word with the problem-state bit set and the current instruction address field (also in the status word) set to the address in main storage of the user program. The new status word immediately changes the state of the central processing unit to the problem state, and execution continues with the specified address in the user program. There are, of course, other methods of implementing operational control in a computer system, but the above technique is a typical representation. Other terms that are frequently associated with operational control are *monitor mode* and *master and slave modes.*

External Events

The use of a data channel to permit the overlap of processing and input/output activity was mentioned earlier. The central processing unit sends information to the data channel on what input or output it needs to have performed, and then continues with normal processing. The data channel subsequently performs the requested input or output operation simultaneously. The situation is analogous to a supervisor instructing one worker to perform a certain task. After the instructions are received, both employees go about their respective duties. When the worker is finished with the task, he or she interrupts the supervisor for further instructions. The data channel operates in a similar manner. When an input or output operation is complete, it interrupts the execution of the central processing unit. In a computer system an independent event that interrupts normal computer processing is called an *interruption.* An interruption can occur for one of many reasons:

1. The computer detects an erroneous condition in an executing program.
2. A component external to the computer (such as a data channel) requires attention or signals completion.
3. The error correction circuitry of the computer detects a hardware error.
4. A program executing in the problem state requires services that can be performed only in the supervisor state and executes an instruction that causes an interruption to be initiated.

Computers are designed and built to recognize a fixed number of different kinds of interruptions. The actual number varies depending upon the primary market for the computer and ranges from as low as five to as high as 99. One method of handling interruptions relies on the fact that each type of interruption is associated with two fixed locations in main storage. Each of these locations is designed to hold a replica of the status word. One of the fixed locations is referred to as the "old status word," and the other is referred to as the "new status word." When an interruption occurs, the "current status word," maintained in the central processing unit on a dynamic basis as a program is executed, is stored in the old status word location, and the status word located at the new status word location replaces the current status word in the central processing unit. The process of swapping status words is depicted in Figure 5.5. The current address field of

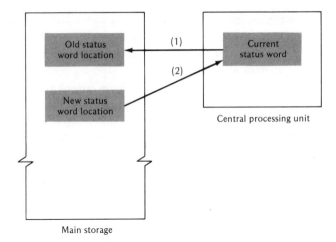

FIGURE 5.5 **The swapping of status words after an interruption.**

the new status word contains the address of the first instruction in a routine designed to process that type of interruption, and the supervisor-state bit is usually set. Interruptions are normally processed in the supervisor state, and the central processing unit continues processing in the interruption handling routine. The old status word reflects the state of the central processing unit when the interruption occurred, so that execution of that program can be resumed when the interruption processing has been completed.

Computer Instructions

Another major difference between computers lies in the instruction repertoire, or, put in a slightly different manner, the basic operations the computer is designed to execute. The instruction repertoire of large general-purpose computers is extensive and can be justified by the fact that the computer is used for a wide range of applications. Small and medium-sized computers have more restricted instruction repertoires, and many operations performed with one instruction in a large computer require two or three instructions in a smaller computer. Computer instructions can be grouped into five convenient classes that seem to be invariant among computers. They are described in the following list:

1. *Arithmetic instructions* include operations used for performing arithmetic on a digital computer. Also included in this category are instructions for making arithmetic comparisons and for converting values from one number base to another.

2. *Logical instructions* perform operations on bytes and bits that include data movement, logical comparisons, testing, and data editing.
3. *Branching instructions* provide the capability for altering the sequential flow of program execution.
4. *Input and output instructions* initiate input or output operations by passing appropriate commands to data channels and allow the status of specific devices to be tested. Input and output instructions are normally implemented as privileged instructions.
5. *Status switching instructions* permit the status word and storage keys (see next section on "storage") to be loaded and stored under program control. Instructions in this category are also privileged and effectively change the status of the computer system.

Most general-purpose computers have a basic set of instructions that allow most computational processes to be programmed. Since most programs are written in a higher-level language—such as Common Business Oriented Language, or COBOL—the instruction repertoire is usually not of concern to most users of the computer. An area in which the instruction repertoire is of concern, however, is that of efficiency. If several instructions are needed to execute a basic computational operation, then the actual execution time of a program is proportionately high. On the other hand, an extensive set of instructions requires more circuitry and is more sophisticated to build. The end result, of course, is that the choice of a particular computer is a trade-off of cost, basic computing speed, and computational efficiency.

MAIN STORAGE

Although the central processing unit controls the operation of the computer, the organization and implementation of main storage implicitly determines the manner in which the central processing unit functions. When discussing main storage, two characteristics are of prime importance:

1. The physical technique (or device) used to implement main storage.
2. The physical arrangement of the storage elements that constitute main storage.

These characteristics determine how main storage is organized and addressed and how it can be accessed. The objective of main storage must again be stated: it should be directly addressable by the central processing unit, and it must operate at a speed approaching that of the central processing unit.

Organization, Addressing, and Access Width

The manner in which main storage is organized determines how it is accessed. The process of accessing main storage by the central processing unit* is performed as follows:

1. Place the address of the desired data item in a *memory address register.*
2. Initiate a "fetch" operation.
3. Main storage is accessed and the desired data item is placed in a *memory data register* for reference by the central processing unit.

How much data are placed in the memory data register? With a word-oriented computer, the addressed word from main storage is placed in the memory data register. With byte-oriented computers, the concept of an "access width" is used. *Access width* refers to the amount of data that is transferred between main storage and the central processing unit with each access. In small byte-oriented computers, the access width can be as small as one or two bytes; while in large byte-oriented computers, the access width can be as high as 16 bytes. Access width is significant for the following reas/n. Suppose an instruction using 8-byte operands is executed. Execution of the instruction on a large computer would require one storage reference. Whereas on a small computer, execution of the instruction might require as many as four references. Therefore, even if the basic speeds of the central processing units are the same, main storage determines how quickly the instruction can be executed.

The significance of access width is also related to whether main storage is implemented by using circuitry or whether physical media such as magnetic cores are used. There are a variety of physical processes available for implementing main storage, such as magnetic cores, thin film, or plated wire. The use of magnetic cores is assumed in the following section; in fact, main storage is frequently referred to as *core storage.*

Access Time

When magnetic cores are used as the storage technology, access time is determined by the storage cycle time that involves read-out and write-back operations. The write-back operation is required to reset the cores because of the read-out process, which sets the cores to zero. The process of read-out and write-back is depicted in Figure 5.6. At time t_i, the central processing unit sends a signal to the main storage

* Actually, any component that accesses main storage would perform the same steps.

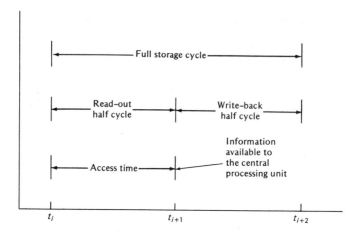

FIGURE 5.6   Main storage access time.

unit to initiate a storage cycle. At time t_{i+1}, the information is available to the central processing unit, and processing may continue as outlined below. The time from t_i to t_{i+1} is referred to as *access time.* The write-back half cycle extends from t_{i+1} to t_{i+2}; during that time the main storage unit is busy and another access cannot be made.

When main storage is implemented using electronic circuitry, then the read-out and write-back half cycles do not apply, and a full storage cycle consists only of access time. Obviously, electronic circuitry is the preferred method of implementing main storage from a performance point of view. Although modern manufacturing methods permit the fabrication of solid state chips that contain circuits, electronic circuitry is more expensive than magnetic core technology.

Main Storage Interleaving

One of the methods used to reduce the effective storage cycle time is to employ a technique called *interleaving.* The storage cycle time comprised of read-out and write-back half cycles applies to a single storage unit; when multiple storage units are designed into a computer system, they can be accessed in parallel.

Assume that main storage is designed as two independent units— called two-way interleaving. Suppose further that odd-numbered addresses are in the first unit and even-numbered addresses are in the second unit. If sequential main storage locations are accessed, then read-out cycles can be overlapped with write-back half cycles, as depicted in Figure 5.7. This technique effectively eliminates the write-back half cycle, so that the effective cycle time for main storage that is two-way interleaved approaches half the amount of cycle time needed if storage were not interleaved. Ultrahigh-speed computers em-

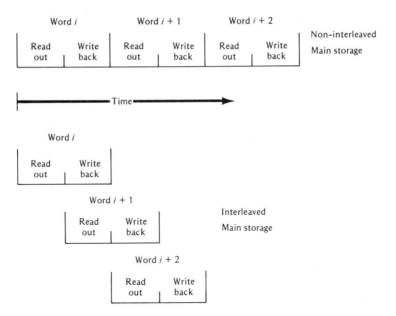

FIGURE 5.7   Access to noninterleaved and interleaved main storage.

ploy as high as 16-way interleaving with access widths of up to 128 bytes.

DATA CHANNELS

The data channel, which is essentially a small, hard-wired computer, is used to compensate for the difference in speeds between electromechanical input and output devices and the purely electronic operation of the central processing unit and main storage. In addition, modern operating techniques, such as multiprogramming and time sharing, require asynchronous input and output operations and device independence. These facilities are provided through the use of a data channel.

In most computer systems, the data channel is a logical extension to the central processing unit and main storage and is independent of input and output devices attached to the system. In large-scale computing systems, data channels are designed as separate components. In many small-scale systems, the data channels are integrated into the central processing unit.

Channel Operation

A data channel is designed to operate independently of other data channels and the central processing unit. It uses a channel program composed of channel commands placed in main storage, in the same manner that the central processing unit uses a computer program composed of instructions. Typical channel commands are read, write, control, sense, and transfer in channel. These commands are covered below.

An input/output operation is initiated in the central processing unit by a privileged instruction that specifies the channel and device addresses on which the operation is to take place. The address in main storage of the channel program is also provided to the channel at this time. If the channel and device are free, then the central processing unit continues with the next instruction, and the data channel takes charge of the input/output operation. This is how the frequently mentioned compute and input/output overlap is achieved in the computer.

The format of a typical channel command is given in Figure 5.8. The *command code* field specifies the input/output operation to be performed. The *data address* field specifies the beginning address in main storage of data to be written out, or in the case of a read operation, the beginning address of where the data are to be placed. The *count* field specifies how many bytes (or words) are to be transferred between main storage and the input/output medium during the operation. The *flags* field specifies a variety of things, such as: (1) whether the channel program is continued; (2) whether an interruption should be generated when the operation is complete; (3) whether the data should be skipped (that is, read from the input/output medium but not placed in main storage); and (4) whether a data record should be "split" between two or more areas in main storage.

The data channel operates like a "data manager"; it decodes channel commands and sends orders to input/output control units and devices. For a *read operation,* the data channel accepts data from the control unit and accumulates them in a buffer within the channel. When the buffer is full, the central processing unit is interrupted and the accumulated data is placed in main storage. For a *write operation,* the data channel fetches a "buffer's worth" of data from main storage and feeds it to the control unit on a byte (or character) basis. Data channel organization is shown in Figure 5.9, where two concepts are depicted: the standard input/output interface and the access width.

Standard Input/Output Interface and Access Width

The *standard input/output interface* refers to the amount of data that can pass at any point in time between a data channel and a device attached

Command code	Data address	Flags	Count

FIGURE 5.8   Typical channel command format.

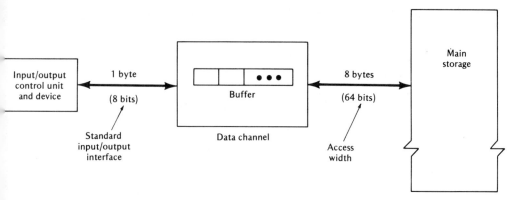

FIGURE 5.9   Data channel organization. Access width typically varies from 2 to 128 bytes and is dependent upon the design and organization of main storage.

to it. Usually all devices attached to the computer system adhere to the standard input/output interface, permitting a wide range of devices from different manufacturers to be utilized. Most modern computer systems use a standard input/output interface of one byte (or character). The *access width,* covered earlier with regard to main storage, is a function of the design and organization of main storage. All components that access main storage must be designed to use the access width provided. Because the access width is usually greater than that of the standard input/output interface, the data channel includes a buffer to compensate for the electronic speeds of main storage and the electromechanical speeds of input and output devices.

It is obvious from the preceding discussion that a data channel actually operates like a small computer through the process of decoding and executing channel commands. In some large-scale scientific computer systems (or "number crunchers," as they are sometimes called), small programmable computers—termed *satellite computers*—have been used to achieve the same purpose as the data channel.

Channel Design Factors

Normally, several data channels and the central processing unit compete for access to main storage. Therefore, when a data channel gains access to main storage, it is desirable to transfer enough information to make the effort worthwhile. (This fact relates to the access width mentioned earlier.) As a result, the data channel requires storage facilities for each input/output operation that include a count, a main storage address, the main storage address of the current channel command, control and status data, and a buffer for incoming or outgoing data. This storage combined with logical and functional facilities constitutes a data channel and is a substantial investment in physical equipment.

The speed of input/output devices varies from 10 bytes per second (BPS), in the case of a low-speed data communications terminal, to 3 million BPS, in the case of a high-speed disk storage device. In order to justify the cost of a data channel it is necessary to share data channel facilities for low-speed devices. The reason is obvious. For high-speed devices, the logical and functional facilities are fully utilized; whereas with low-speed devices, the same facilities are idle for a good portion of the time.

Subchannel Concept

The data channel facilities that are necessary to sustain an input/output operation are referred to as a *subchannel.* Logical circuitry of the data channel is shared among the subchannels; storage areas are used to record the state of an input/output operation and are not shared. The manner in which subchannels are implemented is used to distinguish between three types of data channels: the selector channel, the byte-multiplexer channel, and the block-multiplexer channel.

Selector Channel.   The *selector channel* is used with high-speed input/output devices, such as magnetic disks or drums, that provide high data-transfer rates that exceed 300,000 bytes per second. The selector channel includes one subchannel and can manage only one data-transfer operation at a time. Once a logical connection is made between an input/output device and the selector channel, the channel is regarded as being "busy" until the input/output operation is complete.

Byte-Multiplexer Channel.   The *byte-multiplexer channel* is used for controlling several low-speed devices that do not justify the exclusive use of a data channel because of the low speeds involved. (The key point is that a data channel can sustain a given data rate from one fast device or several slow devices.) A byte-multiplexer channel contains several subchannels and can sustain an input/output operation on each of its subchannels concurrently. A device remains connected to a subchannel for the duration of an input/output operation but uses only the logical and functional facilities of the data channel during the transfer of a single byte of information. In reality, therefore, the data channel services one subchannel, then another subchannel, on a "multiplexed" basis.

Block Multiplexer Channel.   The *block-multiplexer channel* combines the concepts of the selector and byte-multiplexer channels. Here, a block refers to a complete data record. The block-multiplexer channel is shared by several high-speed devices in the same manner that a byte-multiplexer channel is shared by several low-speed devices—except that blocks are multiplexed rather than bytes. The logical and functional facilities of a block-multiplexer channel are freed during nondata-transfer operations, such as a disk seek, for use by another subchannel.

Input/Output Completion and Interruption

The central processing unit and data channels operate asynchronously; the central processing unit initiates an input/output operation in the data channel, and from then on the units function independently of each other. The central processing unit is in control—much like the traditional supervisor-employee relationship. In fact, the central processing unit can halt an input/output operation in most computers through an instruction designed for that purpose.

Normally, however, the data channel operates until it has completed an input/output operation and then "informs" the central processing unit that it is finished. The central processing unit is informed of the completion of an input/output operation through an input/output interruption, one of the types mentioned earlier.

MULTIPLE COMPUTER SYSTEMS

The manner in which a computer system is organized and used determines to a large extent how effective the computer system is as a computing resource. The situation is more a matter of functional organization than it is of physical structure. If a task is assigned to a high-cost (and in most cases, a high-performance) component that could be performed equally well by a lower-cost component, then the effectiveness of the system could be improved by functional reorganization within realistic limits. The concept could be viewed as the "systems approach" to computer utilization, because the objective is to maximize the performance of the entire system. One method of increasing computer performance is to add another computer to the total system configuration. The additional computer is usually a small computer to which routine tasks are assigned. In other types of multiple-computer systems, only a central processing unit is added and main storage is shared between the computers involved.

Peripheral Computers

A *peripheral computer*, in its traditional form, is used to replace low-speed input/output devices, such as a card reader and line printer, with a higher-speed device, such as magnetic tape. The peripheral computer is a relatively small system used to read input cards and place them on magnetic tape and also to read print lines placed on magnetic tape and print them on its line printer. Thus, input to the main computer is magnetic tape and printed output is also placed on magnetic tape for subsequent printing.

The use of a peripheral computer is justified because a nominal figure for the input rate of punched cards is between 300 and 1,200 80-column cards per minute, which amounts to 1,600 characters per second or less. Printed output ranges from 1,000 to 2,400 120-character lines per minute, which amounts to 4,800 characters per second or less. An average figure for magnetic tape input and output is in the neighborhood of 100,000 characters per second.

Peripheral computers are still used but the technique of input and output buffering with the data channel has partially eliminated their need in recent years.

Satellite Computers

A *satellite computer* is a small programmable computer attached to the main computer. Each satellite computer is used to manage input/output operations and perform data editing for a given set of devices. Normally, several satellite computers are employed when this technique is used.

Satellite computers are similar in concept to the data channel; they normally include features for interrupting the main computer and for sharing portions of main storage. In fact, satellite computers substitute for data channels in some computer systems.

Attached Support Processors

An *attached support processor* (see Figure 5.10) is a computer system that is attached to the main computer via a channel-to-channel adapter or with shared main storage. Usually, when the channel-to-channel

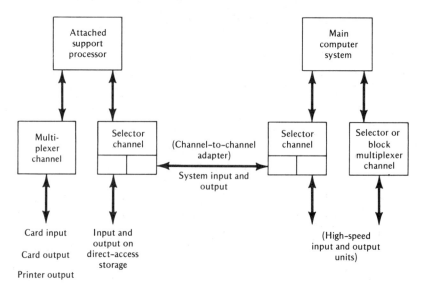

FIGURE 5.10   Attached support processor.

adapter is used, the attached computer performs input/output and editing for the main computer. The low-speed input and output devices of the main computer are replaced by the adapter connection, so that data can be transferred between the systems at electronic speeds. The attached support computer performs low-speed input and stacks the information on a direct-access storage device, in anticipation of a request from the main computer for input data. Similarly, output lines received by the attached support computer from the main computer are stacked up on a direct-access device for subsequent printing or punching. The attached support computer serves as a buffering system for the main computer and is not normally used for the processing of user programs.

Multiprocessing Systems

A computer system that includes more than one central processing unit is referred to as a *multiprocessing system.* The concept of multiprocessing is employed to increase either the reliability or the performance of the system. As depicted in Figure 5.11, the central processing units in a multiprocessing system share main storage, and consequently, they can service the same set of jobs.

When multiprocessing is used to improve system performance, the central processing units operate asynchronously and effectively share the work load. In many operating environments, such as an airline reservation system, response is critical. In fact, the success or failure of an enterprise may be dependent upon a computer. In cases such as this, an extra central processing unit is available to take over in the event of malfunction in the primary central processing unit. Thus, both central processing units must have access to the same information (main storage, direct-access storage, magnetic tape units, and other storage units) and must be able to exchange control signals when one central processing unit fails.

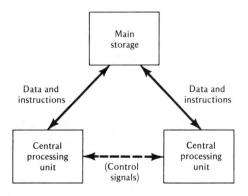

FIGURE 5.11   Conceptual view of a multiprocessing system.

Modern computer systems contain circuitry for error checking and correction. When the hardware detects an operational error, it attempts to correct the error condition through sophisticated logical procedures. When an error condition cannot be corrected, a malfunction is signaled. Sometimes, an error occurs in a bank of main storage or in an input/output or mass storage device. If possible in these cases, the failing component is logically disconnected from the system, under program control, and computer operation continues in a less efficient manner. The key point, obviously, is that in many applications, it is preferable to operate in a degraded state than to fail completely.

Vocabulary   The student should be familiar with the following terms in the context in which they were used in the chapter.

access time	main storage
access width	memory address register
arithmetic/logic unit	memory data register
attached support processor	multiple computer system
block multiplexer channel	multiprocessing system
buffer	new status word
byte multiplexer channel	peripheral computer
central processing unit	problem state
command code field	read out
control unit	satellite computer
count field	selector channel
current status word	serial device
data address field	standard input/output interface
data channel	status word
direct-access device	subchannel
flags field	supervisor state
index register	system
input/output control unit	terminal device
input/output device	unit record device
interleaving	write back
interruption	

Questions   1. What is a buffer?

2. What is a rationale for the supervisor and problem states?

3. In what way does the data channel provide the overlap of processing and input/output operations?

4. In what way do access width and the standard input/output interface contribute to the need for a data channel?

5. What is a subchannel?

Exercises   1. Describe the relationship between the supervisor state, the data channel, and the interruption.

2. Draw a flow diagram of the processes involved in performing an input/output operation.

3. Describe how interleaving and access width contribute to access time.

4. Give the similarities and differences between the block-multiplexer channel and the byte-multiplexer channel.

5. Describe techniques that are used for minimizing the input/output bottleneck.

Related Reading   Gear, C. W. *Computer Organization and Programming.* New York: McGraw-Hill, 1969.

Katzan, H. *Computer Organization and the System/370.* New York: Van Nostrand Reinhold, 1971.

Stone, H. S. *Introduction to Computer Organization and Data Structures.* New York: McGraw-Hill, 1972.

Input and Output— Media and Devices

lmost anyone who has registered at a college, paid a telephone bill, or made a purchase at a large department store has dealt with computer media of some kind. The first concern, of course, involves entering recorded information into the computer; that is where input devices come into the picture. Output devices are used for the reverse process—getting information from the computer. Using input and output in this sense is familiar to most people, but the words also refer to processes carried on within the computer itself. Because main storage is limited in size, data are also placed on mass storage devices when not being used. Magnetic tape and direct-access storage (such as magnetic disk) are used for this purpose. In general, the process of reading data into main storage is referred to as input, regardless of whether it is from a mass storage device or it involves manual preparation. Similarly, the process of writing data from main storage to an external device is referred to as output, again regardless of whether the device is for mass storage or for human use.

INTRODUCTION

In dealing with input/output concepts, it is important to distinguish between the medium and the device used to read or write it. For example, a punched card is a medium for recording information; a card reader or a card punch is a device.

In this chapter four media and associated devices are presented in detail: punched cards, magnetic tape, magnetic disk, and the line printer. A variety of other devices are covered briefly to acquaint the reader with current thinking regarding input and output devices. Telecommunications facilities are widely used these days, and much of the concern over large data banks is related to the manner in which they can be accessed via ordinary telephone lines and a terminal device. Telecommunications and terminal devices are also covered in this chapter.

INPUT AND OUTPUT ORGANIZATION

Figure 6.1 depicts a simplified input/output subsystem, including input/output control units and devices. An input/output control unit is designed to control the operation of one or more devices of a given class. Typical input/output control units are magnetic tape control units, disk control units, and unit record control units. Normally, input/output devices share control units, since all devices are not being used at a particular point in time.

An input/output device operates as a "slave" to its control unit; the control unit sends an order to the device to perform an elementary operation—such as read, write, rewind, or seek—and the device rou-

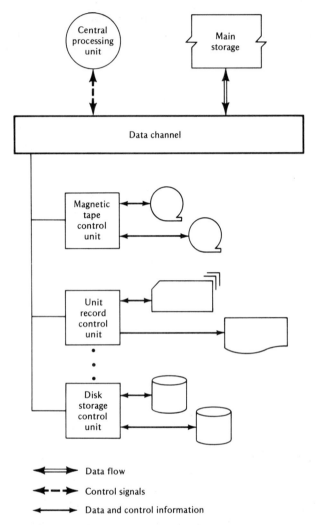

FIGURE 6.1   Simplified input/output subsystem. (The viewpoint is conceptual, since unit record and disk devices usually do not utilize the same channel.)

tinely performs the requested operation. If a device happens to be busy when an order is received, it returns a busy indication (that is, a flag) to the control unit. The control unit can then save the requested operation for subsequent execution, or it can return a busy signal to the data channel. An input/output control unit is frequently integrated into the device itself; in addition, an input/output control unit and a set of devices are sometimes housed in the same cabinet, and one often hears of a "disk system" or a "tape system." In general, however, control units and devices interact as just described, regardless of the engineering design employed.

Classification of External Storage Media

External storage media and devices are classified by whether they use unit records or volumes. When the external storage medium takes the form of a punched card or a printed line, it is referred to as a *unit record* and is used with a *unit record device*. As examples, line printers produce printed lines, and card reader/punches read and punch cards.

When the external storage medium can store several sets of records, as is the case with magnetic tape, it is referred to as a *volume*. As an example, a familiar storage volume is a reel of magnetic tape that is read and written by a magnetic-tape unit. An important consideration is whether a storage volume is removable. Although the number of input/output devices in any computer system is limited by the available equipment, the number of storage volumes is not limited as long as a given storage volume can be removed from its associated device.

Code Conversion

One of the major functions performed by an input/output control unit is code conversion. In most cases, information is not recorded on a storage medium in exactly the same form that it exists in main storage. The punched card is an ideal example. In main storage a character exists in a 6-bit or an 8-bit coded form; on a punched card a character is recorded as a column of 12 bits. A unit record control unit makes the necessary code conversions.

The preceding discussion implies great flexibility in the kinds of devices that can be connected to a computer. All that is needed to make a device compatible with a given computer system is to have an input/output control unit that can perform the necessary code conversions.

PUNCHED CARDS

The standard punched card, frequently referred to as the IBM card, measures 7 and ⅜ by 3 and ¼ inches and is 0.007 inch thick. A punched card costs about $\frac{1}{10}$ of a cent. The corners may be rounded or square and one corner is usually cut to detect when a card is upside down. A card is organized into 80 columns, numbered 1 through 80, with 12 punching positions in each column, numbered 12, 11, and 0 through 9. Information is recorded by punching rectangular holes in the card; one column represents one character. Thus, in a single column there are 12 positions that can be punched. By established convention, combinations of the various punches represent the characters of the computer alphabet. Figure 6.2 depicts the various card code combinations. For example, the letter B is represented by punches in the 12 row and the 2 row. Similarly, the character 7 is represented by a punch

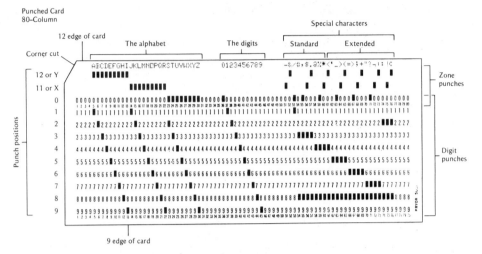

Punched Card
80-Column

FIGURE 6.2   **Hollerith card code. (This alphanumeric punched card code was invented by Dr. Herman Hollerith in 1889.)**

in the 7 row, and the character * is represented by punches in the 11 row, 8 row, and the 4 row.

The primary use of punched cards is as an input media for data prepared through human participation. Figure 6.3 shows a typical keypunch machine, which contains a keyboard like an ordinary typewriter. Blank cards are entered into the keypunch machine, and appropriate holes are punched when a given key is depressed. Figure 6.4 gives a typical input card. It contains three fields: name, social security number, and hours. (A *field* is a group of columns that represents one data item.) Punched cards are convenient for human use because individual cards can easily be added, deleted, replaced, and sorted. A typical card reader/punch is depicted in Figure 6.5. The objective of the card reader is to detect (that is, recognize) the contents of a card and place the corresponding information in main storage. Figure 6.6 shows the internal

Courtesy of IBM Corporation

FIGURE 6.3   **Typical keypunch machine for punching cards.**

```
JOHN E. SMITH          486127192 56
 I  II   I I

 II I      I

0 0 0 0 0 0 0 0 0 0 0 0 0 ▌0 0 ▌0 0 0 0 0 0 0 0 0 0 0 0 0 0 0 0 0 0 0 0 0 0 0 0 0 0 0 0 0 0 0 0 0 0 0 0 0 0 0 0 0 0 0 0 0 0 0 0 0 0 0 0 0 0 0 0 0 0 0 0 0 0 0
 1 2 3 4 5 6 7 8 9 10 11 12 13 14 15 16 17 18 19 20 21 22 23 24 25 26 27 28 29 30 31 32 33 34 35 36 37 38 39 40 41 42 43 44 45 46 47 48 49 50 51 52 53 54 55 56 57 58 59 60 61 62 63 64 65 66 67 68 69 70 71 72 73 74 75 76 77 78 79 80
1 1 1 1 1 ▌1 1 1 1 1 1 1 1 1 1 1 1 1 1 1 1 1 1 1 1 1 1 1 1 1 1 1 1 1 1 1 ▌1 1 ▌1 1 1 1 1 1 1 1 1 1 1 1 1 1 1 1 1 1 1 1 1 1 1 1 1 1 1 1 1 1 1 1 1 1 1 1 1 1 1 1 1
2 2 2 2 2 2 2 2 2 2 2 2 2 ▌2 2 2 2 2 2 2 2 2 2 2 2 2 2 2 2 ▌2 2 2 ▌2 2 2 2 2 2 2 2 2 2 2 2 2 2 2 2 2 2 2 2 2 2 2 2 2 2 2 2 2 2 2 2 2 2 2 2 2 2 2 2 2 2 2 2 2
3 3 3 3 3 3 3 3 3 3 3 ▌3 3 3 3 ▌3 3 3 3 3 3 3 3 3 3 3 3 3 3 3 3 3 3 3 3 3 3 3 3 3 3 3 3 3 3 3 3 3 3 3 3 3 3 3 3 3 3 3 3 3 3 3 3 3 3 3 3 3 3 3 3 3 3 3 3 3 3 3
4 4 4 4 4 4 4 4 4 4 4 4 4 4 ▌4 4 4 4 4 4 4 4 4 4 4 ▌4 4 4 4 4 4 4 4 4 4 4 4 4 4 4 4 4 4 4 4 4 4 4 4 4 4 4 4 4 4 4 4 4 4 4 4 4 4 4 4 4 4 4 4 4 4 4 4 4 4 4 4 4
5 5 5 5 5 5 5 5 ▌5 ▌5 5 5 5 5 5 5 5 5 5 5 5 5 5 5 5 5 5 5 ▌5 5 5 5 5 5 5 5 5 5 5 5 5 5 5 5 5 5 5 5 5 5 5 5 5 5 5 5 5 5 5 5 5 5 5 5 5 5 5 5 5 5 5 5 5 5 5 5 5 5
6 6 6 6 6 ▌6 6 6 6 6 6 6 6 6 6 6 6 6 6 6 6 6 6 6 ▌6 6 6 6 6 6 6 ▌6 6 6 6 6 6 6 6 6 6 6 6 6 6 6 6 6 6 6 6 6 6 6 6 6 6 6 6 6 6 6 6 6 6 6 6 6 6 6 6 6 6 6 6 6 6 6
7 7 7 7 7 7 7 7 7 7 7 7 7 7 7 7 7 7 7 7 7 7 7 7 7 7 7 7 7 ▌7 7 7 7 7 7 7 7 7 7 7 7 7 7 7 7 7 7 7 7 7 7 7 7 7 7 7 7 7 7 7 7 7 7 7 7 7 7 7 7 7 7 7 7 7 7 7 7 7
8 8 8 8 8 8 8 ▌8 8 8 ▌8 8 8 8 8 ▌8 8 8 8 8 8 8 8 8 8 8 8 ▌8 8 8 8 8 8 8 8 8 8 8 8 8 8 8 8 8 8 8 8 8 8 8 8 8 8 8 8 8 8 8 8 8 8 8 8 8 8 8 8 8 8 8 8 8 8 8 8 8 8
9 9 9 9 9 9 9 9 9 9 9 9 9 9 ▌9 9 9 9 9 9 9 9 9 9 9 9 9 9 9 9 ▌9 9 9 9 9 9 9 9 9 9 9 9 9 9 9 9 9 9 9 9 9 9 9 9 9 9 9 9 9 9 9 9 9 9 9 9 9 9 9 9 9 9 9 9 9 9 9 9
 1 2 3 4 5 6 7 8 9 10 11 12 13 14 15 16 17 18 19 20 21 22 23 24 25 26 27 28 29 30 31 32 33 34 35 36 37 38 39 40 41 42 43 44 45 46 47 48 49 50 51 52 53 54 55 56 57 58 59 60 61 62 63 64 65 66 67 68 69 70 71 72 73 74 75 76 77 78 79 80
```

PRYOR 5ט

FIGURE 6.4   Typical input card.

workings of a card reader/punch. Holes in the card are sensed by brushes that protrude through the card and make an electrical connection, or by photo-electric cells. Reading is performed on the right side of the unit. Cards to be read are placed in the read hopper; a card is read when a read signal is received from the computer, via the data channel and control unit. The card passes through two read stations and is finally deposited in an output stacker. Each card is read twice so that the results can be compared as a means of error checking. Punching is performed on the left side of the unit. Blank cards are placed in the punch hopper; a card is punched when a punch signal is received from the computer, again via the data channel and control unit. The card is punched at one station and read at another to verify that the card was punched correctly. The punched card is also deposited in an output stacker. The cards may be routed to alternate stackers (that is, pockets) under computer control.

Courtesy of IBM Corporation

FIGURE 6.5   Combined card reader/punch unit.

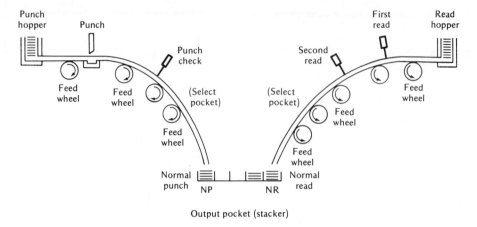

FIGURE 6.6   Internal mechanism of the card reader/punch.

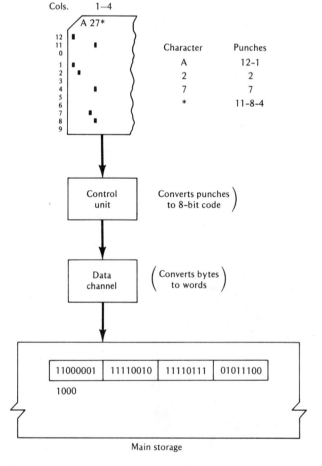

Character	Punches
A	12–1
2	2
7	7
*	11–8–4

FIGURE 6.7   The code conversion process in reading a punched card.

Figure 6.7 depicts the process of reading a card. The card is initially read by the card reader, and the information on it is sent to the control unit. The input/output control unit performs a code conversion from 12-bit card columns to 8-bit bytes. Each byte is sent individually to the data channel, which deposits it in a buffer. When the number of bytes corresponding to the access width is received, the central processing unit is interrupted, and the characters are placed in main storage. (In this example, the read operation instructs the computer to place columns 1 to 4 of the card into locations 1000 to 1003 of main storage.) As far as data transfer is concerned, all input/output control units and devices appear essentially the same to the data channel. The process of reading is reversed for punching.

Punched cards are used as an input medium, a storage medium, and occasionally as an output medium. A major disadvantage of punched cards as a storage medium is that they are cumbersome to handle and occupy a relatively large space when a large volume is involved.

MAGNETIC TAPE

Magnetic tape is a recording medium similar to that used with an ordinary tape recorder. Computer magnetic tape is ½ inch wide and consists of a plastic base with an iron oxide coating. The length of a magnetic tape varies up to approximately 2,400 feet. One character's worth of information is recorded laterally across the tape and a group of characters (called a *block)* is recorded in one write operation. Successive blocks are separated by approximately ¾ of an inch of blank tape, called an *interblock gap.*

Figure 6.8 gives a set of 7-bit magnetic tape codes. Iron oxide particles are magnetized in one direction or the opposite direction to represent the presence or absence of a bit. Longitudinal rows are labeled CBA8421 for identification and the C row denotes parity. *Parity* refers to whether the number of bits that is set in a lateral row across the tape is odd or even. The tape is always written with even (or odd) parity, using the C bit for codes that are odd (or even). When the tape is subsequently read, an error condition is raised for all characters without the correct parity.

Magnetic tape is read and written by a magnetic tape unit, such as those depicted in Figure 6.9. One reel serves as the supply reel and the other serves as the take-up reel. The tape is written or read as it passes over a magnetic read-write head, as depicted in Figure 6.10.

The process of reading a magnetic tape is similar in concept to that of reading a punched card. The control unit performs a code conversion from 6-bit code (7 bits including the parity) to 8-bit bytes.*

---

* Nine-track tape, which does not require a code conversion, is also in widespread use.

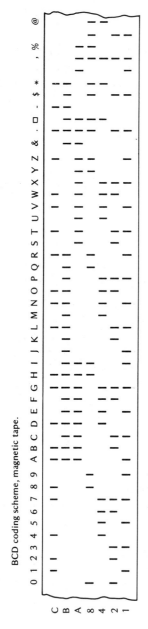

BCD coding scheme, magnetic tape.

FIGURE 6.8   Magnetic tape codes.

Courtesy of IBM Corporation

FIGURE 6.9   Representative magnetic tape units.

Magnetic tape is a sequential device, in the sense that the tape unit must pass over the $(i-1)$st data item before the ith data item can be accessed. In the example of Figure 6.11, the "next" information on tape (A27* in this case) is read into locations 1000 to 1003. Again, the conversion process is reversed for writing.

Magnetic tape is characterized by the width of the tape, the recording density, and the tape speed. As mentioned above, magnetic tape

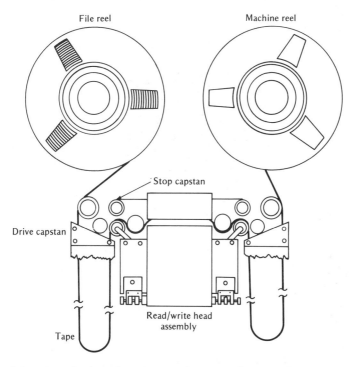

FIGURE 6.10   Internal mechanism of a representative magnetic tape unit.

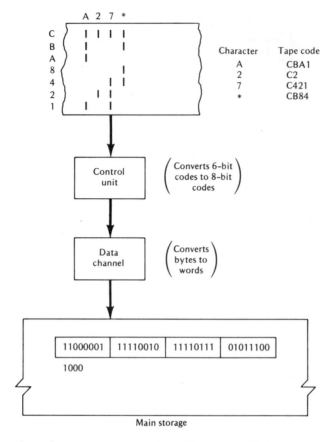

Character	Tape code
A	CBA1
2	C2
7	C421
*	CB84

FIGURE 6.11   The code conversion process in reading a magnetic tape.

with a width of ½ inch is the most widely used. However, tape up to 1 inch in width has been used to increase the data transfer rate. *Density* refers to the number of bytes recorded per inch. Typical values range from 200 bytes per inch (BPI) to 3,200 BPI. Tape speed varies from 37.5 inches per second to 200 inches per second. Overall, the data rate of magnetic tape varies from 7,500 bytes per second to 320,000 bytes per second.

The primary advantages of magnetic tape are that it is inexpensive (the average 2,400-foot reel costs about $12) and that it can store a large amount of information for its size. A tape reel ranges from 8 to 12 inches in diameter and can hold from 1 to 20 million bytes. Magnetic tape, unlike punched cards, is reusable by simply writing over previously stored information.

Magnetic tape is useful for storing large amounts of data that can be accessed sequentially. Typical applications that lend themselves to the use of magnetic tape involve the processing of large data files, such as those that might be found in payroll, personnel management, customer billing, and inventory control.

MAGNETIC DISK

Although magnetic tape provides reasonably high data transfer rates and is a relatively inexpensive storage medium, it is ineffective when data must be accessed directly. Recall that with magnetic tape, the computer (or more precisely, the magnetic tape unit) must pass over the $(i - 1)$st data item to be able to access the ith data item, unless perhaps, the tape unit was initially positioned at the $(i - 1)$st item. Many applications, such as information storage and retrieval, require that data be accessed directly. A reasonably good example is an insurance company that uses a computer to store policy data. When policyholders inquire about their policies, their records must be retrieved directly, and the policy files of most insurance companies are usually large.

One of the most widely used devices for direct access is magnetic disk. The recording medium is a set of metal disks coated with magnetic material, such as ferrous oxide. The disks are mounted on a rotating spindle, as depicted in Figure 6.12. Data are recorded on tracks on the disk surfaces and are read or written as the disks rotate. The concept of disk storage is similar to that of a phonograph record, except that the tracks are concentric instead of spiral. The stack of disks is referred to as a *disk volume,* and if the volume is removable, it is referred to as a *disk pack.*

Data are recorded on both surfaces of a disk (except perhaps the top and bottom surfaces of a volume, which are used for protection), and a single access arm controls two read/write heads, one for the upper surface and one for the lower surface. The access arms form a comb-type assembly that moves in and out together. A single read/write head is used to access a single surface.

Each track can store the same number of bits and is identified by a track address. Typically, track addresses range from 000–199. Each

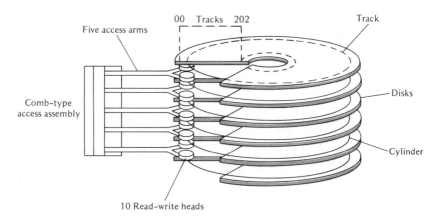

FIGURE 6.12   Disk storage mechanism.

surface is also identified by a head address (that is, the read/write head used to read the surface); the implication is that the heads are switched electronically when a given surface is to be read. Thus, a particular track is identified by (and located by) a track number and a head number. A magnetic disk is read or written by first moving the access arms to the proper track address prior to the input or output operation and by then switching on the desired read/write head. The process of moving the read/write head to the proper place is referred to as the *disk seek*. The time necessary to retrieve information from disk storage is therefore a function of three variables: seek time, the time necessary for the disk to rotate to the desired position on a track, and data-transfer time. Rotation speed is about 2,400 revolutions per minute, and recording density varies from 3,500 to 15,000 bytes per track. As a result, the data-transfer rate of disk storage varies from 300,000 bytes per second to 1.5 million bytes per second. Average seek time varies from 25 to 60 milliseconds.

A disk storage module has three major components: (1) the disk volume, (2) the access arms and read/write heads, and (3) the disk mechanism that causes the recording surfaces to rotate and works in conjunction with the access arms and read/write heads to record and retrieve data. A disk storage unit is usually classed by several factors:

1. Number of disk storage modules per unit
2. Number of recording surfaces per module
3. Capacity of each track and the number of tracks per surface
4. Seek time and rotation speed
5. Whether the disk volume is removable or not

Figure 6.13 depicts two disk storage units, one that contains a single-disk module and the other that contains eight-disk modules. Both utilize removable disk packs, such as the one shown in the same figure. The major advantage of removable disk packs is that they can be removed from the disk storage unit, so that the total disk capacity of a computer system is not limited by the number of disk units. Disk packs range in capacity from approximately 7 million bytes to approximately 100 million bytes. Therefore, a single storage facility, such as the eight-disk module of Figure 6.13, can hold as many as 800 million bytes. Not all disk volumes are removable. Nonremovable disk volumes generally provide faster access but have a smaller capacity.

Data that are stored on magnetic disk can be stored and retrieved sequentially or directly, depending upon the needs of a particular application. However, the cost of magnetic disk is approximately 20 times that of magnetic tape, all factors considered. (For example, the cost of a small disk pack with 10 recording surfaces that can hold about 7 million characters ranges from $350 to $500. The average 2,400-foot magnetic tape reel also holds about 7 million characters. These figures

Courtesy of NCR Corporation

Courtesy of IBM Corporation

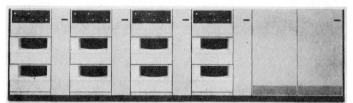

Courtesy of IBM Corporation

FIGURE 6.13 **Disk storage.**

obviously depend upon how the respective media are used.) For computer applications that require direct-access capability, there is no alternative. For applications that require only sequential access, the choice between magnetic tape and magnetic disk is a matter of input/output time and cost.

Magnetic disk is used primarily as a storage medium, for storing information on either a temporary or a permanent basis.

LINE PRINTER

From a human point of view, the most widely used output device that produces readable material is the line printer. As the name implies,

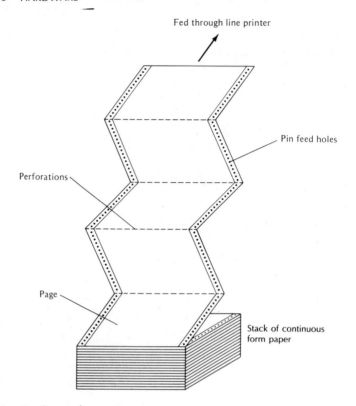

Fed through line printer

Pin feed holes

Perforations

Page

Stack of continuous
form paper

FIGURE 6.14   Continuous form paper.

the line printer prints a line at a time and is normally used for high-volume output. The speed of line printers varies from 60 to 5,000 lines per minute. To sustain these high rates, continuous form paper is used. A *continuous form* (see Figure 6.14) is a long piece of paper with pin feed holes on the edges and with perforations to provide the required form size. Continuous forms can be preprinted to provide reports of various kinds. Common examples of preprinted forms are student grade reports and paychecks. A typical line printer is depicted in Figure 6.15.

A line printer prints a line of information (usually 120 or 132 characters) at one time by one of three methods:

1. Impact printing
2. Chemical or photographic techniques
3. Laser technology

The impact technique is more widely used because it generally produces better quality printing at a lower line speed. Impact printing uses a print chain, a print wheel, or a print drum and involves impacting the paper (and the ribbon) with the printing mechanism, or vice versa.

Courtesy of IBM Corporation

FIGURE 6.15   Line printer.

Figure 6.16 shows a print chain that contains several sets of print characters mounted on a chain that moves horizontally in front of the paper. An electromechanically-controlled hammer behind the paper forces the paper against the type face as the character to be printed passes in front of the proper position on the paper. The speed of impact line printers usually varies between 500 and 3,500 lines per minute. Line speeds less than 500 lines per minute are used for small computers or special purposes.

Chemical or photographic techniques generally are used in printers

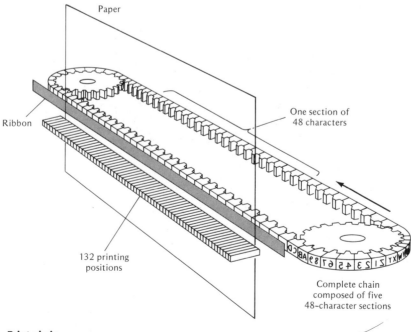

Paper

Ribbon

One section of
48 characters

132 printing
positions

Complete chain
composed of five
48-character sections

FIGURE 6.16   Print chain.

with ultra-high speed in the range of 3,000 to 5,000 lines per minute. Nonimpact techniques usually result in lower printing quality; however, this situation is changing, and it is expected that the use of nonimpact printers may surpass the use of impact printers as the quality of the former improves.

The use of advanced laser technology in printers permits an entire page to be printed at one time, while allowing output paper of different sizes. Laser printers are a new technological innovation, and very few technical details of how they operate have been released at this time for proprietary reasons.

Figure 6.17 depicts the process of printing a line. As in previous cases, data is sent from main storage to the data channel and then on to the control unit through the standard interface on a byte basis. Information is collected in a buffer in the control unit until a complete line is formed; then, the print mechanism is activated to print the line.

The line printer is the primary output device for printed material because of the fact that there usually is a large amount of printing

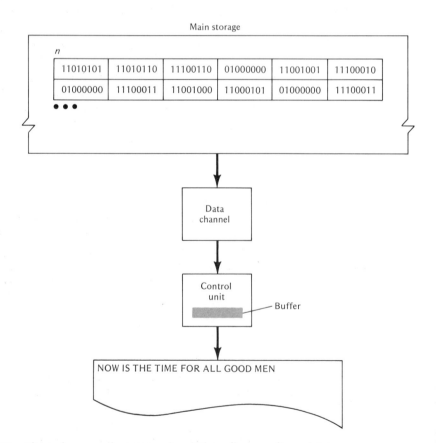

FIGURE 6.17   The code conversion process in printing a line on a line printer.

to be done. Typewriter-like devices that print on a character-by-character basis are frequently used for low-volume output. The printed page is also a storage medium, of a sort, but it is difficult to read the information back into the computer without rekeypunching the information. Optical readers, which are presented in the next section, are occasionally used for this purpose.

MISCELLANEOUS INPUT AND OUTPUT DEVICES

Because of the standard interface mentioned in the previous chapter, a wide variety of devices have been developed that provide input storage and output facilities. The market for peripheral devices of this type is large, and engineers have been known to develop input and output devices in their basement prior to embarking on a new business venture. This section summarizes a variety of well-known devices.

Keytape and Keydisk

Punched cards are the primary means of entering original data into the computer; however, card reading is relatively slow. An alternative approach to data entry is to use a *keytape device,* wherein the data is placed directly on magnetic tape. The data is entered via a keyboard and placed into a small memory by the keytape unit. The data is also displayed on a CRT screen so that the operator can inspect the input data for accuracy. CRT is an acronym for cathode ray tube, which is a display device similar in concept to a common television tube. When the operator has finished typing a line, it is entered directly on magnetic tape. A variation to the keytape approach is to use a *keydisk system,* wherein the data is placed directly on magnetic disk. A limiting factor with keydisk systems is that disk storage units are expensive, and it is difficult to justify independent units for the data entry operation. A recent technique is to connect several keydisk entry stations to a minicomputer that writes the entered data on a few disk units. Thus, the disk units are shared among many keydisk stations.

Optical and Magnetic Character Readers

An *optical reader* is a device that reads letters, numbers, and special characters from printed, typed, or handwritten documents. The optical reader scans the document, compares the result with prestored images, and enters appropriate data into the computer. Documents with invalid characters are rejected.

A *magnetic ink character reader* reads characters printed with ink containing metallic materials. The most common example of magnetic ink characters is found at the bottom of bank checks. These characters can be read visually and by a magnetic ink character reader. Special magnetic ink character readers have been developed for the banking industry.

Paper Tape

A medium that is used for input, storage, and output is punched *paper tape*. Punched paper tape is similar to magnetic tape in concept except that data are recorded by actually punching holes in the tape. The advantage of paper tape to cards is that paper tape does not have an 80-character limit on data records. The major disadvantages of paper tape are that errors are difficult to correct and that readers and punches are relatively slow, operating at approximately 500 and 300 characters per minute, respectively. Some types of computer terminals permit punched paper tapes to be prepared "off-line" prior to entry to the computer, minimizing errors when the user is connected to the computer.

Magnetic Drum

A *magnetic drum* is a mass storage device that uses a metal cylinder coated with a magnetizable material as a storage medium. Data are stored in circular tracks, referred to as *bands,* that are generally analogous to tracks on disk. The magnetic drum is housed in an upright cabinet and frequently contains its own control unit. Data-transfer rates are generally faster than disk storage and range from 300,000 to 1.5 million bytes per second. Access time is somewhat faster than disk, as is storage capacity. The drum, per se, is not removable, and a drum storage unit is generally more expensive than disk storage. Magnetic drum storage is usually used to store programs and tables.

Magnetic Strip and Card Devices

Magnetic strip and *magnetic card* devices are high-capacity electro-mechanical devices. A magnetic strip consists of a plastic strip coated with iron oxide, similar to magnetic tape. A magnetic card consists of a card coated with iron oxide. Both devices consist of several storage media (that is, strips or cards) mounted in a removable cartridge holder. When an instruction from the computer is received, a strip or card drops from the holder and is moved under a read/write head. Each strip or card can be addressed directly. The cost of magnetic strip and magnetic card storage is less than disk storage. Because of the mechanical access mechanism, access times are high. Devices of this type are used for applications that require immediate access to high-volume data.

Graphic Devices

Two types of graphic display units are graph plotters and drafting machines. Units of this type are either on-line or off-line. On-line devices are connected directly to the computer. Off-line devices use a magnetic tape as input; the magnetic tape is written by a computer program as a separate operation.

Graphic devices operate under control of instructions, such as "move the pen to point (10,5)." By synthesizing sequences of such instructions, the device can be made to prepare a desired figure. *Graph plotters* usually operate by drawing straight lines from point to point. *Drafting machines* allow a variety of plane curves to be drawn.

One of the advantages of using graphic display units is that a figure can be redrawn as many times as necessary by simply rerunning the program, whereas a skilled artist or draftsman would invariably include differences when making copies of the same figure.

Microfilm

Printed output from the computer can be voluminous, and a means of solving the volume problem is to write the output directly on microfilm. The process is referred to as *computer output microfilm* and is abbreviated as COM. Computer output microfilm operates as follows:

1. The data is converted to a form that can be displayed on a CRT screen.
2. The pictures appear on a CRT.
3. The face of the CRT is photographed.
4. The film is processed and developed.

Steps 2 through 4 are performed by a COM device, available as an ordinary peripheral device. COM output can be produced in one of the well-known forms of microfilm technology—that is 16, 35, 70 or 105 mm film, microfiche, or aperture cards (punched cards with microfilm windows).

COM devices operate at very high speeds, up to 1,000 lines per second, which is approximately 50 times faster than the average line printer. One of the primary advantages of COM output is that printed and graphic output can be conveniently incorporated on the same report.

Other Devices

Several other well-known devices exist, ranging from CRT devices to audio response units. Devices such as these, which are normally used with data communications facilities, are covered in the next section. Not all input and output devices have been covered here, but the devices that a computer user is most likely to encounter have been dealt with. The references given at the end of the chapter offer additional information on input and output devices.

DATA COMMUNICATIONS FACILITIES

Data communications refer to the use of teleprocessing facilities, such as ordinary telephone lines, for the transmission of data between remote locations. Technologically, data communications are not new and have been used with military/defense systems since the early 1950s. With the widespread use of computers in nonmilitary organizations, the use of data communications facilities are a natural technical extension. Data communications have made possible many of the popular computer applications—such as time sharing, computer networks, message transmission and switching, and information-based systems like airline reservations and brokerage information systems. Data communications are a complex issue because interfacing two different types of equipment invariably leads to problems and because many of the privacy and security problems relate to data communications. Privacy and security problems would exist without data communications (or without computers); however, the widespread use of data communications simply makes the problems worse. The benefits to be derived from the use of data communications, however, greatly outweigh the difficulties, and this means of communication is here to stay.

Data communications facilities are used for three major reasons:

1. To provide computational facilities to a user at a remote location
2. To permit information to be entered or retrieved from a data management system on a dynamic basis from a remote location
3. To transfer data between locations at a high rate of speed

On the surface the three areas appear to be diverse, but from a technical point of view, they are essentially the same and can be generally categorized as *communications systems*.

A communications system has five components:

1. Message source
2. Encoder
3. Signal channel
4. Decoder
5. Message destination

A conceptual model of a communications system is given in Figure 6.18. In a computer communications system, the source or the destination is a computer system, and the channel is either a telegraph or ordinary telephone. Telegraph and telephone facilities usually are designed as open wires, coaxial cable circuits, and microwave systems.

As depicted in Figure 6.19, data is represented as a train of bits for data transmission. Successive bits represent a character, as covered previously with respect to computer codes. Data can be transmitted in one of three modes: asynchronous start-stop, synchronous, and parallel. When *asynchronous transmission* is used, one character is transmitted between source and destination at a time, and extra bits called "start" and "stop" bits are used to achieve calibration between transmitter and receiver. Asynchronous transmission is almost always used when a human is involved in the communications process. When *synchronous transmission* is used, an entire block of characters is transmitted between source and destination without employing start and stop bits. The block is accumulated in a buffer prior to transmission, and the synchronization of transmitter and receiver is precisely controlled by oscillators. Obviously, synchronous transmission is more efficient, since there are no start and stop bits and no pauses as a result of human response time. Synchronous transmission is frequently used when human intervention is not used in the transmission process. *Parallel transmission* uses several communications channels to transmit a character—usually one channel exists for each bit in the code.

Data communications lines (that is, the communications channel) are classified as to the *data rate,* or speed of transmission, they can

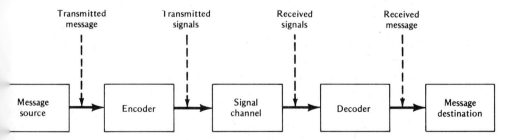

FIGURE 6.18   **Conceptual model of a communications system.**

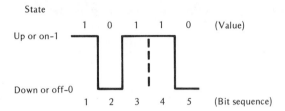

FIGURE 6.19   Data can be represented as a train of bits for data transmission.

sustain. Three classes are usually identified: subvoice grade, voice grade, and wide band. *Subvoice-grade lines,* customarily used for teletype service, transmit at rates from 45 to 180 bits per second. *Voice-grade lines,* used for ordinary telephones, transmit at rates from 110 to 9,600 bits per second. *Wide-band lines* are used for high-volume data and transmit at rates of 12,500 to 250,000 bits per second. The most significant characteristic of data communications lines is whether they are switched or private. *Switched lines* go through public exchanges and are located practically everywhere. Telegraph and public telephone lines fall into this category. *Private* (or leased) *lines* avoid the public switching network and are frequently used for high-volume traffic. Private lines are normally available in the three grades given above. Many companies lease lines when many calls are made between remote offices.

Data can be transmitted over conventional telephone lines. A key problem, however, is that computers operate digitally (that is, by pulses) and communications lines operate by analog transmission (that is, by waves). Therefore, data must be converted from digital to analog form prior to transmission and back to digital form when the data is received. The process is depicted in Figure 6.20.

The process of converting digital signals to analog signals is called *modulation;* the process of converting analog signals to digital signals is called *demodulation.* A hardware device that performs modulation/demodulation is called a *modem;* it must be attached to both ends of the communications line. Two types of modem are widely used: a

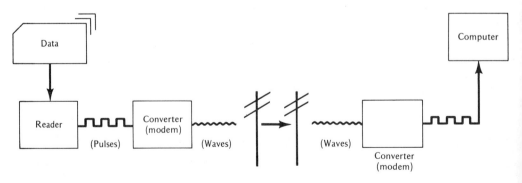

FIGURE 6.20   Data transmission.

dataset and an acoustical coupler. A *dataset* is a fixed connection between the telephone line and a unit of computer equipment and is supplied by the telephone company. An *acoustical coupler* is attached to a computer terminal device and converts digital signals to audible tones. Since the acoustical coupler is not attached to a communications line, the terminal device can be portable. The acoustical coupler mechanism allows the receiver of an ordinary telephone to be clamped into it to establish the line connection.

Use of an acoustical coupler has great advantages. Salespeople can have a battery-powered computer terminal with an acoustical coupler in their cars. All they need do to access the computer is to stop at a telephone booth, dial the number of the computer, clamp the receiver into the acoustical coupler, and they are ready to use the computer.

Data communications systems can take several forms: computer to computer, input/output device to computer, terminal device to computer, and so on. From the computer's point of view, a data communications terminal is essentially treated as an ordinary input/output device, such as a card reader or printer.

There are a variety of terminal devices, ranging from keyboard/typewriter devices to audio response units. Figure 6.21 shows five major devices: a data entry station, a CRT device, an audio response unit, a data collection unit, and an intelligent terminal.

A *keyboard/typewriter terminal device* resembles an ordinary typewriter in all respects, except that the terminal device is connected to the computer via data communications lines. The unit serves for both input and output. For input, users type the information they want sent to the computer. As each character is typed, it is printed at the terminal and sent to the computer. When the line is complete, the user presses RETURN to return the carriage and to send a special code to the computer indicating "end of line." Output is under the control of a computer program. As each character is sent to the terminal device, it is handled immediately. Printable characters are typed; control characters tell the terminal to "carriage return," "double space," and so on.

A *CRT terminal device* contains a display device that resembles a portable television set and a keyboard. The display device essentially replaces the carriage and paper of the previous device. As each character is typed for input, it is displayed on the screen. As above, pressing RETURN completes the line and returns a position indicator to the beginning of the next line. As lines are displayed, preceding lines are successively "rolled up" until the top line disappears at the top of the screen. The output lines are displayed in a similar manner. CRT-type devices are more costly than keyboard/typewriter devices and provide no "hard copy"—that is, printed output; however, CRT-type devices allow faster display speeds.

An *audio response unit* is used to provide convenient, low-volume output. A device of this type consists of a small magnetic drum and an audio speaker unit. The drum contains a small number of prere-

CRT terminal device

Courtesy of IBM Corporation

Data collection
station

Courtesy of IBM Corporation

Audio response unit

Courtesy of IBM Corporation

Intelligent
terminal

Courtesy of Hewlett-Packard

Keyboard/typewriter
terminal device

Courtesy of IBM Corporation

FIGURE 6.21   A variety of terminal devices.

corded syllables, words, or phrases. To generate a particular message, the computer sends an appropriate sequence of codes to the audio response unit, which selects the corresponding sounds from the drum and outputs them through the speaker unit. Audio response units are commonly used with stock quotation or credit verification systems.

A *data collection station* is an input device located in a remote location, such as an assembly plant or a medical ward in a hospital. Normally, data is entered through keys, dials, or switches. The data is stored at the computer on a recording medium such as tape or disk for subsequent processing.

An *intelligent terminal* is a terminal device that can be programmed to perform relatively minor data verification and editing functions. The use of an intelligent terminal, when appropriate, provides better service to the user and reduces the work load on the main computer. Intelligent terminals are commonly used in data entry systems to verify input data. Another interesting use of intelligent terminals is for computer consoles designed for use by executives. The terminal is programmed to dial the computer automatically when the executive turns the device on for use.

The above devices are only a few of the devices that can and have been used with data communications facilities. Remote tape units, card readers, and line printers are also in widespread use.

One of the more exotic uses of data communications facilities involves computer-to-computer communications without human intervention. Systems of this type are referred to as *computer networks*. Again, computer programs are necessary for instructing the computer when and what to do. One computer is simply programmed to dial the telephone number of the other computer to establish a data communications link. Once the link is established, appropriate programs are designed to make requests for information or respond to requests for information, as the case may be.

Vocabulary   The student should be familiar with the following terms in the context they were used in the chapter.

acoustical coupler	data communications
asynchronous transmission	dataset
audio response unit	demodulation
card reader/punch	density
code conversion	disk pack
communication system	disk seek
computer output microfilm	disk volume
continuous form	drafting machine
CRT device	field
data collection terminal	graph plotter

intelligent terminal
keydisk
keypunch machine
keytape
line printer
magnetic disk
magnetic drum
magnetic ink optical reader
magnetic strip device
magnetic tape
modulation
optical reader
paper tape
parallel transmission

pin feed holes
private line
subvoice-grade line
switched line
synchronous transmission
tape speed
terminal device
track
unit record
unit record device
voice-grade line
volume
wide-band line

Questions

1. In what way do the standard input/output interface and the input/output control unit appear to attack the same problem?
2. What are the advantages and disadvantages of the following media: punched cards, magnetic tape, and magnetic disk.
3. What is the width of a computer magnetic tape?
4. In everyday words, what is a disk seek?
5. Why is continuous form paper used?

Exercises

1. The chapter emphasized the difference between a device and a medium. Give as many analogous "combinations" as you can that exist in the noncomputer world. Example: pencil and paper. What about pen, ink, and paper?
2. Interpreting a punched card is the process of determining the recorded information. Interpret the following card:

3. Suppose columns 10–17 of the following card were read into computer storage, byte locations 5320–5327.
Give the contents in binary form of those byte locations.

```
      I
      I
0000000000 0 00 0 000000000000000000000000000000000000000000000000000000000000000000000000
 1 2 3 4 5 6 7 8 9 10 11 12 13 14 15 16 17 18 19 20 21 22 23 24 25 26 27 28 29 30 31 32 33 34 35 36 37 38 39 40 41 42 43 44 45 46 47 48 49 50 51 52 53 54 55 56 57 58 59 60 61 62 63 64 65 66 67 68 69 70 71 72 73 74 75 76 77 78 79 80
111111111111 1 11111111111111111111111111111111111111111111111111111111111111111111111111
2222222222 2 2222 2 222222222222222222222222222222222222222222222222222?222222222222222222
33333333333333333333333333333333333333333333333333333333333333333333333333333333
444444444444444 4 444444444444444444444444444444444444444444444444444444444444444444
55555555555555555555555555555555555555555555555555555555555555555555555555555555
66666666666666666666666666666666666666666666666666666666666666666666666666666666
77777777777777777777777777777777777777777777777777777777777777777777777777777777
8888888888888988888888888888888888888888888888888888888888888 6 888888888888888888
999999999 ■ ■ 9999999999999999999999999999999999999999999999999999999999999999999
 1 2 3 4 5 6 7 8 9 10 11 12 13 14 15 16 17 18 19 20 21 22 23 24 25 26 27 28 29 30 31 32 33 34 35 36 37 38 39 40 41 42 43 44 45 46 47 48 49 50 51 52 53 54 55 56 57 58 59 60 61 62 63 64 65 66 67 68 69 70 71 72 73 74 75 76 77 78 79 80
```

4. The contents of byte location 5320–5327, of question 3, are written on magnetic tape. Give a picture of that segment of tape showing the recorded information.

5. Given a magnetic tape unit that records at 800 BPI and moves at 75 inches per second, compute the data rate of that unit.

6. Data is recorded on magnetic tape in blocks of 80 characters with ¾-inch gaps between the blocks. The recording density is 800 BPI. What percentage of the tape is blank (that is, contains gaps) and what percentage contains recorded information?

7. What is the storage capacity of the following disk pack?
   Recording surfaces: 10
   Tracks per surface: 200
   Bytes per track: 3,620

8. Prepare a short but in-depth report on one of the following devices:
   Keytape or keydisk device
   Optical or magnetic character reader
   Paper tape (including codes)
   Magnetic drum
   Magnetic strip or card device
   Graph plotter device
   COM

9. Your instructor will give you the telephone number of a computer data communications line. Dial the number and describe what happens.

10. Visit the computer center or a terminal room. Prepare a short report on a dataset or an acoustical coupler.

Related Reading

Flores, I. *Data Structure and Management.* Englewood Cliffs, N.J.: Prentice-Hall, 1970.

Katzan, H. *Computer Organization and the System/370.* New York: Van Nostrand Reinhold, 1971.

Martin, J. *Introduction to Teleprocessing.* Englewood Cliffs, N.J.: Prentice-Hall, 1972.

7

Survey of Modern Computing Devices

* This chapter may be skipped without a loss of continuity.

wide variety of computational devices are presently available, ranging from simple calculators to large-scale computers. In fact, some of today's scientific programmable calculators are equivalent in computing power to small-scale scientific computers of 15 years ago. This chapter gives a brief survey of calculators, microcomputers, minicomputers, and medium-scale and large-scale computers.

CALCULATORS

Calculators range from simple adding machine-like devices to powerful programmable calculators with the capacity of holding a large number of program steps and with printing capability.

Simple Calculators

A simple calculator, such as the one pictured in Figure 7.1, contains facilities for addition, subtraction, multiplication, division, and possibly square root and percentage calculations. A calculator of this type normally performs calculations as they are entered in "algebraic entry" notation. For example, this entry:

will display a result of 18. The calculations take place in an accumulator, which holds the value displayed.

Simple Memory

A useful enhancement to many calculators is a single memory register for storing a constant value or the intermediate result of a calculation.

Courtesy of Texas Instruments Incorporated

FIGURE 7.1   Simple calculator.

Courtesy of Texas Instruments

FIGURE 7.2   Simple calculator with memory.

Figure 7.2 shows a calculator of this type. A typical set of additional instructions the calculator can respond to are: memory clear, memory recall, memory add, and memory subtract.

Student Calculators

The National Council of Teachers of Mathematics has endorsed calculators as a valuable instructional aid for mathematics education. A typical student calculator is given in Figure 7.3. It contains facilities for powers and roots, logs, trig functions, and memory functions—in addition to the standard arithmetic operators. Parentheses are also available for use in cases such as the evaluation of: $\sqrt{(5-2)^2 + (9-5)^2}$ which would be keyed in algebraic entry notation as

Courtesy of Texas Instruments Incorporated

FIGURE 7.3   Student calculator (algebraic entry notation).

Algebraic entry is characterized by the fact that the arithmetic function is placed between the numbers in a two-number operation, as in 2×2.

Another approach to the representation of arithmetic expressions is to use Reverse Polish Notation (RPN), wherein the arithmetic function follows both members of a two-number operation, as in

$$\boxed{3} \quad \boxed{\uparrow} \quad \boxed{2} \quad \boxed{\times}$$

which is a representation of 3×2. One of the advantages of RPN is that fewer keystrokes are required for complex expressions. The evaluation of $\sqrt{(5-2)^2 + (9-5)^2}$ would be keyed in RPN as:

$$5 \quad \boxed{\uparrow} \quad 2 \quad \boxed{-} \quad \boxed{x^2} \quad 9 \quad \boxed{\uparrow} \quad 5 \quad \boxed{-} \quad \boxed{x^2} \quad \boxed{+} \quad \boxed{\sqrt{x}}$$

The use of Reverse Polish Notation is similar to the way arithmetic is performed in many adding machines. Figure 7.4 depicts an RPN calculator.

Programmable Calculators

The power of calculators increased considerably with the invention of the programmable calculator, which in most cases also includes an addressable register for storing data. Typically, from 8 to 26 data values can be stored during the execution of a program.

A programmable calculator has a "program" or "learn" mode in which all calculator steps entered are saved as a program. When switched to the "run" mode, the calculator can perform the steps automatically. Figure 7.5 depicts a typical programmable calculator.

Courtesy of Hewlett-Packard

FIGURE 7.4   Student calculator (Reverse Polish Notation).

Courtesy of Texas Instruments Incorporated

FIGURE 7.5   Typical programmable calculator.

Continuous Memory

One of the problems with a programmable calculator is that the program must be entered each time it needs to be used. This process can be tedious so at least one calculator manufacturer has developed a calculator with a "continuous memory" that retains a program when the calculator is turned off (see Figure 7.6).

Program Storage

Regardless of whether a calculator had continuous memory or not, a need existed for a medium on which programs could be stored from the calculator, entered into the calculator, and exchanged between per-

Courtesy of Hewlett-Packard

FIGURE 7.6   Calculator with continuous memory.

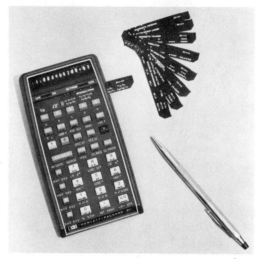

Courtesy of Hewlett-Packard

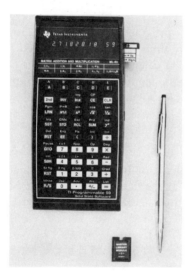

Courtesy of Texas Instruments Incorporated

FIGURE 7.7   A tape is used for storage with some calculators.

sons. As demonstrated in Figure 7.7, a small magnetic tape is used for this purpose. The tape can be used for program storage and for storing the contents of calculator registers.

Printing Capability

Modern calculators even have a printing capability as depicted in Figure 7.8. In one calculator, a thermal printer is built into the unit. In another calculator, the calculator can be plugged into a printer unit for printing capability.

Wrist Calculator

One of the most sophisticated calculators, because of its small size, is the wrist calculator (Figure 7.9), which incorporates the functions of a wristwatch, calculator, timer/stopwatch, calendar, and alarm. The wrist calculator permits calculations to be performed on decimal data, time, time intervals, and dates and also includes a memory register for storing any of the four kinds of data. Because of the watch function, memory is naturally continuous in a wrist calculator.

Courtesy of Hewlett-Packard

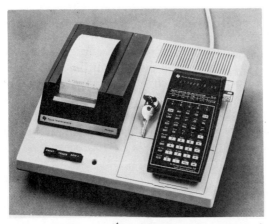

Courtesy of Texas Instruments Incorporated

FIGURE 7.8   **Calculator with printing capability.**

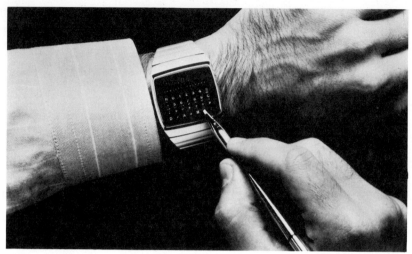

Courtesy of Hewlett-Packard

FIGURE 7.9   Wrist calculator.

A Final Note

Calculator technology provides considerable insight into the potential of miniaturized circuitry and electronics fabrication techniques. Clearly, a calculator is not a computer because of obvious functional limitations. Nevertheless, the development of calculators has definitely allowed electrical engineers to streamline micro-miniaturized systems, and these new developments are reflected in modern microcomputers.

MICROCOMPUTERS

The modern fabrication technique of being able to place a large number of circuits in a small area—known as *large scale integration,* or LSI—has given rise to the practice of placing an entire central processing unit on a single chip. (A *chip* is a slice of silicon ranging from $\frac{1}{10}$ of an inch on a side to $\frac{1}{4}$ of an inch on a side.) A central processing unit on a chip is known as a *microprocessor,* and this development has given birth to a whole list of exciting new computer applications. For example, microprocessors are used in TV games and in automobiles to control spark advance. Figure 7.10 shows a microprocessor on a chip.

Microcomputer Design

A schematic of a microcomputer is given in Figure 7.11. One of the unique characteristics of microcomputers is the use of *read-only memory*

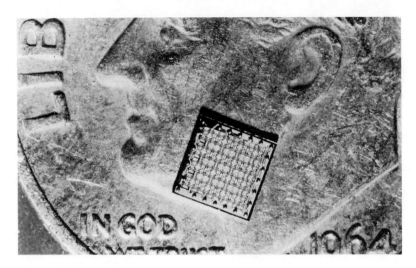

FIGURE 7.10   Microprocessor on a chip.

(ROM) and *random-access memory* (RAM). Collectively, ROM and RAM serve as "main storage" in the model, given earlier, of a digital computer. Read-only memory can only be read by the microprocessor and is preloaded to contain the operating systems type of programs—including language processors. Random-access memory can be read and written by the microprocessor and is used to hold user programs and data. Normally, ROM and RAM are regarded as physical extensions of each other.

Another defining characteristic of a microcomputer is that a data channel is not used, to keep the cost and size down, and all input and output must pass through the microprocessor.

Personal Computers

Figure 7.12 depicts a typical personal/home microcomputer. Large scale integration has reduced costs to the extent that a system like the one

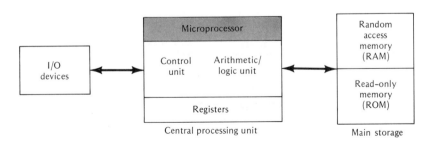

FIGURE 7.11   Simplified schematic of a microcomputer.

Courtesy of Radio Shack, a Division of Tandy Corporation

FIGURE 7.12   Typical personal/home computer system.

shown sells for less than $600 and typically includes the following components:

1. Microprocessor
2. Professional keyboard
3. Read-only memory (approximately 4 thousand bytes)
4. Random-access memory (approximately 4 thousand bytes)
5. Power supply and necessary controls
6. CRT display for input and visual output
7. Audio tape cassette player for storage of programs and data

The ROM storage contains programs that provide the user with the capability of entering and executing programs in Beginner's All-purpose Symbolic Instruction Code, or BASIC language.

Some of the typical applications for personal/home computers are:

1. Personal finance, such as checkbook balancing and budgeting
2. Student classroom assistance—with, for example, arithmetic and language
3. Home utility functions, such as metric and recipe conversion
4. Game playing and entertainment

In general, no knowledge of electronics or of computers is needed to make effective use of a personal computer.

Hobby Computers

A *hobby computer* has the same general characteristics as a personal computer except that a greater knowledge of electronics and of computers is normally required to effectively use software and to connect the computer to different kinds of electronic equipment. Figure 7.13 depicts a typical hobby/business computer system.

Some of the applications earmarked for hobby computers, at this point in their development, are:

1. Interactive graphics
2. Computer control of household apparatus
3. Music synthesis
4. Speech recognition
5. Audio output
6. Game playing and recognition

An average hobby computer ranges in price from $1000 to $10,000 and may include the following components:

1. Microprocessor, power supply, and necessary controls
2. Up to 64 thousand bytes of ROM
3. Up to 64 thousand bytes of RAM
4. Disk storage
5. Special printer—that is, prints a line one character at a time
6. Keyboard
7. Variety of display and other input and output devices

Courtesy of Radio Shack, a Division of Tandy Corporation

FIGURE 7.13   Typical hobby/business computer system.

There is currently a substantial interest in hobby computers, but only time will determine whether the useful applications can sustain the high level of interest.

Microcomputers for Business

Because of the relatively low cost of hobby computers and the capability of putting together a system that exactly meets the needs of a particular business, a microcomputer is considered to be ideal for a small business looking for its first computer. Although quality software and effective repair service continue to be problem areas, the acquisition of a microcomputer is a viable option for many small businesses.

SMALL BUSINESS COMPUTERS

Microcomputer technology has been used by computer manufacturers to develop small business computers, complete with programs, that can be integrated into a business system in a short period of time. Two advantages of small business computers are the low cost and the availability of high-quality service by computer manufacturers.

Desk-Top Computers

A desk-top computer is a logical extension of the concept of a calculator with the power of a general-purpose computer. A computer in this category is normally used for problem solving through an easy-to-use programming language, such as BASIC.

A desk-top computer is usually a self-contained unit that holds a microcomputer with up to 64 thousand bytes of storage, a keyboard, a display, and a tape or disk unit. The system operates on ordinary household electrical current and is light enough to be portable. Figure 7.14 depicts a typical desk-top computer.

Optional equipment to a desk-top computer typically includes a serial printer, disk storage, and data communications capability. The price range of a desk-top computer is nominally from six to twenty thousand dollars.

Data Processing Machines

Small business computers for data processing nominally range in price from ten thousand to fifty thousand dollars and incorporate components—such as printers, card reader/punches, and disk storage units—

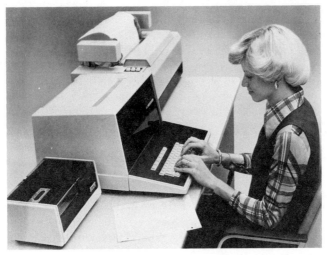

Courtesy of NCR Corporation

FIGURE 7.14   **Typical desk-top computer.**

to satisfy the data processing needs of a small business firm. Figure 7.15 shows a typical small business computer.

Data processing programs are available for computers in this category for applications such as accounts receivable, accounts payable, general ledger, payroll, and inventory control. All a business need do is acquire the computer system and programs and learn how to use them. Systems in this category are frequently referred to as *turnkey systems.*

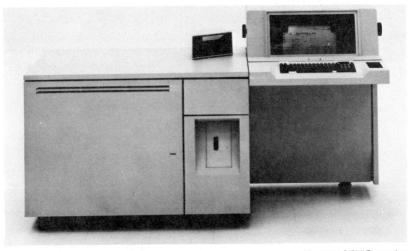

Courtesy of IBM Corporation

FIGURE 7.15   **Typical small business computer.**

MINICOMPUTERS

The rapid growth in computer applications created the need for a computer system that could be dedicated to a specific application for a reasonable investment of money and space. Clearly, a general-purpose computer was needed, but one that was not as sophisticated as medium-scale or large-scale systems. These needs led to the development of the minicomputer.

Characteristics

There is substantial agreement over the characteristics of a minicomputer, even though many types of minicomputers are currently being marketed. Some of the more general characteristics are:

1. It is physically small.
2. It is a general-purpose computer.
3. It is a word-oriented computer with a small word size—such as 16 bits.
4. It has a main storage size of from 4,000 to 64,000 words.
5. It sells for a price ranging from $4,000 to $50,000.
6. It operates as a binary computer.

Minicomputers are functionally fast machines and usually provide data channel capability. Figure 7.16 depicts a typical minicomputer.

Applications

Minicomputers are normally configured for a given application so that the capability of connecting a wide range of devices is expected. Some typical minicomputer applications are:

1. Run a scoreboard for a sports arena
2. Control the operation of a bank's cash machine
3. Generate mailing lists for a mail order house
4. Control a factory operation
5. Collect laboratory data
6. Perform stockholder data processing for a large corporation
7. Provide problem solving capability for students in a high school

Most minicomputers do not require air conditioning or special electrical facilities.

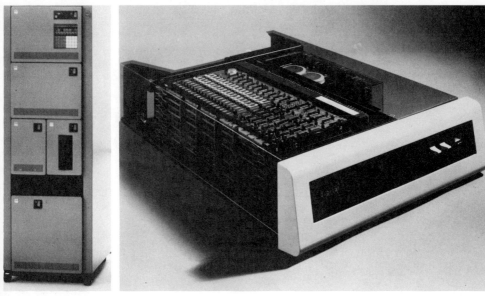

FIGURE 7.16   Typical minicomputer.

MEDIUM-SCALE AND LARGE-SCALE COMPUTERS

Medium-scale and large-scale computers offer several advantages for organizations that can afford them:

1. More computations per dollar
2. Increased flexibility
3. Increased computing power
4. Concurrent access
5. Overlapped operations
6. Capability of storing large amounts of data
7. High speed for timely results

Figures 7.17 and 7.18 depict medium-scale and large-scale computer systems, respectively. The considerations given in Chapter 6, "The Computer as a System," apply primarily to medium-scale and large-scale computer systems.

The difference between a medium-scale and a large-scale computer is primarily a matter of degree rather than one of basic function. A large-scale computer has in general a faster central processing unit, more main storage, more channels, and more devices than a medium-scale computer. The subject of organization is also important, and a large-scale computer is organized so that more functions can be performed in parallel. However, there are no hard and fast rules, and

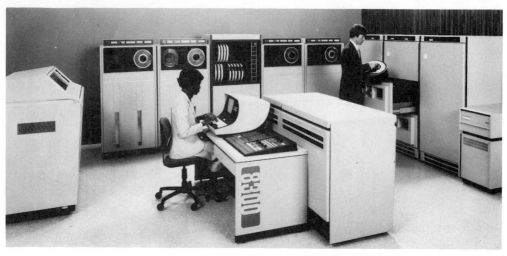

Courtesy of NCR Corporation

FIGURE 7.17   Medium-scale computer.

either type of system may possess any of the above characteristics.
    Some of the factors that are normally associated with medium-scale and large-scale systems are the following:

1. A computer operations staff is required.
2. The data processing organization would normally require specialists in the following areas: systems analysis, programming, business analysis, and data management.
3. Data processing standards are required.
4. A secure physical facility is needed.

The above topics are covered in Chapter 22.

Courtesy of IBM Corporation

FIGURE 7.18   Large-scale computer.

Vocabulary   The student should be familiar with the following terms in the context in which they were used in the chapter.

algebraic entry   programmable calculator
calculator   RAM
hobby computer   Reverse Polish Notation (RPN)
microprocessor   ROM
minicomputer   small business computer
personal computer

Questions   1. What, do you imagine, is the primary difference between a small business computer and a minicomputer?

2. Are there any analogous products to the personal/hobby computers mentioned in the chapter?

3. What function does ROM perform?

4. What does the schematic of a microcomputer tell us about inherent limitations on its speed?

5. What are some of the considerations that would apply to the design and development of a wrist computer, as compared to a wrist calculator?

Exercises   1. List feasible applications for microcomputers in business.

2. List the criteria you would use in deciding between a microcomputer or a small business computer for your firm's accounting functions.

3. One of the open questions in data processing is large-scale centralized computing vs. minicomputer decentralized computing. List the criteria you would use for making such a choice.

Related Reading

Foster, C. C. *Computer Architecture.* New York: Van Nostrand Reinhold, 1976.

Hilburn, John L., and Julich, Paul M. *Microcomputers/Microprocessors: Hardware, Software, and Applications.* Englewood Cliffs, N.J.: Prentice-Hall Inc., 1976.

Katzan, H. *Computer Systems Organization and Programming.* Chicago: Science Research Associates, 1976.

Part

3

Programming

Programming Concepts

T he process of preparing an application for the computer is generally known as programming. The notion of programming is fairly well known, but specificity is usually lacking. The objective of this chapter is to introduce the concept of programming and to place the concepts in perspective with the larger problem of developing a total computer application.

DEVELOPMENT OF A COMPUTER APPLICATION

The popular conception of a computer is that it is an extremely complex, almost unknowable device that can solve any problem or perform any task put to it. While the computer is indeed a very complex machine, it simply does not solve problems or perform tasks automatically. An application must be developed, and the development usually takes place in several phases—only one of which is programming. This section gives an overview of application development. The subject is covered in more detail in later chapters.

Major Phases of Application Development

The development of a computer application typically involves several people and a variety of different activities. Developing applications does not preclude a one-person operation but usually more than one person is involved. The steps in application development include the following types of activities, which normally take place in the order given:

1. Problem definition
2. Systems analysis
3. Functional specification
4. Programming
5. Debugging and testing
6. Documentation
7. Systems implementation

Each type of activity is discussed briefly below.

Problem Definition

A potential problem requiring a computer solution manifests itself through a need of some kind. For example, scientists may need to summarize their experimental data within a given time period or to a special degree of accuracy, or a businessperson may need to resolve a paperwork problem that continually increases in scope and magnitude. A bowling alley proprietor may wish to streamline the bowling league operations, thereby attracting more leagues. A direct-mail firm may wish to computerize its mailing labels, replacing inefficient and outdated methods. The problem definition phase is often characterized by the fact that the people who recognize the need are usually limited in one or more of several ways, including:

1. They do not have the resources to solve the problem and must sell the new concept to higher management or administration.
2. They recognize the need but are not sure of the best solution.
3. They are not sure that their needs can be satisfied with a computer.
4. They are not certain of how a computer solution to their problem would fit into the total organization.
5. They are not confident of the validity of their need, are not sure that they can justify the solution, and prefer an outside opinion.

The best course of action to take in these cases is to state the need precisely or formulate the problem exactly and then to call in a systems analyst from within the organization or an outside consultant to gather and analyze the facts relevant to the proposed application.

Systems Analysis

The process of analyzing a proposed computer application is performed by a person experienced in computer technology, applications, and organizational issues. More specifically, the systems analyst or consultant performs the following functions:

1. Determines whether the proposed application can be done
2. Develops the general methodology to be employed
3. Determines how the proposed computer application can be effectively integrated into the operational structure of the organization

If, during the process of performing the above functions, it is determined that the proposed project is a viable one, then the systems analysis phase also includes a detailed flow analysis of the system or program and a specification of the inputs required and the outputs produced.

Functional Specification

Functional specification is the precise specification of the steps that comprise a computer program. In a data analysis application, for example, functional specification would involve determining the statistical techniques and mathematical equations to be employed and the manner in which they would be used. In an inventory control application, functional specification would involve the specification of methods for computing inventory levels, reorder points, and backorder requests. In a payroll application, functional specification would be the identification of taxes and other deductions and the precise specification of the methods for computing gross and net pay. Functional specification is not restricted to mathematical calculations and also includes techniques for storing and retrieving data and for editing and generating reports. A functional specification of a computational procedure is usually referred to as an *algorithm*.

Programming

Programming is the process of writing down the steps that comprise a computer program. If detailed program specifications were generated from the systems analysis and functional specification phases, then computer programming involves the straightforward coding of the program in a suitable programming language. If general specifications were produced during the systems analysis and functional specification phases, then the programming phase would also involve the writing of detailed procedures in addition to coding. Computer programming is a detailed process that can easily result in a program that contains inadvertent errors. In fact, most programs contain errors that must be detected and removed.

Debugging and Testing

The process of running a program to determine if it contains errors is known as testing or program check-out, and the task of removing errors is known as debugging. Testing and debugging is achieved through the use of test cases that determine if the program operates correctly for each possible type of computation for which it was designed. Errors can occur in a variety of ways, including the following: incorrectly written program, faulty algorithm, poor systems analysis, and incorrect specification of applicable data values.

Documentation

The documentation phase includes the development of procedures for using the system or program and the preparation of reports describing the procedures and internal structure of the program. Effective documentation is necessary when a person other than the original programmer is required to make changes in it.

Systems Implementation

Systems implementation is the process of putting the system or program into production. Some student, engineering, and scientific programs are developed and debugged, and computed results are obtained; then the program is discarded. These are referred to as "one shot" jobs. For these programs, documentation and implementation procedures are minimal. Other programs, such as those associated with information systems, data processing, and other applications may be used for years, going through change cycles to satisfy current needs. In the latter case, the effectiveness of a program should be monitored to insure that the changing needs of the organization are satisfied.

PROCEDURES AND ALGORITHMS

The steps that comprise a computational procedure must be delineated before the procedure can be programmed for the computer. Since the notion of writing down the steps that constitute a process of some kind is not unique to the computer field, not all procedures are appropriate for computer implementation. To better understand computational procedure, it may be useful to describe two processes that do not lend themselves to programming.

Noncomputational Procedures

Two familiar examples of procedures from everyday life are found in a cookbook and a mechanics repair manual. As an example of a recipe, consider the following procedure for preparing fried chicken:

Williamsburg Fried Chicken

Joint the Chickens neatly, wash and drain. Soak in Milk for half an Hour. Dredge them well with Flour to which Salt and Pepper have been added. Fry in an iron Skillet in boiling Fat almost deep enough to cover the Pieces of Chicken. Turn each Piece at least three Times. Fry to a nice brown, drain on brown Paper and serve with Gravy sent up in a separate Boat.[1]

As an example of a repair procedure, consider the following procedure for car storage preparation:

1. Helen Bullock, *The Williamsburg Art of Cookery* (Williamsburg, VA: Colonial Williamsburg, Inc., 1958), p. 46.

Car Storage Preparation—30 Days or Less

1. Wash car and inflate tires to 40 pounds pressure.
2. Provide proper cooling system protection.
3. Run engine until completely warmed up; then drain and refill with fresh oil which, according to the label on the can, is intended for service "SE."
4. Run engine again with fresh oil until completely warmed up; drive car to place of storage and park. Do not restart again until end of storage period.
5. Be sure parking brake is in released position and the car is on level surface.
6. If car is to be stored in a hot area, the fuel tank, lines, pump, filter, and carburetor should be drained.
7. Disconnect battery and prevent battery from discharging or freezing by keeping it fully charged.[2]

These procedures have two common characteristics:

1. They are each written to perform one particular task.
2. They are each fairly general in nature, requiring a certain amount of expertise from the person involved.

These are two major areas in which a computer procedure differs from procedures found in everyday life.

Specification of a Computational Procedure

In order for a procedure to be useful for computational purposes, it must be very specific in the sense that every condition and every possibility must be specified (or taken care of). Table 8.1 contains a representative percentage withholding table for income taxes. The table specifies the amount that should be withheld from a monthly employee's pay for either single or married persons. (Similar tables exist for weekly, biweekly, and semimonthly payroll periods.) The procedure is complete since all wage values are considered. It should be pointed out that the tables indicate the computations that should be performed but do not necessarily specify how they should be performed.

Computer Procedures

Because a computer is a detailed and precise machine, the steps that comprise a computer procedure must be sufficiently detailed at each stage of a computation to permit the required calculations to be performed. Also computer procedures do not solve one problem; they are designed to solve a whole class of similar problems. The procedure

2. *1973 Cadillac Shop Manual* (Detroit, Michigan: General Motors Corporation, 1972).

TABLE 8.1 REPRESENTATIVE PERCENTAGE WITHHOLDING TABLE FOR INCOME TAXES

MONTHLY Payroll Period

(a) SINGLE person—including head of household:

Wages less allowances:	Income tax to be withheld:	
Not over $108 0		

Over—	But not over—	Income tax to be withheld:	of excess over—
$108	–$292	16%	–$103
$292	–$500	$29.44 plus 20%	–$292
$500	–$792	$71.04 plus 23%	–$500
$792	–$1,042	$138.20 plus 21%	–$792
$1,042	–$1,203	$190.70 plus 26%	–$1,042
$1,208	–$1,500	$233.80 plus 30%	–$1,208
$1,500	....	$321.46 plus 36%	–$1,500

(b) MARRIED person—

Wages less allowances:	Income tax to be withheld:	
Not over $208 0		

Over—	But not over—	Income tax to be withheld:	of excess over—
$208	–$417	17%	–$208
$417	–$750	$35.53 plus 20%	–$417
$750	–$1,146	$102.13 plus 17%	–$750
$1,146	–$1,500	$169.45 plus 25%	–$1,146
$1,500	–$1,875	$257.95 plus 28%	–$1,500
$1,875	–$2,167	$362.95 plus 32%	–$1,875
$2,167	....	$456.39 plus 36%	–$2,167

for adding two signed (that is, positive or negative) numbers a and b serves as an example:

1. If a and b have the same sign, go to step 5. (If a and b have different signs, continue with step 2.)
2. Subtract the smaller magnitude from the larger magnitude. (Continue with step 3.)
3. Give the result the sign of the number with the larger magnitude. (Continue with step 4.)
4. Stop.
5. Add the magnitudes of the numbers a and b. (Continue with step 6.)
6. Give the result the sign of number a. (Continue with step 7.)
7. Stop.

The procedure, in this case, is fairly detailed and would work for any two numbers a and b. For example, $(-5) + (-4) = -9$, $16 + (-11) = 5$, $10 + 20 = 30$, and so forth. A specific procedure of this type that exists as a finite list of instructions specifying a sequence of operations and that gives the answer to any problem of a given type is called an *algorithm*. Computer programs are based on the concept of an algorithm.

Algorithms

The notion of an algorithm has been known since antiquity, even though in modern times the term is most frequently used with computers. As an example, consider the familiar algorithm used to generate a sequence of numbers known as Fibonacci numbers, which have amazing applications in the physical world. For example, Fibonacci numbers can be used to describe the arrangement of stems on a branch and the growth in the rabbit population. The growth in a rabbit population is particularly illustrative. A rabbit takes approximately one month to mature, and once matured, a pair of rabbits can beget a litter every month thereafter. Assume for simplicity that each litter contains exactly two rabbits—one male and one female. Thus, the time necessary for a newborn litter to have a litter of its own would be two months: one month to mature and one month to have a litter. The growth in population is demonstrated as follows:

Month	Number of Rabbit Pairs	Remark
1	1	Initial pair: birth to maturity
2	1	Initial pair: starts 1st litter
3	2	Initial pair has 1st litter; 1st litter matures

Month	Number of Rabbit Pairs	Remark
4	3	Initial pair has 2nd litter; 1st litter starts litter
5	5	Initial pair has 3rd litter; 1st litter has its 1st litter; 2nd litter starts its litter; etc.
3	8	etc.
7	13	etc.

The sequence of the numbers of rabbit pairs follows the Fibonacci sequence, depicted as follows:

1 1 2 3 5 8 13 21 24 . . .

The pattern can be developed by inspection. After the first two numbers, each succeeding number is the sum of the previous two numbers. Thus, if F_i denotes the ith Fibonacci number then $F_1 = F_2 = 1$, and

$$F_i = F_{i-1} + F_{i-2}$$

for all i greater than 2. An algorithm for computing Fibonacci numbers that are less than 100 is given as follows:

1. Set N1 to 0. (This is not a Fibonacci number, and is used only to start the process.)
2. Set N2 to 1. (This is the first Fibonacci number.)
3. Write down N2.
4. Set N3 equal to N1 + N2.
5. If N3 is greater than 100, then stop the calculations.
6. Write down N3.
7. Replace N1 by N2.
8. Replace N2 by N3.
9. Continue the calculations with step 4.

An algorithm exists for each computational problem that has a general solution. The solution may exist as a set of mathematical equations that must be evaluated or as a set of procedural steps that satisfy a preestablished procedure—such as the well-known procedure for calculating income tax liability.

As another example, consider the Euclidean algorithm stated as follows:

Given two positive integers a and b, find their greatest common divisor.

There are as many problems of this type as there are pairs of positive integers a and b. The algorithm involves the construction of a descending sequence of numbers. The first is the larger of the two numbers; the second is the smaller; the third is the remainder from dividing the first by the second; the fourth is the remainder from dividing the second by the third; and so forth. The process ends when there is a zero remainder. The greatest common divisor is the last divisor in the sequence. For example, the descending sequence of numbers for the greatest common divisor of 44 and 28 is written as: 44 28 16 12 4 0. The last divisor is 4, which is the result. The algorithm can be summarized in the following list of instructions:

1. Write down a and b.
2. If b is greater than a, exchange them.
3. Divide a by b giving the remainder r.
4. If r is equal to zero, stop; b is the greatest common divisor.
5. Replace a by b; (that is, $b \rightarrow a$).
6. Replace b by r; (that is, $r \rightarrow b$).
7. Go to step 3.

The actual calculations can be listed as follows:

Greatest common denominator of 44 and 28:			Greatest common denominator of 10 and 8:		
a	b	r	a	b	r
44	28	16	10	8	2
28	16	12	8	2	0
16	12	4		Result is 2.	
12	4	0			
	Result is 4.				

Now, several of the characteristics of this algorithm (and algorithms in general) can be given:

1. The algorithm consists of a finite number of steps.
2. The instructions are precise.
3. The instructions are unambiguous.
4. The procedure will work for any two numbers, a and b.

The Euclidean algorithm demonstrates another important characteristic of an algorithm. The number of operations that are actually performed in solving a particular problem is not known beforehand; it depends on the input data and is discovered only during the course of computation. This may appear to be a contradiction, but it is not. The number of instructions in an algorithm is finite; however, some instructions may be executed more than once and others may not be executed at all.

DESCRIPTIVE METHODS

For many applications a simple list of the steps that comprise an algorithm is sufficient for stating that algorithm in a clear and unambiguous manner. However, when the procedure is complex and different options exist, then a list of instructions is hard to follow. An analogous example is a list of directions for locating a particular place in an unfamiliar city. When the directions are complex, a road map is usually preferred.

Flow Diagrams

A flow diagram is used in the computer field for describing a complex process. A flow diagram—or a *flow chart*—may be comprised of symbols that represent the following functions:

1. *Flow direction.* The flow of control is represented by an arrow. The arrowhead denotes the symbol to which control is passed.
2. *Process.* The rectangular process symbol denotes a computational operation.
3. *Input/output.* An input or output operation is denoted by a parallelogram with slanted edges. Making information available for processing—that is, read in—is an input function. The recording or display—that is, read out—is an output function.
4. *Decision.* The diamond-shaped decision symbol is used to denote a change in direction of flow on a conditional basis.
5. *Start-stop.* The terminal symbol denotes the beginning or end of a computational process.
6. *Connection.* The small circle serves as a connector between different points in a flow chart.

The flow charting symbols are shown graphically in Figure 8.1.
   A flow chart of the algorithm for generating Fibonacci numbers is given in Figure 8.2. One of the greatest benefits of the use of flow charts is that the existence of repetitive operations can be detected at a glance. Figure 8.3 depicts another repetitive algorithm that computes the largest factor of an integer N. As in the previous examples, the flow chart gives a visual description of a procedure, and the type of operation performed at each stage of the computation is clearly evident by the flow charting symbol used.

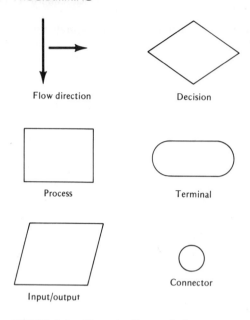

Flow direction   Decision

Process   Terminal

Connector

Input/output

FIGURE 8.1   Flow charting symbols.

Decision Tables

It is usually suggested that beginning programmers draw a flow chart of the method of problem solution before the program is written to insure that they have the logic of the problem in good order. For large programs, flow charts are almost mandatory—even for experienced programmers. In spite of its usefulness, however, a flow chart has its disadvantages. First, a flow chart can easily become a "bushy mess," especially for a program in which the internal logic is complex. Second, the use of a flow chart essentially requires that the programmer describe the problem and develop the program at the same time. A method of describing a problem without specifying its implementation uses the concept of a decision table. A *decision table* is a tabular display of the decision criteria and the resultant actions of a problem situation. A decision table is composed of a set of mutually exclusive and collectively exhaustive rules. Each rule specifies a set of conditions and the actions to be taken if those conditions arise. As an example, consider the decision table for whether or not to carry an umbrella, given in Figure 8.4. The set of conditions occupies the upper left quadrant and the set of actions occupies the lower left quadrant; they are called the *condition stub* and *action stub*, respectively. Each vertical rule is composed of *condition entries* and *action entries*, as shown in Figure 8.5. An irrelevant condition (that is, one that can be either yes or no) is denoted by a hyphen. Returning to the decision table in Figure 8.4, the condition

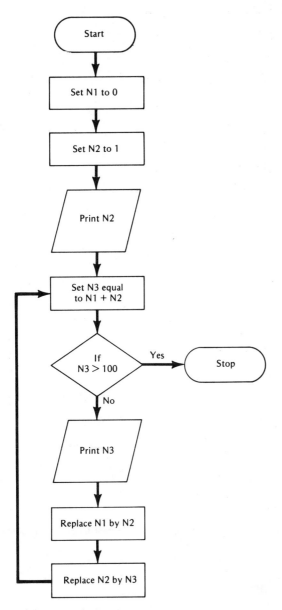

FIGURE 8.2   Flow chart of the algorithm for generating Fibonacci numbers.

that it is not rainy outside, that rain is forecast, but that the weather is sunny denotes that the action "do not carry an umbrella" should be taken.

As a realistic example, consider the problem of who should file a U.S. tax return and whether to use form 1040 (long form) or 1040A

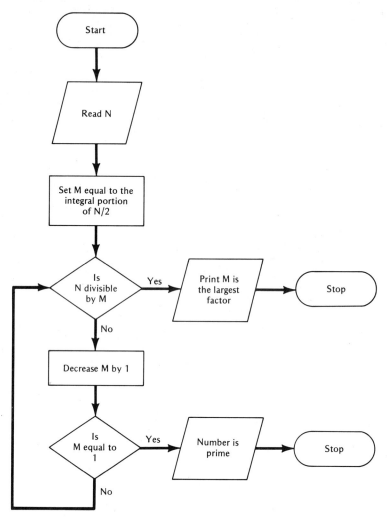

FIGURE 8.3   Flow chart of an algorithm for computing the largest factor of an integer N.

	Umbrella Table	Rule			
		1	2	3	4
Conditions	Raining outside	Y	N	N	N
	Rain forecast	–	Y	Y	N
	Sunny outside	–	Y	N	–
Action	Carry umbrella	X		X	
	Do not carry umbrella		X		X

FIGURE 8.4   Decision table for deciding whether to carry an umbrella.

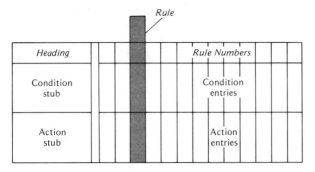

FIGURE 8.5   **Format of a decision table.**

(short form).* An individual must file a return if one or more of the following conditions hold:

1. Citizen a resident of the U.S.
2. Earned $600 or more if under 65 years of age.
3. Earned $1,200 or more if 65 years of age or older.
4. A tax refund is desired.

An individual is permitted to use the short form (1040A) if the following conditions hold:

1. Income is less than $10,000; *and*
2. Income consists of wages subject to withholding and not more than $200 total of other wages, interest, and dividends; *and*
3. The taxpayer wishes to use the tax table or take the standard deduction instead of itemizing deductions.

This problem is conveniently described (see Figure 8.6) in two decision tables: the first to determine if a return should be filed and the second to determine which form should be used.

The use of decision tables is particularly appropriate when it is necessary to insure that all possible conditions that can occur have been accounted for. In fact, many students have commented that a decision table would be useful in many legal contracts and make more sense than the legal jargon.

---

* The specifications for filing income tax returns is purposely "out of date," so that it will not be used in a real life situation. *Do not use this information for filing your income tax return.*

Return Table	1	2	3	4	5	6	7
Citizen or resident of U.S.	Y	Y	Y	Y	Y	Y	N
Age less than 65	Y	Y	Y	N	N	N	–
Earned $600 or more	Y	N	N	–	–	–	–
Earned $1200 or more	–	–	–	Y	N	N	–
Refund desired	–	Y	N	–	Y	N	Y
File return (go to form table)	X	X		X	X		X
Do not file return			X			X	

Conditions / Action (left margin labels)

Form Table	1	2	3	4
Income less than $10,000	Y	Y	Y	N
Not more than $200 of other wages, interest, etc.	Y	Y	N	–
Tax table or standard deductions	Y	N	–	–
Use Form 1040 (long)		X	X	X
Use Form 1040A (short)	X			

Conditions / Action (left margin labels)

FIGURE 8.6   A set of decision tables for filing income tax.

COMPUTER PROGRAMS AND PROGRAMMING LANGUAGES

A computer representation of an algorithmic process is a *computer program.* More specifically, a program is a meaningful sequence of statements in a special language designed to tell the computer how to accomplish a certain task. Internal to the computer, a program is executed by a set of specific, computer-oriented instructions that effectively control the operation of the computer. The process of converting a program written in a programming language to its set of internal computer-oriented instructions is covered in a later chapter.

Introductory Concepts

The statements in a program parallel the steps in an algorithmic process. Consider the problem of computing the largest factor of an integer N, given in Figure 8.3. The algorithm and the program in the BASIC language are listed as follows:

Algorithm	BASIC Program
1. Write down the number N.	10 READ N
2. Set M equal to the integer portion of N/2.	20 LET M = INT(N/2)
3. If N is divisible by M, go to step 8.	30 IF N/M = INT(N/M) GOTO 80

Algorithm	BASIC Program
4. Decrease M by 1.	40 LET M = M − 1
5. If M is greater than 1, go to step 3.	50 IF M > 1 GOTO 30
6. Print number is prime.	60 PRINT N; 'IS PRIME'
7. Stop.	70 STOP
8. Print "largest factor is" M.	80 PRINT 'LARGEST FACTOR OF'; N; 'IS'; M
9. Stop.	90 STOP
	100 END

A computer listing and execution of the program is given in Figure 8.7, and except for the DATA statement that supplies a data value for the program, it is identical to the program given above.

A second example of a computer program is given in Figure 8.8. It represents a simple payroll program written in the BASIC language that computes net pay as gross pay minus taxes and deductions. The program reads in the employee's name, hours, rate, tax percentage, and deductions and also pays time and one-half for all hours over 40. At this stage, full comprehension of the program should not be expected; however, a fairly good idea of how the program works can be obtained by reading through the statements.

The structure of a program can be ascertained from the examples. The program exists as a series of statements that perform three basic functions: (1) input, (2) processing, and (3) output. In the examples, the READ statement performs the input function; the PRINT statement performs the output function; and the LET, IF, GOTO, and STOP statements perform the processing functions. As mentioned previously, the DATA statement provides data on which the programs can operate. Finally, the END statement denotes the end of the program.

```
0010 READ N
0020 LET M = INT(N/2)
0030 IF N/M = INT(N/M) GOTO 0080
0040 LET M = M − 1
0050 IF M > 1 GOTO 0030
0060 PRINT N; 'IS PRIME'
0070 STOP
0080 PRINT 'LARGEST FACTOR OF'; N; 'IS'; M
0090 STOP
0100 DATA 477
0110 END
RUN
LARGEST FACTOR OF 477 IS 159

  READY
```

FIGURE 8.7   Computer listing and execution of the largest factor program.

```
0010  PRINT USING FLP, 0190
0020  PRINT FLP,
0030  READ N$,H,R,P,D
0040  IF N$ = ' ' GOTO 0130
0050  IF H≤40 GOTO 0080
0060  LET P1 = 40*R + (H − 40)*R*1.5
0070  GOTO 0090
0080  LET P1 = H*R
0090  LET T = P1*P/100
0100  LET P2 = P1-T-D
0110  PRINT USING FLP, 0200,N$,H,R,T,D,P1,P2
0120  GOTO 0030
0130  STOP
0140  DATA 'A. ABLE',40,3.75,20,17
0150  DATA 'B. BAKER',35,2.5,10,17
0160  DATA 'C. CHARLY',50,6,30,25
0170  DATA 'D. DAWG',80,1,5,0
0180  DATA ' ',0,0,0,0
0190  :   NAME      HRS   RATE   TAXES   DEDUCT   GROSS    NET
0200  :##########   ###   ##.##  ###.##  ###.##   ###.##   ###.##
0210  END
```

NAME	HRS	RATE	TAXES	DEDUCT	GROSS	NET
A. ABLE	40	3.75	30.00	17.00	150.00	103.00
B. BAKER	35	2.50	8.75	17.00	87.50	61.75
C. CHARLY	50	6.00	99.00	25.00	330.00	206.00
D. DAWG	80	1.00	5.00	0.00	100.00	95.00

FIGURE 8.8   Computer listing and execution of a payroll program.

Note on Programming Languages

The BASIC programming language, used in the previous examples, was designed as an easy-to-use language for problem solving in an academic, business, or scientific environment. There are several other widely used programming languages that are designed for particular classes of computer applications. Some of the better known programming languages are:

1. FORTRAN—(derived from FORmula TRANslating system) a mathematically-oriented language designed for scientific and engineering applications
2. COBOL—(derived from COmmon Business Oriented Language) a programming language for data processing in business
3. APL—a powerful mathematically-oriented language for scientific and business applications
4. PL/I—a multipurpose programming language for programs that span the traditional boundaries between applications

One of the primary advantages of modern computer technology is that a user can, in most cases, select an appropriate language for a particular type of computer application.

This book surveys two widely used programming languages that are used in data processing: BASIC and COBOL. BASIC, which is an acronym for *B*eginner's *A*ll-purpose *S*ymbolic *I*nstruction *C*ode, was developed at Dartmouth College under the direction of J. G. Kemeny. It was designed as an easy-to-learn language for the academic environment but has achieved great popularity as a professional programming language for business analysis and data processing. COBOL, which stands for *CO*mmon *B*usiness *O*riented *L*anguage, is the most widely used programming language for data processing. COBOL was originally developed with the support of the U.S. Department of Defense and through extensive collaboration by computer users and manufacturers.

Vocabulary   The reader should be familiar with the following terms in the context in which they were used in the chapter.

algorithm	flow chart
algorithm development	problem definition
BASIC	procedure
COBOL	programming
debugging and testing	systems analysis
decision table	systems implementation
documentation	

Questions   1. Why would the various phases of application development be important to business management?

2. What is the major difference between problem definition and systems analysis?

3. What is the major difference between algorithm development and programming?

4. Why is the recipe for Williamsburg fried chicken not an algorithm?

5. Could the procedure for car storage preparation be an algorithm? Why?

Exercises   1. Prepare a flow chart to input five numbers and find the maximum value.

2. Prepare a flow chart of the procedure necessary for dropping or adding a course at your school.

3. Prepare a decision table of the procedure for "making change."

4. Convert the monthly percentage withholding table to a flow diagram.

5. Convert the monthly percentage withholding table to a decision table.

Related Reading

Tonge, F. M., and Feldman, J. *Computing: An Introduction to Procedures and Procedure-Followers.* New York: McGraw-Hill Book Company, 1975.

Trakhtenbrot, B. A. *Algorithms and Automatic Computing Machines.* Boston: D. C. Heath and Company, 1963.

Wilde, D. U. *An Introduction to Computing: Problem-Solving, Algorithms, and Data Structures.* Englewood Cliffs, N.J.: Prentice-Hall Inc., 1973.

Programming Techniques

LANGUAGE CONCEPTS

Alphabet
Statements

DATA

Numeric Data
Descriptive Data

VARIABLES AND IDENTIFIERS

Variables
Identifiers

**OPERATORS, EXPRESSIONS, AND
REPLACEMENT**

Operators
Expressions
Replacement and Data Movement

DATA ORGANIZATION

Arrays
Structures

STRUCTURED PROGRAMMING

The Structure Theorem
Sequence
Ifthenelse
Dowhile
Dountil and Case
Application of the Concepts
Implementation of Structured Programming
Structural Programming Coding Conventions in the
COBOL Language

This chapter presents an introduction to programming languages and covers a relatively recent programming technique known as *structured programming*. Information on programming language concepts that are common to BASIC and COBOL, which are covered in detail in the next two chapters, has been placed in this chapter. This chapter also includes a few topics that are fundamental to data processing in general and provide good background for the subject.

LANGUAGE CONCEPTS

A *language* can be defined as a set of conventions used for communication. The conventions normally involve (1) the characters or letters, used for synthesizing language constructs, and (2) the rules that must be followed for developing the constructs in a meaningful way. Computer languages employ similar operating conventions.

Alphabet

The characters that can be used to construct statements are termed the *alphabet* of the language being used. Although there is much similarity between the alphabets of different computer languages, significant differences also exist.

Most programming languages use an alphabet that includes approximately 48 characters. The characters that comprise an alphabet are grouped into letters (such as A, B, and so forth), digits (such as 1, 2, and so forth), and special characters (such as $+$, $*$, %, and so forth). The size of the alphabet has very little to do with the computer since a 6-bit character permits 64 combinations (2^6) and an 8-bit byte permits 256 combinations (2^8). In many cases, however, the size of the alphabet is related to the number of printable characters on the card punch machine, the terminal device, or the line printer.

Statements

A program is a set of *statements* that serve to inform the computer of the processing to be performed. Statements are punched on cards or typed in at the computer terminal. Different statements must be separated in some way, and a convenient means of doing that is to start each statement on a new card or a new line. In many programming languages the end of a card (or line) denotes the end of a statement, unless a continuation is specified in some way, and a program is composed of a collection of data records (that is, cards or lines). In some programming languages a program is a string of characters formed by linking the data records that comprise the program. Each statement is terminated by a semicolon. Thus, a given data record may contain one or more statements or parts of statements.

In subsequent chapters much of the discussion will concern statements and statement structure, and very little will be presented on the precise manner in which a statement is entered. This is because it is the statement itself that is of prime concern, and its means of representation is merely an operational convention.

DATA

In general a data processing program processes two types of data: numeric data and descriptive data. *Numeric data* would include items such as gross pay, the number of units of inventory, and a commission percentage. Thus, a numeric data item could be used in an arithmetic computation, such as when *hours* are multiplied by *rate* to obtain *gross pay*. *Descriptive data* would include items such as name, address, and age. Thus, a descriptive data item could *not* be used in an arithmetic computation.

Numeric Data

In ordinary arithmetic, calculations are performed on numbers represented as sequences of decimal digits, with possibly a decimal point and possibly an algebraic sign. A number of this type is called a *decimal number*. Thus, a decimal number x can be represented by an expression of the form:

$$x = n + 0.d_1 d_2 d_3 \ldots$$

where n is a signed or unsigned whole number and the d_is are digits in the range 0–9. The following constants are regarded as decimal numbers:

7	.00138
− 19	− 93000
+ 54.137	

Unneeded parts, such as the sign, decimal point, or fraction, need not be written—except as required by a particular application or programming language. A decimal number without a fraction is termed an *integer*.

Descriptive Data

A descriptive data item exists as a string of characters, and for that reason it is frequently referred to as *character data*. When a character constant is written in a computer program, the characters comprising the constant value are enclosed in quotation marks, such as:

"INVENTORY ANALYSIS"

A character constant, when written in a computer program, is frequently referred to as a *literal*. When character data is recorded on a storage medium—such as cards, tape, or disk—the quotation marks are not recorded.

VARIABLES AND IDENTIFIERS

In mathematics the name given to an unknown quantity is *variable*. For example, one might say, "Let x equal the . . . ." In actual practice the concept is more general and enables principles to be developed independently of a particular problem.

Variables

The term *variable,* in contrast to the word *constant,* implies that a number can assume a set of values or, in other words, that the value of a variable is not constant but is subject to change. The equation:

$$y = 3x^2 + 2x + 5$$

for example, defines a second-degree polynomial for all real values of x. The letters x and y are variables.

A variable is also used as a symbolic name in everyday discourse. Thus, variables such as x or y are frequently used to represent an unknown quantity or to help in explaining a complex idea for which ordinary language is inadequate.

Identifiers

Symbolic names are frequently used in computing and are referred to as *identifiers,* because they identify something. In higher-level languages symbolic names are used for a variety of purposes—hence the more general name of identifier.

The most familiar type of identifier is used to name a data element that can change during the course of computation; it is termed a *variable,* as discussed above. Other identifiers are used to name statements (that is, statement identifiers), data files, "key" words, attributes, and other entities. Sample identifiers are:

I	MOVE
FOR	ADD
TO	SUM

Thus, in the BASIC statement:

FOR I = 1 TO N

the tokens FOR, I, TO, and N are identifiers and the number 1 is a constant. Of the four identifiers, FOR is a *statement identifier* that identifies a particular type of statement, I and N are variables, and TO is an identifier used as a *separator,* which is used to separate similar constructs such as two numbers in succession. Similarly, in the COBOL statement:

MOVE "INVENTORY ANALYSIS" TO TITLE

the tokens MOVE, TO, and TITLE are identifiers and "INVENTORY ANALYSIS" is a literal. Of the three identifiers, MOVE is a statement identifier, TITLE is a variable (or *data name* as it is called in COBOL), and TO is a separator.

OPERATORS, EXPRESSIONS, AND REPLACEMENT

A computer can perform a variety of operational functions, known as *computing* or *computation.* Some of these functions are: (1) arithmetic and logical operations, (2) data movement, (3) sequence and control functions, and (4) input and output. Normally, these operational functions are available to users through statements in a programming language, and when users desire to specify a particular type of operation, they pick the most appropriate statement for that purpose. Arithmetic and logical operations are particularly important since they are made available to users in several ways (not necessarily in a single language) and are frequently used in several types of statements.

Assume that one desires to add the value of variable A to the value of variable B. This operation could be specified in several ways, such as:

$$A + B \qquad\qquad (1)$$
or
$$\text{ADD A TO B} \qquad\qquad (2)$$

Method (1) is similar to ordinary mathematical notation and is the most frequently used method in programming. Method (2), which is a COBOL statement, is less convenient when several mathematical operations need to be performed or when a user wants to include mathematical operations in one of the other statements in a programming language. As a means of specifying a stand-alone operation, however, method (2) has the advantages of being convenient, straightforward, and readable.

Operators

In a programming language a symbol that denotes a computational operation is known as an *operator*. Thus, in the statement:

A + 1

for example, + is an operator; the variable A and the constant 1 are *operands* to the operator. If A has the value 7, then A + 1 has the value 8. More specifically, an operand is a quantity upon which an operation is performed. An operand can be either a variable or a constant. Some operations, such as addition and subtraction, require two operands and are written with the operator symbol separating the operands. The expression A + B, to use an earlier example, denotes that the value of variable B should be added to the value of variable A. (The example is, of course, abbreviated since there is no indication of what to do with the result.) Other operators require a single operand, such as negation and are written with the operator preceding the operand. The expression −A, for example, computes the expression 0 − A and is used to change the sign of A. If A = 10, then −A equals −10.

In data processing, operators are classed into three general categories:

1. *Arithmetic operators* such as + (for addition and identity), − (for subtraction and negation), * (for multiplication), / (for division), and ** (for exponentiation).
2. *Comparison operators* that compare two data items (also referred to as relational operators), that is,

    < for less than
    ≤ for less than or equal to
    = for equal to
    ≥ for greater than or equal to
    > for greater than
    ≠ for not equal to
3. *Logical operators* that determine the truth of one or more assertions, that is,

    ∧ for and
    ∨ for or
    ∼ for not (or complement)

The representations of some of these operators vary between programming languages; for example, the logical operator "and" is represented by AND in COBOL, and the exponentiation operator is represented by ↑ in BASIC. In all cases, however, the mathematical meaning of the operations is the same. Table 9.1 gives informal definitions for the various operators.

TABLE 9.1   COMPUTATIONAL OPERATORS

	Operation	# of Operands	Form	Definition (R = result)	Example (↔denotes equivalence)
ARITHMETIC OPERATORS	Addition	2	A + B	R = A + B	2 + 3 ↔ 5
	Subtraction	2	A − B	R = A − B	6 − 4 ↔ 2
	Multiplication	2	A * B	R = A × B	4 * 3 ↔ 12
	Division	2	A/B	R = A ÷ B	9/2 ↔ 4.5
	Exponentiation	2	A ** B	R = A^B	3 ** 2 ↔ 9
	Negation	1	−A	R = 0 − A	−A ↔ −3, where A = 3
	Identity	1	+A	R = 0 + A	+A ↔ −5, where A = −5
LOGICAL OPERATORS	And	2	Q ∧ T	R is true if Q and T are both true and is false otherwise.	T ∧ Q ↔ false
	Or	2	Q ∨ T	R is true if either Q or T is true and is false otherwise.	T ∨ Q ↔ true
	Not	1	~Q	R is true if Q is false; R is false if Q is true.	~T ↔ false
COMPARISON OPERATORS	Less than	2	A < B	R is true if A is less than B and is false otherwise.	3 < 2 ↔ false
	Less than or equal to	2	A ≤ B	R is true if A is less than or equal to B and is false otherwise.	3 ≤ 3 ↔ true
	Equal to	2	A = B	R is true if A is equal to B and is false otherwise.	3 = 2 ↔ false
	Not equal to	2	A ≠ B	R is true if A is not equal to B and is false otherwise.	3 ≠ 2 ↔ true
	Greater than or equal to	2	A ≥ B	R is true if A is greater than or equal to B and is false otherwise.	2 ≥ 3 ↔ false
	Greater than	2	A > B	R is true if A is greater than B and is false otherwise.	3 > 2 ↔ true

For the logical operators: T = true and Q = false

Expressions

As in mathematics, operators and operands can be combined to form an expression denoting that a sequence of operations is to be performed. For example, A + B * C means that the product of B and C is to be added to A. Implied here is the fact that computational operations are executed in a prescribed sequence and that operators possess a priority that determines the order in which the operations are executed. A simple priority scheme is:

Priority	Operator
highest	**
↓	* or /
lowest	+ or −

which means that ** is executed before * or /, and so forth. Thus, the expression 2 + 3 * 4 has the value 14. Programmers can use the priority of operators to their advantage. For example, the mathematical expression $ax^2 + b$ can be written in a programming language as A * X * * 2 + B while maintaining the intended order of operations. In other cases, such as $\frac{(a + 1)^2}{a + b}$, it is necessary to depart from the established order of execution. This need is served with parentheses that can be used for grouping. Expressions within parentheses are executed before the operations of which they are a part. The above example can be written in a programming language as (A + 1) * * 2 / (A + B). Similarly, the expression (2 + 3) * 4 has the value 20. The use of parentheses can be extended to as many levels of nesting as are required by a particular sequence of operations.

Replacement and Data Movement

Expressions are permitted in some statements in a programming language because a computed value is frequently needed. For example, the following statement in the BASIC language:

IF A + B > 13.5 GOTO 510

directs the flow of program control to the statement numbered 510 if the value of the expression A + B is greater than 13.5. However, the most frequent use of the expression is to specify that a set of computations are to be performed and that the value of a variable is to be replaced with the result. Thus, in the statement:

LET A = B + C

the value of A is replaced with the *value* of the expression B + C;

this is called an *assignment statement.* The equivalence sign ($=$) denotes replacement but does imply equivalence since values and not expressions are involved. Thus if B contains the value 10 and C contains the value 20, then execution of the statement $A = B + C$ causes A to be replaced with the value 30; B and C retain their original values.

In mathematics an identity such as:

$$(a + 1)(a + 2) = a^2 + 3a + 2$$

is commonly used. Statements of this type are strictly illegal in programming languages. The assignment statement takes the general form:

$$v = e$$

which means that the value of variable v is replaced with the value of the expression e, computed at the point of reference. The precise forms that v and e can assume are discussed later with respect to the different programming languages. In general, an expression e can be a constant, a variable, or a meaningful combination of constants, variables, operations, and parentheses. All of the following are valid expressions:

P	2 * * ML
25	(A1 + B2) * C3 − D4
I * J	A * B * * 2 − 1
DOG + CAT	(A)

An assignment statement, such as:

NAME = C1

causes no computation to be performed and simply replaces NAME with the value C1. (C1 retains its original value.) A comparable facility is provided in the COBOL language with a separate statement of the form:

MOVE C1 TO NAME.

Similarly, the statement:

ADD A TO B.

given previously, is equivalent to the assignment statement:

B = B + A

In fact, the statement $B = B + A$ means: "Add A to the current value of B and replace the old value of B with the result of the addition."

One of the objectives of the above discussion is to emphasize the fact that each programming language has characteristics of its own; these characteristics are one of the reasons that a user would select a particular language in which to write a program. However, several other factors—such as availability, efficiency, programming standards, and so forth—would normally be considered in the choice of a language.

DATA ORGANIZATION

A value such as a person's age or the name of a part is known as a *single value*. A value of this kind can be represented as a constant or a variable. When many values are being considered, it is very cumbersome and inefficient to assign a name to each value.

Arrays

In a great many cases data take the form of a family of related data items. For example, a measurement taken at different locations at successive intervals might be recorded as follows:

Location—Date	Temperature
New York—January 1	29°
Miami—January 1	69°
Chicago—January 1	26°
Los Angeles—January 1	60°
New York—March 31	41°
Miami—March 31	79°
Chicago—March 31	38°
Los Angeles—March 31	67°
New York—June 1	75°
Miami—June 1	92°
Chicago—June 1	80°
Los Angeles—June 1	88°

Storing the information in the above form is cumbersome and would occupy an excessive amount of storage. In this case, an array, such as the following:

	TEMP	1	2	3
	1	29	41	75
Location	2	69	79	92
Index	3	26	38	80
	4	60	67	88

Date Index

would be considerably more convenient. The temperature in Miami, which has a location index of 2, on March 31, which has a date index of 2, is easily retrieved as 79°. A key point is that only the array, as a whole, need be given a name—in this case TEMP. In computing, the concept of an array is extended to include n dimensions. The process of retrieving an element of an array, termed *selection,* uses the name of the array and the relative position of the desired element in the array. Indexes used to select an element from an array are termed a *subscript* and can be expressed as constants, variables, or expressions. The established practice is to reduce an index to an integer before selection takes place. The number of indexes in a subscript must equal the number of dimensions in the array. Thus, 'TEMP (3, 2),' in the above example, would select the value 38. When writing a subscript, the indexes are separated by commas and the entire set of indexes are enclosed in parentheses following the array name. The convention is used since subscripts or superscripts in the usual sense cannot be entered into the computer.

An array has several properties of interest. The array A, defined as:

$$a_{1,1} \quad a_{1,2} \quad a_{1,3}$$
$$a_{2,1} \quad a_{2,2} \quad a_{2,3}$$

can be used as an example. The first property is the *number of dimensions,* of which A has 2. Each dimension is further characterized by an *extent,* which is the number of array elements in a dimension. Another property is *homogeneity,* which refers to the fact that each element of an array must have the same data attribute. Thus, for example, an array must contain all numeric or all character values. Obviously, distinct values may differ. The last property of an array is how it is stored. Two methods are in widespread use: *row order* and *column order.* Row order, also known as index order or lexicographic order, denotes that the elements of an array are stored in consecutive locations in main storage in a row-like fashion. Both BASIC and COBOL languages use row order. It is necessary to know how an array is stored in a given language for the following reason. Consider these statements in BASIC:

```
DIM A( 13, 4 )              (1)
MAT READ A                  (2)
```

Statement (1) defines an array with 13 rows and 4 columns. Statement (2) specifies that data is to be read from a data set into computer storage to occupy matrix A. Data must be placed in the data file in a prescribed sequence so that a value is placed in the intended array position. Therefore, the order in which the array elements are stored must be known.

Structures

Many computer applications, such as data processing, use an aggregate of data in which individual data items do not necessarily have identical sizes or identical data types. A data aggregate of this type is known as a *structure* and is frequently associated with a data record. More specifically, a structure is a collection of variables (possibly of different types and sizes) organized in a hierarchy. A typical structure is specified as follows:

```
01  PAYDATA.
    02  EMPLOYNO SIZE IS 8 CLASS IS NUMERIC.
    02  NAME.
        03  FINIT SIZE IS 1 CLASS IS ALPHABETIC.
        03  MINIT SIZE IS 1 CLASS IS ALPHABETIC.
        03  LAST SIZE IS 15 CLASS IS ALPHABETIC.
    02  DEP SIZE IS 2 CLASS IS NUMERIC USAGE IS
        COMPUTATIONAL.
    02  RATE PICTURE IS 9999V99 USAGE IS COMPUTATIONAL.
    02  GROSS.
        03  PAY PICTURE IS 99999V99 USAGE IS
            COMPUTATIONAL.
        03  FEDTAX PICTURE IS 99999V99 USAGE IS
            COMPUTATIONAL.
        03  FICA PICTURE IS 999V99 USAGE IS
            COMPUTATIONAL.
        03  STATETAX PICTURE IS 9999V99 USAGE IS
            COMPUTATIONAL.
        03  CITYTAX PICTURE IS 999V99 USAGE IS
            COMPUTATIONAL.
```

Figure 9.1 shows how this structure would be stored. For some purposes, such as input and output, it is convenient to treat a data aggregate as a single unit, as in the following input statement in COBOL:

```
READ PAYFILE INTO PAYDATA AT END GO TO DONE.
```

In this case, the complete data record is read into the storage reserved for the structure named PAYDATA. In other cases, it is necessary to be able to reference specific data fields in the structure, such as the following statement which updates the gross pay:

```
ADD RATE TO PAY.
```

In a structure the relative position of the data element in the hierarchy is specified with a level number, such as 01, 02, or 03. Data items with the same relative level number are at the same level in the hierarchy. Structures are presented in more detail with the COBOL language.

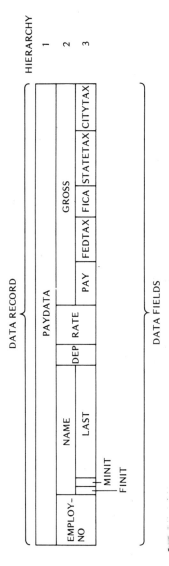

FIGURE 9.1 Illustration of a typical hierarchic structure showing record and field levels.

STRUCTURED PROGRAMMING*

Structured programming is a method of computer programming that contributes to a program's reliability, maintainability, and readability. The technique exists as a set of mathematically based rules that apply to programming during each step of the process. A major advantage of structured programming is that it simplifies the control structures in a program, so that instead of using GOTO statements that effectively branch "all over the place," a program is composed of well-defined blocks of statements, such as those achieved through the use of the conventional DO (or FOR) loop. (A *loop* is a sequence of computer instructions that repeats itself over and over.) Structured programming requires a systematic and disciplined approach to programming. The objective and the result is that a more precise form of programming is achieved with structured programming than by using conventional programming practices.

The Structure Theorem

The concept of structured programming is based on the *Structure Theorem,* which states that a program with one entry and one exit (that is, a *proper program*) is functionally equivalent to a program constructed from the following logic structures:

1. A sequence of two or more functions
2. A conditional branch of the form
      If p THEN a ELSE c
3. Repeated execution of a function while a condition is true; that is, the DO WHILE statement

The basic idea behind structured programming is that a program can be represented as a function with one entry and one exit, as shown in Figure 9.2, and that it can be constructed by systematically applying the three logic structures, listed above. In actual practice, the logic structures are frequently supplemented by two additional logic structures that facilitate programming.

Entry ⟶ function ⟶ Exit

FIGURE 9.2   A function is a program segment with one entry and one exit.

---

* This section can be omitted without a loss of continuity.

FIGURE 9.3   **The sequence function.**

Sequence

The *sequence function,* shown in Figure 9.3, is equivalent to stating that two functions, each with one entry and one exit, can be regarded as a single function. Formally, the *sequence proposition* states that the *firstpart* followed by the *secondpart* does the sequence function.

Ifthenelse

The *ifthenelse function* (See Figure 9.4) provides a conditional facility that includes two subfunctions in its definition. Formally, the *ifthenelse proposition* states the following: Whenever the *iftest* is true, the *thenpart* does the ifthenelse function; and whenever the *iftest* is false, the *elsepart* does the ifthenelse function. Thus, the IFTHENELSE statement is equivalent to a function, as defined earlier. In this logic structure, *thenpart* and *elsepart* are functions.

Dowhile

The *dowhile function* (see Figure 9.5) provides a looping facility analogous to the DO or FOR loops in most programming languages. In its most elementary form, the dowhile function serves as a compound statement. Formally, the *dowhile proposition* states the following: Whenever the *whiletest* is true, the *dopart* followed by the *dowhile* does the dowhile function; and whenever the *whiletest* is false, the identity does the do-

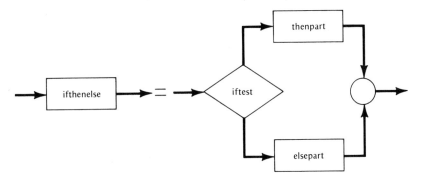

FIGURE 9.4   **The ifthenelse function.**

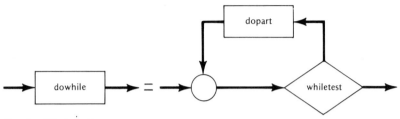

FIGURE 9.5   The dowhile function.

while function. In the latter case, the false result from the *whiletest* causes an exit from the function. In this logic structure, *dopart* is a function.

Dountil and Case

Structured programming is the repeated application of the ifthenelse function and dowhile function to produce a program that exists as a function. The *dountil function* (Figure 9.6) and the *case function* (Figure 9.7) are encountered sufficiently often that they warrant unique structures. The *dountil function* is an alternate form of looping in which the function is executed while the *untiltest* is true. The *case function* is a multi-branch-multijoin structure that is equivalent to a set of nested ifthenelse functions.

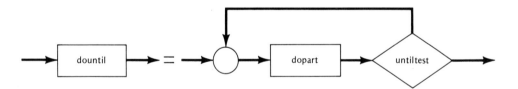

FIGURE 9.6   The dountil function.

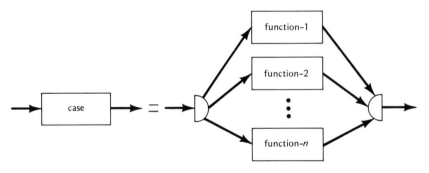

FIGURE 9.7   The case function.

Application of the Concepts

As an example of how the preceding concepts can be used to synthesize or analyze a structured program, consider the following program in text form:

```
if p then
      a
      do while(q)
            b
      end do
else
      if r then
            c
      else
            do while(s)
                  d
            end do
      end if
      e
end if
```

The flow diagram form of the program is given in Figure 9.8. Analyzing the flow diagrams in Figure 9.8 from bottom-to-top, the diagrams become more easily understood because less detail is included. Synthesizing the program from top-to-bottom, detail is added in each successive step. The transition is made between the various flow diagrams by repeated application of the structure theorem.

Implementation of Structured Programming

One of the most significant characteristics of a structured program, which was exhibited in the preceding example, is that the program is highly readable. The text can be read from top-to-bottom without any "jumping around." There is a noted lack of GOTO statements, which are the major cause of the excessive branching found in many programs. Readable programs are useful during development, testing, and maintenance. In fact, different functions can be assigned to different programmers that are working cooperatively on a project.

Another factor that contributes to readability is the practice of indenting statements, so that the statements that correspond to a particular function can be easily identified. The end result is that a reader can easily grasp the logic of a program, at any level of detail, by studying the segments that correspond to the functional structure of a program.

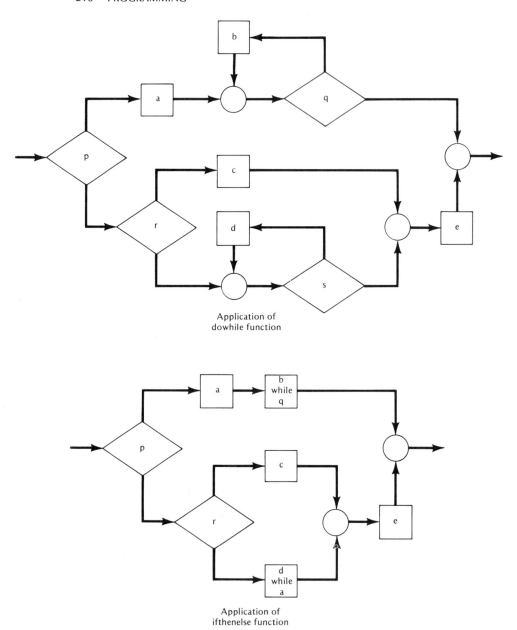

Application of
dowhile function

Application of
ifthenelse function

FIGURE 9.8(a) Analysis of a structured program.

The use of structured programming and appropriate coding practices become a set of "project rules" when enforced by management control. Although most programming projects benefit from structured programming, large-scale software development projects are particularly amenable to the techniques because of the relatively large numbers of routines and programmers involved.

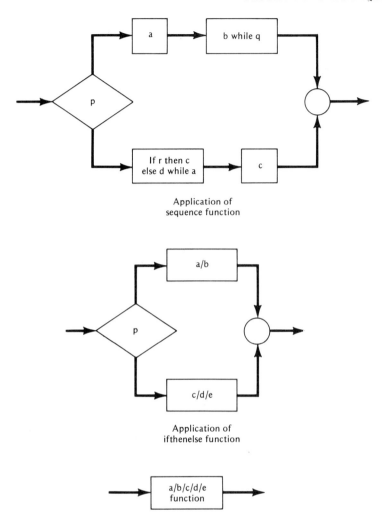

Application of
sequence function

Application of
ifthenelse function

Structured Programming Coding Conventions in the COBOL Language

The structured programming coding conventions in the COBOL language presented here can be reviewed after the study of the COBOL language (Chapter 11) has been completed. The conventions use the reference diagrams for the *ifthenelse* and *dowhile* functions, which are given in Figure 9.9. The development of coding conventions for the dountil and case functions is left as an exercise.

The coding convention for the ifthenelse function is defined in COBOL as:

```
IF p
    code for F₁
ELSE
    code for F₂
```

Alternately, the ELSE clause may be omitted.

The coding convention for the dowhile function uses the PERFORM statement and includes the function F in a remote location in the Procedure Division. The function has two options: (1) while clause only; and (2) while clause with indexing. The PERFORM statement in COBOL contains an UNTIL option rather than a WHILE option so that the coding convention uses a "not p" condition. The two options are defined in the above order as follows:

```
PERFORM paragraph-F UNTIL(NOT p).

PERFORM paragraph-F
    VARYING identifier-1 FROM identifier-2 BY identifier-3
    UNTIL (NOT p).
```

Because of the UNTIL option to the PERFORM statement in COBOL, the dountil function is relatively straightforward to implement.

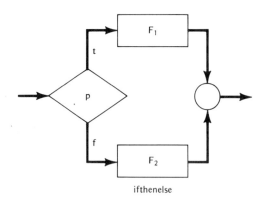

ifthenelse

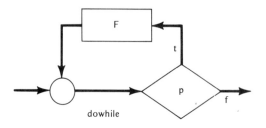

dowhile

FIGURE 9.9   Reference diagrams for the COBOL coding conventions.

Vocabulary   alphabet
arithmetic operator
array
case function
character data
comparison operator
decimal number
dountil function
dowhile function
expressions
extent
homogeneity
identifier
index

ifthenelse function
language
literal
logical data
logical operator
number of dimensions
operator
replacement
sequence function
statement
structures
Structure Theorem
subscript
variable

Questions   1. Do all languages, including natural languages, have an alphabet?

2. With respect to data, where do the terms numeric and character come from?

3. What is a literal?

4. If a variable is a symbolic name, then why is the term *identifier* used instead of *variable* in naming various constituents of programming languages?

5. To what arithmetic statement is the following COBOL statement equivalent:

MULTIPLY A BY B

6. What are the differences between an array and a structure?

7. What is the *Structure Theorem?*

8. What is the primary difference between the dowhile and dountil functions?

9. Why are "project rules" important to an organization engaged in computer programming?

Exercises   1. Classify the operators (infix or prefix) in the following expressions:

$-A * B$ $A * (-B)$
$3.14 * PT$ $A / (-B * C)$
$(A + B * C) - 1$ -13.4

2. Given the matrix:

$$A = \begin{pmatrix} -7 & 3 & 9 & 6 \\ 5 & 1 & 4 & 3 \\ 2 & 8 & 7 & 5 \end{pmatrix}$$

where the row bounds are 1 and 3 and the column bounds are 1 and 4, give A(2, 3), A(3, 2), and A(1, 2).

3. Develop a logic structure diagram for the dountil function using one or more of the following functions in combination: sequence, ifthenelse, and dowhile.

4. Develop a logic structure diagram for the case function using one or more of the following functions in combination: sequence, ifthenelse, and dowhile. If necessary, limit the number of cases to a small value, such as three.

5. Develop coding conventions for the dountil and case functions in COBOL.

Related Reading

Baker, F. T. "System Quality Through Structured Programming." *Proceedings of the 1972 Fall Joint Computer Conference,* AFIPS vol. 39, pp. 339–343.

Donaldson, J. R. "Structured Programming," *Datamation,* vol. 19, no. 12 (December 1973): 52–54.

Elson, M. *Concepts of Programming Languages.* Chicago: Science Research Associates, 1973.

McCracken, D. D. "Revolution in programming," *Datamation,* vol. 19, no. 12 (December 1973): 50–52.

Miller, E. F., Jr., and Lindamood, G. E. "Structured programming: Top-down Approach." *Datamation,* vol. 19, no. 12 (December 1973): 55–57.

Sammet, J. E. *Programming Languages: History and Fundamentals.* Englewood Cliffs, N.J.: Prentice-Hall, Inc., 1969.

10

BASIC

The BASIC language achieves its greatest utility from the simple fact that it is easy to learn, easy to use, and easy to remember. (BASIC is an acronym for *B*eginner's *A*ll-purpose *S*ymbolic *I*nstruction *C*ode.) BASIC is particularly appropriate for the student or the data processing person who wants to utilize the advantages of computer processing without becoming a computer expert.

BASIC LANGUAGE STRUCTURE

BASIC was originally developed at Dartmouth College under the direction of Professors John G. Kemeny and Thomas E. Kurtz. BASIC has been under continuous development, and several implementations of the language are currently available at universities, through computer service companies, and in business concerns. Enhancements have been made to the original concept of BASIC, and one frequently hears of an "extended BASIC," "super BASIC," "advanced BASIC," and so forth; occasionally, one even hears of a "basic BASIC."

This chapter of the book covers the original Dartmouth version of BASIC plus many of the subsequent extensions to the language. Variations exist between different implementations of the language. Any person making extensive use of the language should consult the reference manual for the system being used.

Fibonacci Numbers

As an example of the general appearance of a BASIC program, consider the Fibonacci sequence introduced earlier and depicted as follows:

    1   1   2   3   5   8   13   21   34   . . .

The pattern is clear: after the first two numbers, each succeeding number is the sum of the previous two numbers. A BASIC program that generates Fibonacci numbers less than or equal to 50 is given as follows:[1]

```
 10   LET N1=0
 20   LET N2=1
 30   PRINT N2
 40   LET N3=N1+N2
 50   IF N3>50 THEN 100
 60   PRINT N3
 70   LET N1=N2
 80   LET N2=N3
 90   GOTO 40
100   END
```

1. It is not necessary that the first few programs be completely understood. Only general concepts are required since all topics are covered in later sections.

Output

1
1
2
3
5
8
13
21
34

The above program is fairly obvious and will not be discussed further. After the next example, however, several statements, including those used above, will be described.

A Classic Problem

As an illustration of the manner in which BASIC can be used to solve a problem, consider this classical problem: Manhattan Island was sold by the Indians to the settlers in 1626 for $24 worth of beads and trinkets. At a given interest rate, what is the island worth today? A simple solution is presented in the following program:

```
10   LET P = 24
20   LET R = .06
30   FOR Y = 1627 TO 1979
40     LET P = P + P * R
50   NEXT Y
60   PRINT P
70   END
```

Output:[2]

2.05675E+10

The statements numbered 10 and 20 assign the values 24 and .06 to the principal (P) and the interest rate (R), respectively. The interest for a given year is computed as P * R, and the principal at the end of a given year is computed as P + P * R. Statements 30 through 50 constitute a *program loop;* the principal is recomputed as the year (Y) advances from 1627 to 1979. After the loop is completed (that is, the number of iterations specified in statement 30 has been satisfied), the resulting principal (P) is printed in statement 60.

The PRINT statement can also be used to have several data items printed on the same output line by including those items in the PRINT

2. 2.05675E + 10 is the floating point form of 20,567,500,000.

statement, separated by commas or semicolons. Thus if statement 60 read,

60 PRINT "PRESENT VALUE OF MANHATTAN =";P

then the output would be,

PRESENT VALUE OF MANHATTAN = 2.05675E + 10

Data items enclosed in quotation marks are printed as descriptive information, whereas the *numerical value* of an expression is printed. (Recall that a variable, such as P, is an expression.)

In the preceding program, the data of the problem was built into the program (that is, a beginning principal of 24 and an interest rate of .06). If the user desired to repeat the calculations for different interest rates, then a set of data values would have to be established with a DATA statement, such as

DATA .05, .06, .07, .08

and the data set would have to be accessed with a READ statement, such as

READ R

Thus, a program to compute the present value of Manhattan Island for different interest rates is given as follows:

```
10   DATA.05,.06,.07,.08
20   FOR I = 1 TO 4
30      LET P = 24
40      READ R
50      FOR Y =1627 TO 1979
60         LET P = P + P * R
70      NEXT Y
80      PRINT "PRESENT VALUE OF MANHATTAN =";P
90   NEXT I
00   END
```

Output:

```
PRESENT VALUE OF MANHATTAN = 7.24492E + 08
PRESENT VALUE OF MANHATTAN = 2.05675E + 10
PRESENT VALUE OF MANHATTAN = 5.65828E + 11
PRESENT VALUE OF MANHATTAN = 1.50937E + 13
```

The program includes a nested FOR loop that has the form:

$$A \begin{cases} \text{FOR. . . .} \\ \text{. . . .} \\ \quad B \begin{cases} \text{FOR. . .} \\ \text{. . . .} \\ \text{. . . .} \\ \text{NEXT. . .} \end{cases} \\ \text{. . . .} \\ \text{NEXT. . .} \end{cases}$$

The interpretation of the nested loops is as follows: For every iteration of loop A, loop B is executed from start to finish. Thus, if A is executed n times and loop B is executed m times, then a given statement contained in loop B is executed $n \times m$ times.

Several statements were used in the above examples:

LET—assigns the value of an expression to a variable

FOR—begins a program loop and specifies how many times it is executed

NEXT—ends a program loop and tells the computer to return to the beginning of the loop for the next iteration

PRINT—causes output data to be printed

DATA—creates a set of data

READ—causes data specified in a DATA statement to be accessed (read) and assigned to specified variables

END—ends a BASIC program

Each of these statements is described in more detail in later sections.

Characters and Symbols

A computer program is a coded form of an algorithm for solving a given problem on a computer. The statements of a program are encoded in the alphabet of the language using established conventions. It is necessary to distinguish between characters of the alphabet and symbols of the language. A *character of the alphabet* is an entity that has a representation internally and externally to the computer. The letter "A," for example, is a character of most language alphabets. The majority of characters have no meaning in their own right; for example, the letter "A" only has meaning through the manner in which it is used, which may be as part of a variable, the name of a statement, and so forth. Table 10.1 lists the BASIC alphabet, which consists of approximately 50–55 characters depending upon the equipment involved.

A *symbol of the language* is a series of one or more characters that

TABLE 10.1   Characters of the BASIC alphabet

Alphabetic Characters (26) A B C D E F G H I J K L M N O P Q R S T U V W X Y Z *Digits* (10) 0 1 2 3 4 5 6 7 8 9 *Special Characters* (19)

Name	Character
Blank	(no visual representation)
Equal sign	=
Plus sign	+
Minus sign	−
Asterisk	*
Solidus (slash)	/
Up arrow	↑
Left parenthesis	(
Right parenthesis	)
Comma	,
Point or period	.
Single quotation mark (apostrophe)	'
Double quotation mark	"
Semicolon	;
Question mark	?
"Less than" symbol	<
"Greater than" symbol	>
"Not equal" symbol	≠
Currency symbol (dollar sign)	$

has been assigned a specific meaning. Typical symbols are the plus sign (+) and the comma, used as a separator. A symbol consisting of more than one character is termed a *composite symbol,* and it is assigned a meaning not inherent in the constituent characters themselves. Typical composite symbols are ** for exponentiation and >= for "greater than or equal to." The symbols of the BASIC language are listed in Table 10.2.

In most implementations of BASIC, lower-case letters can be used interchangeably with upper-case letters. Spaces are ignored in BASIC, except with quotes, so that they can be inserted by the user to promote easy reading.

Data Types and Constant Values

Two types of data are permitted in BASIC, arithmetic data and character-string data. An *arithmetic data item* has a numeric value and is refer-

TABLE 10.2   Symbols of the BASIC language

Symbol	Function	Alternate[a]
+	Addition or prefix +	
−	Subtraction or prefix −	
*	Multiplication	
/	Division	
↑	Exponentiation	**
>	Greater than	GT
>=	Greater than or equal to	GE
=	Equal to (also see below)	
<>	Not equal to	≠ or NE
<	Less than	LT
<=	Less than or equal to	LE
;	Separates elements of list or subscripts	
.	Decimal point	
;	Separates elements of list	
=	Assignment symbol	
"	Used to enclose literals	
( )	Enclose lists or group expressions	

[a] Some versions of BASIC use alternate composite symbols; frequently, the characters used are a function of the input devices available to the user.

enced through the use of a variable or a constant and may be generated as an intermediate result or as part of a computational procedure. BASIC accepts arithmetic constants in three principal forms:

1. As a constituent of a non-DATA statement, such as the number 5 in

    LET A = B + 5

2. As a constant in a DATA statement, such as

    DATA 25,−13.289,.734E − 4

3. In response to an input request (from an INPUT statement), such as

    ? − 75,4.56

In general, the arithmetic constant is written in the usual fashion, that is, as a sequence of digits possibly preceded by a plus or minus sign and possibly containing a decimal point. (An arithmetic constant is specified in decimal, and the user need not be concerned with how it is stored.) Sample arithmetic constants are −13.5, 12345, 1., +36, .01, −5, and 0. In addition, an arithmetic constant can be scaled by a power of 10 by following the constant with the letter E followed by the power, which must be expressed as either a positive or negative integer. Thus, the constant x E y is equivalent to the expression $x \times 10^y$ in mathematics. To cite some examples, .12E– 4 is equivalent to .000012, –3E2 is equivalent to –300, +1.234E3 is equivalent to 1234, and –1E+1 is equivalent to –10. The sign of an arithmetic constant is frequently omitted in expressions by applying elementary rules of arithmetic. Thus, instead of writing A + (–5), most users simply write A – 5. Similarly, A – (–5) would ordinarily be written as A + 5.

In an arithmetic constant, the E (if used) must be preceded by at least one digit. Thus, 1E2 is a valid constant, whereas E2 is not.

A *character-string data item* is stored as a string of characters and can include any character recognized by the computer equipment. A character-string data item is referenced through the use of a variable or a constant. BASIC accepts character-string constants in three principal forms:

1. As a constituent part of a non-DATA statement, such as

    LET F $ = "TEA FOR TWO"

    or

    IF P $ = "END" THEN 100

2. As a constant in a DATA statement, such as

    DATA "BIG", "BAD"

3. In response to an input request (from an INPUT statement), such as

    ? " EACH HIS OWN"

A character-string constant must be enclosed in quotation marks. Any character within the quotes, including the blank character, is considered to be part of the character string. The length of a character string is the number of characters between the enclosing quotation marks. If quotation marks are to be included in the string, then the included mark must be represented as two consecutive quotation marks. The two consecutive quotation marks are a lexical feature of the language and are stored as a single character. Sample character-string constants are:

Character-String Constant	Length	Would Print As
"TEA FOR TWO"	11	TEA FOR TWO
"123.4"	5	123.4
"""DARN IT"""	9	"DARN IT"
"DON'T"	5	DON'T

Character-string data are frequently used for printing descriptive information, such as page and column headings, and are occasionally referred to in BASIC as *label data.*

Names

A *name* is a string of alphabetic or numeric characters, the first of which must be alphabetic. In BASIC, names are used to identify scalar variables, array variables, and functions.

A *scalar arithmetic variable* name (also referred to as a simple variable) consists of a single letter or a single letter followed by a single digit. A, I, Z1, and K9 are valid simple variables, while A10, DOG, and 3A are not. The initial value of a simple variable is zero, and it can only be used to represent arithmetic data.

A *scalar character-string variable* name (also referred to as a simple character variable) consists of a single letter followed by a dollar sign (that is, the currency symbol). The maximum length of a character string that can be assigned to a character-string variable is 18. The initial value of a simple character variable is 18 blanks. Thus, A$, I$, and S$ are valid simple character variables, while A1$, 5$, and IT$ are not.

Arrays

An *array* is a collection of data items of the same type (that is, all arithmetic data items or all character-string data items) that is referenced by a single array name. An *arithmetic array* can have either one or two dimensions and uses an identifier that consists of a single letter. An element of an array is referenced by giving the relative positive of that element in the array. If the array has one dimension, then an element is referenced by appending a subscript enclosed in parentheses to the array name as follows:

$$a\ (e)$$

where a is the array name and e is an expression evaluated at the point of reference. Thus, the array reference $a(e)$ selects the eth element of array a. If the array has two dimensions, then an element is selected in a similar manner with an array reference of the form:

$$a\ (e_1,\ e_2)$$

where a is the array name and e_1 and e_2 are expressions evaluated at the point of reference. Thus, the array reference of $a(e_1,\ e_2)$ selects the element located in the e_1th row and the e_2th column of a. The following are valid array references: A(I), B(W4), C(P+1), C(I,J), E(T3/

R+13, 3*X ↑2—1), F(A(2*Q)), and G(B(1), 4). The last two examples depict subscripted subscripts. All elements of an arithmetic array are initially set to zero when the program is executed.

A *character-string array* (referred to as a character array) can have one dimension and uses an identifier that consists of a letter followed by a dollar sign. Each element of a character array can contain up to 18 characters and is initially set to 18 blanks when the program is executed. As with an arithmetic array, an element of a character array is referenced by specifying the relative position of that element in the array with a construction of the form:

$$a\$(e)$$

where *a*$ is the array name and *e* is an expression evaluated at the point of reference. The following are valid character array references: B$(3), C$(I), D$(2*J—1), and D$(A(K)).

The extent of an array can be declared implicitly or explicitly. An *explicit array declaration* is made through the use of the dimension (DIM) statement, which is used to give the extent of each dimension of the array. Thus, the statement:

```
DIMP(3,4),Q(36),T$(17)
```

defines a two-dimensional arithmetic array P with three rows and four columns, a one-dimensional arithmetic array Q with 36 elements, and a character array T$ with 17 elements, each element of which can contain a character string of 18 characters. The lower subscript bound for all array dimensions is one; the upper subscript bound is the value declared with the DIM statement. The DIM statement is presented in a later section on arrays.

An *implicit array declaration* is made when an array reference with either a single or a double subscript is made to an undeclared array. An array referenced in this way with a single subscript is assigned an extent of 10 with lower and upper subscript bounds of 1 and 10, respectively. An array referenced in this way with a double subscript is assigned row and column extents of 10; each dimension has lower and upper bounds of 1 and 10, respectively.

Operators and Expressions

Arithmetic and comparison operators are included as part of the BASIC language. Arithmetic operators are defined on arithmetic data and are classed as binary operators and unary operators. A *binary arithmetic operator* is used in the following manner:

operand ⊕ operand

where an operand is defined as an arithmetic constant, a function reference, an element of an arithmetic array, or an expression enclosed in
parentheses, and $\oplus$ is one of the following arithmetic operators: +,
−, *, /, or ↑. A *unary arithmetic operator* is used in the following manner:

−operand

where "operand" has the same definition as given above. The use of
a unary operator is restricted to the following cases:

1. As the leftmost character in an expression, provided that two
    operators do not appear in succession; or
2. As the leftmost character in a subexpression enclosed in parentheses
    such that the unary operator follows the left parenthesis.

An example of case 1 is −A+B↑C while an example of case 2 is
A*(−B↑(−3). The result of a binary or unary arithmetic operation is
a numeric value.

   An *arithmetic expression* can be an arithmetic scalar variable, an element
of an arithmetic array, a numeric constant, a function reference, or a
series of these constituents separated by binary operators and parentheses and possibly prefixed by unary operators. Thus, any of the
following are valid expressions in BASIC:

A1   −(C1+I−1)   −SQR (X↑3)−J
B+25   SIN (X3)   ((Y+3)*Y+16)*Y−1

As stated previously, parentheses are used for grouping, and expressions within expressions are executed before the operations of which
they are a part. For example, the expression 2 * (3 + 4) equals 14.
When parentheses are not used in an arithmetic expression, an operand
may appear as though it is an operand to two operators; that is, for
example, the operand B in an expression such as:

A+B*C

In this case, operators are executed on a priority basis as governed
by the following list:

Operator	Priority
↑ (that is, **)	Highest
unary −	↓
*,/	
binary +, binary −	Lowest

Thus, in the expression A+B*C the expression B*C is executed first, and the result of that subexpression is added to A. Operators of the same priority are executed in a left-to-right order.

A *character expression* is a character variable, a character array member, or a character constant. Except when they are used in a PRINT statement, character strings are handled in a special way:

1. If the character string contains less than 18 characters, it is padded on the right with blanks so that it can be stored as 18 characters.
2. If the character string contains more than 18 characters, it is truncated on the right so that its length is 18 characters.

(Character strings used in a PRINT statement are given a length determined by the enclosing quotation marks and the above conventions do not apply, that is, no padding or truncation occurs.)

A *comparison expression* has the form:

operand $\oplus$ operand

where the "operands" can be either arithmetic expressions or character expressions (the operands cannot be mixed), and $\oplus$ is one of the following comparison operators: =, <>, >=, >, <=, or <. The result of a comparison expression is either a "true" value or a "false" value, which is used in the conditional IF statement. Thus, if A = 10, B = 15, C $ = "TEA", and D $ = "DOG", then the following valid comparison expressions give the indicated results:

A = B yields the value "false"[1]
A ↑ 2 + A * B >= B ↑ 2 yields the value "true"
C $ <> D$ yields the value "true"
(A + 2.5) ↑ 2 > 101.5 yields the value "true"
C $ < D $ yields the value "false"[2]

In an arithmetic comparison expression, the arithmetic expressions that serve as operands to the comparison operation are evaluated first; then the comparison operation is performed.

Statement Structure

BASIC is designed to be a language for time-sharing, and the structure of the language reflects that mode of operation. *Time-sharing* means

1. Arithmetic comparisons use the arithmetic value of the operands.
2. When BASIC (and as a matter of fact, any programming language) is implemented, an ordering sequence among characters is defined. Frequently, the ordering sequence is based on the numerical values of the bit representations of the characters.

that many users share the resources of the computer. Each statement in BASIC is prefixed with a *statement number* that serves two purposes:

1. BASIC statements are executed in an order determined by the arithmetic value of the statement number; and
2. The statement number is used to reference another statement in statements such as

   GOTO 500

In the first case, the statement number serves as a "line number," so that statements need not be entered in any specific order to facilitate the insertion, deletion, and modification of statements.

The form of a BASIC statement is:[3]

  statement-number [statement-identifier] [statement-body]

where *statement-number* is an unsigned integer;[4] *statement-identifier* is a word that identifies a particular type of statement; and *statement-body* is a series of characters that comprise the body of the statement. Sample statements are:

```
500   LET A = B + C * D
300   LET K3 = 16
783   GOTO 100
910   IF A > = B THEN 300
440   STOP
999   END
```

Thus, a statement is constructed from a statement identifier, a statement body, or both. Neither a statement identifier nor a statement body is required, and thus a blank line (except for the statement number) is permitted to improve readability and to serve as a point of reference in a program. Blank lines are ignored by the computer.

A good programming practice is to insert comments to help a person remember what a particular set of statements does. A comment (that is, a remark) can be inserted anywhere in a program with a statement of the form:

  statement-number REM[any character] . . .

---

3. The syntactical conventions used to describe programming languages are covered in Appendix A.
4. Usually, one to four decimal digits are permitted in a statement number.

For example, the following statements are comment lines:

```
350   REM THIS PROGRAM IS INCORRECT
890   REMARK FNG IS THE GAMMA FUNCTION
```

Comment lines are ignored by the computer.

Program Structure

A program in the BASIC language is characterized by the fact that a complete program must be entered before any part of the program is executed and by the fact that it is usually transparent to the user how the program is executed. In general, the conventions given below apply regardless of whether the operational mode is time-sharing or batch processing. The time-sharing mode is used as an example.

After the user identifies himself or herself to the computer, the word "READY" is typed by the computer so that the user knows that the computer is ready to accept a command telling it what to do. (Obviously, commands differ between different implementations of the language.) Assume the user types the word NEW, telling the computer that the program being developed is a new program, followed by the name of the new program. Another "READY" message is typed by the computer and the user can proceed to enter the program. (If the user had typed the word OLD followed by a program name, then the old program would be retrieved from direct-access storage for use by the terminal user.) The user enters information line by line. Each statement must be preceded with a statement number, which is saved as part of the statement. The only restriction on a program is that it must end with an END statement; in other words, the highest numbered statement in a program must be the END statement.

When the user has entered the complete program, a command is entered to either RUN the program or to LIST the program. After the computer has performed a requested action, it types "READY" to inform the user that he or she can again enter either statements or commands.

The user can add or change a statement at any time by simply typing the statement number (of the line to be inserted or modified) followed by the new statement. When the program is run or listed, the statements are sorted by statement number, and new statements replace old ones. A statement is deleted by typing its statement number with a blank line.

Once the execution of a program is started, the program runs until a STOP statement is executed, an END statement is reached, or a condition arises that prevents further execution. The following example depicts the preceding concepts:

Computer: READY
User: NEW TRNGL
Computer: READY
User: 100 DATA 3,4,5,12,7,24
User: 200 READ B,H
User: 300 LET D = SQR(B↑2+H↑2)
User: 400 PRINT B,H,D
User: 500 GOTO 200
User: 999 END
User: RUN
Computer: 3   4   5
             5   12   13
             7   24   25

Computer: OUT OF DATA IN LINE 200

Computer: READY

User: 150 PRINT "BASE", "HEIGHT", "DIAG"
User: RUN

Computer: BASE   HEIGHT   DIAG
Computer: 3   4   5
Computer: 5   12   13
Computer: 7   24   25

Computer: OUT OF DATA IN LINE 200

User: LIST
Computer: 100 DATA 3,4,5,12,7,24
Computer: 150 PRINT "BASE", "HEIGHT", "DIAG"
Computer: 200 READ B,H
Computer: 300 LET D = SQR(B↑2+H↑2)
Computer: 400 PRINT B,H,D
Computer: 500 GOTO 200
Computer: 999 END
Computer: READY

Thus, the structure of a program in the BASIC language is inherent in the fact that it is a collection of statements ordered by a statement number (that is, line number).

INPUT AND OUTPUT STATEMENTS

This section and the following sections describe the various statements that comprise the core of the BASIC language. The statements are grouped by the functions they perform, and examples of the use of each type of statement are given.

Input and output statements are used to enter data into the computer and to display results to the user. Four statement types are presented: PRINT, DATA, READ, and INPUT

PRINT Statement

The PRINT statement is used to display results on a person's output unit, which is usually a terminal device. The form of the PRINT statement is:

```
PRINT expression [{,|;}expression] . . .
```

where "expression" is an arithmetic or a character-string expression. The syntax of the PRINT statement denotes that the following cases are valid:

```
PRINT   A              PRINT   C,D1+3
PRINT   25             PRINT   H;I
PRINT   2*B            PRINT   J,K;L
PRINT   A,B,C,D,E      PRINT   "ABC";M
PRINT                  PRINT   2*A↑3+4*A+5
```

The key point is that expressions must be separated by a punctuation character that can either be a comma or a semicolon. Normally, the PRINT statement is used in a program as follows:

```
10   PRINT "3↑2=",3↑2
20   END
```

and a result such as:

```
3 ↑ 2 =    9
```

is produced. A comma is used as punctuation, and the output values are printed in columns. Each column has a width of 18 characters. When it is desired to run the fields together, a semicolon is used as a separator, as in the following example:

```
10   PRINT "3↑2=";3↑2
20   END
RUN

3↑2=9
```

When a PRINT statement is completed, the carriage is normally moved up to the next line. The user can prevent the carriage from advancing by ending the PRINT statement with either a comma or a semicolon. The following example illustrates the latter point:

```
10   FOR I = 1 TO 5          10   FOR I = 1 TO 5
20       PRINT I             20       PRINT I;
30   NEXT I                  30   NEXT I
40   END                     40   END
RUN                          RUN

     1                            1 2 3 4 5
     2
     3
     4
     5
```

A PRINT statement with no statement body simply advances the carriage line. Thus, in the following example:

```
10   PRINT "FIRST LINE"
20   PRINT
30   PRINT "NEXT LINE"
40   END
RUN

FIRST LINE

NEXT LINE
```

a line on the printed page is skipped as a result of the "null" print statement (line 20).

DATA Statement

The DATA statement is used to create a data list, internal to the computer, and has the form:

```
DATA constant [,constant] . . .
```

where "constant" is an arithmetic or character constant. All data specified in DATA statements are collected into a single list; the order of the data constants is determined by the logical order of the DATA statements in the program. The internal data list can be accessed by the READ statement during the execution of a program. Actually, the DATA statement is a nonexecutable statement, and the internal data list is created before the program is executed. Thus, DATA statements can be placed anywhere in a program. The logical order of DATA statements is determined by the relative magnitude of associated statement numbers.

READ Statement

The READ statement is used to assign values to scalar and array variables and has the form:

```
READ variable [,variable] . . .
```

where "variable" is an arithmetic or character scalar variable or a subscripted array variable. A pointer is associated with the internal data list constructed from the DATA statements in a program. Initially, this pointer is set to the first value in the data list. As READ statements are processed, successive values from the data list are assigned to the variables in the READ statements. Logically, the values in the data list are used up as READ statements are executed. Each value from the data list must be the same type as the variable to which it is assigned. Thus, it is the user's responsibility to insure that data values are sequenced in the required order. If an attempt is made to "read" data when the data list is exhausted or the type of a data value and the variable to which it is assigned do not agree, then a READ error results, and execution of the program is terminated. A READ error also occurs when an attempt is made to "read" data when no DATA statement exists in the program. Examples of the DATA and READ statements have been given previously. The following example depicts the use of character-string constants, as well as arithmetic constants:

```
 5   PRINT "GRADE REPORT"
 6   PRINT
10   READ N$,T1,T2,T3
20   PRINT N$
30   PRINT "AVERAGE IS"; (T1 + T2 + T3)/3
35   PRINT
40   GOTO 10
50   DATA "R.ADAMS"
51   DATA 80,90,76
52   DATA "J. COTTON"
53   DATA 50,71,68
54   DATA "M.DODGER"
55   DATA 100,86,96
99   END
RUN

GRADE REPORT

R.ADAMS
AVERAGE IS 82

J.COTTON
AVERAGE IS 63
```

M.DODGER
AVERAGE IS 94

OUT OF DATA IN LINE 10

Input Statement

In some cases the data values to be used in a program are not known beforehand and must be entered by the user on a dynamic basis—that is, while the program is being executed. The INPUT statement allows the user to interact with an executing program and permits data values to be entered. The INPUT statement operates like the READ statement except that data is entered from the user's console instead of from an internal data set. The INPUT statement is placed in a program at the point that the data is needed. The computer types a question mark (?), and the execution of the program is suspended until the required data is entered. Since a program can include several INPUT statements, most people precede the INPUT statement with a PRINT statement identifying the data that should be entered. The form of the INPUT statement is:

```
INPUT variable [,variable] . . .
```

where "variable" is an arithmetic or character scalar variable or a subscripted array variable. The following example depicts the use of the INPUT statement:

```
10   PRINT "ENTER A,B"
20   INPUT A,B
30   PRINT "A + B = "; A + B
40   PRINT "A * B = "; A * B
50   GOTO 10
60   END
RUN

ENTER A,B
?2,3

A + B = 5
A * B = 6
ENTER A,B
?3, 4
A + B = 7
A * B = 12
?STOP
PROGRAM HALTED
```

The above program includes what is known as an *input loop;* in other words, program control is always directed to the statement numbered 10 and then to statement 20 (with the GOTO statement in line 50) to input new values for A and B. The user can terminate the loop by typing STOP instead of entering a data value.

ASSIGNMENT STATEMENTS

The assignment statement permits a data value to be assigned to a scalar variable or to a subscripted array variable. Assignment statements include the simple LET statement and the conventional assignment statement.

Simple LET Statement

The LET statement has the form:

LET variable = expression

where "variable" is a scalar arithmetic variable or a subscripted arithmetic array variable, and "expression" is an arithmetic expression; or where "variable" is a scalar character-string variable or a subscripted character-string array variable, and "expression" is a character-string expression. The statement means: "Replace the value of the variable with the value of the expression evaluated at the point of reference in the program." The following examples depict valid LET statements:

```
LET A = 10
LET B $ = "TEA FOR TWO"
LET C1 = .00125 * A + 3
LET D (14) = 191.8
LET E$ (I + 1) = "JOKER"
LET P (K, 3 * J + 1) = A * B (L − 2) ↑ I
```

Conventional Assignment Statement

The use of the word LET in the assignment statement is a notational convenience and is not required in most implementations of BASIC. The form of the conventional assignment statement is:

variable = expression

where "variable" and "expression" are the same as defined above. Examples of valid assignment statements are:

A = 10
B$ = "TEA FOR TWO"
P (K, 3 * J + 1) = A * B (L − 2) ↑ I

and so forth.

PROGRAM CONTROL

As was mentioned previously, statements in a program are executed
sequentially until a statement is executed that alters the sequential
flow of execution. Six statements are included in the BASIC language
to control the manner in which a program is executed: GOTO, IF,
END, STOP, FOR, and NEXT. The GOTO and IF statements are presented in this section and are used to alter the flow of program execution
on an unconditional and on a conditional basis, respectively. The END
and STOP statements are also covered briefly. The FOR and NEXT
statements are used for looping and are described in the next section.

GOTO Statement

The GOTO statement has the form:

```
GOTO statement-number
```

where "statement-number" must be the line number associated with
a statement in the program. If the statement number used as the operand
to the GOTO statement does not exist in the program, then the condition is recognized and continued execution of the program is not permitted. Several examples of the GOTO statement are given in previous
sections.

IF Statement

The IF statement allows program control to be altered on a conditional
basis, depending on the value of a "conditional" expression. The format
of the IF statement is:

```
IF comparison-expression THEN statement-number
```

If the "comparison-expression" has the value "true" (in other words,
the condition holds), then program control passes to the statement
whose statement number is specified. If the statement to which control
is branched is a nonexecutable statement (such as a DATA statement),
then program control is passed to the first executable statement follow-

ing the specified nonexecutable statement. If the "comparison-expression" is "not true" (in other words, the condition does not hold), then the execution of the program continues with the first executable statement that logically follows the IF statement.

The following example, which computes the average of a list of values, depicts the use of a simple IF statement, as well as an assignment statement, a GOTO statement, and a remark statement. The list is terminated when the value −999 is reached.

```
10  READ V
20  IF V = −999 THEN 70
30  REM S AND N ARE INITIALLY ZERO
40  S = S + V
50  N = N + 1
60  GOTO 10
70  PRINT "AVERAGE IS"; S/N
80  DATA 24, 42, 68, 50, −999
90  END
```

Output:

AVERAGE IS 46

Other examples of the IF statement are given in subsequent sections.

END and STOP Statements

Every program written in the BASIC language must end with the END statement, which has the following format:

The END statement serves two purposes:

1. It denotes the logical end of the program, such that statements with statement numbers greater than that of the END statement are ignored by the computer.
2. It causes execution of a program to be terminated when program control flows to it.
   The STOP statement, which takes the form:

```
STOP
```

causes execution of the program to be terminated. The STOP statement can be located anywhere in the program, making it unnecessary to branch to the END statement to terminate the execution of a program.

LOOPING

Many algorithms require that a sequence of steps be repeated. An algorithm of this type is usually programmed in one of two ways: (1) the program steps are duplicated the required number of times; and (2) the program is written so that the same program steps are executed iteratively. The second method is preferred in complex programs or when the necessary number of iterations is not known beforehand.

Introduction to Iterative Procedures

A series of statements to be executed repetitively is termed a *loop;* the statements that comprise the loop are termed the *body of the loop;* and one pass through the loop is termed an *iteration.* The number of iterations is governed by a *control variable* that usually operates as follows:

1. The control variable is set to an *initial value.*
2. The value of the control variable is compared with a limit value. If the limit value is exceeded, then the loop is not executed, and the first executable statement following the body of the loop is executed.
3. The body of the loop is executed.
4. The value of the control variable is incremented by a specified value—frequently referred to as an *increment* or a *step.* (The implication is that the program "steps" through the loop as the "control variable" assumes a set of values.)
5. The value of the control variable is compared with a limit value. If the limit value is exceeded, then the loop is terminated, and program execution continues with the first executable statement following the body of the loop. Otherwise, execution of the loop continues with step 3.

The following BASIC program depicts a simple loop:

```
10   REM SUM OF EVEN INTEGERS <=N
15   PRINT "ENTER N";
20   INPUT N
30   S=0
40   I=2
50   IF I>N THEN 90
60   S=S+I
70   I=I+2
80   IF I<=N THEN 60
90   PRINT "SUM="; S
```

```
100   PRINT
110   GOTO 15
120   END
RUN

ENTER N? 5
SUM = 6

ENTER N? 10
SUM = 30

ENTER N? 2
SUM = 2

ENTER N? 1
SUM = 0

ENTER N? STOP
PROGRAM HALTED
```

The program depicts each of the above steps. The statement numbered 40 initializes the control variable I (step 1). The statement numbered 50 tests the control variable I against the limit N (step 2). Statement number 60 is the body of the loop (step 3). Statement number 70 increments the control variable (step 4) with a "step value" of 2. Statement number 80 tests the control variable against the limit (step 5); if the value of the control variable is less than or equal to the limit value, then program control is returned to the statement numbered 60 to repeat the loop.

Looping is such a frequently used technique in computer programming that special statements are defined to control the manner in which loops are executed.

FOR and NEXT Statements

Two statements are included in BASIC to facilitate the preparation of program loops. The FOR statement is used to start a loop; it specifies the control variable, its initial value, its limit value, and the step. The NEXT statement is used to close a loop; it specifies the control variable that should be "stepped." The previous loop written with the use of FOR and NEXT statements is given as follows:

```
10   REM SUM OF EVEN NUMBERS < = N
20   PRINT "ENTER N";
30   INPUT N
40   S = 0
50   FOR I = 2 TO N STEP 2
60      S = S + I
```

```
 70   NEXT I
 80   PRINT "SUM = "; S
 90   PRINT
100   GOTO 20
110   END
 RUN

ENTER N? 5
SUM = 6

ENTER N? 10
SUM = 30

ENTER N? STOP
PROGRAM HALTED
```

The statements between the FOR and the NEXT statements comprise the body of the loop.

The format of the FOR statement is given as:

```
FOR arithmetic-variable = arithmetic-expression
   TO arithmetic-expression [STEP arithmetic-expression]
```

where "arithmetic-variable" must be a scalar variable and "arithmetic-expression" must be a scalar expression. If the STEP clause is omitted, it is assumed to be +1. The format of the NEXT statement is:

```
NEXT arithmetic-variable
```

where "arithmetic-variable" is the same scalar variable that is used in the corresponding FOR statement.

The FOR and NEXT statements are used in pairs to delineate a FOR loop. The FOR statement establishes the control variable and specifies the initial value, limit value, and step value. (The three values are referred to as *control parameters.*) The NEXT statement tells the computer to perform the next iteration. The control parameters are evaluated when the FOR statement is executed and cannot be changed in the body of the loop. *However, the value of the control variable can be modified from within the body of the loop.* FOR loops can be nested—that is, there can be more than one loop—but they must not overlap each other.

Effective Use of FOR and NEXT Statements

It is important to recognize that the use of a FOR/NEXT loop is a means of achieving control in a computer program. It can be used in some cases to eliminate the need for the GOTO statement, as shown in the following program that computes *n* factorial:

```
 10   FOR I = 1 TO 2 STEP 0
 20     PRINT "ENTER N";
 30     INPUT N
 40     F = 1
 50     FOR J = 2 TO N
 60       F = F * J
 70     NEXT J
 80     PRINT N; "FACTORIAL IS"; F
 90     PRINT
100   NEXT I
110   END
RUN

ENTER N? 5
5 FACTORIAL IS 120

ENTER N? 7
7 FACTORIAL IS 5040

ENTER N? 1
1 FACTORIAL IS 1

ENTER N? STOP
PROGRAM HALTED
```

The above program depicts a nested loop (that is, a *double loop*, as it is frequently called). The outer loop is executed until a "STOP" is entered in response to the INPUT statement. The same effect could have been achieved with a FOR statement, such as:

FOR I = 1 TO 10000

where the loop is not expected to execute for the full 10,000 iterations but will be terminated by a special condition, as shown. In a similar fashion a FOR loop can be used to count the number of times a series of statements is executed; for example:

```
10   DATA 8, 10, 7, 20, 15, 0
20   REM COMPUTE AVERAGE AND NUMBER OF VALUES
30   FOR N = 1 TO 100
40     READ V
50     IF V = 0 THEN 80
60     S = S + V
70   NEXT N
80   PRINT "AVERAGE = "; S/(N − 1); "NUMBER OF VALUES = "; N − 1
90   END
RUN

AVERAGE = 12   NUMBER OF VALUES = 5
```

In addition, the FOR statement, as defined above, allows several useful options, three of which are:

1. There can be a nonintegral STEP.
2. There can be a negative STEP.
3. The value of the control variable can be changed in the FOR loop.

All three cases are shown in the following example:

```
10   FOR D = 2 TO −2 STEP −.5
20     IF D <> 0 THEN 40
30        D = −1
40        PRINT 1/D
50   NEXT D
60   END
RUN

0.5
0.666667
1
2
0
−2
−1
−0.6666667
−0.5
```

Other examples of the FOR loop are included in the next section on arrays.

ARRAYS

Arrays are an important feature of most programming languages since a great many computer applications utilize the concept of a family of related data, referred to by a single name—the *array variable*. The subject of arrays is briefly considered in Chapter 9; this section goes into more detail on how arrays are defined and used. First, a very brief review. An *arithmetic array* can have either one or two dimensions; an arithmetic variable name must consist of a single letter. A *character array* must have one dimension only; its variable name must consist of a single letter followed by a dollar sign ($).

Implicitly Defined Arrays

An implicitly defined array is one that is used without being declared. A one-dimensional implicitly defined array has an extent of 10 with lower and upper subscript bounds of 1 and 10, respectively. A two-dimensional implicitly defined array has both row and column extents of 10; lower and upper subscript bounds for each dimension are also 1 and 10, respectively.

Implicitly defined arrays are allowed in BASIC for practical reasons:

1. "Small" arrays are frequently used, especially in an academic environment, and it is a convenience to be able to use an array of this type without having to define it. Also, by not having to specify the size of a "small" array, fewer characters have to be entered into the computer, and the chances of making a simple mistake are lessened.
2. Computer storage is sufficiently large to easily handle the storage requirements of implicitly defined arrays.
3. For large arrays, which *do* have to be declared, storage must be managed judiciously.

As an example of a case where the use of an implicitly defined array could be useful, consider the storage and retrieval of a parts list that takes the following form:

Part Index	Part Name	Quantity	Unit Price
1	Place ZR41T	10	.49
2	Hinge J33	5	1.26
3	.5 × 3 Bolt	103	.12
4	Washer .5 Alum	97	.01
5	Nut .5 Hex	103	.03
6	PT 4001 T	21	.25

The program, which follows, first stores the "part name" as a string array and the "quantity" and "unit price" as a two-dimensional array. Then the user is allowed to input a part index, and the computer prints out the name, quantity, and the value of the inventory.

```
 10   REM ENTER INVENTORY DATA
 20   READ N
 30   FOR J = 1 TO N
 40      READ P$(J),D(J,1),D(J,2)
 50   NEXT J
 60   REM RETRIEVE DATA
 70   PRINT "ENTER PART INDEX";
 80   INPUT I
 85   IF I > N THEN 150
 90   PRINTS P$(I), "QUANTITY = "; C(I,1); "UNIT PRICE = "; D(J,2);
         "TOTAL VALUE = "; D(I,1) * D(I,2)
 95   PRINT
100   GOTO 70
```

```
150   PRINT "INDEX ERROR"
151   GOTO 70
200   DATA 6
201   DATA PLACE ZR41T", 10,.49
202   DATA "HINGE J33",5,1.26
203   DATA ".5 × 3 BOLT",103,.12
204   DATA "WASHER .5 ALUM",97,.01
205   DATA "NUT .5 HEX",103,.03
206   DATA "PT 4001 T",21,.25
999   END
RUN

ENTER PART INDEX? 4
WASHER .5 ALUM QUANTITY = 97   UNIT PRICED = 0.01
        TOTAL VALUE = 0.97

ENTER PART INDEX? 7
INDEX ERROR
ENTER PART INDEX? 3
.5 × 3 BOLT   QUANTITY = 103   UNIT PRICE = 0.12
        TOTAL VALUE = 15.36

ENTER PART INDEX? STOP
PROGRAM HALTED
```

The value of the elements of an implicitly defined arithmetic array are set initially to zero, and the value of the elements of an implicitly defined character-string array are set initially to 18 blanks.

Explicitly Defined Arrays

An array is explicitly dimensioned with the DIM statement that has the following form:

```
DIM array-specification [,array-specification] . . .
```

where "array-specification" is defined as:

  arithmetic-variable (integer-constant [,integer-constant])

or

  character-variable (integer-constant)

where "integer-constant" must not be zero. The following example depicts valid array specifications:

  DIM A(17), B$(54), C(15,25), D(3,20), E(1000)

A one-dimensional array is specified as:

DIMa(n)

or

DIM a\$(n)

and has an extent of n with lower and upper subscript bounds of 1 and n, respectively. An element of a (or a\$) is selected by an array reference of the form $a(e)$ (or $a\$(E)$), where e is an arithmetic expression that is evaluated at the point of reference and truncated to an integer. Similarly, a two-dimensional array is specified as

DIM $a(m,n)$

and has row and column extents of m and n, respectively. The lower and upper subscript bounds for the row extent are 1 and m, respectively, and the lower and upper subscript bounds for the column extent are 1 and n, respectively. An element of a is selected by an array reference of the form $a(e_1,e_2)$, where e_1 and e_2 are arithmetic expressions evaluated at the point of reference and truncated to integers.

The following example computes prime numbers using the Sieve of Eratosthenes (which is a means for finding prime numbers by writing down odd numbers from 3 up and by erasing the third number after 3, the fifth number after 5, the seventh number after 7, and so forth). The program requests a number N and then computes and prints the prime numbers less than or equal to N.

```
10   DIM P (1000)
20   PRINT "ENTER N";
30   INPUT N
40   IF N > 1000 THEN 990
50   FOR I = 2 TO N
60      P(I) = I
70   NEXT I
80   L = SQR (N)
90   FOR I = 2 TO L
100     IF P (I) = 0 THEN 140
110     FOR J = I + I TO N STEP I
120        P(J) = 0
130     NEXT J
140   NEXT I
150   PRINT
160   PRINT "PRIMES LESS THAN";N
170   FOR I = 2 TO N
180     IF P (I) = 0 THEN 200 ·
190     PRINT P (I);
200   NEXT I
```

```
210   PRINT
220   GOTO 20
990   PRINT "TOO LARGE"
991   GOTO 20
999   END
RUN

ENTER N? 100

PRIMES LESS THAN 100
2 3 5 7 11 13 17 19 23 31 37 41 43 47 53 59 61
67 71 73 79 83 89 97

ENTER N? 2000
TOO LARGE
ENTER N? 15


2 3 5 7 11 13

ENTER N? STOP
PROGRAM HALTED
```

The program also depicts nested FOR loops and the variable control parameters that were mentioned in the preceding section.

As a final example of the use of one-dimensional arrays, the following program reads a list of numbers and sorts them in ascending order. The program utilizes an exchange technique, depicted as follows:

The program initially sets a flag (F) to zero. When an exchange is made, F is set to 1. If both passes are made through the data without making an exchange, then the values are sorted and the program terminates. Otherwise, the process is repeated. The advantage of the exchange technique is that the process is efficient if the data is sorted or partially sorted beforehand.

```
10   DIM W(100)
20   READ N
```

```
 30   IF N > 100 THEN 990
 40   FOR I = 1 TO N
 50      READ W(I)
 60   NEXT I
 70   F = 0
 80   FOR I = 1 TO N − 1 STEP 2
 90      IF W(I) < = W (I + 1) THEN  140
100         T = W(I)
110         W (I) = W (I + 1)
120         W (I + 1) = T
130      F = 1
140   NEXT I
150   FOR I = 2 TO N − 1 STEP 2
160      IF W (I) < = W (I + 1) THEN 210
170      T = W (I)
180      W (I) = W (I + 1)
190      W (I + 1) = T
200      F = 1
210   NEXT I
220   IF F < > 0 THEN 70
230   PRINT "SORTED VALUES"
240   FOR I = 1 TO N
250      PRINT W (I);
260   NEXT I
270   STOP
500   DATA 12
501   DATA-7,3,9,6,5,1,4,3,8,0,2,7
990   PRINT "TOO MANY VALUES"
999   END
RUN
```

```
SORTED VALUES
-7 0 1 2 3 3 4 5 6 7 8 9
```

Two dimensional arrays are defined and used in a similar manner, and the student is directed to the readings for more information on this subject. One of the features in the full BASIC language is a set of matrix input/output statements that permit a complete array to be read or printed with one BASIC statement.

FUNCTIONS*

The computer is frequently used in applications that require the use of a mathematical function, such as the sine, cosine, or square root. In the computer, functions such as these are usually approximated to a given degree of accuracy with an algorithm such as the following series expansion for the trigonometric sine:

* This section can be omitted without a loss of continuity.

$$\sin x = x - \frac{x^3}{3!} + \frac{x^5}{5!} - \frac{x^7}{7!} + \ldots$$

Two options exist:

1. Users can program their own mathematical functions.
2. A set of frequently used functions can be provided as part of the programming language.

Usually, the second option is selected since not all users are versed in computer approximations, and it is convenient not to have to bother with them. Moreover, approximations can be coded efficiently in assembler language and placed in a program library to be shared by all users.

Built-in Functions

Functions that are supplied as part of the programming languages are referred to as *built-in functions.* The form of a function reference is the function name followed by an arithmetic expression in parentheses. The expression is evaluated at the point of reference, and the specified function is applied to the value of the expression. The function returns a value that can be used as an operand in the expression. Thus, the expression 2 + SQR (25) has the value 7, where SQR is the square root function.

Function name for a built-in function is comprised of three letters that have mnemonic relationship to the function they name. The form of a function reference is:

```
function-name (arithmetic-expression)
```

where "function-name" is one of the mathematical functions defined in the implementation of the language. Table 10.3 lists the built-in functions included in the original Dartmouth version of BASIC. All of the functions listed in Table 10.3 operate on a single value.

The following list gives some mathematical expressions that include functions and their equivalent representation in BASIC:

Mathematical Expression	*BASIC Expression*
$\sqrt{1 - \sin^2 x}$	SQR(1 − SIN(X) ↑ 2)
$\dfrac{\cos 30°}{\sqrt{a^2 + b^2 - 2ab \cos c_1}}$	COS(30*(3.14159/180)) or COS(3.14159/6)
	SQR(A ↑ 2 + B ↑ 2 − 2*A*B*COS(C1))
$\tan^{-1}(x/y)$	ATN(X/Y)
$\dfrac{e^x - e^{-x}}{2}$	(EXP(X) − EXP (−X))/2
$(\lvert x \rvert)^2 \uparrow 3$	ABS(X) ↑ 3

TABLE 10.3   Built-in functions

Function Reference	Definition
SIN (x)	Computes the sine of x radians.
COS (x)	Computes the cosine of x radians.
TAN (x)	Computes the tangent of x radians.
ATN (x)	Computes the arctangent in radians of the argument x; the result is in the range $-90°$ to $+90°$.
EXP (x)	Computes the value of e raised to the x power; that is e^x.
LOG (x)	Computes the natural logarithm (that is, $1n\,|x|$) of the absolute value of x.
ABS (x)	Computes the absolute value of x (that is, $|x|$).
SQR (x)	Computes the square root of x, where $x \geqslant 0$.
INT (x)	Computes the largest integer $\leqslant x$.
SGN (x)	Returns the sign of x; if $x < 0$, then $SGN(x) = -1$; if $x = 0$, then SGN (x) $= 0$; and if $x > 0$, then SGN (x) $= +1$.

When a function reference is used as an operand, as in SIN(X) ↑ 2 or ABS(X) ↑ 3, the function is applied first, and the result of the function is used in the arithmetic operation. In other words, a function reference has a higher priority than any of the arithmetic operators.

ınternal Constants

An *internal constant* is a frequently used arithmetic value that is defined in the BASIC language. Three internal constants that are often used are pi, *e,* and the square root of 2, listed as follows:

Identifier	Approximate Value (short form)
&PI	3.14159
&E	2.71828
&SQR2	1.41421

Internal constants eliminate the need to remember and enter frequently used arithmetic values. An internal constant is treated as an ordinary operand.

The use of functions and internal constants is demonstrated in the next section.

APPLICATIONS

This section further demonstrates how the BASIC language is used by giving some routine applications.

Roots of an Equation

The roots of a quadratic equation of the form:

$$ax^2 + bx + c = 0$$

are given by the quadratic formula:

$$\text{root} = \frac{-b \pm \sqrt{b^2 - 4ac}}{2a}$$

For example, the equation $x^2 + 5x + 6 = 0$ can be factored as $(x + 2)$ $(x + 3) = 0$, and the roots are known as $x = -2$ and $x = -3$. The BASIC program given in Figure 10.1 uses the quadratic formula to solve a quadratic equation.

Mean and Standard Deviation

The arithmetic mean and standard deviations of a set of numbers are computed, respectively, by the formulas:

$$\bar{x} = \left(\sum_{i=1}^{n} A_i \right) \Big/ n$$

```
LIST

100 READ A,B,C
200 IF A = 0 THEN 990
300 LET R1 = (−B + SQR(B ↑ 2 − 4*A*C))/(2*A)
400 LET R2 = (−B − SQR(B ↑ 2 − 4*A*C))/(2*A)
500 PRINT "A="; A;" B="; B;" C="; C;" ROOT1="; R1;" ROOT2="; R2
600 GOTO 100
700 DATA 1,5,6
800 DATA 1,3,−40
900 DATA 0,0,0
990 END
READY

RUN
A = 1 B = 5  C = 6      ROOT1 = − 2 ROOT2 = − 3
A = 1 B = 3  C = − 40 ROOT1 = 5    ROOT2 = − 8


STOP AT LINE 990
READY
```

FIGURE 10.1   **A BASIC program demonstrating the use of the quadratic formula to solve a quadratic equation.**

and

$$\sigma = \sqrt{\frac{\sum_{i=1}^{n} A_i^2}{n} - (\bar{x})^2}$$

LIST

```
10 DIM A(100)
20 READ N
25 IF N = 0 THEN 260
30 LET S1 = 0
40 LET S2 = 0
50 FOR I = 1 TO N
60    READ A(I)
70    LET S1 = S1 + A(I)
80    LET S2 = S2 + A(I)*A(I)
90 NEXT I
100 REM COMPUTE ARITHMETIC MEAN
110 LET X = S1/N
120 REM COMPUTE STANDARD DEVIATION
130 LET Y = SQR(S2/N − X*X)
140 REM OUTPUT FOLLOWS
150 PRINT "DATA"
160 FOR I = 1 TO N
170    PRINT A(I);
180 NEXT I
190 PRINT
200 PRINT "MEAN="; X: "STANDARD DEVIATION="; Y
205 GOTO 20
210 DATA 5
220 DATA 6,7,10,20,2
230 DATA 10
240 DATA 34,56.1,8,123,7,19.453,7.985,5,23,70.001
250 DATA 0
260 END
READY

RUN
DATA
 6 7 10 20 2
MEAN = 9 STANDARD DEVIATION = 6.0663
DATA
 34 56.1 8 123 7 19.453 7.985 5 23 70.001
MEAN = 35.3539 STANDARD DEVIATION = 35.97575

STOP AT LINE 260
READY
```

FIGURE 10.2   **A BASIC program that computes the mean and standard deviation of a set of numbers.**

```
10   PRINT "ENTER WAGES"
20   INPUT W
30   IF W > 108 THEN 60
40   T = 0
50   GOTO 250
60   IF W > 292 THEN 90
70   T = .16*(W − 108)
80   GOTO 250
90   IF W > 500 THEN 120
100   T = 29.44 + .20 (W − 292)
110   GOTO 250
120   IF W > 792 THEN 150
130   T = 71.04 + .23 (W − 500)
140   GOTO 250
150   IF W > 1042 THEN 180
160   T = 138.20 + .21 (W − 792)
170   GOTO 250
180   IF W > 1208 THEN 210
190   T = 190.70 + .26 (W − 1042)
200   GOTO 250
210   IF W > 1500 THEN 240
220   T = 233.86 + .30* (W − 1208)
230   GOTO 250
240   T = 321.46 + .36 (W − 1500)
250   PRINT "WITHHOLDING IS"; T
260   PRINT
270   PRINT "MORE? 1-Yes, 0-No"
280   INPUT A
290   IF A = 1 THEN 10
300   END
```

FIGURE 10.3   A BASIC Program to compute withholding for a single person.

The BASIC program given in Figure 10.2 computes $\bar{x}$ and σ by accumulating the sum and sum of squares of the values A_i as they are read in from an internal data list created by DATA statements.

Payroll Calculations

Table 8.1 gives representative percentages for income tax withholding for a payroll application. Figure 10.3 gives a BASIC program that computes the withholding for single persons. (This program serves only as an example since it can be programmed more efficiently through the use of arrays.)

Vocabulary   The reader should be familiar with the following terms in the context in which they are used in the chapter.

arithmetic data item	increment
arithmetic expression	initial value
array	INPUT
binary operator	internal constant
body of the loop	iteration
built-in function	LET
character	limit value
character expression	loop
character-string data item	name
comparison expression	NEXT
composite symbol	PRINT
control variable	quotation marks
DATA	READ
DIM	scalar
END	statement
explicit array declaration	statement number
FOR	step
GOTO	STOP
IF	symbol
implicit array declaration	unary operator

Questions

1. Study the program to determine the present value of Manhattan given in the chapter. Why is it necessary to include the following program loop?

```
FOR Y = 1627 TO 1973
   LET P = P + P *R
NEXT Y
```

2. Distinguish between a "character" and a "symbol."

3. Can you think of any advantage that the use of the up arrow (↑) has for representing exponentiation over the use of the double asterisk (**)?

4. With regard to the use of exponential notation for writing constants, the following statement can be made: "In an arithmetic constant, the E (if used) must be preceded by at least one digit." Why?

5. What function does the dollar sign ($) serve for naming character-string data items?

6. What is the only statement that must be present in a BASIC program?

7. How do you delete a statement in a BASIC program?

8. How do you replace a statement in a BASIC program?

9. In what order are the statements that comprise a BASIC program executed?

10. Which of the following expressions are invalid?

```
A+ −B      ((( 34 )))   0$+1
+/A        A$ < 63      T$(3)
A(B(2))    −E + F       X(−4)
D(E + 1)   W(−1)        X+Y−1>13.4
```

11. What is an "implicit array declaration"?

Exercises
1. Give an example of a character constant.
2. Give errors (if any) in the following BASIC statements:

```
LET AB = 16
LET A3 = K + 10,000
LET F$ = 'DON'T"
REED A, B, C
DATA 4E − 3
LET A = W + 3.12.3
LET K13 = − 3E − 1
```

3. Discuss the execution of the following program segment using the material given in the chapter:

```
LET A = 3
LET B = 6
LET C = B/A + C
PRINT D
```

4. Write a BASIC program to compute the product of the numbers 2E3, 173.89, −14.839, 63.1, and .123E−1 and to print the result.

5. A depositor puts $10 per month in the bank. Interest is 6% per year compounded monthly. Write a BASIC program to compute the amount the depositor has in the account after 20 years.

6. Write a BASIC program that computes N! (that is, N factorial) and operates as follows: The computer requests that the user enter a number (N). After verifying that the number is a positive integer, the computer computes N!, prints it, and then requests another number. Error diagnostics should be printed if the number is not a positive integer.

7. Write a BASIC program to compute the sum of the numbers less than 100 that are divisible by 7.

8. Given a set of numbers of the form:

$$\text{DATA } n, x_1, x_2, \ldots x_n$$

(allow for at least 100 values) write a BASIC program that computes and prints the following:

(a) Sum of numbers in the list
(b) Largest number
(c) Smallest number
(d) Number of numbers equal to 20
(e) Number of numbers greater than 50 and less than 75

9. Given a set of pay records of the form:

DATA employee-number,name,hours,hourly-rate,tax-rate

such as:

DATA 4439, "JOHN JONES",45,2,10,0.18

Write a BASIC program that computes the following values for each employee:
(a) Gross salary
(b) Tax
(c) Take-home pay
Produce the results as a payroll listing that gives for each employee (that is, each line of the listing): employee number, name, hours, gross salary, tax, and take-home pay. Label the columns. Pay time and one-half for hours over 40. Have the program terminate when a zero employee number is read.

10. Write a BASIC program to read in the following table and sort the entries by key:

Key	Value
10	−13.43
7	81.914
16	−50.1
2	13964.2
9	63.173
24	−.4E−2
11	0
6	2

Related Reading

Gateley, W. Y., and Bitter, G. G. *BASIC for Beginners.* New York: McGraw-Hill, 1970.

Katzan, H. *The IBM 5100 Portable Computer: A Comprehensive Guide for Users and Programmers.* New York: Van Nostrand Reinhold, 1977.

Nolan, R. L. *Introduction to Computing through the BASIC Language.* New York: Holt, Rinehart, and Winston, 1974.

Sass, C. J. *BASIC Programming and Applications.* Boston: Allyn and Bacon, 1976.

Walker, T. M. *Fundamentals of BASIC Programming.* Boston: Allyn and Bacon, 1975.

11

COBOL

INTRODUCTION

COBOL and Data Processing
Execution

OVERVIEW OF THE COBOL LANGUAGE

COBOL Reference Format

SAMPLE COBOL PROGRAM

Identification Division
Environment Division
Data Division
Procedure Division

LANGUAGE FUNDAMENTALS

Character Set
Words
Names
Nouns
Constants
Special Registers
Punctuation
Data Reference
Comment Lines

This chapter gives an overview of COBOL to familiarize the student with the concepts, but not necessarily the details, of the language. COBOL is a more extensive language than BASIC, and a detailed treatment of it, comparable to Chapter 10, would be inappropriate in a book not devoted exclusively to the subject. The student who is interested in additional information on the COBOL language is directed to the readings at the end of the chapter. This chapter also includes a brief discussion of optional COBOL language fundamentals for readers who wish to pursue the subject individually.

INTRODUCTION

As a programming language, COBOL is relatively easy to learn and use and readable in the sense that a reasonably good understanding of a COBOL program can be obtained by reading a listing of that program. COBOL is an extensive language designed for data processing with special features for sorting, writing reports, handling tables, segmenting programs, and managing libraries—in addition to a full complement of descriptive, computational, and input/output facilities.

COBOL and Data Processing

COBOL is a language used for data processing, whereas BASIC is used generally for numeric computation. One of the characteristics of data processing is that most applications are file oriented in the sense that a program operates on one or more files and either modifies them or produces new ones. Files are composed of records, and in data processing records usually adhere to a well-defined format. For example, a payroll program that produces paychecks requires a carefully designed format so that characters are placed in appropriate places on a previously specified form. Thus, data description is of prime importance in COBOL. Actual computation also differs from that performed with the BASIC language. In data processing, numeric computation performs a minor role, and input/output, data movement, editing, and conversion play a major role. Looping is also different in data processing. In numeric computations, a program frequently iterates until a solution is obtained. In data processing, a set of computations is usually developed for each record in a file, and the program loops back to read the next record and perform the required computations.

Execution

The average data processing program tends to run longer on the computer than the average scientific program—although there are notable exceptions—and relatively more data processing programs are used on a long-term basis than in scientific computing. As a result, almost all COBOL programs are compiled into machine code before execution.

OVERVIEW OF THE COBOL LANGUAGE

This section gives an overview of the COBOL language by presenting a relatively straightforward COBOL program and then discussing it. COBOL language elements are presented in subsequent sections.

Cobol Reference Format

A program in the COBOL language is prepared as 80-character data records and punched on cards, placed on magnetic tape, and so on. A program is a set of consecutive data records—like, for example, a deck of cards. COBOL statements are prepared using a *reference format*, for convenience and standardization:

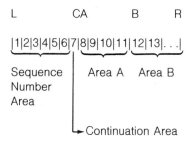

where:

> L denotes the leftmost character position of a line.
> C denotes the seventh character position relative to L.
> A denotes the eighth character position relative to L.
> B denotes the twelfth character position relative to L.
> R denotes the rightmost character position in a line.

Four areas are defined: the sequence number area, continuation area, area A, and area B. The areas are used as follows:

1. A six-digit sequence number occupies the sequence number area. The manner in which the sequence number is used is implementation-dependent.
2. Division, section, and paragraph names begin in area A.
3. COBOL sentences—that is, a set of COBOL statements—are written in area B.

4. Any statement that requires more than one line is continued by starting subsequent lines in area B. In this case, the rightmost character of the preceding line is interpreted as though it were followed by a space. A line is usually "broken" between words or literals. In this case, nothing special need be done. However, a word or literal may be continued on another line by placing a hyphen in the continuation area (column 7); in this case, the first nonblank character in area B of the current line is the successor of the last nonblank character of the preceding line without any intervening space. A nonnumeric literal is continued by making the first nonblank character of area B of the continuation line a quotation mark; the nonnumeric literal is continued with the first character after that quotation mark.

The following examples demonstrate these concepts:

```
L    CA    B

001050  ENVIRONMENT DIVISION.
    .
    .
    .
001100  FILE-CONTROL.
001110      SELECT IN-FILE ASSIGN TO READER.
001120      SELECT OUT-FILE ASSIGN TO PRINTER.
    .
    .
    .
001500  PROCEDURE DIVISION.
    .
    .
    .
001640  GET-DATA-PAR.
001650      READ IN-FILE AT END GO TO CLOSE-UP.
    .
    .
    .
001870      IF MALE ADD A TO B, MOVE GOOD TO BAD, . . . ,
001880      ADD TOP TO BOTTOM.
    .
    .
    .
003410  CLOSE-UP.
003420      CLOSE IN-FILE, . . . . . . DISPLAY 'END 0
003430-      'F Job' UPON KEY BOARD.
```

The following notes further explain the use of the COBOL reference format:

1. Line 001050 demonstrates a division name that must start in area A.

2. Line 001100 is a paragraph name that also must start in area A.

3. Lines 001110 and 001120 are COBOL statements that must be written in area B.

4. Line 001500 is another division name.

5. Line 001640 is a paragraph name. It must start in area A and can extend into area B, as required.

6. Line 001650 is a COBOL statement; it is *not* continued. (In fact, it is a sentence because it ends with a period.)

7. Line 001870 is a COBOL sentence; the last statement of this line is continued as line 001880. The continuation line begins in area B and *the hyphen in the C area is not used* because the statement is broken between words.

8. Line 003410 is another paragraph name; it is referred to in line 001650.

9. Line 003420 contains the beginning of a COBOL sentence, composed of COBOL statements. It is continued in line 003430 and a hyphen is used in the continuation area of the continuation line (that is, column 7) because the statement is broken in a nonnumeric literal. (Note that line 003430 begins with a quotation mark, which is required when a nonnumeric literal is continued.)

The COBOL examples that follow depict only the A and B areas; however, in actual practice, the programmer is usually required to use sequence numbers.

SAMPLE COBOL PROGRAM

Figure 11.1 gives the flow diagram of a sample payroll program. The program is designed to process payroll information on a weekly basis and produces a listing that contains the following information for each input "pay card": social security number, payroll code (that is, either weekly or hourly), name, and total pay. The listing also contains a title and column headings.

Input to the program is a "pay card" that contains the following information in the specified columns:

col. 1–9: Social security number (9 columns)
col. 15–44: Employee's name (30 columns)
col. 47: Payroll code (1 column: W denotes weekly, H denotes hourly)
col. 50–55: Payrate (6 columns: if weekly, this field contains weekly salary; if hourly, this field contains hourly rate)
col. 58–61: Hours worked (4 columns)

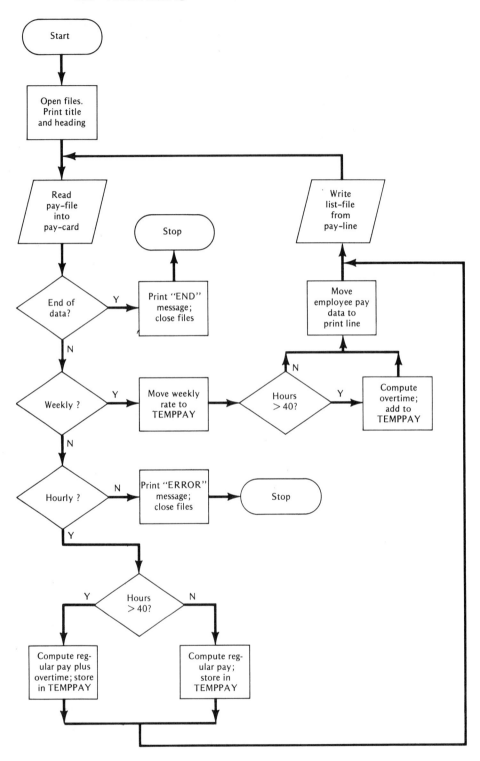

FIGURE 11.1   Flow diagram of sample payroll program.

The program operates as follows:

1. Employees who are paid weekly receive their weekly salary regardless of hours worked. However, if hours worked exceed 40, then the employee receives an overtime premium computed as follows:

$$(\text{hours} - 40) \times \left(\frac{\text{weekly salary}}{40}\right) \times 1.5$$

2. If employees are paid hourly, then their pay is computed as: hours times rate plus time and one-half for hours over 40.

A COBOL program to compute a pay listing, as outlined, is given in Figure 11.2. The complete program is composed of four divisions: identification, environment, data, and procedure. The blank line between the divisions is included for readability and is not required. Blank lines are ignored by the computer. The divisions must be presented to the COBOL compiler in the given order. Each division is discussed in the following paragraphs.

Identification Division

The purpose of the identification division is to identify the source program and the outputs of the compilation process. The only required lines in this division are the division header and the program identification, which assigns a name to the program. The identification division for the payroll program (Figure 11.2) is repeated as follows:

```
IDENTIFICATION DIVISION.
PROGRAM-ID. PAYROLL.
AUTHOR. J. ANALYST.
INSTALLATION. ABC CORP.
REMARKS. INTRODUCTORY COBOL EXAMPLE.
```

The *program name* line is written:

PROGRAM-ID. *program name.*

where "program name" is a user-defined COBOL name. The rules for forming a "name" are covered later.

The identification division is computer independent and causes no computer instructions to be generated. The user may use this division to include in the program listing the date the program was written,

```
IDENTIFICATION DIVISION.
PROGRAM-ID. PAYROLL.
AUTHOR. J.ANALYST.
INSTALLATION. ABC CORP.
REMARKS. INTRODUCTORY COBOL EXAMPLE.

ENVIRONMENT DIVISION.
CONFIGURATION SECTION.
SOURCE-COMPUTER. ABC-123.
OBJECT-COMPUTER. ABC-123.
INPUT-OUTPUT SECTION.
FILE-CONTROL.
        SELECT PAY-FILE ASSIGN TO CARD-READER.
        SELECT LIST-FILE ASSIGN TO LINE-PRINTER.

DATA DIVISION.
FILE SECTION.
FD    PAY-FILE
        LABEL RECORDS ARE OMITTED
        DATA RECORD IS PAY-CARD.
01    PAY-CARD.
        02  S-S-NO    PICTURE 9(9).
        02  FILLER    PICTURE X(5).
        02  NAME      PICTURE X(30).
        02  FILLER    PICTURE X(2).
        02  PAY-CODE PICTURE A(1).
            88 WEEKLY VALUE IS "W".
            88 HOURLY VALUE IS "H".
        02  FILLER  PICTURE X(2).
        02  RATE    PICTURE 9999V99.
        02  FILLER  PICTURE X(2).
        02  HOURS PICTURE 999V9.
        02  FILLER  PICTURE X(19).
FD    LIST-FILE
        LABEL RECORDS ARE OMITTED
        DATA RECORD IS PAY-LINE.
01    PAY-LINE.
        02  FILLER      PICTURE X(6).
        02  SOCSECNO PICTURE 9(9).
        02  FILLER      PICTURE X(6).
        02  PAY-CODE   PICTURE A(1).
        02  FILLER      PICTURE X(6).
        02  EMPL-NAME PICTURE X(30).
        02  FILLER      PICTURE X(2).
        02  TOTALPAY    PICTURE $$,$$$.99.
        02  FILLER      PICTURE X(63).
WORKING-STORAGE SECTION.
77    TEMPPAY PICTURE 9999V99.
01    TITLE.
```

FIGURE 11.2   Sample COBOL program.

```
        02   FILLER PICTURE X(30) VALUE IS SPACES.
        02   FILLER PICTURE X(15)
             VALUE IS "PAYCHECK REPORT".
        02   FILLER PICTURE X(87) VALUE IS SPACES.
   01   HEADING.
        02   FILLER PICTURE X(5) VALUE IS SPACES.
        02   FILLER PICTURE X(11)
             VALUE IS "S.S. NUMBER".
        02   FILLER PICTURE X(2) VALUE IS SPACES.
        02   FILLER PICTURE X(8)
             VALUE IS "PAY CODE".
        02   FILLER PICTURE X(10) VALUE IS SPACES.
        02   FILLER PICTURE X(4) VALUE IS "NAME".
        02   FILLER PICTURE X(20) VALUE IS SPACES.
        02   FILLER PICTURE X(9)
             VALUE IS "GROSS PAY".
        02   FILLER PICTURE X(63) VALUE IS SPACES.
   01   ERR-MESS.
        02   FILLER PICTURE X(5) VALUE IS SPACES.
        02   FILLER PICTURE X(5) VALUE IS "*****".
        02   FILLER PICTURE X(32)
             VALUE IS "DATA ERROR—CHECK AND RERUN JOB".
        02   FILLER PICTURE X(5) VALUE IS "*****".
        02   FILLER PICTURE X(85) VALUE IS SPACES.
   01   END-MESS.
        02   FILLER PICTURE X(30) VALUE IS SPACES.
        02   FILLER PICTURE X(18)
             VALUE IS "END OF PAY LISTING".
        02   FILLER PICTURE X(74) VALUE IS SPACES.
PROCEDURE DIVISION.
INITIALIZE.
        OPEN INPUT PAY-FILE.
        OPEN OUTPUT LIST-FILE.
PRINT-TITLE-AND-HEADING.
        WRITE PAY-LINE FROM TITLE
          AFTER ADVANCING 0 LINES.
        WRITE PAY-LINE FROM HEADING
          AFTER ADVANCING 2 LINES.
        MOVE SPACES TO PAY-LINE.
        WRITE PAY-LINE.
READ-PAY.
        READ PAY-FILE AT END GO TO END-OF-JOB.
        IF WEEKLY GO TO COMPUTE-WEEKLY-PAY.
        IF HOURLY GO TO COMPUTE-HOURLY-PAY.
        WRITE PAY-LINE FROM ERR-MESS.
          AFTER ADVANCING 2 LINES.
        CLOSE PAY-FILE, LIST-FILE.
        STOP RUN.
COMPUTE-WEEKLY-PAY.
```

FIGURE 11.2   *(Continued)*

```
            MOVE RATE TO TEMPPAY.
            IF HOURS GREATER THAN 40.0
                COMPUTE TEMPPAY = TEMPPAY + (RATE / 40) *
                (HOURS - 40) * 1.5.
            GO TO PRINT-PAY.
      COMPUTE-HOURLY-PAY.
                IF HOURS GREATER THAN 40.0
                    COMPUTE TEMPPAY = RATE * 40 +
                    (HOURS - 40) * RATE * 1.5
                    ELSE COMPUTE TEMPPAY = RATE * HOURS.
      PRINT-PAY.
            MOVE SPACES TO PAY-LINE.
            MOVE S-S-NO TO SOCSECNO.
            MOVE PAY-CODE IN PAY-CARD TO PAY-CODE IN
                PAY-LINE.
            MOVE NAME TO EMPL-NAME.
            MOVE TEMPPAY TO TOTALPAY.
            WRITE PAY-LINE. GO TO READ-PAY.
      END-OF-JOB.
            WRITE PAY-LINE FROM END-MESS AFTER ADVANCING
                2 LINES.
            CLOSE PAY-FILE, LIST-FILE.
            STOP RUN.
```

FIGURE 11.2   *(Concluded)*

programmer name, compilation date, installation, and any other information that is desired.

Environment Division

The environment division is the part of a source program that specifies the equipment being used. It includes information necessary for the computer to run the program. This division allows memory size, input/output units, hardware switches, and so forth to be specified. User names may be assigned to particular hardware units and to data files on specific input/output devices. The environment division tends to be machine or operating system dependent and is usually modified when a COBOL program is converted to run on another computer system.

The environment division for the payroll program is given as follows:

```
ENVIRONMENT DIVISION.
CONFIGURATION SECTION.
SOURCE-COMPUTER. ABC-123.
OBJECT-COMPUTER. ABC-123.
INPUT-OUTPUT SECTION.
      SELECT PAY-FILE ASSIGN TO CARD-READER.
      SELECT LIST-FILE ASSIGN TO LINE-PRINTER.
```

The configuration section specifies that the source and object computer is the ABC-123. In general, these entries take the form:

SOURCE-COMPUTER.   computer-name.
OBJECT-COMPUTER.   computer-name.

where "computer-name" is a set of characters recognized by the compiler. The source and object computers need not be the same and can also specify different hardware configurations. The source computer is the computer on which the COBOL program is translated to the computer's language. The object computer is the computer on which the program is executed.

The input-output section is used to assign symbolic file names to input/output devices to be used in the program. The form of the SELECT statement is:

SELECT file-name ASSIGN TO device-name.

where "file name" is the name assigned to a file by the programmer, and "device name" is a name for a particular class of devices recognized by the compiler. In this example, the statements:

```
SELECT PAY-FILE ASSIGN TO CARD-READER.
SELECT LIST-FILE ASSIGN TO LINE-PRINTER.
```

specify that PAY-FILE is to be assigned to a card reader and LIST-FILE is to be assigned to a line printer. PAY-FILE and LIST-FILE are symbolic names of data files that *must be* described in the data division. The SELECT statement must begin in area B of the reference format.

Names of hardware units, such as CARD-READER, vary between different compilers, computer systems, and operating systems.

Data Division

The data division describes the information on which the program operates. *All data files, data records, and temporary storage must be described.* This division is usually independent of a particular implementation of COBOL.

The data division consists of two sections: file and working storage. The *file section* gives the attributes of input/output files and of the data records that comprise these fields. The *working storage section* defines the main storage used during the execution of a program. (Review Figure

11.2 to determine the relative position of the file and working storage sections and their general appearance.)

File Section.   The file section of the data division of the pay listing program is given as follows:

```
FILE SECTION.
FD   PAY-FILE
     LABEL RECORDS ARE OMITTED
     DATA RECORD IS PAY-CARD.
01   PAY-CARD.
     02  S-S-NO          PICTURE 9(9).
     02  FILLER          PICTURE X(5).
     02  NAME            PICTURE X(30).
     02  FILLER          PICTURE X(2).
     02  PAY-CODE        PICTURE A(1).
         88 WEEKLY VALUE IS "W".
         88 HOURLY VALUE IS "H".
     02  FILLER          PICTURE X(2).
     02  RATE            PICTURE 9999V99.
     02  FILLER          PICTURE X(2).
     02  HOURS           PICTURE 999V9.
     02  FILLER          PICTURE X(19).
FD   LIST-FILE
     LABEL RECORDS ARE OMITTED
     DATA RECORD IS PAY-LINE.
01   PAY-LINE.
     02  FILLER          PICTURE X(6).
     02  SOCSECNO        PICTURE 9(9).
     02  FILLER          PICTURE X(6).
     02  PAY-CODE        PICTURE A(1).
     02  FILLER          PICTURE X(6).
     02  EMPL-NAME       PICTURE X(30).
     02  FILLER          PICTURE X(2).
     02  TOTALPAY        PICTURE $$,$$$.99.
     02  FILLER          PICTURE X(63).
```

Two files are described: PAY-FILE and LIST-FILE. The letters FD denote "file description," followed by the file name and its attributes. The record description of all records that belong to a file follow the FD statement. A record description is a structure that must begin with a 01 level entry that contains the record name. In this case the first FD statement describes the file named PAY-FILE and specifies that its data record is PAY-CARD. The record description of PAY-CARD follows the FD statement for PAY-FILE. The length of record PAY-CARD is implicitly given by the data items of which it is composed. The second FD statement describes the file named LIST-FILE and specifies that its data record is PAY-LINE. The record description of PAY-LINE follows the FD statement for LIST-FILE.

Most COBOL entries use reserved words. For example, in the FD statement:

```
FD   LIST-FILE
     LABEL RECORDS ARE OMITTED
     DATA RECORD IS PAY-LINE.
```

the only words supplied by the programmer are LIST-FILE and PAY-LINE; the remainder of the words in the statement are COBOL reserved words, which represent names that cannot be used for any other purposes.

Data items within a record (02 level entries in this case) are either assigned a name or given the word FILLER in place of a name. The word FILLER can be assigned to a field when that field is not used in a program. Consider the input record named PAY-CARD. It has a length of 80 characters, and each character position in the record is accounted for by a variable name or by a filler. The implication is that the record is read into an area of storage, and when a variable is referenced, the correct field in the record is accessed. In other words, the record description serves as a template. The same concept holds true for output.

Each data item or field in a record is described with a PICTURE clause. As picture characters, 9 denotes a numeric character, A denotes an alphabetic character, X denotes any character in the COBOL alphabet, and V denotes an implied decimal point. Repetition of the same picture character is specified as follows:

$$\underbrace{CCC...C}_{n} \leftrightarrow C(n)$$

so that PICTURE X(4) is equivalent to PICTURE XXXX and PICTURE 9(5)V9(4) is equivalent to PICTURE 99999V9999.

The 88-level items in PAY-CARD denote condition names. The following specification:

```
02   PAY-CODE PICTURE A(1).
     88 WEEKLY VALUE IS "W".
     88 HOURLY VALUE IS "H".
```

is interpreted as follows: The name of the condition that PAY-CODE="W" is WEEKLY and the name of the condition that PAY-CODE="H" is HOURLY. ("W" and "H" are nonnumeric literals.)

Thus, in the procedure division of the program, the programmer can write:

```
IF WEEKLY . . .
```

instead of

```
IF PAY-CODE="W" . . .
```

The output record PAY-LINE contains the data item:

```
02  TOTALPAY PICTURE $$,$$$.99.
```

that denotes data editing. When a value is moved to TOTALPAY, it is edited such that leading zeros are suppressed and the rightmost leading zero is replaced with a dollar sign. The comma is an insertion character; a comma is inserted into the edited result if digits appear to the right and to the left of it. The use of picture editing is consistent with the technique of computing, editing, or converting, and then storing, mentioned earlier; so that editing or conversion is not performed during the actual output operation.

The output record PAY-LINE contains 132 characters—the precise length of a print line.

Working Storage Section. The working storage section of the data division describes storage used during execution of a program but not assigned to a particular file. Both data records and independent storage can be defined. Consider the working storage section of the pay list program:

```
WORKING-STORAGE SECTION.
77    TEMPPAY     PICTURE 9999V99.
01    TITLE.
      02  FILLER PICTURE X(30) VALUE IS SPACES.
      02  FILLER PICTURE X(15)
          VALUE IS "PAYCHECK REPORT".
      02  FILLER PICTURE X(87) VALUE IS SPACES.
01    HEADING.
      02  FILLER PICTURE X(5) VALUE IS SPACES.
      02  FILLER PICTURE X(11)
          VALUE IS "S.S. NUMBER".
      02  FILLER PICTURE X(2) VALUE IS SPACES.
      02  FILLER PICTURE X(8)
          VALUE IS "PAY CODE".
      02  FILLER PICTURE X(10) VALUE IS SPACES.
      02  FILLER PICTURE X(4) VALUE IS "NAME".
      02  FILLER PICTURE X(20) VALUE IS SPACES.
```

```
    02   FILLER PICTURE X(9)
         VALUE IS "GROSS PAY".
    02   FILLER PICTURE X(63) VALUE IS SPACES.
01  ERR-MESS.
    02   FILLER PICTURE X(5) VALUE IS SPACES.
    02   FILLER PICTURE X(5) VALUE IS "*****".
    02   FILLER PICTURE X(32)
         VALUE IS "DATA ERROR—CHECK AND RERUN JOB".
    02   FILLER PICTURE X(5) VALUE IS "*****".
    02   FILLER PICTURE X(85) VALUE IS SPACES.
01  END-MESS.
    02   FILLER PICTURE X(30) VALUE IS SPACES.
    02   FILLER PICTURE X(18)
         VALUE IS "END OF PAY LISTING".
    02   FILLER PICTURE X(74) VALUE IS SPACES.
```

The data item TEMPPAY is assigned six digits of independent storage because it has a level number of 77. The implied decimal point is after the fourth digit from the left. The record descriptions of TITLE, HEADING, ERR-MESS, and END-MESS describe records that will be moved to PAY-LINE before the "write" operation. None of the fields in either record is assigned a name, other than FILLER, because none of them is going to be referred to in the program. However, the fields of these records are assigned a value with the VALUE clause. The VALUE clause can only be used in the working storage section and may not be used in the file section, except in an 88-level item— that is, the specification of a condition name. Each of the records— that is, TITLE, HEADING, ERR-MESS, and END-MESS—is precisely 132 characters in length—the same length as PAY-LINE.

If the fields in one of the records under discussion (HEADING, for example) were not assigned a value with the VALUE clause, it would have to be given a name and then be assigned a value during the execution of the program. The clause:

```
VALUE IS SPACES
```

uses a figurative constant, which is SPACES (or SPACE—they are equivalent). A *figurative constant* is a frequently used value that is assigned a data name. Other frequently used figurative constants are ZERO and QUOTE. Figurative constants are discussed again later.

Independent storage (77-level items) may not be used in the file section.

Procedure Division

The procedure division specifies the steps that the computer is to follow. The procedure division is composed of statements, sentences, paragraphs, and sections; it corresponds to the "program" in other programming languages except that declarative information is omitted. By itself, the procedure division is an incomplete specification of a program because information in other divisions of the COBOL program is needed.

Of all the divisions of a COBOL program, the procedure division is more like meaningful English. Verbs are used to denote actions, and sentences, paragraphs, and sections correspond to complex procedures.

The procedure division begins with the statement:

```
PROCEDURE DIVISION.
```

and is composed of sections and paragraphs. The paragraphs of the payroll program are described separately. The first paragraph is given as follows:

```
INITIALIZE.
    OPEN INPUT PAY-FILE.
    OPEN OUTPUT LIST-FILE.
```

where INITIALIZE is the paragraph name. The paragraph contains two OPEN statements. The OPEN statement prepares the specified file for either input or output. Functionally, this statement serves to "connect" the input/output device, assigned to the specified file in the environment division, to the program. Each COBOL statement begins with a verb, such as OPEN, that denotes the function the statement is to perform. The verb is followed by words that augment the verb and specify operands on which the computer is to operate.

The next paragraph of the procedure division is:

```
PRINT-TITLE-AND-HEADING.
    WRITE PAY-LINE FROM TITLE
        AFTER ADVANCING 0 LINES.
    WRITE PAY-LINE FROM HEADING
        AFTER ADVANCING 2 LINES.
    MOVE SPACES TO PAY-LINE.
    WRITE PAY-LINE.
```

where PRINT-TITLE-AND-HEADING is the paragraph name. The paragraph consists of four statements: WRITE, WRITE, MOVE, and WRITE—in that order. The paragraph simply prepares the title for the report. When doing input and output in COBOL, a good rule to remember is that the program *reads files* and *writes records*. Therefore, a write statement is associated with a particular data file through the DATA RECORDS ARE . . . clause in the FD statement, and the user must write a data record declared with the appropriate file. The first statement (that is, the WRITE statement) is equivalent to the following:

```
MOVE TITLE TO PAY-LINE.
WRITE PAY-LINE AFTER ADVANCING 0 LINES.
```

The ADVANCING 0 LINES clause tells the printer to go to the top of the next page. Similarly, the ADVANCING 2 LINES clause tells the printer to skip two lines before printing. The last statement, that is,

```
WRITE PAY-LINE
```

contains no ADVANCING clause, and one line is advanced automatically before printing.

The succeeding paragraph named READ-PAY reads an input record and branches to the procedure defined for each type of input card. Incorrect input is recognized, and error processing is performed.

```
READ-PAY.
      READ PAY-FILE AT END GO TO END-OF-JOB.
      IF WEEKLY GO TO COMPUTE-WEEKLY-PAY.
      IF HOURLY GO TO COMPUTE-HOURLY-PAY.
      WRITE PAY-LINE FROM ERR-MESS
        AFTER ADVANCING 2 LINES.
      CLOSE PAY-FILE, LIST-FILE.
      STOP RUN.
```

The READ statement reads the next input record into a storage area for that file. Each input file has a storage area. The data record defined with PAY-FILE is a template that allows information to be accessed by name. The first IF statement uses the condition name WEEKLY; it is the same as if the programmer had written:

```
IF PAY-CODE = "W" GO TO COMPUTE-WEEKLY-PAY.
```

If the condition is true, the statement(s) following the IF clause is (are) executed. Otherwise, the computer goes to the next sentence. The operand to the GO TO statement, in this case COMPUTE-WEEKLY-PAY, is a paragraph or section name. There are no statement numbers in COBOL, per se. However, the programmer can achieve the same purpose by using a paragraph name. At this point a paragraph or section name is nothing more than a statement label. Later, statements are described that utilize the concept of a paragraph or section.

The second IF statement in the READ-PAY paragraph tests for the HOURLY condition and executes in a similar manner to the first IF statement. If the input record is neither weekly nor hourly, an error condition exists, and an error message is printed. The CLOSE statement terminates processing of the specified files and logically disconnects the input/output devices from the program. The STOP RUN statement terminates processing of the program.

The COMPUTE-WEEKLY-PAY paragraph is the first case of actual computation being performed.

```
COMPUTE-WEEKLY-PAY.
    MOVE RATE TO TEMPPAY.
    IF HOURS GREATER THAN 40.0
        COMPUTE TEMPPAY = TEMPPAY + (RATE / 40) *
    (HOURS − 40) * 1.5.
    GO TO PRINT-PAY.
```

The MOVE statement moves the weekly rate to the temporary pay location. Numeric values are aligned by decimal point. The IF statement causes the COMPUTE statement to be executed if hours are greater than 40. The COMPUTE statement is analogous to the assignment statement or the LET statement in BASIC. Several restrictions exist on the writing of expressions. Operators (such as, =,+,−,*,/) must be preceded and followed by at least one space. The left parenthesis must not be followed by a space, and the right parenthesis must not be preceded by a space. At this point, it is fairly obvious that hyphens can be used in names, but the reader has probably wondered about the minus operation. Placing a space before and after the minus sign, that is, A − B is used to distinguish the expression A *minus* B from the name A-B, since a name may not contain imbedded spaces.

In COBOL, the following hierarchy is established among operators:

Operator	Hierarchy
**	Highest
* or /	↓
+ or −	Lowest

and parentheses are used for grouping as in BASIC. The GO TO PRINT-LINE transfers program control to the named paragraph.

The COMPUTE-HOURLY-PAY paragraph demonstrates a compound IF statement, that takes the form:

$$\text{IF condition} \begin{Bmatrix} \text{statement-1} \\ \textit{NEXT SENTENCE} \end{Bmatrix} \begin{Bmatrix} \textit{OTHERWISE} \\ \textit{ELSE} \end{Bmatrix}$$

$$\begin{Bmatrix} \text{statement-2} \\ \textit{NEXT SENTENCE} \end{Bmatrix} .$$

and is depicted in Figure 11.3. In this format "statement-1" and "statement-2" can each be one or more COBOL statements. The COMPUTE-HOURLY-PAY paragraph is given as follows:

```
COMPUTE-HOURLY-PAY.
      IF HOURS GREATER THAN 40.0
         COMPUTE TEMPPAY = RATE * 40 + (HOURS − 40) *
         RATE * 1.5
      ELSE COMPUTE TEMPPAY = RATE * HOURS.
```

If HOURS is greater than 40, the statement

```
COMPUTE TEMPPAY = RATE * 40 + (HOURS − 40) * RATE * 1.5
```

is executed, and program control passes directly to the next sentence. If HOURS is not greater than 40, then the statement following the word ELSE is executed, and program control is passed to the next sentence.

The PRINT-PAY paragraph is:

```
PRINT-PAY.
      MOVE SPACES TO PAY-LINE.
      MOVE S-S-NO TO SOCSECNO.
      MOVE PAY-CODE IN PAY-CARD TO PAY-CODE IN PAY-LINE.
      MOVE NAME TO EMPL-NAME.
      MOVE TEMPPAY TO TOTALPAY.
      WRITE PAY-LINE. GO TO READ-PAY.
```

An area in storage is associated with the output record PAY-LINE. The first statement moves spaces to PAY-LINE to remove residual characters from previous write statements. The statement:

```
MOVE S-S-NO TO SOCSECNO
```

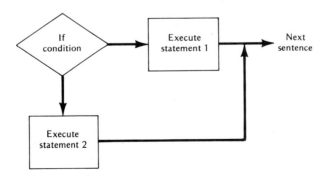

FIGURE 11.3   The compound IF statement.

moves the numeric field S-S-NO to the numeric field SOCSECNO. The contents of S-S-NO are left unchanged. The fields are aligned by decimal point, which is assumed, in this case, to be to the right of the rightmost digit in the field. The statement:

```
MOVE PAY-CODE IN PAY-CARD TO PAY-CODE IN PAY-LINE
```

involves a movement of alphabetic information from left to right in the fields. The clause PAY-CODE IN PAY-CARD constitutes a qualified name that is required because the data item PAY-CODE is used in two structures. Thus, the qualification IN PAY-CARD denotes the structure in which PAY-CODE is found. The statement:

```
MOVE NAME TO EMPL-NAME
```

involves alphanumeric information that is also moved from left to right. The following general rules apply to data movement of character data. Consider the statement:

```
MOVE A TO B
```

Rules:

1. If the length of A is greater than the length of B, then A is truncated on the right during the replacement operation.
2. If the length of A is less than the length of B, then B is padded on the right with spaces.

Numeric fields are aligned by decimal point and padded on the left or right with zeros. The final MOVE statement:

```
MOVE TEMPPAY TO TOTALPAY
```

causes editing to be performed. Alignment is made by decimal point, and zero suppression is performed on the left as denoted in the PICTURE clause for TOTALPAY. The WRITE statement transfers PAY-LINE to the associated file. After the WRITE statement is executed, the information in PAY-LINE is no longer accessible. The GO TO statement demonstrates that more than one statement and more than one sentence can be written on one line.

The final paragraph:

```
END-OF-JOB
    WRITE PAY-LINE FROM END-MESS AFTER ADVANCING
    2 LINES.
    CLOSE PAY-FILE, LIST-FILE.
    STOP RUN.
```

is entered when an "end of data" condition is reached in the READ statement of paragraph READ-PAY. This paragraph writes a message, closes files, and terminates execution of the program.

In data processing the "end of data" condition is frequently used to terminate processing of a file. An algorithm is defined for the processing of a single data record and is repeated for each record in the file.

LANGUAGE FUNDAMENTALS*

This section describes the basic facts necessary for using COBOL. The material applies to all four divisions of a COBOL program. A key concept in COBOL is that of a word. The language is designed so that a programmer can express a program as a series of words familiar to the COBOL compiler. (This fact is obvious from the example of the preceding section.) Words are grouped to form statements; statements are grouped to form sentences; and so on. The term *word* is defined more explicitly after the COBOL character set is presented.

Character Set

The complete COBOL character set consists of the following 51 characters:

Character	Meaning or Name
0.1, . . . ,9	Digit
A,B, . . . ,Z	Letter
	Space character (blank)
+	Plus sign
—	Minus sign or hyphen
*	Asterisk
/	Slash (stroke, virgule, solidus)
=	Equal sign
$	Currency sign (dollar sign)
,	Comma
.	Period or decimal sign
;	Semicolon
"	Quotation mark
(	Left parenthesis
)	Right parenthesis
>	Greater than symbol
<	Less than symbol

---

* This section may be omitted without a loss of continuity.

However, most implementations of COBOL permit other characters in alphanumeric data items.

Two sets of COBOL characters can be referred to by name to facilitate programming. *Numeric characters* consist of the digits 0 through 9. *Alphabetic characters* consist of the letters A through Z. Later, a class test is defined that allows the programmer to test if all characters in a data item are numeric or alphabetic.

The characters in the COBOL alphabet are also placed in categories on the basis of the function they serve in the language. Some characters serve more than one purpose. The characters used in *words* are: the letters A through Z, the digits 0 through 9, and the hyphen (-). The characters used for *punctuation* are:

Character	Meaning
	Space
,	Comma
;	Semicolon
.	Period
"	Quotation
(	Left parenthesis
)	Right parenthesis

Rules for using the punctuation characters are given in a later paragraph. The characters used for *editing* are:

Character	Meaning
B	Space
0	Zero
+	Plus
—	Minus
CR	Credit
DB	Debit
Z	Zero suppression
*	Check protection
$	Dollar sign (currency sign)
,	Comma
.	Decimal point

Editing characters are used to aid the programmer in generating data processing output. COBOL allows four characters to be used as *arithmetic operators* in the COMPUTE statement and in conditional expressions. Arithmetic symbols are:

Character or Symbol	Meaning
+	Addition
—	Subtraction
*	Multiplication
/	Division
**	Exponentiation

Comparison (or relational) *operators* are permitted in conditional expressions (or *conditions,* as they are called in COBOL); the following characters are used:

Character	Meaning
>	Greater than
<	Less than
=	Equal to

Words

In COBOL, a *word* is a construct that can be "read," similar to a word in a human language. More formally, a word is a series of not more than 30 characters chosen from the character set for words. A word may not begin or end with a hyphen. It is important to consider how a word is recognized, since many statements are composed of several words. A word is terminated by a space or by the following punctuation characters: a period, a right parenthesis, a comma, or a semicolon. It should be noted that this is an important rule. For example, it makes the expression $A + B$ unusable (a fact which was also known because operators must be preceded and followed by a space). Also, when using a subscripted variable of the form:

data-name   (subscript)

the rule implicitly states that the "data-name" must be followed by a space, and this is indeed one of the COBOL rules on the use of subscripts.

In the study of programming languages, it seems as though everything is classified in one way or another, and sometimes in more than one way. A convenient classification for words is to distinguish between reserved words and names. A *reserved word* is part of the COBOL language and may not be used by the programmer as the name of something. A *name* is a word defined by the programmer.

Reserved words are further classified as to whether they are keywords, optional words, or connectives. A *keyword* is required in the statement or clause of which it is a part. In most cases the omission of a keyword or the substitution of another word for a keyword changes the meaning of a clause or a statement, or causes that construction to be interpreted as being syntactically incorrect. A keyword can be a verb, such as READ, ADD, or MOVE; a required word, such as TO in the MOVE statement; or a word that is assigned a functional meaning, such as NUMERIC, SPACE, or POSITIVE. An *optional word* can be included in a clause or statement at the programmer's option and is used to improve readability and understanding. For example, in the statement:

```
READ MFILE RECORD INTO DATA-AREA.
```

READ and INTO are keywords, MFILE and DATA-AREA are names, and RECORD is an optional word that can be omitted but not replaced by another COBOL word. A *connective* is used to qualify a data name, to link two or more consecutive operands, and to form compound comparison expressions. A *qualifier connective* uses the words OF and IN to establish a unique reference to a data item. A *series connective* uses the comma (,) to link two or more operands in a single statement, such as:

```
ADD A,B GIVING C.
```

It may seem unusual to classify a comma as a reserved word; however, the COBOL standard makes this classification, and it is included for completeness.) A *logical connective* is one of the words AND, OR, AND NOT, and OR NOT that is used to form complex conditions.

Names

A *name* is a word that contains at least one alphabetic character—not necessarily the first character in the word. There are several types of names in COBOL:

1. A *data name* identifies a data item. It is declared in the data division and used in the procedure division.
2. A *file name* identifies a data file. It is declared in the environment and data divisions and used in the procedure division.
3. A *record name* identifies a data record. It is declared in the data division and used in the procedure division.
4. A *procedure name* is either a paragraph or section name. In the environment and data divisions, section names are predefined as part of the COBOL language. In the procedure division, paragraph and section names are defined contextually by their presence in the program and are used as operands in some statements.
5. A *condition name* is a data name assigned to a particular value or a set of values of a data item. A condition name is defined as an 88-level item in the data division and is used as a condition in the IF statement.
6. A *special name* is a name assigned to a specific hardware component in the environment division.

"Extended COBOL" also allows user-defined names to be assigned to a program unit, library, report, sort file, or saved area (for random access input/output processing).

Nouns

A user-defined name is an instance of a set of operands frequently referred to as *nouns*. More specifically, a *noun* is used as an operand in a COBOL statement and is *usually* a COBOL word, as defined previously. A noun can be a user-defined name, a constant, or a special register (the last two are covered in the next two sections). Names are classified in the preceding paragraph.

Constants

There are three types of constants in COBOL: numeric literals, nonnumeric literals, and figurative constants. A *numeric literal* is a fixed-point value composed from the numeric characters 0 through 9, the plus sign, the minus sign, and the decimal point in accordance with the following rules:

1. It must contain from 1 to 18 numeric characters.
2. It may be signed or unsigned. If a sign is used, it must be the first character in the numeric literal. An unsigned numeric literal is positive.
3. It must not contain more than one decimal point. If the decimal point is omitted, the numeric literal is an integer.
4. The value of a numeric literal is a number to the base ten using the positional number system.

A *nonnumeric literal* is a series of 1 to 120 characters from the COBOL alphabet, excluding the quotation mark; it is bounded by quotation marks. For example, the following are nonnumeric literals:

```
"TEA FOR TWO"
"123.4$"
"ADD A TO B".
```

All nonnumeric literals are classed as alphanumeric data items.

A *figurative constant* is a value to which a data name has been assigned. Figurative constants are reserved words, as defined previously. A figurative constant is used as an ordinary data name, that is, without quotation marks, and the singular and plural forms are equivalent. The following figurative constants are defined in COBOL:

ZERO	Represents the character 0, or one or more occurrences
ZEROES	of the character 0, depending on context.
ZEROS	

SPACE SPACES	Represents one or more spaces (blank characters) depending on context.
HIGH-VALUE HIGH-VALUES	Represents one or more occurrences of the character that has the highest value in the computer's set of characters.
LOW-VALUE LOW-VALUES	Represents one or more occurrences of the character that has the lowest value in the computer's set of characters.
QUOTE QUOTES	Represents one or more occurrences of the quotation mark character. The word QUOTE cannot be used in place of the quotation mark as a delimiter.
ALL literal	Represents one or more occurrences of the string of characters representing the nonnumeric literal. The literal may be a figurative constant, in which case the word ALL is superfluous.

In all cases the class of a figurative constant must agree with the requirements of the statement in which it is used.

Special Registers

A *special register* is a storage area recognized and generated by the COBOL compiler for use in several of the COBOL statements. The only special register included in the COBOL "nucleus" of basic requirements is TALLY, defined as an unsigned integer of five digits in computational form. The register TALLY may be used anywhere that a data name of integral value can be used. Extensions to COBOL allow additional special registers, such as LINE-COUNTER, PAGE-COUNTER, CURRENT-DATE, and TIME-OF-DAY.

Punctuation

Because of the use of reserved words in COBOL, punctuation is a minor concern—provided that a few simple rules are followed. Punctuation rules that are specific to a particular division of a COBOL program are covered when that division is presented in detail. A key point is that the space character, the comma, the semicolon, and the period are used in the same way that they would be used in the English language. The general rules are:

1. When a period, semicolon, or comma is used, it must not be preceded by a space but must be followed by a space.
2. A left parenthesis must not be followed immediately by a space, and a right parenthesis must not be preceded immediately by a space.

3. Two or more successive spaces are treated as a single space—except in nonnumeric literals.

4. At least one space must appear between two successive words, nouns, or parenthetical clauses.

5. An operator, including the equals sign denoting replacement, must be preceded and followed by a space.

6. A comma may be used between successive operands in a statement. A comma followed by a space is equivalent to a space.

7. A comma or a semicolon may be used to separate a series of clauses. (Successive clauses are frequently used in the environment and data divisions to specify the attributes of a data item, file, or hardware name.)

8. A comma or semicolon may be used to separate a series of statements—although the only punctuation needed between successive statements is a single space.

9. Sentences, paragraphs, sections, and divisions must always end with a period.

The flexibility of the punctuation rules in COBOL permits many installations to adopt fairly rigid but useful documentation standards. For example, a frequently used convention in many installations is to separate successive clauses and operands with a comma and to end each statement with a semicolon. Effective documentation is an installation management problem, but this is a case where the versatility of a programming language has partially solved a nonprogramming problem.

Data Reference

The reserved words IN and OF were mentioned previously as qualifier connectives. A name must be qualified when it does not, by itself, provide a unique reference to the data item or paragraph that it names. Qualification is achieved by following a data name or a paragraph name by one or more phrases composed of a qualifier preceded by IN or OF. (IN and OF may be used interchangeably.) The general rule for qualification is:

$$\begin{Bmatrix} \text{data-name} \\ \text{condition-name} \end{Bmatrix} \begin{bmatrix} \begin{Bmatrix} OF \\ IN \end{Bmatrix} \text{data-name} \end{bmatrix} \dots$$

for data and condition names, and

$$\text{paragraph-name} \left[\left\{ \begin{array}{c} OF \\ IN \end{array} \right\} \text{section-name} \right]$$

for paragraph names. For example, in the structures

```
01   BIGA        01   BIG B
     02 A . . .        02 HIGH
     02 B . . .           03 A . . .
                          03 C . . .
                     02 LOW
                        03 B . . .
                        03 D . . .
```

qualification is needed for the compiler to distinguish between the data items A and B in records BIGA and BIGB. Thus, a reference to A and B in record BIGA must be written A IN BIGA and B IN BIGA, respectively. Similarly, data item A in record BIGB must be qualified and can be referred to as A IN HIGH IN BIGB. Only enough qualification is needed to make a reference unique. Thus, provided that no other conflict exists, the reference B IN BIGB is equivalent to B IN LOW IN BIGB.

A paragraph name cannot be duplicated within a section of the procedure division. Therefore, at most, one level of qualification is needed for a paragraph name. The statements:

```
BIG SECTION.
FAST-PAR.
  MOVE A TO B, . . .
    .
    .
    .

LITTLE SECTION.
FAST-PAR.
  ADD A TO B, . . .
    .
    .
    .

OTHER SECTION.
SLOW-PAR.
    .
    .
    .
  GO TO FAST-PAR. IN LITTLE.
    .
    .
    .
```

depict an example of a case where qualification is needed for a paragraph name. When a section name is used as a qualifier, the word SECTION must not appear. When a paragraph name is referred to from within its own section, it need not be qualified; that is, for example,

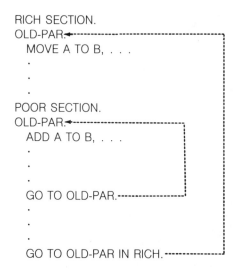

```
RICH SECTION.
OLD-PAR.◄-----------------------------------¬
    MOVE A TO B, . . .                        ¦
    .                                         ¦
    .                                         ¦
    .                                         ¦
POOR SECTION.                                 ¦
OLD-PAR.◄------------------------¬            ¦
    ADD A TO B, . . .            ¦            ¦
    .                            ¦            ¦
    .                            ¦            ¦
    .                            ¦            ¦
    GO TO OLD-PAR.---------------┘            ¦
    .                                         ¦
    .                                         ¦
    .                                         ¦
    GO TO OLD-PAR IN RICH.--------------------┘
```

The following rules apply to qualification:

1. Each qualifier must be of successively higher level and must be within the same hierarchy (record or section) as the name that it qualifies. (However, as mentioned, only enough qualification is needed to make a name unique.)
2. The same name must not appear at two levels in the same hierarchy so that that name would appear to qualify itself.
3. If a name requires qualification, then it must be qualified each time it is used in a program.
4. A data name used as a qualifier cannot be subscripted. However, the complete data reference can be subscripted.
5. A name can be qualified even though it is unique and qualification is not needed.

Subscripts.   Another form of data reference requires subscripting and involves selecting an element of an array. An array is defined with the OCCURS clause in the data division, as in the following example:

```
01   BIG-REC.
     02   TABLE OCCURS 50 TIMES.
          03   SYMBOL PICTURE X(8).
          03   VALUE PICTURE S9(5).
```

that defines a one-dimensional array of structures (a single level table, as it is called) of the form:

Index	Symbol	Value
1	XXXXXXXX	S99999
2	XXXXXXXX	S99999
3	XXXXXXXX	S99999
.	.	.
.	.	.
.	.	.
50	XXXXXXXX	S99999

An individual element of an array is selected with a subscript, represented either by a numeric literal with an integral value, by the special register TALLY, or by a data name. A subscript is enclosed in parentheses following the array name or following a sub-element of the array. Thus, the reference TABLE(I) selects the Ith structure in the array of structures named TABLE, and the reference SYMBOL IN TABLE (I) selects the data item SYMBOL in the Ith structure of TABLE. If SYMBOL in TABLE is unique, then the last reference can be simplified as SYMBOL(I).

Up to three dimensions are permitted for arrays, and if there is more than one subscript in an array reference, they must be separated by commas. In general, a reference to an array variable takes the form:

$$\left[\begin{Bmatrix} \text{data-name} \end{Bmatrix} \begin{matrix} OF \\ IN \end{matrix} \text{data-name} \right] \ldots \left[(\text{subscript[,subscript[,subscript]]}) \right]$$

Comment Lines

The programmer may insert commentary information into the identification and procedure divisions of a COBOL program. In the identification division the REMARKS clause is used, and the commentary information can take the form of a set of sentences that ends with the beginning of the environment division.

In the procedure division the keyword NOTE is used to mark the beginning of commentary information. If the NOTE sentence is the first sentence in a paragraph, then the entire paragraph is considered to be commentary information. If the NOTE sentence appears other than as the first sentence of a paragraph, then the comment ends with the first period followed by a space.

Vocabulary   The reader should be familiar with the following terms in the context in which they were used in the chapter.

area A

area B

COBOL reference format

condition name

configuration section

continuation area

data division

environment division

figurative constant

file section

filler

identification division

input-output section

paragraph

picture clause

procedure division

sequence number

working storage section

Exercises

1. What is meant by the remark that "COBOL programs are self-documenting"?

2. What is the difference between a data name and a constant?

3. In what margins (A or B) do each of the following start:

division	sentence
section	statement
paragraph	continuation line

4. In your own words state the role of each of the divisions in a COBOL program.

5. What purpose does a "PICTURE clause" serve?

6. List all of the COBOL rules, formal and informal, that are given in the chapter.

7. Why is qualification necessary? What kinds of qualification are there?

8. Give three figurative constants.

9. Can you think of any reason why the length of a nonnumeric literal is from 1 to 120 characters?

10. Give errors in the following constants (if any):

    123.456   89.9—

    —9.14   6319283764192004

    5,143.00   +123.

11. Which of the following are valid data names?

    | JONES | PL/I | ZERO |
    | K-25 | SIX | 15-M |
    | 12BLOT | A+B+C | ADD |

12. True or false: data names and paragraph names are constructed using the same COBOL rules.

13. Indicate which of the following nonnumeric literals are invalid and give the reason why.

    "TEA FOR TWO"   "COMMON BUSINESS ORIENTED LANGUAGE"

    "12+ +AB"   "THE ANS="F3.4"DOLLARS"

    SPACES

Related Reading

Ashley, R. *ANS COBOL (A Self-Teaching Guide).* New York: John Wiley and Sons, 1974.

Davis, G. B., and Litisky, C. R. *Elementary COBOL Programming: A Step by Step Approach.* New York: McGraw-Hill, 1971.

Lindahl, T. F. *An Introduction to American National Standard COBOL.* Menlo Park, Calif.: Cummings Publishing, 1973.

Murach, M. *Standard COBOL.* Chicago: Science Research Associates, 1971.

Smith, M. Z. *Standard COBOL: A Problem-Solving Approach.* Boston: Houghton Mifflin, 1974.

Spitzbarth, L. M. *Basic COBOL Programming: Self-Instructional Manual and Text.* Reading, Mass.: Addison-Wesley Publishing, 1970.

Part

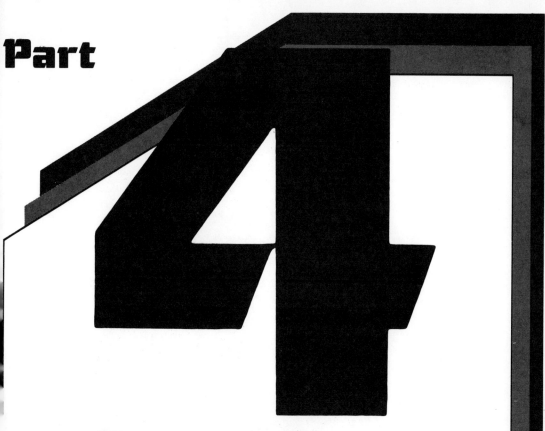

Computer Software

Assembler Language and Language Processors

Languages for computer programming vary in both scope and complexity. At one end of the spectrum is assembler language, which resembles the instruction format of the computer. At the other end are complex programming languages that can be used to describe computational procedures in an unambiguous fashion. Two higher-level programming languages were covered in preceding chapters. This chapter covers assembler language and gives an overview of language processors.

ASSEMBLER LANGUAGE

Assembler language is designed to allow programs to be written in the machine language of the computer without having to deal with internal codes and machine addresses. There are several reasons why a user might write a program in assembler language rather than in a programming language:

1. A higher-level programming language is not available for the computer.
2. The user requires a functional capability or option that is outside of the scope of a programming language.
3. Using special features of a particular computer, an experienced programmer can produce a more efficient program in assembler language than he can in a programming language.

Assembler language is used primarily for systems programs for a given computer, such as language processors, operating systems, and data communications and graphics packages. Most applications programs are written in a language such as COBOL or BASIC because it is more economical to write programs in these languages and because a program can be transferred to another machine with a minimum of effort. The economics of the situation include lead time, personnel requirements, program verification, etc.—all of which can be translated into economic variables. Thus, programs written in a standard programming language are said to be more "portable" than programs written in assembler language.

Program Structure

An assembler language program is a series of statements that describe the procedure the computer should follow at each stage of a computation. All entities in the program must be described, including constants, storage areas, and indicators. This requirement is not a characteristic of most programming languages, since the compiler usually takes care of generating temporary storage areas, constants, and indicators.

A program written in assembler language is translated into an equivalent program in machine language by a program called an *assembler program* or simply an *assembler.* The assembler is a *language processor,* as defined later in this chapter. A program written in assembler language does not have to make sense to the assembler, which makes a straightforward translation of the program to machine language. A compiler, on the other hand, does perform an analysis of the structure of a program.

Two things should be noted. For the most part, each statement in an assembler language program causes one machine instruction to be generated by the assembler. There are minor exceptions that occur because some statements provide information to the assembler and do not correspond to computer instructions. Also, assembler language is largely dependent upon the computer, and assembler language operation codes normally correspond to actual computer instructions.

Statement Format

Entries in an assembler language program can be made symbolically, whenever appropriate, which is one of the primary advantages of using assembler language. A statement in assembler language is designed to supply the following information to the assembler:

1. The relative location of an instruction or data item; this entry allows the statement to be referenced in the program and normally does not reflect where the program is to be loaded in main storage.
2. The operation code of a machine instruction or a statement providing information to the assembler.
3. The operands required by the operation code.

Statements are read by the assembler on a line-by-line basis. In addition to the statement itself, a line of input may also contain comments and a sequence number. Some assemblers inspect the sequence numbers to verify that lines are in the correct sequence and that a line is not inadvertently left out.

Entries in the statement portion of a line are usually formatted in one of two ways:

1. The *columnar form* places the entries in columns, as in the following example:

Location	Operation	Operands
HERE	RD	ABLE
	RD	B
	L	ABLE
	M	B
	A	CHARLY
	ST	DOG
	BR	HERE
	.	
	.	
	.	

2. The *free form* uses a set of rules that allow a statement to be essentially "mapped" into a columnar representation. A typical set of rules is: (a) The location field always starts in column one or a line; (b) Fields must be separated by at least one blank character; (c) If no entry exists in the location field, the operation field must not begin before column two. This is shown in the following representation of the above program:

```
HERE RD ABLE
   RD B
   L ABLE
    M B
  A CHARLY
      ST DOG
  BR HERE
    .
    .
    .
```

The columnar form is a special case of the free form.

Types of Instructions

Assembler language normally incorporates three types of instructions: machine instructions, assembler instructions, and macro instructions. *Machine instructions* correspond to actual computer instructions. Typical examples are L (for load), A (for add), M (for multiply), and ST (for store). Machine instructions tell the computer what to do. *Assembler instructions* provide information to the assembler on how the program should be assembled. Assembler instructions tell the assembler what to do. *Macro instructions* allow a predefined set of statements to be used in an assembler language program. This topic is not covered further in this book.

Absolute and Relocatable Programs

Programming conventions and requirements vary between different computer systems and between different applications. For some applications, a program must be written so that it can be placed in a specific area of main storage. On-board computers in ships, planes, and space vehicles might fall into this category. For the majority of computer applications, a program can be placed in any appropriate area of main storage, as long as instructions that reference specific locations are adjusted accordingly.

An assembler language program that is written for a specific area of main storage is referred to as an *absolute program.* All symbolic names in an absolute program correspond to fixed addresses in main storage. Thus, in the example below the assembler instruction ORG (for origin) tells the assembler to assemble the program so that it can be placed in main storage locations beginning with 100.

```
      ORG   100
A     EQU   6320
LP    L     A
      A     B
      .
      .
      .
```

Similarly, the assembler instruction EQU (for equivalence) tells the assembler to equate the symbol A to the machine address 6320. As a result, the load instruction would be assembled for location 100, and the add instruction would be assembled for location 101, assuming that a word-oriented computer is involved. Note here that symbols identify addresses and not values, so that when the load instruction is generated by the assembler, its operand field contains the address 6320.

An assembler language program that is written to be loaded into an area of main storage that is not specific is referred to as a *relocatable program.* Symbols in a relocatable program refer to addresses that are relative to the beginning of the program rather than to fixed locations in main storage.

When an assembler assembles a program, it substitutes numeric operation codes for symbolic operation codes and numeric operands (such as machine addresses) for symbolic operands. Machine instructions are synthesized in this manner and are written along with control information on output media, such as cards, tapes, or disks, for subsequent loading into the computer.

Assembler Instructions

Assembler instructions, frequently referred to as *pseudo-operations,* do not always cause machine code to be generated by the assembler. As mentioned above, assembler instructions provide information to the assembler and can be grouped into four classes: 1) program control instructions, 2) symbol defining instructions, 3) data defining instructions, and 4) listing control instructions.

Program Control Instructions.   The precise manner in which the program should be assembled is specified by program control instructions. Two frequently used program control instructions are ORG and END. The ORG instruction specifies the origin, or beginning location, of a program. The END instruction denotes the end of the program.

Symbol Defining Instructions.   A symbol can be assigned a specific address or be made equivalent to the address of another symbol by using a symbol defining instruction. Two frequently used symbol defining instructions are EQU and SYN. The EQU instruction (for equate or equivalence) is used to assign an address to a symbol. The SYN instruction (for synonym or synonymous) is used to assign the address of one symbol to another symbol.

Data Defining Instructions.   Data defining instructions are used to introduce data into an assembler language program or to define storage areas for later use. Data can be specified in any of a wide variety of forms. For example, all of the following forms assign the fixed-point value 5 to the symbol FIVE:

Location	Operation	Operand
FIVE	CONST	5
FIVE	DEC	5
FIVE	DC	F'5'
FIVE	DC	B'101'

Here, DC denotes "define constant," B denotes "binary," and F denotes "fixed point." Similarly, the following instruction establishes a storage area composed of 100 fixed-point locations. DS denotes "define storage."

Location	Operation	Operand
APRI	DS	100F

Listing Control Instructions.   Listing control instructions are used in preparing the printout of the program and provide the following instructions:

1. Supply a "title" for each page of the program listing
2. Command the assembler to skip a line in the program listing
3. Command the assembler to eject the page on the line printer so that the next line printed begins on a new page

Typical listing control instructions are TITLE, SPACE, and EJECT.

Sample Assembler Language Program

As an example of the assembler instructions covered here, several parts of a hypothetical assembler language program are given below. The statements are numbered for reference.

Location	Operation	Operand	
	TITLE	'SAMPLE PROGRAM'	(1)
	ORG	2500	(2)
CRIT	EQU	7531	(3)
	L	VAL	(4)
	S	CRIT	(5)
	A	S23	(6)
	.		
	.		
	.		
	EJECT		(20)
*	THIS SEGMENT PREPARED BY A.B. JONES		(21)
IMPT	SYN	CRIT	(22)
DELTA	EQU	8000	(23)
	L	ALPHA	(24)
	S	IMPT	(25)
	.		
	.		
	.		
	SPACE	2	(70)
*	TEST PROCEDURE BEGINS HERE		(71)
	ORG	4000	(72)
	L	SUPPL+4	(73)
	.		
	.		
	.		
VAL	DC	F'67.34'	(121)
S23	DC	F'0'	(122)
ALPHA	DS	F	(123)
SUPPL	DS	50F	(124)
	END		(125)

Although this program is not complete, the general structure of an assembler language program and most assembler instructions are shown. The TITLE instruction in statement (1) specifies a title that is printed at the top of each page of the listing. The ORG instruction in statement (2) tells the assembler to assign addresses to the program beginning with 2500. The EQU instruction in statement (3) assigns the address 7531 to the symbol CRIT. When CRIT is used as an operand in a symbolic instruction, the assembler uses 7531 in the address field of the corresponding machine instruction. In the computer listing of the program, the EJECT instruction in statement (20) would cause subsequent printing to begin on the top of the next page. The SYN instruction in statement (22) specifies that the symbol IMPT should be assigned the same address as CRIT, that is, 7531. Statements (121) and (122) specify fixed-point constants. Statement (123) reserves one storage location and assigns it the name ALPHA. Statement (124) reserves 50 locations and assigns the symbolic name SUPPL to the beginning address. The END instruction in statement (125) denotes the end of the program.

Address Arithmetic

Statement (73) in the sample program gives the instruction:

    L   SUPPL+4

The statement specifies that something should be loaded into the accumulator. Remember that we are dealing with addresses in assembler language, and the objective is to generate machine language instructions. Thus, the operand SUPPL + 4 means that the address of SUPPL plus the value 4 is generated as the address in the corresponding machine instruction.

Most versions of assembler language also permit *absolute addresses* to be used. This means that a programmer can use an actual machine address as an operand in an instruction, such as

    L   6385

which means "load the contents of location 6385." Values that are to be used literally must be denoted with a special character, such as an equals sign. For example:

    L   =F'25'

is equivalent to

```
        L    V1
        .
        .
        .
V1  DC   F'25'
```

where V1 is an arbitrary name.

Comment Lines

The preceding program includes statements with an asterisk (*) in the first column of the line. These are comment lines that are ignored by the assembler. A comment line is normally used by a programmer to include descriptive information.

A Final Remark

The preceding information represents a general overview of assembler language. Most data processing persons do not use assembler language; however, the basic concepts should be recognized for dealing effectively with programmers who must use it for special applications.

LANGUAGE PROCESSORS

One of the most important factors contributing to the widespread use of assembler language and of programming languages is that much of the detail of programming can be subordinated to another computer program, known as a "language processor." A *language processor* is a program that accepts another program as input; the output of a language processor is either a translated version of the input program or a set of computed results. The concept is an important one because a computer system is a complicated device for which preparing a program that can control it in an effective and useful manner is a complex task. The use of an appropriate language facilitates the programming process and allows the computer to be available to more people. The fact that a computer can help to prepare its own program—via the language processor—is a notion worthy of considerable thought, especially since the concept can be extended to several levels of program preparation.

Terminology

A program that is expressed in assembler language or in a programming language is referred to as a *source program*. The source program is read by a language processor from cards, tape, a direct-access storage device, or a terminal device via telecommunications facilities. Language processors are grouped into three categories: assemblers, compilers, and interpreters. An assembler or compiler are *language translators,* because they produce an output program, called an *object program,* that is a translated version of the source program.

Assembler language programs are translated into equivalent machine language programs. Programming language programs are translated into equivalent machine language or into assembler language programs. Most compilers produce machine language programs. Occasionally compilers are designed to produce assembler language output, which must then be run through the assembler to produce a machine language program. A program listing normally accompanies an assembly or a compilation. The program listing is used for program checking and debugging and frequently provides the machine language produced by the translation process. The object program is recorded for subsequent input to the computer for execution on cards, tape, or a direct-access storage device. The terminology of the translation process is shown in Figure 12.1.

The following sections describe the three principal language processors: assemblers, compilers, and interpreters.

Assembler Programs

An *assembler program* (usually referred to as an *assembler*) converts a program written in assembler language to an equivalent program in machine language. The translation process is called *assembly* or the *assembly process.* Assembly is usually performed in two passes over a source program. In the first pass, relative addresses are assigned to symbols in the location field. In the second pass, symbolic operation codes are replaced by internal machine codes and symbolic operands are replaced

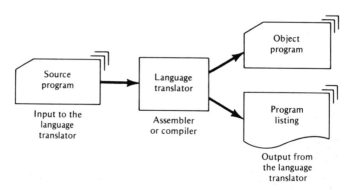

FIGURE 12.1   The language translator accepts a source program as input and produces an object program and a program listing as output.

by the corresponding addresses that were determined during pass one. The object program and the program listing are also produced during pass two. Various forms of error checking and analysis are performed during both passes.

Compiler Programs

A *compiler program* (usually referred to simply as a *compiler*) converts a program written in programming language either to machine language or to assembler language. In the second case, the resulting assembler language program must be further processed by the assembler. Figure 12.2 shows sample assembler language statements that would be generated by a single statement in a programming language. In contrast to assembly, which generates one machine instruction for each assembler language source statement, the compiler usually generates several machine instructions for each source statement in a programming language. Compilation is generally considered to be more complicated than assembly, since programming language structure tends to be more complex than assembler language structure. Although a compiler is necessarily dependent on the language being compiled, the following steps are usually involved.

1. The compiler reads the source program on a statement-by-statement basis and performs the following processing for each statement:
   a. lexical analysis to identify keywords, names, constants, punctuation characters, and so on
   b. syntactical analysis to identify the type of statement and determine that its structure is admissible
   c. places constituents of statements in lists and tables to facilitate the generation of machine code and to allow a global analysis of the program
2. A flow analysis of the program is performed to check for inter-statement errors and to provide information on how machine registers should be assigned.

Higher-Level Language	Assembler Language		
I=J*K+L	L	6,J	(Load reg. 6 with J)
	M	5,K	(Mult. regs. 5–6 by K)
	A	6,L	(Add L to reg. 6)
	ST	6,I	(Store reg. 6 in I)

FIGURE 12.2   Sample assembler language statements that would be generated for a single statement in a higher-level language.

3. Program optimization is performed and machine instructions are generated.
4. An object program and a program listing are produced.

A compiler and an assembler have one important feature in common: each has the complete source program at its disposal. Therefore, the various steps in the assembly and compilation processes can be executed at the discretion of the person designing the assembler or the compiler. Only after a source program has been completely analyzed by an assembler or compiler and an object program is produced is that object program actually executed.

Interpreter Programs

One type of language processor that allows program modification *during* execution is the interpreter. The *interpreter* is a language processor that executes a source program without producing an object program. An interpreter operates as follows:

1. The interpreter reads the source program on a statement-by-statement basis and performs the following processing for each statement:
   a. The statement is scanned, identified, analyzed, and interpreted to determine the operations that should be performed.
   b. The required operations are executed by the interpreter and the intermediate results are retained.
2. The next statement that is interpreted depends on the results of the statement just executed (such as in the case of a GOTO statement).

Although different interpreters vary in internal design, the key point is that an object program is not produced and that all statements are not necessarily processed by the interpreter. The interpretive technique is frequently used with a simple, easy-to-use language (such as a desk calculator language) or in an operational environment (such as time-sharing) where programs are not likely to be rerun many times.

Translation and Execution

In most cases a language translator and the program it produces run on the same computer, and the normal sequence of operations is:

1. Translate source program to object program.
2. Load object programs into main storage.
3. Execute the programs loaded in step 2.

The translation process, however, is not restricted to the computer on which the object program is to be executed. In some cases, a program is assembled or compiled on one computer and executed on another. The only restriction is that the format of the object program and the computer on which it is executed must correspond. An example of a case where translation and execution take place on different computers occurs with some small military computers that do not contain the necessary capability to support the translation process. In these cases, an assembler program designed to produce object programs for the smaller computer is programmed to run on a larger general-purpose system with the capability to translate.

An assembler that runs on a general-purpose computer to generate a machine language program for another computer is called a *cross assembler.* Similarly, a compiler that runs on a general-purpose computer to generate a machine language program for another computer is called a *cross compiler.*

Vocabulary

absolute program	listing control instruction
address arithmetic	location field
assembler	machine instruction
assembler instruction	macro
assembler language	object program
comment	operand field
compiler	operation field
cross assembler	program control instruction
cross compiler	pseudo operation
data defining instruction	relocatable program
interpreter	sequence number
language processor	source program
language translator	symbol defining instruction
list	

Questions and Exercises

1. Give three computer applications for which the use of assembler language would be appropriate. Characterize these applications. Can you draw any conclusions?

2. Develop a set of assembler language statements to perform the following calculation:

    $$PAY = RATE \times HOURS \times 1.5 + BONUS$$

3. What purpose does the "operation field" serve?

4. Distinguish between a machine instruction and an assembler instruction.

5. What kind of instruction would be used to print the name of a source program on each page of the listing of an assembler language program?

6. What is the difference between the following statements:
    A = SUPPL+4
    L   SUPPL+4
7. What characteristics do assemblers and compilers have in common?
8. Distinguish between lexical and syntactical analysis.

Related Reading

Graham, R. M. *Principles of Systems Programming.* New York: John Wiley and Sons, 1975.

Lee, J. A. N. *The Anatomy of a Compiler.* New York: Van Nostrand Reinhold, 1967.

Wegner, P. *Programming Languages, Information Structures, and Machine Organization.* New York: McGraw-Hill Book Company, 1968.

Operating Environment

he notion of computer operations and associated software was presented in an earlier chapter. This chapter provides additional information on the interrelationship between the computer software, the operation of the computer, and the required organizational structure. Some of the related concepts implied in earlier chapters are clarified here.

THE CONCEPT OF A JOB

Although it would be convenient to give instructions to the computer system with some means of verbal input, it is not feasible using today's technology. Therefore, instructions must be entered through one of the input devices. In this section, punched cards are used to illustrate how programs and instructions are entered into the operating system.

Control Information

The work performed by the computer for one user in one time span is called a *job*. A *job* is a single run on the computer. The operating system needs the following information to run a job:

1. Identity of the user
2. Control information
3. Program(s)
4. Data

The control information tells the operating system what the user wants the computer to do. The operating system reads the control information and initiates the execution of programs that perform the required functions.

Deck Setup

Figure 13.1 shows the deck setup for a hypothetical operating system. The $JOB card identifies the users and provides accounting information telling whom to charge for the execution of the job. The $COBOL card tells the operating system to read in the COBOL compiler from magnetic tape or disk. The statements of the COBOL program are read by the COBOL compiler, and the machine language program that results from the compilation is placed on disk or magnetic tape for subsequent loading and execution. A print out of the program is produced as a by-product so that the user has a record of the program. The print out is also used for testing and debugging the program.

Normally, a program such as the compiler passes control back to the operating system to read the next "control" card. In this case, the next card is the $LOAD card, which causes the loader program to be read in. The loader program loads the machine language program, previously placed on magnetic tape or disk, into main storage and turns program control over to it for execution. Now the user program has control of the computer. It reads its own data and produces computer results, as mentioned previously. When the user program has completed its execution, it exits the operating system for the next job, and the above process is repeated.

Operational Procedures

Each computer center has its own operational procedures, and how a user submits a job differs widely. In some centers, card decks are placed on a table outside the computer room. In others, the user submits his or her deck through a window established for that purpose. When the computer is in a remote location, a messenger may pick up jobs at a central station and transport them to the computer. Results are normally returned in the same manner.

Batch Processing

In the computer room, a computer operator collects a set of jobs and enters them into the computer as a "batch of jobs." The entire process is referred to as *batch processing.* In most modern computer installations,

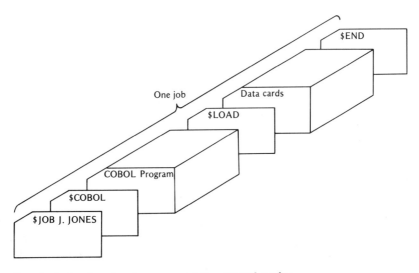

FIGURE 13.1   **Sample deck setup showing representative control cards.**

jobs are read in and placed on disk storage. When the operating system needs the next job, it goes to disk storage to get it.

An example of a batch of jobs might be a payroll job, an inventory job, an engineering computation, and a file maintenance and update run. A set of jobs such as these would be executed in a sequence based, at least in part, upon the order the jobs were submitted for execution at the computer center.

THE OPERATING SYSTEM

The *operating system* is a set of programs designed to manage the resources of the computer system and to provide job-to-job transition. These programs are frequently referred to as *control programs,* since they control the operation of the entire computer system. Although operating systems vary widely between installations and computer vendors, there are four types of facilities, or routines, that are usually provided: system management, job management, data management, and user service.

System Management

System management routines control the operation of the computer system and provide logical interface between the hardware and the other routines of the operating system. System management routines monitor hardware functions, perform actual input/output operations, schedule jobs for execution, control peripheral input/output devices, allocate main storage, and handle abnormal conditions that arise during computation.

Job Management

Job management routines provide a logical interface between a job (processing program) and the system management routines. Job management routines control and monitor the execution of a job, read control cards, and handle job terminations.

Data Management

Data management routines provide a software interface between processing programs and external storage. Data management routines control data transfer operations, maintain catalogs and libraries, manage input/output device assignment, and allocate space on mass-storage devices.

Even though data management is generally concerned with input and output, it uses system management functions for that purpose so that all input and output is managed on a system-wide basis.

User Service

User service routines comprise utility programs, necessary for using a computer system, and service programs that facilitate the programming process. Utility programs include disk initialization, core dumps, card-to-tape, diagnostics, and so on. Service programs perform sort/merge, editing, loading, and many other similar functions.

Multiprogramming

Early operating systems were characterized by the fact that jobs were loaded into main storage and executed on a sequential basis. In spite of automatic job-to-job transition and input/output systems, normal delays in the processing of a job caused the central processing unit (CPU) to "wait" for intermittent short periods of time and resulted in ineffective use of main storage. Modern operating systems (see Figure 13.2) utilize a technique known as *multiprogramming* to allow several jobs to share the resources of the computer system and to allow card reading, printing, and punching to proceed simultaneously with system operation. In a multiprogramming system, a scheduler routine gives control of the central processing unit to another program when the executing program encounters a *natural wait*—such as when waiting for an input operation. Thus, the more expensive units in the system are fully utilized. Input jobs are maintained in a queue on direct-access storage and output is maintained in a similar queue on the same or another device. When the operating system needs another job to process, it is selected from the input queue on either a sequential or priority basis.

Remote Job Entry/Remote Job Output

Batch processing causes delays. First, a user's job must be transported to the central computer and entered into the system. Next, the job must wait in the input queue until its turn for processing. Last, the output queue must be printed or punched and the results sent back to the originator. A recent technique known as *remote job entry* allows a job to be transported from a remote location to the central computer over ordinary telephone lines. An analogous technique, known as *remote*

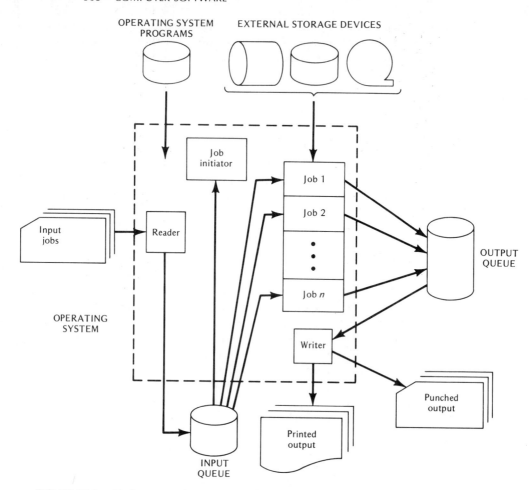

FIGURE 13.2   **Modern operating system environment.**

job output, provides a means for sending results back to the originator over telephone lines. The user, or originator, must have an appropriate terminal device for sending and receiving information from the central computer.

When using remote job entry, a job enters the input queue directly and "people" delays are avoided. This technique is frequently employed when a centralized computer is used to provide service to offices in different locations.

TIME SHARING

Although remote job entry/remote job output solves some of the problems of transporting programs and data to and from the central computer, the scheduling bottleneck at the computer still causes delays—especially when small one-shot programs are involved. *Time sharing* allows the user at a remote location to enter into a conversation with the computer (figuratively speaking) using, again, a terminal device and telephone lines.

Characteristics of Time Sharing

In a time-sharing system, computer time is scheduled differently than in an operating system. When time sharing, each user is given a short burst (called a *time slice*) of computer time on a periodic basis. The computer switches between programs so fast that the user is given the illusion that he has the computer to himself. In reality, however, he is sharing the computer with many other users. Time sharing is most frequently used during program development by professional programmers and problem solvers, such as analysts, scientists, or engineers, or to enter or retrieve information from the system on a demand basis. Time sharing is particularly useful in an academic environment. A student can sit at a terminal and, within a short period of time, solve an assigned problem using the computer. The greatest benefit of time sharing is that when an error is encountered, it can be corrected immediately so that progress on the problem can continue. When using batch processing, an error is discovered only when a completed job is returned to the user. If an error occurs at least one more run must be made to correct the error.

Figure 13.3 shows the terminal printout for a typical time-sharing terminal session. Four major steps are involved:

1. *Sign-on.* The user establishes a data connection to the computer and identifies himself to the system.
2. *Program initiation.* The user specifies that he wants to use an old program or prepare a new one. The user also gives the name of the new program so that it may be retrieved from or stored in a library (on direct-access storage) for easy access.
3. *Program preparation.* The user enters a new program on a statement-by-statement basis or enters modifications or corrections to an old program.
4. *Program execution.* The program is actually executed by the computer.

A user may run one program or several programs. In other words, user needs may change depending on the results obtained. The concept of a job does not apply and the notion of a terminal session is used instead. A *terminal session* is the time between when a user first signs on to the computer and when the user finally logs off. A terminal session may extend from minutes to hours. The important thing is that the computer is not idly waiting while a user is thinking about what he wants to do next; it is doing work for other users. This is

[User dials computer and makes line connection.]

```
HELLO
GOOD MORNING ON AT 9:13 MON.          Sign-on and user identification pro-
   06-11-73                              cedure
USER NUMBER? 08520
SYSTEM? BASIC                          User chooses BASIC language and a
NEW OR OLD? NEW                          new program named FACT.
NAME? FACT
READY                                  Computer is ready to accept program


100  PRINT "ENTER K"
110  INPUT K
120  LET F = 1
130  FOR I = 1 TO K
140  LET F = F*I
150  NEXT I
160  PRINT K; "FACTORIAL ="; F         Program to compute K factorial,
170  PRINT                               entered by user.
180  GO TO 100
190  END
RUN
FACT 9:30 MON. 06-11-73
ENTER K                                User enters data
?4
   4 FACTORIAL = 24                    Result
ENTER K
?6
   6 FACTORIAL = 720
ENTER K
?0
   0 FACTORIAL = 1
ENTER K                                User terminates input loop
?STOP

TIME 1 SEC.                            Central processing unit time
```

FIGURE 13.3   Sample terminal session for a time-sharing system.

what is known as time sharing—people are sharing time on the computer.

Time Sharing System

A time-sharing system is similar in concept to the operating system discussed earlier in this chapter. System management routines manage the resources of the computer system and determine which user programs use the central processing unit and when they use it. Job management routines read and interpret control information supplied by people from terminals. Data management routines manage input and output operations and maintain libraries of programs on direct-access storage. When people want to use one of their programs, all they need to do is supply its name; data management routines make the program available for use. The basic objective is different, however. In an operating system, the objective is to keep the computer busy and to get as much work done by the computer as possible. In a time-sharing system, the objective is to keep the user busy and the time-sharing system is designed to provide that service. A time-sharing system provides a more people-oriented service, but this service is costly because computer resources are used in switching between users.

Users

There are many users of a time-sharing system. A distinction must be made, however, between the users who *can* use the system and the users who *are* using the system at any point in time. The time-sharing system contains a list (or a table) of the identification codes of people who can use the system. The number of identification codes may be as large as 2,000. At any point in time, however, only a small subset of these people can be actively using the computer. Large time-sharing systems allow as many as 200 active users. A small time-sharing system may limit the number of active users to between five and ten.

For purposes of demonstration, assume a time-sharing system with 100 active users. The number 50 would work just as well. The programs of 100 users could not possibly occupy main storage at one time. Therefore system management routines must manage main storage on a dynamic basis, and programs and data must be moved back and forth between main storage and direct-access storage. This process is referred to as *swapping*. When a person requests the services of the computer, his programs and data must be "swapped in." When main storage space is needed for another user, programs and data must be "swapped out." Swapping takes computer time and requires space on direct-access media.

Scheduling

Another function that must be performed by system management routines is scheduling. Active users can be placed into three groups:

1. *Active*—user's program currently being executed
2. *Ready*—user's program waiting to use the computer
3. *Waiting*—programs "inactive" because the computer is waiting for the user to respond.

Active and ready programs can use the central processing unit. A program is placed in the "waiting" group when the computer issues a "read" instruction to a user's terminal. In the time it takes a user to read and react to a message from the computer, several programs can be serviced.

There are several methods of scheduling in time-sharing systems. A straightforward method is given here. "Ready" programs are given control of the central processing unit on a round-robin basis. The technique operates as follows: a small value, such as 100 milliseconds, is put into a computer timer. Then the central processing unit is turned over to a program. The program executes and the timer counts down. When the timer reaches zero or the program needs input data, the program's time slice is over and the central processing unit is given to the next program on the ready list. As shown in Figure 13.4, several activities are taking place at any point in time in a time-sharing system:

1. A program that has finished its time slice is being swapped out.
2. A program is currently going through a time slice.
3. A program is being swapped in for its next time slice.

The computer goes through the procedure so rapidly that there is no appreciable delay in response time, that is, the time it takes the computer to respond to a person's input. There is a saturation point, however. When the number of users passes the saturation point, response time increases markedly. A typical response-time curve of a time-sharing system is shown in Figure 13.5.

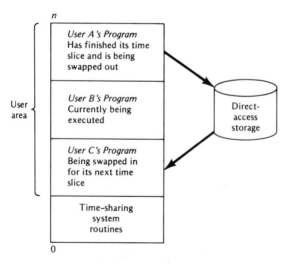

FIGURE 13.4 Simplified diagram of main storage in a time-sharing system.

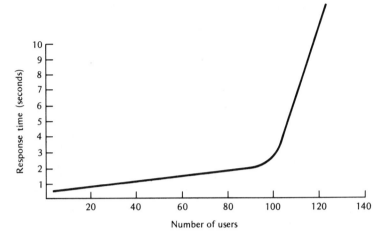

FIGURE 13.5   **Response-time curve for a typical time-sharing system.**

Classification of Time-Sharing Systems

Time-sharing systems are classed as either closed or open. A *closed system* provides computer service exclusively through one or two programming languages. An *open system* allows the user at a remote terminal to utilize all facilities of the computer system, including assembler language, a variety of input/output devices, and data management capabilities. Most time-sharing facilities provide closed service since the intended audience are general users, such as engineers, analysts, or students. An open system is slightly more complicated and is intended for the professional programmer.

Many organizations employ large-scale computers for data processing applications and continually strive to use them more efficiently. The bread-and-butter jobs, such as payroll and inventory control, are run in a multiprogramming mode of operation. Time-sharing service is provided for technical problem solving and for program development in one of three ways: (1) in conjunction with multiprogramming on the same computer; (2) through an "in-house" computer system dedicated to time sharing; or (3) from an outside time-sharing service. Time-sharing service companies frequently offer relatively low rates because of a competitive market situation.

THE COMPUTER INSTALLATION

It is probably not necessary to state that people are needed to utilize computers effectively. As in any other occupation, there are "divisions of labor," job classifications, specialists, clerks, and so on. In fact, many well-thought-out computer applications, such as magazine subscription systems, are turned into chaotic situations by the conflicts and misunderstandings of the people involved. Even in the simplest case where an engineer, analyst, or student prepares his or her own program, a computer operator is needed to actually run the program on the computer. At the opposite extreme, the manager of accounts receivable in the accounting department may come to the computer department with the intuitive feeling that a well-designed program would help in performing the work for which he or she is responsible. This person needs much more than an operator. He or she needs someone to determine what should be done, someone to prepare and debug the program, someone to prepare the data for the program, and someone to run the program on a periodic basis. Most computer applications fall somewhere in between these examples, and since most college graduates these days have some exposure to the computer, they can appreciate what is involved.

The People Problem

Computers and data processing are regarded as a high technology area in the sense that a person has to know something about the subject to get something done. There are areas in modern society where an unknowledgeable person can stumble along with the hope that everything will eventually turn out all right. In the area of data processing, the opposite result is very likely to take place. Another important point is that, sooner or later, difficulty is encountered with most computer applications. The operator goofs and mounts the wrong tape or drops a deck of cards. The program has a logic error that is not detected until the program is in production for two years. A clerical person prepares the data incorrectly. A systems analyst, through a misunderstanding with the problem originator, inadvertently omits one of the cases that can arise. When a program "bombs out," as they say, everyone involved has a tendency to blame someone else. The programmer blames the operator; the systems analyst blames the programmer; the problem originator blames the systems analyst; and everyone blames the clerk. The solution, naturally, is an organization chart and precise job descriptions.

Data Processing Department

Figure 13.6 gives an organization chart for a typical data processing installation. *Data processing managers* are responsible for the personnel and equipment in their departments. This is typically a management position, and the data processing manager spends much time with

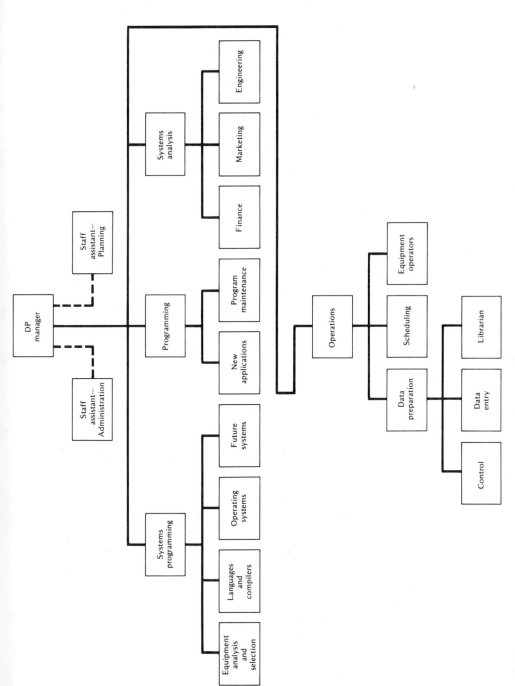

FIGURE 13.6   Organization chart of a typical data processing department.

budgets, planning, and personnel responsibilities. The data processing department primarily performs a service function for the organization and the data processing manager owes allegiance to the total organization. Departments such as finance, marketing, and engineering are the customers of the data processing department, and the data processing manager serves as an administrative link between these departments and cost/effective computer utilization. The data processing manager uses administrative and planning assistants at the staff level for tasks that range from ordering supplies to producing five-year plans for the department. The data processing department is typically organized into four areas: systems programming, systems analysis, programming, and operations.

Systems Programming.   *Systems programming* is responsible for the following technical functions:

1. Equipment analysis and selection.
2. Development, acquisition, and effective utilization of programming languages, compilers, and applications systems.
3. Selecting and maintaining operating systems and time-sharing facilities.
4. Development of technical specifications for future computers, systems, and applications.
5. Establishment of programming standards.

Systems programming is primarily a technical area. The most experienced programmers and systems analysts tend to be "promoted into" the systems programming group. The work in the systems programming group is usually computer-oriented, and the personnel are regarded as computer specialists.

Systems Analysis.   *Systems analysis* is responsible for computer-based systems that support the activities of other departments. For example, in the billing department, a systems analysis would analyze and describe the flow of information from a credit purchase to payment, which might include the following stages:

1. Purchase
2. Entry of purchase record to computer
3. Collection of charges
4. Preparation of bill
5. Stuffing and mailing
6. Recording of payment
7. Computer entry of payment record
8. Update of customer's record
9. Summary and reporting

The *systems analyst* would develop the optimum flow for an operation of this type and attempt to use the data processing capability of the computer whenever its use would be cost-effective for the organization. Systems analysts are applications-oriented and are not necessarily computer experts. They tend to be specialists in the area of the organization to which they apply their talents. The systems analyst normally prepares program specifications and forms layouts and serves as a communications liaison between the programmer and the problem originator. The systems analyst usually obtains projects in either of three ways:

1. The data processing manager discovers an area that might lend itself to computer processing and has a systems analyst look into it.
2. A department manager intuitively feels that a computer program or system might improve the operation and requests the services of a systems analyst.
3. The systems analyst, because of experience and interest, feels that one or more of the "systems and procedures" of the organization would benefit from in-depth study.

Programming.   *Programming* is concerned with the development of computer programs. Although practically anyone can prepare a simple program, complicated programs require the services of programming specialists who are trained to prepare programs with a minimum of wasted effort. The *programmer* is concerned with detailed specification of the program, coding, debugging, testing, and documentation. A programmer may work directly with a problem originator, such as an engineer, or with a systems analyst when many people are involved in the application, such as the billing procedure given above. Once the validity of a program has been verified, the programmer turns a program over to operations personnel for production use. For example, consider a payroll program. Once the program is complete and is turned over to operations, the programmer is not involved in day-to-day running of the program unless something goes wrong.

Operations.   *Operations* personnel are organized into data preparation, scheduling, and equipment operators. *Data preparation personnel* are concerned with the paperwork both into and out of the computer, such as data entry and keypunching. Most data preparation sections also have a librarian who records the status of production programs and data files. *Scheduling personnel* are concerned with the running of production programs. Most organizations have certain programs that must be run on a regular basis, such as payroll, billing, and inventory control programs. *Equipment operators* actually operate the computer equipment. Normal functions performed by an operator are:

1. Starting the computer and loading the systems programs
2. Mounting tapes and disk packs

3. Responding to informational requests from the operating system
4. Entering jobs into the computer
5. Recognizing when the computer is malfunctioning and calling repair personnel

Each of the areas of the data processing department has a hierarchy. For example, there are junior programmers, associate programmers, lead programmers, senior programmers, and programming managers.

Advancement and Management

In many large organizations, a college degree is required for programmers, systems analysts, or management personnel. This requirement has been relaxed in some small organizations because of a lack of qualified personnel. Many organizations, however, feel the requirement is good since it allows a career path to be established so that an individual is not "dead ended."

In most organizations and in most fields (engineering, accounting, and so on), the normal progression is upward through the ranks of management. This sequence does not necessarily hold in the computer field. Where it does hold, many problems exist. First, many qualified computer people decline to move into management and prefer to pursue technical careers in systems programming or systems analysis. Although many have conjectured why this is so, the most probable reason is that the computer field has progressed and is progressing very rapidly and that many people find the technical aspects interesting and challenging. Another problem is that technological obsolescence occurs very quickly—in a time span as short as five to seven years. Thus, many people who have moved into management positions find their technological knowledge obsolete in just a few years and become severely threatened by younger people with more up-to-date technical knowledge. This is a strong reason why many technical people are reluctant to move into management positions. This phenomenon will probably continue to some extent until the pace of technological advancement in the computer field begins to show signs of slowing down.

Other Computer People

The computer people mentioned here reflect a typical computer installation, which represents only one group of people in the computer field. There is also a multitude of people who design, produce, and sell computers, input and output devices, computer programs, and computer supplies. There are service bureaus that sell time-sharing service and do contract programming. The computer field also employs consultants

ONMENT9

and requires auditors. There are computer magazines, computer newspapers, and companies that specialize in used computers. Other companies produce computer furniture, computer floors, and computer security devices. There are companies that lease computers and others that will come in and run your computer installation for you. Finally, there are companies that will come and analyze how well you are running your computer.

Vocabulary The student should be familiar with the following terms in the context in which they were used in the chapter.

batch processing	operations
closed system	programming
control card	remote job entry
data preparation	remote job output
data processing manager	scheduling
equipment operators	scheduling personnel
job	systems analysis
job management	systems management
multiprogramming	systems programming
open system	time sharing

Questions and Exercises

1. Distinguish between a job and a terminal session.
2. An operating system is organized into system management, job management, data management, and user service. Generalize and try to apply the same type of structure to an organization with which you are familiar. Is the structure a "management structure" or an "operational structure"?
3. Why are sign-on procedures needed in a time-sharing system?
4. Based on the chapter, what "kind" of people would be good as:
   Data processing managers
   Systems analysts
   Programmers
   Computer operators

   Are different personalities needed? What are the problems of overtraining?
5. Prepare an organizational chart for a data processing department with which you are familiar.

Related Reading

Katzan, H. *Operating Systems: A Pragmatic Approach.* New York: Van Nostrand Reinhold, 1973.

Sanders, D. H. *Computers and Management.* New York: McGraw-Hill, 1974.

Watson, R. W. *Timesharing System Design Concepts.* New York: McGraw-Hill, 1970.

Data Management Concepts

The manner in which data is managed in a computer system and in a computer installation determines the degree to which user needs can be satisfied and governs the efficiency of an information system. Input/output and external storage devices are factors that limit the efficiency of most information-based systems, even though devices such as the channel and operational techniques such as multiprogramming are used to increase overall system performance. Therefore, the manner in which input and output are performed, the methods used for data storage and organization, and the techniques used to access data are of prime importance. Data management facilities are normally provided through the services of a computer operating system. Operating systems technology and data management go together like "bread and butter." One reason for this is that input and output operations are the biggest problem in the design of an operating system that effectively manages the use of system resources. Another related reason is that the execution of actual input and output instructions are privileged because problems and data must be protected in a multiprogramming environment. Problems and data *must* be managed by the operating system on a system-wide basis. Other reasons also exist. Modern direct-access storage devices can store millions of bytes of information, and it is convenient and efficient for operating system routines to allocate space on them. Also, because users prefer to reference data files by name, file names and attributes must be stored within the system. File names, attributes, and storage requirements are specified with control cards that are read and processed by job management routines. Data management is usually considered to be part of an operating system.

BASIC CONSIDERATIONS

In data management, a distinction is made between units of data and units of storage. Elements of data structure are scalars, arrays, and structures. For input and output operations, these elements are grouped to form *data records*—also called *logical records*. A set of related data records is called a *file*. An example of these concepts is a single employee's record in a payroll file. Most data processing and information management applications are programmed to deal with data records and files, and are, therefore, "data structure" oriented. This is desirable because programs can be developed independently of how the data is organized and on what type of media it is stored. Then, every time the data organization or media changes, the program does not have to be modified.

The computer system, on the other hand, deals with storage structures. A group of bytes or words comprise a *field*, which is the smallest unit of storage. If a field were broken down further, it would lose its meaning. For example, the characters "PRATT INSTITUTE" on a punched card refer to an entity that actually exists. The characters taken individually are simply letters of the alphabet.

A *block* that is composed of either bytes or bits is the unit of interchange between a main storage and an external storage medium. When the computer system performs a read operation, a whole block is read by the input device, even though the input operation may involve only a part of the block. When reading punched cards for example, the whole card must be read to obtain the first n columns, where n < 80. The same is true for output operations. Each time the computer system executes a write operation, a block is written by the output device. This is a simplification of the input and output processes because the computer does not "zap out" hundreds of thousands of bytes all at once. From the viewpoint of computer programs and data management routines, however, input and output operations involve blocks, and the details of data transfer are subordinated to the hardware of the input/output system.

The term block is often used interchangeably with the term *physical record,* commonly associated with magnetic tape. On tape, consecutive blocks are separated by interblock gaps and control information. On direct-access devices, a data record is recorded as either two or three blocks separated by interblock gaps and control information. A file does not necessarily occupy consecutive tracks on direct-access storage. This is because as a file grows, secondary allocations of direct-access storage space usually do not occupy tracks adjacent to previous allocations. A set of consecutive tracks on direct-access storage is referred to as an *extent.* A file on a direct-access storage medium is composed of one or more extents.

RECORD STRUCTURES

Since records and files exist for performing input and output operations, a correspondence must be made between data records and blocks. The manner in which data records correspond to blocks is referred to as *record structure,* or *data record format.* Three kinds of structure or format exist:

1. A block corresponds to one data record.
2. A block is composed of two or more data records.
3. A block contains a segment of a data record.

When one data record is stored in a block, the record is known as an *unblocked record.* When one or more data records are stored in a block, the records are known as *blocked records.* When a data record is stored in two or more blocks, the record is referred to as a *spanned record.*

Fixed-Length

Data records are grouped (or "blocked") according to one of three formats: fixed-length records, variable-length records, or undefined-length records. The size of a *fixed-length record* is constant for all data records in a block, and the size of the block is also fixed (see Figure 14.1). Fixed-length records may be blocked or unblocked.

A fixed-length record is used when the number of data values in the record do not change in the course of computer processing. A typical example would be an employee personnel record like the one shown in Figure 9.1. Even though specific values may change, the *number* of values does not change so the record always stays the same size.

Variable-Length

With *variable-length records,* the size of a data record is variable in length, and the size of the block is also variable. Normally, a maximum must be stated so that input/output buffer space can be allocated. Variable-length records are shown in Figure 14.2. The *block length* (L) is included in the block, preceding the data, so that the data management system can manipulate the data correctly. The record size (l) of a variable-length record is referred to as a *record descriptor word.* Although block and record descriptor words require storage space, the objective of variable-length records is to conserve storage space.

The basic idea is that with variable-length records the need to carry along unused fields is eliminated. Unused fields must be carried with fixed-length records. Fixed and variable-length records can be blocked or unblocked depending upon the needs of a particular application. Blocked records require less storage space on the external medium because some interblock gaps are eliminated. Also, fewer input/output

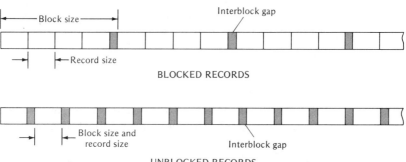

FIGURE 14.1   Fixed-length record structure.

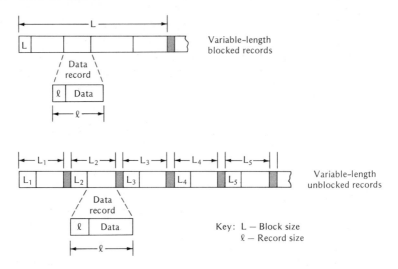

FIGURE 14.2   Variable-length record structure.

operations are required since the execution of a single operation involves the transfer of several data records. On the other hand, the use of blocked records involves increased buffer space and requires additional data manipulation functions.

A variable-length record is used when the number of data values in the record varies according to transactions handled during computer processing. A typical example would be an invoice/billing system in which the number of invoices for a customer, reflected in the customer record, would be dependent upon that customer's activity for the billing period.

Undefined-Length

Undefined-length records are allowed in many operating environments to permit the reading and writing of records that do not satisfy the specifications of fixed and variable-length processing (see Figure 14.3). When undefined-records are used, the user is responsible for performing the housekeeping tasks associated with data management.

Spanned

A *spanned record* is a record format and a blocking technique. Spanned records are used when the length of a block is fixed for some reason.

FIGURE 14.3   Conceptual view of undefined-length records.

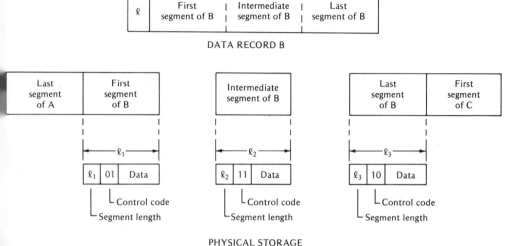

Control codes:

0 — Complete data record
1 — First segment of a multi–segment record
0 — Last segment of a multi–segment record
1 — Intermediate segment of a multi–segment record

FIGURE 14.4   Spanned record.

Typical cases occur when buffer space is limited and when a record must be stored on direct-access storage that exceeds the length of a track (and no overflow feature is available). A spanned record, labeled B, is depicted in Figure 14.4. The record is composed of segments that occupy three consecutive blocks. The data contained in each segment is preceded by a "segment length" field (l) and a "control code" number that allows the record to be processed by data management routines.

BASIC DATA MANAGEMENT FUNCTIONS

Apart from input and output, which can be considered as basic system operations, data management routines perform two basic functions: blocking/deblocking and buffering. *Blocking* is the process of grouping data records to form a block. The reverse process is known as *deblocking*. Blocking and deblocking are performed by data management routines that are invoked by assembler language macro instructions or by statements in a programming language that cause the same basic function to be performed.

Data management routines enable users to perceive their files as a series of data records, and the blocking and deblocking processes are transparent to them. Blocked input is a good example. When the first logical record in a block is referenced by an application program, the entire block is read from external storage and the first data record of the block is passed to the program. When the following records in that block are referenced, data management does not have to perform a read operation, and simply returns the next sequential data record in that block to the requesting program. For output, a block is not written until it is filled with data records.

The process of reading and writing blocks is made more efficient by buffering. A *buffer* is a storage area used to compensate for a difference in the operating speeds of two devices. An *input buffer* is an area of storage used to hold input blocks prior to processing. Blocks are read ahead of time so that when a data management routine needs a block, it is already in storage. An *output buffer* is an area of storage used to hold blocks prior to an output operation. Data management routines initiate the filling of a new block as soon as the preceding one has been filled and without waiting for the associated write operation to be completed. Buffering allows the processing unit to effectively utilize the input-output-compute overlap capability provided by an input/data channel.

FILE ORGANIZATION

Data files are organized according to the manner in which they are used. There are four methods of file organization: sequential, direct, indexed sequential, and partitioned.

Sequential

Sequential organization means that the data records of a file must be referenced in a manner dependent upon the sequence in which the data records are physically stored. Card decks and magnetic tape files are always organized sequentially. Files on direct-access storage devices are frequently, but not necessarily, organized in this manner.

Direct

Direct organization means that a data record may be referenced without "passing over" or referencing preceding information. Data records are located by their physical position on the direct-access storage volume.

Indexed Sequential

Indexed sequential organization permits data records in a file to be referenced sequentially or directly. The defining characteristic of an indexed sequential file is that data records are arranged logically by collating sequence, according to a *key field* contained in each record. Indexes of keys are maintained to provide either direct or sequential access.

When an indexed sequential file is referenced sequentially, the keys in an index are processed in order. Each key is associated with the physical location on a direct-access storage volume of the corresponding data record. When an indexed sequential file is referenced directly, the key is looked up in the index (which is analogous to a table) to determine the physical location of the desired record. Data files with indexed sequential organization must reside on a direct-access volume.

Partitioned

Partitioned organization denotes a data file that is divided into sequentially organized members. Each member is composed of data records. A partitioned data file is a file of files. Each file is assigned a name (such as the name of a program) and each name is stored in a directory, along with the physical location of the beginning of the member. The directory is stored along with the file. After a member is located, the data records are referenced as though that member were organized sequentially. Partitioned files are usually used to store programs.

FILE ACCESS

Two different techniques are used for transferring data between main storage and an external storage medium. These techniques are referred to as *access methods* and are implemented as *access routines* supplied by the data management subsystem of the operating system. The access routines are available through macro instructions recognized by the assembler system. Access methods are classified according to their treatment of buffering and input/output synchronization with processing. The two methods are called queued access and basic access.

Queued Access

The *queued access* technique provides automatic blocking and deblocking on data transfers between main storage and input/output devices. Queued access also provides "look-ahead" buffering and automatic synchronization of input/output operation and processing. This access method routine controls the use of buffers so that sufficient input blocks are in storage at one time to prevent delays in processing unit operation. When using queued access, the user need not test for input/output completion, errors, or exceptional conditions. After completion of an input or output macro instruction, control is not returned to the processing program until the operation is logically complete.

Basic

The *basic access* technique does not provide automatic blocking and de-blocking, nor does it provide anticipatory buffering or automatic event synchronization. Basic access is used when the sequence in which records are processed cannot be predicted in advance. With the basic access technique, users must perform their own blocking and deblocking. Moreover, input and output macro instructions only initiate input/output processing; both operations must be checked for completion with an appropriate macro instruction.

Vocabulary   The student should be familiar with the following terms in the context in which they were used in the chapter.

basic access	indexed sequential organization
block	input buffer
blocked record	logical record
blocking	output buffer
buffer	partitioned organization
buffering	physical record
data structure	queued access
deblocking	record structure
direct organization	sequential organization
extent	spanned record
field	storage structure
file	unblocked record
file access	undefined-length record
file organization	variable-length record
fixed-length record	

Questions
1. How do the following features relate to data management: data channel, supervisor state, and interruption?
2. In what way are the concepts of blocking and buffering similar? In what way are they different?
3. What is the basic objective of variable-length records?
4. When is a spanned record used?
5. What are the operational differences between basic and queued access?

Related Reading
Chapin, N. *Computers: A Systems Approach.* New York: Van Nostrand Reinhold, 1971.

Katzan, H. *Computer Data Management and Data Base Technology.* New York: Van Nostrand Reinhold, 1975.

Kindred, A. R. *Data Systems Management: An Introduction to Systems Analysis and Design.* Englewood Cliffs, N.J.: Prentice-Hall, 1973.

Part

5

Systems and Applications

System Development Life Cycle

INTRODUCTION

ost applications evolve through a set of successive stages from initial conception of the system idea to final cessation of system utilization. The set of stages is known as the *system life cycle*. A high degree of similarity exists between the stages of development of the different systems, especially in the areas of computers, data processing, and information systems. Martin Rubin[1] lists the eight stages in the system life cycle as:

1. Conception
2. Preliminary analysis
3. System design
4. Programming
5. System documentation
6. System installation
7. System operation
8. System cessation

The above stages only approximate the real situation and serve as a general model for organization and planning. For example, the class of activities generally known as "controlling and implementing the solution"[2] is not included in the system life cycle. The practicalities of system development are such that the solution (or system) must be monitored and controlled because it may lose some of its effectiveness due to changes in the operating environment. The process of monitoring and controlling the effectiveness of a system necessarily involves a feedback cycle, which is not included in Rubin's system life cycle. The need for monitoring and control may become necessary as a result of three possible conditions:

1. A previously irrelevant system variable may become relevant.
2. The value of one or more system variables may change and affect the operational logic of the system.
3. The functional components of the system may change or need to be adjusted.

Thus, the feedback cycle is a practical reality that can be viewed both from within the life cycle and from outside the life cycle in its operating

1. Rubin, M. L., *Handbook of Data Processing* (Princeton: Brandon/Systems Press, 1970), vol. 1, p. 4.
2. See Churchman, C. W., et al., *Introduction to Operations Research* (New York: John Wiley and Sons, 1974), pp. 595–622.

environment. Because of this, the design and development methodology does not include methods for describing this aspect of the system development life cycle.

CONCEPTION

The *conception stage* is used to determine whether or not a need exists for a new system. The need can be recognized by the system design and development group (for example, the data processing department) or by the organization that the new system is to service. In the latter case, the manager involved is usually aware of a need, but is not certain whether a new or improved system is feasible. The conception stage is formalized when the systems department and the operational group meet to identify the specific need and to determine whether the systems approach supports the goals of the organization.

When a new system is to exist as a product or service, the conception stage will be a preliminary market analysis and a summarization of the relevant business conditions. In organizations that normally deal in products and services, ideas for "new business" occur frequently, and the conception stage serves to sort out ideas that warrant further study. The conception stage is summarized in Figure 15.1.

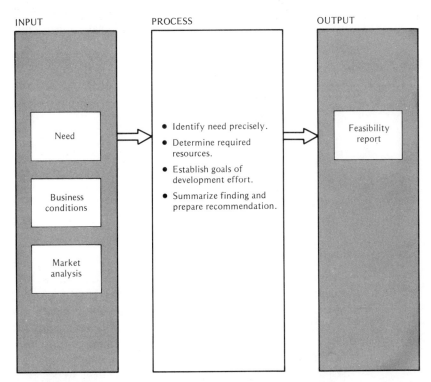

INPUT   PROCESS   OUTPUT

Need

Business
conditions

Market
analysis

- Identify need precisely.
- Determine required resources.
- Establish goals of development effort.
- Summarize finding and prepare recommendation.

Feasibility
report

FIGURE 15.1   **Overview diagram of the conception stage of the system life cycle.**

The result of the conception stage of the system life cycle is usually a report to the sponsoring department that summarizes the needs, resources, and other pertinent information about the proposed system. The report serves as a medium for deciding whether to pursue the proposed system development effort or to drop the idea altogether.

PRELIMINARY ANALYSIS

Preliminary analysis is popularly known as the "feasibility study" and is primarily concerned with three areas:

1. The characteristics of the present system or operating environment
2. Whether a new system should be developed or the present system should be revised
3. Whether the proposed system is viable for the sponsoring organization

The preliminary analysis function is usually performed by a systems analyst assisted by management participation of the sponsoring organization—either through direct participation or by permitting the analyst to work through members of the sponsoring organization. Figure 15.2 gives an overview of the preliminary analysis stage of the system life cycle.

Inputs

Inputs to the preliminary design stage are:

1. Characteristics of the current system
2. Ideas for the proposed system
3. Organization factors
4. Financial considerations

Characteristics of the current system are determined through existing documentation. In the event that documentation does not exist, an extensive analysis is done by the systems analyst. This is an instance in the system life cycle in which effective documentation of the existing system is important for ongoing analysis. Detailed documentation is not necessary, but a general description of the system at the "overview" level is required. *Ideas for the proposed system* are obtained by the analyst as a separate step or as a by-product of the need to describe the existing system. This step is particularly significant when proposed changes

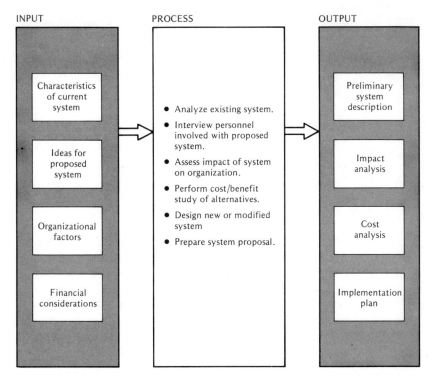

INPUT   PROCESS   OUTPUT

Characteristics
of current
system

Ideas for
proposed
system

Organizational
factors

Financial
considerations

- Analyze existing system.
- Interview personnel involved with proposed system.
- Assess impact of system on organization.
- Perform cost/benefit study of alternatives.
- Design new or modified system
- Prepare system proposal.

Preliminary
system
description

Impact
analysis

Cost
analysis

Implementation
plan

FIGURE 15.2   **Overview diagram of the preliminary design stage of the system life cycle.**

to an existing system are planned. In many cases, actual users of a system are the only ones who are aware of its deficiencies. It is also important to recognize that many users of a system are unaware of the potentialities of a new system and also tend to express the needs, limitations, and deficiencies of the system in their own language. *Organization factors,* which unfortunately are often ignored, include: organizational politics, resistance to change, previous experience with systems work, and the type of employees involved. Organizational factors can "make or break" a system effort if left unrecognized, but generally do not result in organizational problems if considered during the preliminary analysis stage. *Financial considerations* normally include the cost of the current system and standard implementation costs. Expected implementation costs are used to determine how much the proposed system development effort will cost in terms of the organization's resources.

Objectives

The objectives of the preliminary analysis stage are: (1) to investigate the feasibility of developing a system to satisfy the needs identified during the conception stage, and (2) if a new or modified system is both desirable and practical, to propose an effective system that satisfies the stated needs. The functions performed in the preliminary analysis stage usually include:

1. *Analyze* existing system.
2. *Interview* personnel involved with the proposed system.
3. *Assess* impact of new or modified system on the organization.
4. *Perform* cost/benefit study of alternatives.
5. *Design* new or modified system.
6. *Prepare* system proposal.

The specific functions performed by the analyst during the preliminary analysis stage are self-explanatory and are not discussed further. (Interested readers are referred to a reference on the system life cycle, such as Rubin[3] or Benjamin).[4] When data processing is involved in the systems evaluation, then a special effort should be made to determine the optimum resolution of the problem rather than the course of action that would invariably lead to automation. Clearly, the feasibility study may simply reinforce the use of manual procedures.

Outputs

The outputs of the preliminary analysis stage are:

1. Preliminary system description
2. Impact analysis
3. Cost analysis
4. Implementation plan

Each of the four outputs is important, but can realistically be presented to management at different times, depending upon organizational factors. The *preliminary system description* and the cost analysis are the primary inputs to the management decision-making process and effectively determine whether a proposal is accepted or rejected. The two main reasons that system proposals are accepted by management are increased functional capability and reduced cost. At this point, when management is concerned with function and not specific design details, many propos-

3. Rubin, *op cit.*, pp. 19–59.
4. Benjamin.

als are rejected solely on the basis of cost because the functional capability of the system is not clearly understood. In short, the analyst is presenting structure and implementation in the preliminary description rather than function. Required equipment and personnel can be included either in the preliminary system description or in the cost analysis. *Impact analysis* concerns the effect of the proposed system upon organizational operations. In the case of a product or service the impact analysis provides justification for the proposed system in the form of a competitive analysis. *Cost analysis* includes both development costs and operational costs, in addition to a summarization of current costs in the case of an already existing in-house system. In the case of a product or service, the cost analysis would necessarily include expected return on investment, a cost/value analysis, and a study of any risk factors involved. The *implementation plan* is intended to summarize needed resources and establish dates and schedules. It is necessary for the system design and development stages, because of its importance in the success or failure of a systems effort. In short, the implementation plan outlines the remainder of the system life cycle for management comments, suggestions, and approval.

SYSTEM DESIGN

The system design stage of the system life cycle is concerned with the hierarchical structure of the system: the functions that are performed at each level and by each component of the system. The system design effort utilizes the preliminary system description, developed during the feasibility study, and molds that description into a set of design specifications that can be used during the development stage.
  System design involves five major functions:

1. Analysis of system objectives and respecification of these objectives as design constraints
2. Investigation of possible modes of system operation and requirements for physical facilities
3. Establishment of the operational capability of the system and physical equipment needed.
4. Specification of the functional structure of the system and development of a precise description of each system component
5. Documentation of the design of the system

Figure 15.3 gives an overview diagram of the design stage of the system life cycle.

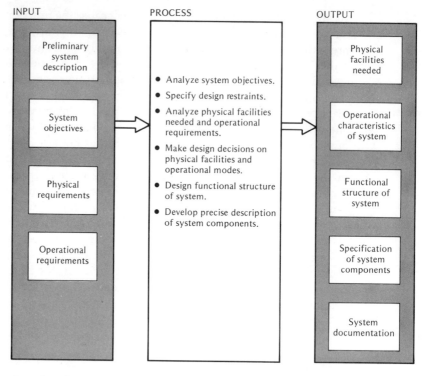

INPUT   PROCESS   OUTPUT

FIGURE 15.3   Overview diagram of the design stage of the system life cycle.

Inputs

Inputs to the design stage include four major items:

1. Preliminary system description, mentioned above
2. System objectives
3. Physical requirements
4. Operational requirements

The set of *system objectives* governs the design of a system and aids in insuring that the system that management decides upon is the same system that will be produced. The objectives may be contained in the preliminary system description or they may be developed by the system designer. The system objectives may also specify the inputs and outputs of the system, although sometimes at a relatively high level.

In a data processing system, for example, a common objective might be to generate a particular type of management report, which may implicitly dictate that a particular kind of information system be developed from which that report can be obtained. The task of determining the necessary modes of system operation and the physical facilities needed may require that the system designer investigate the possible modes in which the system can operate and the equipment needed to sustain that type of operation. The investigation may additionally include a study of how inputs to the system will be obtained and how outputs will be used. The investigation phase can be conducted through interviews, questionnaires, and reports. To sum up, if the necessary inputs to the design stage are not available beforehand, then the designer must obtain them.

Design decisions regarding physical facilities and operational requirements are based on the preliminary system description, design objectives, and the information obtained in the investigation of physical and operational capabilities. Physical facilities characteristically take the form of computer and storage requirements, physical space needed, and vehicles that will be available. Operational requirements involve the manner in which the physical facilities are used and how information will be organized and accessed. The physical and operational specifications for a system serve as the external description of the system.

The process of specifying the functional structure of a system that will provide the required operational capability through the physical facilities is called a *systems design.* The hierarchical structure of the components that comprise the system is usually given, and each component is described in detail. The inputs, outputs, and internal logic of each component are defined. Internal logic is usually described with equations, flow diagrams, or decision tables, and the whole system is described with a general "system" flow diagram or an input/output diagram. The internal logic of a component utilizes the previously established design decisions that concern physical facilities, operational capabilities, and information structures.

Effective documentation of a system starts at the design stage—and perhaps earlier as the preliminary system description. The objective of documentation at the design level is to give the implementation group something to work with and to provide management with the needed information for decision making. Documentation is thus an important by-product of the design phase and not an effort that takes place after the project has been completed. Another factor that is also frequently included in all phases of system design, especially documentation, is a description of the physical environment in which the system is intended to operate.

The design cycle includes feedback between the prospective user of the system and the system designer. This type of feedback is healthy and helps to insure that systems are not designed in a vacuum. After the system design phase has been completed, the prospective user of the system should have a set of specifications that are understandable and acceptable and, at the same time, are technically practical and satisfy the stated objectives of the system. The same set of specifications serve as input to the implementation stage.

SYSTEM IMPLEMENTATION

The system implementation stage is the one in which the logic and specifications of a system are put to the test of a realistic development effort. Briefly stated, the integrity of the system design is verified. It is an accepted practice for the development team to hold "structured walkthroughs," in which the logic of the system is subjected to the scrutiny of the development team in a face-to-face environment. The precise nature of the implementation stage is dependent upon the type of system being developed.

In hardware systems development, detailed logic diagrams for the components of the system are constructed before the components are built. After each component is built, it is subjected to a functional test to insure that it operates according to specifications. The various components of a system are assembled according to a pre-established plan, and the complete system is "system tested" to insure that the interfaces between the components are properly designed and that the system meets its operational objectives.

In the implementation of computer software systems, detailed diagrams of each component are constructed and the design specifications are implemented as software modules. Each module is unit tested, to insure that it functions properly, prior to integration of the modules of the system. The complete system is then system tested, as mentioned above.

Software systems development has evolved as a bottom-to-top process wherein the "lower-level" modules in the hierarchical structure of a system are implemented before "higher-level" modules (see Figure 15.4). The difficulties with bottom-to-top development are that many module interfaces must be developed simultaneously, often by more than one person, and that a driver program must be developed to perform the unit testing of a module. Bottom-to-top development is error-prone, because of the module interfaces, and integration of modules to form a complete system is cumbersome because of the fact that all modules must "come together" at the same time.

An alternate approach to systems implementation is to use top-down development (see Figure 15.5). Top-down development is considered by many to be superior to bottom-to-top development because modules are developed in a natural order from the control structures downward. No driver programs are required and the concept of a stub is employed to test module interfaces. A stub is simply a short module that displays a message stating that program control reached that module and then returns to the calling program. One of the primary advantages of top-down development is that the system is always operable, so an integration effort is not required as the last stage of implementation.

Systems implementation also applies to "people systems" in which

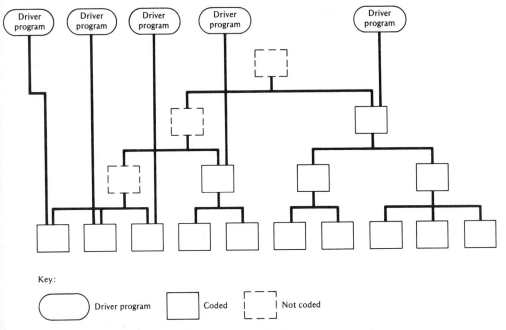

FIGURE 15.4 A conceptual view of a bottom-to-top development, showing the hierarchical structure of the system and driver programs for testing purposes.

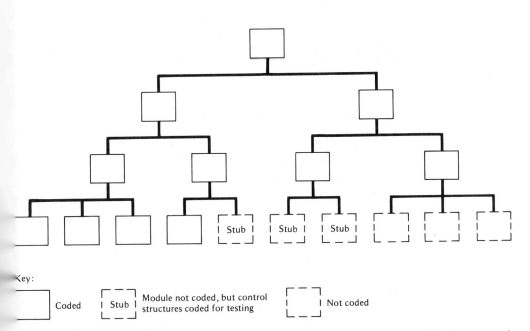

FIGURE 15.5 A conceptual view of top-down development, showing the hierarchical structure of the system and the use of "stubs" for testing.

detailed logic diagrams or detailed module descriptions are replaced by detailed job descriptions. In many human systems, implementation takes the form of reorganization of the management system. Component and module interfaces in hardware and software systems are analogous to people interfaces in human systems, and the system testing phase of hardware and software systems corresponds to the period in human systems in which the informal structure of a management system is developed.

In the implementation of most systems, there is a considerable amount of feedback between the development effort and the systems designers. This is usually because unforeseen circumstances arise and the design of the system must be adjusted accordingly. The need for feedback and adjustment also arises out of limitations in the design of a system, so the implementation stage can also serve as a check on the integrity of the system.

SYSTEM DOCUMENTATION

System documentation is the set of reports that provides general and detailed information on the system. Effective documentation is necessary for installing, maintaining, and using a system and for ongoing analysis of the system's performance. Documentation should satisfy four needs:

1. Reference for management
2. Reference for design, implementation, and maintenance personnel
3. Reference for operators of the system—in the case of hardware or software systems.
4. Reference for users of the system

Unfortunately, system documentation is frequently regarded as a discrete stage in the system life cycle. In reality, effective documentation can be achieved by applying a technically sound methodology at the conception, preliminary analysis, design, and implementation stages of the system life cycle. All the documentation can then be put together during the documentation stage.

SYSTEM INSTALLATION, OPERATION, AND CESSATION

System installation, operation, and cessation are the final three stages in the system life cycle. *System installation* refers to the process of putting a system into operation and includes the activity related to passing shake-down and acceptance tests. In a computer and data processing environment, system installation may also refer to the conversion of data formats to meet the needs of the new system and the adjustment of operating procedures. System installation frequently involves training and demonstrations. Training is usually for operations personnel and emphasizes the operational characteristics of the new or modified system. Demonstrations are usually management-oriented and serve to orient the organization to the added capability provided by the new system and the impact the new system will have on day-to-day operations.

System operation refers to the operation of the new or modified system after installation has been completed. Optimally, the system should be monitored during the initial operational period to insure that the system designers have "zeroed in" on the system needed by the organization. Operator's manuals should be reviewed for accuracy and completeness, and operational standards should be established.

System cessation refers to the fact that all systems have a finite life and are either replaced or modified as the operational environment evolves. Because of the reality that system cessation does occur, a system should be controlled and monitored so that the need for replacement or modification will be recognized in time to insure that continued operation of the system does not degrade the performance of the organization. Monitoring for system cessation differs from monitoring during the initial period of operation; the analysis takes place at a higher level. In fact, system cessation may actually be planned as part of the implementation plan developed earlier in the system life cycle.

To sum up, system installation includes training of operators *and* prospective users, acceptance testing, orientation of the organization to the system, and demonstration of the capability of the new or modified system. System operation is concerned with operational procedures, monitoring, performance evaluation, and standards. Lastly, system cessation is concerned with the ongoing analysis of a system's contribution to the objectives of an organization.

CONCLUSIONS

There is a definite orientation of the system life cycle to the computer field and the systems analysis function to organizational environments. Because of the commonality of systems, however, the concepts apply in general.

Regardless of the type of system involved, system design and documentation plays a major role in most stages of the system life cycle and serves as the primary vehicle for passing information between the various stages. Descriptive documentation techniques include verbal descriptions, syntactical specifications, logic diagrams, drawings and schematics, flow diagrams, decision tables, and HIPO diagrams.

Vocabulary
bottom-to-top development
conception
feasibility study
preliminary analysis
programming
system cessation

system design
system documentation
system installation
system operation
top-down development

References and Reading

Benjamin, R. I. *Control of the Information System Development Cycle.* New York: John Wiley and Sons, 1970.

Churchman, C. W., Ackoff, R. L., and Arnoff, E. L. *Introduction to Operations Research.* New York: John Wiley and Sons, 1957.

Couger, J. D. and Knapp, R. W., ed. *System Analysis Techniques.* New York: John Wiley and Sons, 1974.

Katzan, H. *Systems Design and Documentation: An Introduction to the HIPO Method.* New York: Van Nostrand Reinhold, 1976.

Rubin, M. L. *Handbook of Data Processing Management,* Volume 1, *Introduction to the System Life Cycle.* Princeton, N.J.: Brandon/Systems Press, 1970.

HIPO– A Descriptive Technique

The HIPO technique was developed to display, in a graphical manner, what a system or program does and what data it uses and creates. HIPO can be used as a design aid and as a documentation tool. When the HIPO technique is used, the description of a system can be used throughout the life cycle of that system. Thus, documentation of the system is generated as a by-product of the design and implementation phases and not solely as a separate phase in the system life cycle. A formal step called "documentation" is still important in the system life cycle. Using the HIPO technique, however, documentation is only *finalized* in the documentation phase; it originates with the beginning of the system development life cycle.

INTRODUCTION

HIPO represents a *new* technique for describing systems. Conventional methods such as flow diagrams, decision tables, and words are frequently ineffective for operational reasons. During systems design, because conventional techniques are usually used only to give the structure of a system, designers and implementors are collectively working "in the dark," as far as function is concerned. Designers are concerned about whether a system has a "hole" in it. What this means is that frequently it is not known if the system is lacking in a needed functional capability until the testing phase. Thus, a neglected operational function that has been "missed" during design and implementation and discovered during testing may cause rework and modification and result in slipped schedules and cost overruns. During systems modification, it is often difficult to get at the source of a problem in a large and complex system because needed modifications are given in functional terms while the documentation describes the structure of the system. An excessive amount of time may be spent looking for needed information in order to isolate the component that must be modified. The basic problem is that most documentation is in words, with accompanying flow diagrams and decision tables. As such it is concerned with the elements that comprise the system. However, when an operational capability is required, the person using that capability (i.e., the problem originator) deals only with the *function* that is performed and not with *how* it is performed. Thus, the systems person is required to translate function into structure, logic, and organization—a feat that may be very difficult if the system is large and complex.

Functional Approach

The HIPO technique is intended to show function because designers design function and implementors (for example, programmers) implement and modify function. Since most existing methods for describing systems emphasize structure, they are inadequate for decision making at the systems level because decision makers are mainly concerned with the function of a system. The actual systems development process is a specialized technique that begins with a specification of the needed functional capability and produces the internal structure of a system as part of its development activity. It is outside of the domain of most decision makers.

Once we have a method for describing the function of a system, however, it is readily apparent that the method can be transferred to systems that are not exclusively computer or data processing oriented. Most systems that are developed in the course of human activity are open, in the sense that they interact with their environment. The HIPO technique is particularly relevant to describing open systems and their components which may also be systems, because it permits the inputs, processes, and outputs of the system to be specified. The inputs and outputs describe how a component interacts with its environment; the processes describe what the component does.

It must be emphasized that HIPO can be used only to describe function—not structure, logic, or organization. All systems possess a formal organization which may or may not be functionally oriented. When HIPO is used as a design technique, formal organization tends to reflect the functional orientation of the system. In most, but not all, cases this is a desirable attribute.

Concept of a Function

A function is defined as a process that accepts one or more inputs and produces one or more outputs. The commonly used arithmetic operations of addition and the square root are familiar examples of functions, as illustrated in Figure 16.1. More specifically, as Figure 16.2 shows, a function is a mapping between two sets: the set of inputs and the set of outputs. Thus, the HIPO technique is relevant to describing function because it lists the inputs and outputs and also describes the process involved in accepting input and generating output. When HIPO is used, the traditional functional description that shows inputs

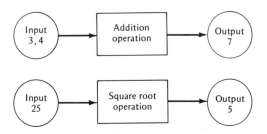

FIGURE 16.1   **Commonly used arithmetic operations are examples of functions.**

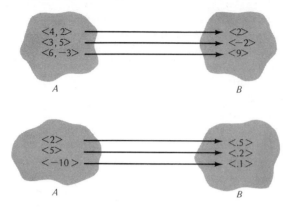

FIGURE 16.2   **Formally, a function is a mapping between two sets. In this case, the function is $f(A) \rightarrow B$ for the minus and reciprocal operations, respectively.**

and outputs is supplemented with a hierarchy diagram that gives the functional breakdown of the system and shows how the functional components fit together.

THE HIPO PACKAGE

A HIPO package is a means of describing a system or program by subdividing the function of that system or program in a meaningful manner. A typical HIPO package consists of the following components:

1. Visual table of contents
2. Overview diagrams
3. Detail diagrams with extended descriptions

The *visual table of contents* is similar to an organization chart and gives the hierarchical structure of the functions that comprise a system or program. *Overview diagrams* describe the inputs, processes, and outputs for the major functions in an application. *Detail diagrams* with extended descriptions show specific functions but point to implementation that takes the form of actual routines, flow diagrams, and supporting text.

Input-Process-Output Diagrams

The input-process-output concept, which is the basis of a HIPO package, is shown conceptually in Figure 16.3. The box on the left lists the inputs to a particular function and the box on the right lists the outputs of that function. The box in the middle lists the steps that comprise the function; in the case of high-level diagrams, the steps point to other lower-level diagrams. Figure 16.4 gives an input-process-

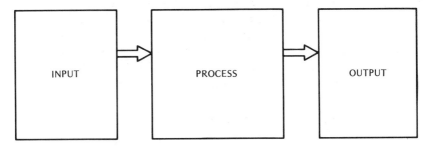

FIGURE 16.3   Input-process-output diagrams are the basis of HIPO packages.

output diagram for a charge account processing system that could be either automated or nonautomated. If an input-process-output diagram represents an overview diagram, then each step in the process would be further described by a lower-level overview or detail diagram. If

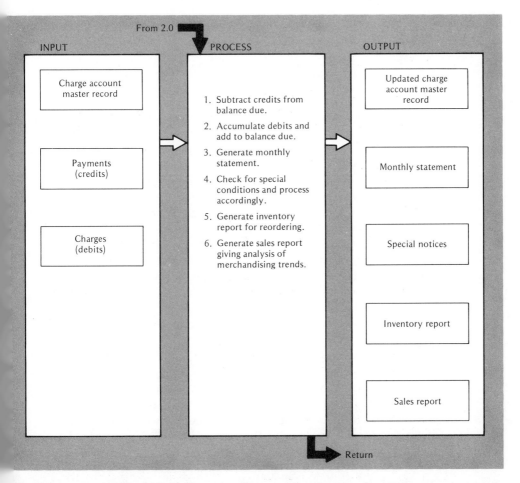

FIGURE 16.4   An example of an input-process-output diagram for a typical charge account processing system.

an input-process-output diagram represents a detail diagram, then each step in the process would be supported by an entry in an extended description of actual implementation represented by flow diagrams, decision tables, and possibly a computer program.

Visual Table of Contents

The objective of the visual table of contents is to supply a top-down hierarchical breakdown of the functions of a system or program. Each box in the hierarchy corresponds to an input-process-output diagram that describes the corresponding function along with its input and output sets. Figure 16.5 illustrates a typical visual table of contents for a credit/billing system that involves both manual procedures and computer data processing. The visual table of contents consists of three components:

1. Hierarchy diagram
2. Legend
3. Optional description section

The major component is the *hierarchy diagram,* which contains the names and identification numbers of overview and detail diagrams in the HIPO package. The hierarchy diagram serves as an organization chart of a system or a program; each function is broken down into subfunctions in the same way that business organizations are broken down into divisions, departments, and groups. A person using or reading a HIPO package can obtain a functional description of components in varying levels of detail by following the chain from the highest functional level down through one or more subfunctions. Thus, the reader need not search through a complete set of input-process-output diagrams to locate the description of a particular function. All that is required is to locate the particular box in the hierarchy diagram, *at the desired level of detail.* The box will contain an identification number of the overview diagram or a detailed diagram that describes the function or subfunction in more detail.

A hierarchy diagram should be read from left to right at each level to determine what the system does. At any given level, the outputs of a functional component serve as input, if appropriate, to the functional component to the immediate right. If it is necessary to obtain additional information, the user of the hierarchy diagram should drop down successive levels until the required detail is available. To sum up, a hierarchy diagram is analyzed from left to right to determine what the system or program does. It is searched from top to bottom to obtain information on a particular functional component. These

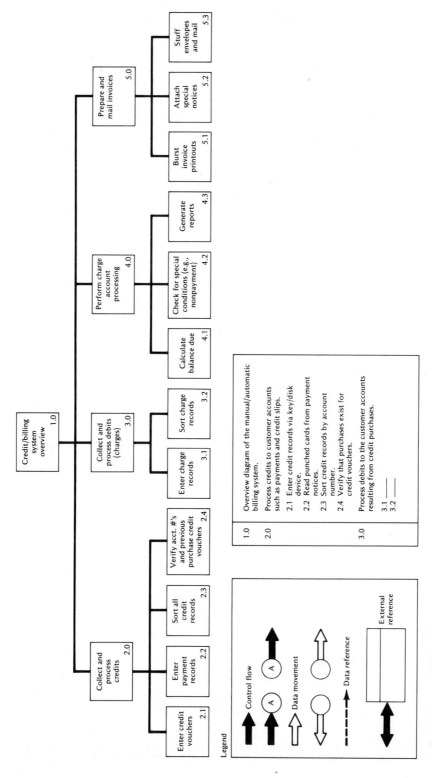

FIGURE 16.5   Visual table of contents.

two main uses of the hierarchy diagram are conceptualized in Figure 16.6.

The *legend* of the visual table of contents (see Figure 16.5) lists the symbols used in the HIPO package and tells how they are used. While a standard set of symbols is ordinarily used, the legend serves as a reference for persons who do not use HIPO diagrams on a regular basis. Another consideration is that since descriptive techniques tend to evolve, a legend makes a complete package meaningful at a later date, regardless of the standards current at that time. This point is particularly relevant when a program is to be modified after it has been in production for several months or years, when the analyst and programmer who were responsible for its development are no longer available. Even though standards may have evolved, the legend still reflects the meaning of those symbols at the time the HIPO package was written.

The optional *description section* provides more information on each

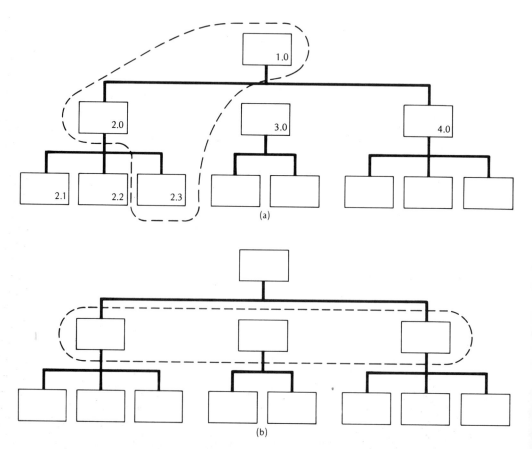

FIGURE 16.6   The hierarchy diagram can be used (a) to locate a particular component, or (b) to understand a system or program at a given level of detail.

function than can be contained in the boxes. Normally, each box in the hierarchy contains only the title of a diagram and its identification number to guide the reader to an overview or detail diagram. Therefore, the description section allows the reader to obtain additional information on a diagram without actually going to that diagram. Each entry in the description section is a one- or two-sentence description of the corresponding box in the hierarchy diagram.

Overview Diagrams

The purpose of overview diagrams is to provide a general idea of the function to be performed at a particular stage of a system or application. A specific overview diagram is located through the hierarchy diagram in the visual table of contents. An overview diagram takes the form of an input-process-output diagram: the inputs are listed at the left and the outputs are listed on the right. The key characteristic of an overview diagram is its generality. There is no indication of how and where the inputs are used or how and where the outputs are generated. The process block in the middle of the overview diagram describes "what" functions are performed, but does not tell "how" they are performed. The input-process-output diagram in Figure 16.4 is an overview diagram; it can be identified by two defining characteristics:

1. The inputs, outputs, and steps of the process are simply listed.
2. There is no explicit indication of where the inputs are used or how the outputs are generated.

Another example of an overview diagram is given in Figure 16.7, which depicts functions that might be performed in a computer program for processing automobile insurance policies.

The steps in the process block normally correspond to lower-level overview diagrams or to detail diagrams and represent subfunctions in the hierarchy diagram of the visual table of contents. When a step in the process block *does* represent a subfunction, it is enclosed in a box with an identifying number in the lower right-hand corner of the box. This number is the identification number of the next lower overview or detail diagram that describes the subfunction.

Detail Diagrams

The purpose of a detail diagram is to give a simple and brief description of a particular function. Specific inputs and outputs are identified, and they are associated with the steps in the process block that use them. Whereas input and output sets for overview diagrams designate files

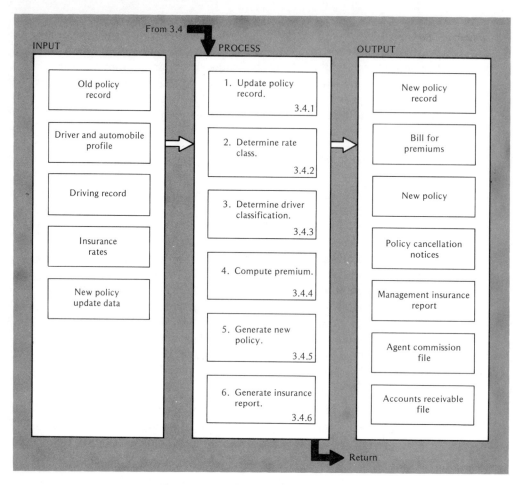

From 3.4

INPUT	PROCESS	OUTPUT
Old policy record	1. Update policy record. 3.4.1	New policy record
Driver and automobile profile	2. Determine rate class. 3.4.2	Bill for premiums
Driving record	3. Determine driver classification. 3.4.3	New policy
Insurance rates	4. Compute premium. 3.4.4	Policy cancellation notices
New policy update data	5. Generate new policy. 3.4.5	Management insurance report
	6. Generate insurance report. 3.4.6	Agent commission file
		Accounts receivable file

Return

FIGURE 16.7 Sample overview diagram for an automobile policy program.

and sometimes records, input and output sets for detail diagrams frequently represent records and fields within records.

An example of a detail diagram is given in Figure 16.8. The diagram represents a typical banking procedure for encoding canceled checks magnetically with the dollar amount of the check and entering the check into the computer system for processing. In this example, the relationship of inputs and outputs to steps in the process block is given specifically, since the objective is to show how the details fit together and to serve as a cross reference to implementation. The process block of a detail diagram may also indicate the use of external or internal subroutines, as in step 3 in Figure 16.8 which shows a sort routine named CHKSORT.

A detail diagram points to implementation through an *extended description* that contains an entry for each step in the process block. Although the contents of each entry in the extended description are not regulated, a typical set of items might include:

1. A *note item* giving additional information on that step.
2. A *routine name* giving the program name that performs a specified function, in a computer environment, or the name of a job description or entry in a procedures manual, in a non-computer environment.

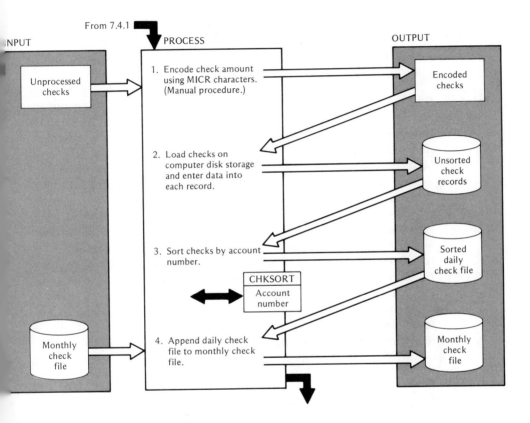

Extended description

Notes	Routine	Label	Flow chart	Ref.
1. Manually encode check amount using MICR recorder.				7.4.1.1
2. Read checks into storage, verify account number, append date, and write records to disk storage.	CHKLOAD	ENTER	CHK7.4.1	7.4.1.2
3. Sort checks using CHKSORT or account number.	CHKLOAD	SORT		7.4.1.3
4. Search to end of monthly check file and copy file. (File is sorted daily by date and account number.)	CHKLOAD	START	CHK7.4.2	7.4.1.4

FIGURE 16.8   Detail diagram for a preliminary bank check processing procedure.

3. A *label* that identifies the starting position for a routine performing that function.
4. A *flow chart* reference that indicates a detailed flow diagram for the step in the process.
5. An optional *reference* to the specific step in the process block.

The detail diagram should not show logic and should give a *simple* and *brief* description of each particular function. If a detail diagram does depict logic, then the description has "gone too far" and shows implementation.

The amount of detail shown in a detail diagram is dependent upon the function being described. Overview and then detail diagrams go from the general to the specific as reflected in the hierarchy diagram in the visual table of contents. If knowledge of a particular field or item of information is necessary for describing a function, then it should be included in the detail diagram. The key point is that only the information necessary to understand a function should be included in the detail diagram; extraneous information confuses the issue and tends to make the diagram harder to understand.

To sum up, the objective of a HIPO package is to communicate—at all levels of detail. As the documentation goes from the general to the specific, as reflected in the hierarchy diagram, the description becomes more dependent upon implementation and points to implementation through the extended description. From the point of view of communication, the practice of describing function rather than implementation is a sound one. Implementation may change because of new hardware, different languages and software, and because of the personnel involved. But function usually remains the same.

DEVELOPMENT OF A HIPO PACKAGE

HIPO is an operational technique that can be employed throughout the life cycle of a system. Since information needed during various phases differs widely, the precise manner in which a HIPO package is developed for a distinct phase is dependent upon the characteristics of that phase. The following three phases are sufficiently different to warrant special consideration: initial design phase, detail design phase, and documentation and maintenance phase.

The *initial design phase* corresponds to the conception and preliminary analysis stages of the system development life cycle, discussed in Chapter 15. The *detail design phase* corresponds to the system design and programming (implementation) stages of the system development cycle. The *documentation and maintenance phase* corresponds to the system documentation, installation, and operation stages of the system development life cycle.

Initial Design Phase

The most fundamental version of a HIPO package is developed during the initial design phase and is called the *initial design package.* The initial design package is prepared by the design group and gives the overall design of the proposed or modified system. Overview diagrams are used by analysts to represent basic design features and the hierarchy diagram is used to show how the various functions fit together. The analyst's ideas go through design reviews until the desired level of functional capability is achieved. The final initial design package is then presented to management and other interested groups for comments and approval.

At the initial design level, the HIPO package lacks the details necessary for implementation but adequately gives the scope of the project and can be used for scheduling and cost estimation. In this phase, the HIPO technique is used as a *design aid.*

The initial design phase may also require knowledge of the *existing* system; in this area the HIPO technique achieves its greatest utility. Through using the hierarchy diagram in the visual table of contents and the overview diagrams that describe the existing system, an analyst or representative of a sponsoring department can easily determine the functions performed by the existing system and can make evaluations and judgments accordingly.

A system described through the HIPO technique can be readily understood by a person who is not knowledgeable in the methods of implementation. This is so because HIPO is used to describe "what" a system does and not "how" the functions are performed.

Detail Design Phase

During the detail design phase, the design and implementation groups complete the design of a system using the initial design package as a base. Usually, the implementation group adds the details necessary for implementation to the initial design package, and then uses the resulting design for implementation. In the computer field, implementation would mean computer programming. In other cases, implementation would involve the synthesis of system components, in whatever form those components might take.

As the system is developed, the implementation group completes the HIPO package by filling in the extended description box and by adding to the initial design as deficiencies become evident during implementation. Frequently, systems do not function properly as designed, and these deficiencies are uncovered only during the course of implementation. Thus, it is important that the implementation group go back to the design group for alterations to the "basic design"; this is the feedback cycle mentioned in Chapter 15. In the process of altering the basic design, the HIPO package must be continually updated to reflect changes in the functions performed by the system. Because a HIPO package shows functions that are not completely dependent upon all of the details of implementation, however, the package is not likely to require a significant number of modifications during system development.

Use of HIPO does not preclude the use of other descriptive techniques, such as flow charts and decision tables. In fact, the implementation group may elect to use these techniques during development of the system. When additional techniques are used, they supplement the HIPO package and may be referenced in the extended description.

The document produced during the detail design phase is known as the *detail design package.* Since HIPO is used to aid in the implementation effort, it serves also as a *development tool* and presents an up-to-date description of the system as it is implemented. The detail design package serves as excellent input to the documentation and maintenance phase, because it is easy to understand, complete and accurate, and exists in a familiar form.

Documentation and Maintenance Phase

The purpose of the documentation and maintenance phase is to prepare for operational use of the system and to record the design and implementation of the system for future modifications and for subsequent development activity. The documents produced during this phase are referred to as *system documents* and include the following:

1. Management overview of the new system
2. Logic manuals that contain the technical information necessary for the maintenance process
3. Reference manuals for users of the system
4. Operator reference manuals that are used for the operation of data processing systems

A HIPO package, by itself, does not constitute any of the system documents but serves as the primary input to the documentation and maintenance phase. The documents that most closely resemble the HIPO package are the *logic manuals* that are used for maintaining the system and for making changes to it. Logic manuals are developed to describe a system and are commonly known as the "documentation of the system." In reality, however, effective documentation should include all the four categories listed above.

When HIPO is used as design aid, development tool, and documentation technique, the design of a system and its documentation start out together and stay together during the system life cycle. The designer's ideas and the implementor's thoughts are recorded when they occur so much of the documentation is generated as a by-product of design and implementation.

The designer's ideas and implementor's thoughts are useful for the management overview, as well as for familiarizing technical writers, who comprise the documentation and maintenance groups, with the scope of the project. The *management overview* is composed mainly of verbal descriptions, but the hierarchy diagram and high-level overview diagrams serve to depict the functions performed by the system in a meaningful fashion and to show the relationships between the various functional components. In cases where the hierarchy and overview diagrams contain more detailed information than is necessary for the management overview, they may have to be redrawn to eliminate some of the detail. Nevertheless, the HIPO technique does serve an important purpose in the managerial description.

The detail design package serves essentially as a set of logic manuals except that the diagrams are edited by the documentation group, and references are made to flow charts, decision tables, and verbal documentations that have been added to the detail design package for clarification. It should be remembered that the detail design package is used for implementation and may be more detailed than necessary for maintenance and for educating new personnel. It is the lower-level detail diagrams that reflect implementation technique and conventions, and these diagrams are deleted when it is necessary to show logic but not show the details of computer programs. A useful aphorism is, "the lower you go in the hierarchy diagram, the more the detail diagrams show implementation rather than function."

HIPO diagrams frequently serve great utility in the development of user and operator *reference manuals,* by providing information to documentation personnel, without constituting a significant portion of the manuals themselves. HIPO diagrams provide, however, an excellent means of presenting an overview of a system and serve an important purpose in introductory sections of user and operator reference manuals.

To sum up, the use of HIPO is a painless way of achieving effective design and documentation. Systems analysts and designers think of the inputs and outputs of a system or program along with the processes involved. By requiring that designers and analysts record their thoughts, ideas, and concepts as HIPO diagrams, and by updating these diagrams through the various stages of design and implementation, documentation is achieved as a by-product of design and implementation rather than as a separate and completely distinct step in the system life cycle. As a result, HIPO documentation is more accurate and tends to reflect meaningful subjects that are less vulnerable to change than is documentation that records solely the details of implementation.

ADVANTAGES OF USING HIPO

There is a natural tendency for a designer, analyst, or technical writer to ask why HIPO should be used at all, since systems have been designed, implemented, and documented for many years without it. Therefore, systems or programming managers who wish to benefit their installations through use of HIPO have a selling job to do. One of the best approaches is to point out the deficiencies in the present methods.

To begin with, conventional methods of design that employ flow charting techniques represent implementation-dependent thinking. Thus, designers and implementors can easily lose sight of the function of the system. When this happens, functional interfaces are frequently "cloudy" because design and implementation activity exists only at the unit level. Documentation will be disjointed because concepts are not tied together, and the technical writer is called in after the system has been completed. Also, designers and implementors use different techniques, at differing levels of detail, to describe their work, and this practice can play havoc with the managerial aspects of system development. Implementation-dependent techniques are inefficient in the sense that it is difficult and time-consuming to obtain information from a logic diagram—that is, unless you know what you are looking for in the first place. Other disadvantages are equally important but are not as visible. The techniques used to design systems are often a hindrance instead of an aid to implementation personnel. The current methodology has no side benefits in the areas of management planning and education to commend it.

The advantages of using the HIPO technique are manifold. The major advantages are:

1. HIPO diagrams are similar in form, as are the various kinds of HIPO packages. Thus, the technique can be used by people with different operational needs.
2. HIPO permits a program or system to be easily understood because a familiar format is employed.
3. HIPO is a "thinking" aid as well as a design, development, and documentation tool.
4. HIPO packages provide a common visual base for education and communication.
5. Use of HIPO promotes efficiency because there is less duplication of information and effort, and more information can be obtained at a glance from a HIPO diagram than from other descriptive techniques.
6. Because a HIPO package is intended to show function, it is not vulnerable to changes inherent in the implementation effort.
7. The HIPO technique is a means of capturing the thoughts of system

designers and allows design and documentation to start out together in the system development life cycle.

8. Use of HIPO facilitates maintenance and testing because a clear definition of functional interfaces is provided and because errors can be detected and isolated on a functional basis.

9. HIPO is a management tool because the functional approach allows planning and scheduling to be made accurately and early in the system development life cycle and because it provides a means of monitoring the development effort.

10. Documentation becomes a by-product of design development and testing because a set of HIPO packages is excellent source material for the documentation group.

The major advantage of HIPO, however, is only implied by the list above: the value of HIPO depends upon how it is used. To a system's designer, it is a design aid. To the implementation group, it is a development aid. To the documentation group, it is a documentation tool.

Case Study

A significant example of the use of the HIPO technique is given in Chapter 18. The objective of the "Sales/Inventory System Case Study" is to demonstrate the HIPO technique. The example also gives a comparison of the use of flowcharting and input-process-output diagrams.

Vocabulary   The student should be familiar with the following terms in the context in which they were used in the chapter.

description section	function
design aid	hierarchy diagram
detail design package	HIPO
detail design phase	HIPO package
detail diagram	initial design package
development tool	initial design phase
documentation and maintenance phase	legend
	overview diagram
documentation technique	system documents
extended description	visual table of contents

Questions and Exercises

1. Name the three components of a HIPO package.
2. Name and describe each of the components of a HIPO package.
3. What is the purpose of the *legend?*

4. What is the purpose of the *description section?*

5. Describe how a module would be located in a HIPO package.

6. Summarize each of the following phases: initial design, detail design, and documentation and maintenance.

7. Write a brief (one page) essay relating the HIPO technique to the system development life cycle.

Related Reading   Katzan, H. *Systems Design and Documentation.* New York: Van Nostrand Reinhold, 1976.

17

Data Processing Applications

DATA PROCESSING FUNCTIONS

System Flowchart
Data Entry
Editing Run
Sort Run
Control Balancing
File Update and Processing
Printing and Reporting

SAMPLE OF DATA PROCESSING APPLICATIONS

Payroll
Accounts Payable

SORTING METHODS

Introductory Remark on Data
Internal Sorting
Merge
External Sort

hrough the use of programming languages and operating systems, it is relatively straightforward to develop a new computer application. An organization must simply be cognizant of the system development life cycle and utilize appropriate descriptive techniques at each stage of the cycle. This does not mean that application development is easy. In fact, it is not. However, it does mean that a high degree of commonality exists in the various steps that comprise a data processing application. This chapter will go a little bit further by delineating the various data processing functions.

DATA PROCESSING FUNCTIONS

There are six basic data processing functions that are common to many data processing applications: data entry, editing, sorting, control balancing, file update and processing, and printing and reporting. The presentation given here uses system flowcharting methods, which are also covered.

System Flow Chart

System flow charts describe the flow of data and the operational procedures in data processing applications. Usually, the following elements are identified: the origin of data, manual operations, storage devices, data transmission procedures, data processing functions, and input/output operations. Figure 17.1 gives a complete description of system flow-charting symbols, divided into three classes: input/output media, input/output devices and device types, and data processing operations. Figure 17.2 is an example of a system flow chart for a data analysis, reporting, and retrieval system. It is typical of system flow charts used in data processing.

Data Entry

Before data can be processed, it must be placed on a suitable media for input operations. The process of putting data in a machine-readable form is known as *data entry*. Data entry is a generic term which refers to several input processes, such as the following:

1. Source documents are keypunched on punched cards and verified. A typical example is the entry of sales receipts for a billing application (see Figure 17.3a).
2. Source documents are placed onto magnetic tape or disk through a data entry device that includes a CRT screen and a keyboard.

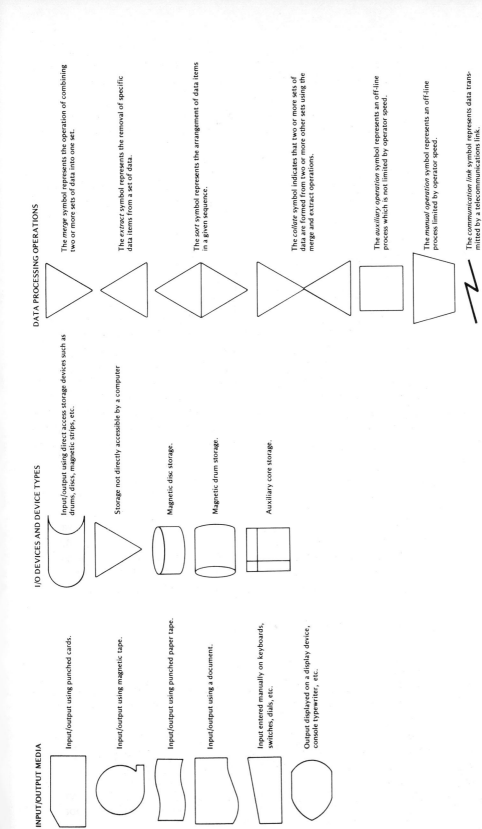

FIGURE 17.1   System flow-charting symbols.

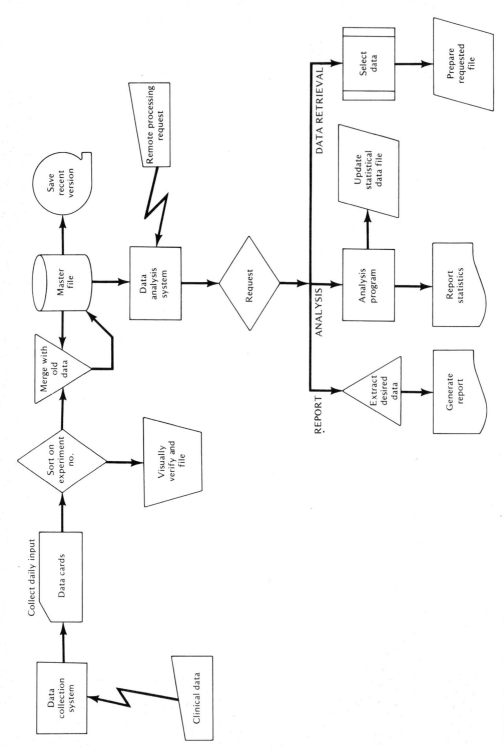

FIGURE 17.2   System flow chart for a data analysis, reporting, and retrieval system.

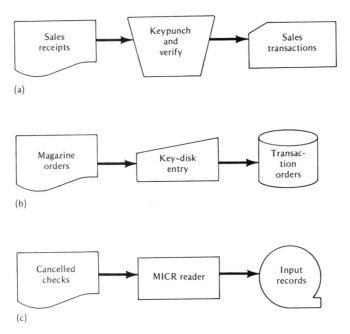

(a)

(b)

(c)

FIGURE 17.3   **System flow charts of typical data entry operations.**

A typical example is the entry of orders for magazines for a circulation/billing/reorder system (see Figure 17.3b).

3. Source documents are read by a special optical reader; the input medium is magnetic tape. A typical example is the bank check reader for checks that have been magnetically encoded[1] (see Figure 17.3c). In some cases, the optical reader is placed on-line and data is entered directly into the computer.

Data entry is almost always accompanied by a manual operation such as keypunching and keyboard entry. Even when documents are fed and read automatically, the machine must be operated manually.

During data entry, precaution must be taken to insure that errors are not inadvertently made. For keypunching, the precaution of verifying is used. Keypunching/verifying takes place in two steps. When keypunching, the operator reads a source document and punches the data onto cards that were previously not punched. When verifying, the operator reads the same source document but uses the previously punched cards as input. As the verifier operator enters data, the data is constantly compared against the corresponding punched card. If a discrepancy occurs, a light turns on to indicate that visual inspection

---

1. The characters placed on the bottom of a check are known as MICR characters. (MICR stands for magnetic into character recognition.) The reader is known as an MICR reader.

is required. For keyboard data entry, the input data is displayed on the screen for visual inspection. If the data is okay, the operator presses a button and the line is then written to tape or disk.

Editing Run

The *editing run* is a specially written program used to insure that the input data is acceptable for processing. The editing that is required for a particular application can take one or more forms, depending upon the data:

1. Checking that dates are valid
2. Checking that customer numbers are valid
3. Checking that amounts are within acceptable limits

In most cases, the editing run is designed to identify transactions that could cause the eventual processing program to produce incorrect results.

Sort Run

The *sort run* is used to place the input transactions, such as sales receipts or cancelled checks, in numerical order by account number. Sorting is an important part of data processing since sets of input are usually not entered into the computer in order. Pre-written sorting programs are almost always available from the computer vendor or from independent companies that sell software.

Control Balancing

Control balancing is the technique of computing a total before and after processing. For payroll processing, a control balance would be the total number of hours. For accounts receivable, a control balance would be the total dollars paid. Often, a control balance is simply the number of transactions processed during one day—computed after data entry, after editing, and after sorting.

File Update and Processing

Figure 17.4 gives a system flow chart for an accounts receivable billing program as an illustrated example of file update and processing. Each

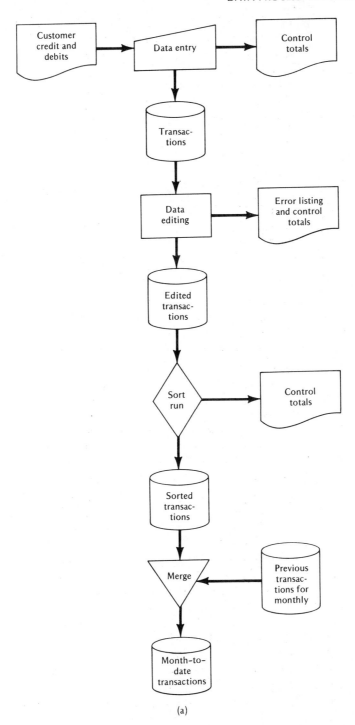

(a)

FIGURE 17.4(a)   System flow chart showing the entry, editing, sorting and merging of transactions.

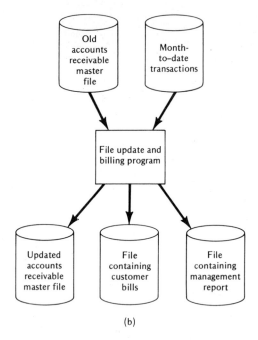

(b)

FIGURE 17.4(b)   System flow chart of file update and processing.

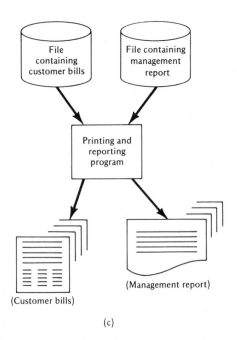

(c)

FIGURE 17.4(c)   System flow chart of printing and reporting.

account has a record in an "accounts receivable master file" that contains information, such as:

Account number
Name and address
Date that the account was established
Date of last credit (payment)
Date of last debit (charge)
Current balance
30-day balance
60-day balance
90-day balance
Over 90-day balance

During the month, transactions consisting of credits (i.e., payments) and debits (i.e., charges) are accumulated on a transaction file through the processes of data entry, data editing, sorting and merging, as depicted in the system flowchart labeled 17.4(a). Then on a periodic basis, usually once a month, the bills are run off and the master file is updated accordingly. This process, referred to as *file update and processing* (see Figure 17.4b), is summarized as follows:

1. The heading for the management report is written to disk for later printing.
2. A transaction record is read from the transaction file.
3. The account's master record is read from the accounts receivable master file.
4. Using descriptive information in the master record, the "bill heading" is written to disk for later printing.
5. The balance carried forward is written to disk for later printing.
6. Succeeding transaction records are read until a record break occurs. (This happens when the account number on a transaction changes to another account.)
7. Credits and debits are accumulated.
8. The total credits are subtracted from the balance carried forward. If the positive difference is greater than a fixed amount (such as 50 cents) a service charge (such as $1\frac{1}{2}\%$) is added and written to disk for later printing.
9. The total debits are added to the result of step 8 and the "amount due" is written to disk for later printing.
10. The variable data in the master record, such as last payment and 60-day balance, are updated.
11. The updated master record is written to the updated accounts receivable master file.

12. A line of management report reflecting this account is written to disk for later printing.

13. The transaction record that caused the record break is used as the next transaction record and the processing continues with step 2.

The process continues until all transaction records are processed and the disk file containing customer bills and the disk file containing the management report are completed.

The function of file update and processing is characterized in the following way:

1. Transactions are processed.
2. A master file is updated to reflect transaction processing.
3. A set of lines to be printed is generated, which may take the form of a management report, customer bills, or inventory records.

Printing and Reporting

As demonstrated in Figure 17.4c, the objective of this function is to generate printed matter. In a small business or minicomputer operating environment, a set of bills or records or a printed report may be generated directly by the file update and processing program. In a more sophisticated operating environment, the data may be written to disk or tape for subsequent printing. The *printing and reporting* operation usually takes one of two forms:

1. The data is written to disk or tape as unformatted data. It is then printed by a specially written processing program that formats the data for the forms used.
2. The data is formatted by the file update and processing program and then written to disk or tape as line images. In this case, the file can be printed by the computer operating system.

The process of printing and reporting is frequently a separate step in a computer application because special printing forms are required— such as billing paper or blank checks.

SAMPLE OF DATA PROCESSING APPLICATIONS

This section gives a brief narrative and system flow chart for a sample of data processing applications. A simplified version of an accounts receivable system was given in the previous section. This section covers payroll and accounts payable systems.

Payroll

Payroll is a typical data processing application. It is commonly identified with data processing, and most people are at least familiar with the basic concepts. It integrates several business departments, such as personnel, payroll, and production.

The payroll master file normally contains the following information which is used during payroll calculations and is updated during a payroll run.

Employee number
Department number
Employee name
Employee home address
Date of hire
Marital status
Dependents
Salary code
Salary rate
Vacation days allotted and used
Sick days allotted
Bond: denomination
          balance
Deductions: bond
            disability
            medical
            credit union
            union dues
            special purchases
Year-to-date totals: vacation days
                     sick days
                     gross pay
                     federal withholding
                     FICA tax
                     state tax
                     city tax
Quarterly totals: gross pay
                  federal withholding
                  FICA tax
                  state tax
                  city tax
Dates: last bond
        last paycheck
        last vacation day
        last sick day

As required by law and organization policy, the output of a typical payroll program consists of:

Paycheck and earnings statement
Payroll register
Deduction register
Tax reports
Management reports
Updated master payroll file

A system flow chart of the typical payroll program is given as Figure 17.5.

It is significant that the origin of input data to the payroll system is from different departments, delineated as follows:

Personnel department: new employees and employee terminations
Payroll department: rate changes
Production departments: time sheets

The above information is entered into the system through a keydisk/keytape operation or through keypunching/verifying. The payroll transactions are then edited and sorted, usually by employee number, prior to payroll processing. The payroll processing program generates the output listed above. The paychecks and earnings statements are generated directly by the payroll program or are written to a separate file for subsequent printing by a special program.

When the payroll is computed centrally in a distributed system, one technique that is used is to transmit the paycheck and earnings statement data to a distributed system via telecommunications facilities and have the checks printed there.

Accounts Payable

The term *accounts payable* refers to amounts owed by an organization. An *accounts payable system* provides the means of disbursing organizational funds and maintaining associated records. An accounts payable system is concerned with the following types of records and transactions:

1. Purchase orders
2. Receiving records
3. Vendor invoices
4. Vendor information
5. Internal cash disbursements

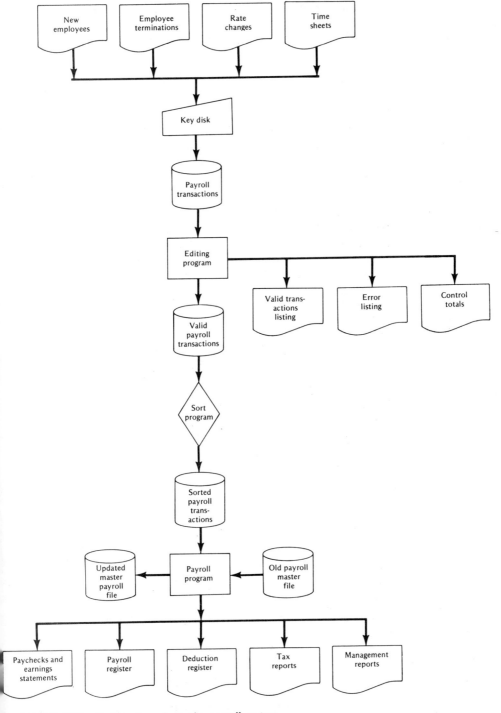

FIGURE 17.5   System flow chart of a payroll system.

Since an accounts payable system is intended to control all payments, with the exception of paychecks, the various items of information are used to perform the following functions:

1. Records purchase orders, receiving records, vendor invoices, vendor credit, and back-order notices from vendors
2. Maintains vendor, open purchase order, accounts payable, external disbursement, and internal disbursement files
3. Generates vendor checks and internal disbursements
4. Produces the following reports:
   Invoice register
   Internal disbursements register
   Cash requirements report
   Accounts payable report (trial balance)
   Distribution summary report
   Department expense report
   Vendor analysis report
   Open purchase order report
   Back order report

The basis of an accounts payable system exists in two files: the vendor file and the open purchase order file. The *vendor file* is used to describe the vendor and payment dates and contains the following information:

1. Vendor name, address, and telephone number
2. Items, description, and prices
3. Discount rates and terms
4. Credit limit
5. Delivery information

The *purchase order file* records purchase orders that represent the vendor's authority to ship goods and issue invoices. A purchase order originates with a *purchase requisition* containing the following information:

1. Name, description, and item numbers of items requisitioned
2. Quantity needed
3. Requisition date and receiving date—date by which items must be received
4. Account number
5. Vendor's name and number (for one-vendor items)
6. Place of delivery

After a purchase requisition is approved, a computer program is run to generate a purchase order and update the open purchase order file. A system flowchart of this operation is given in Figure 17.6.

On a periodic basis (sometimes as often as daily) the accounts payable file is updated with the following information: purchase orders, shipping reports, receiving reports, vendor invoices, vendor credits, back-order notices, and internal disbursement requests. Along with the update, invoice and internal disbursement registers (i.e., reports) are generated. The accounts receivable and open purchase order files

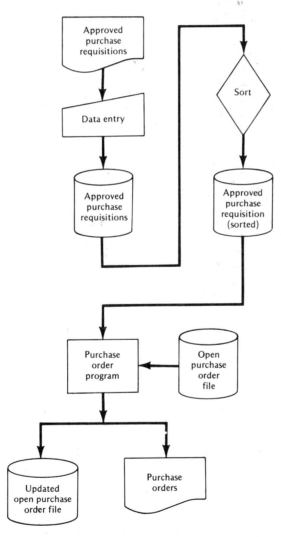

FIGURE 17.6   **System flow chart of computer run to generate purchase orders and update the open purchase order file for an accounts payable system.**

are also updated and vendor checks and internal disbursements may also be generated. In the latter case, checks and disbursements may be written to a file for later printing. The accounts payable system also generates a cash requirements report that is used for financial management. The flow chart of this operation is given in Figure 17.7.

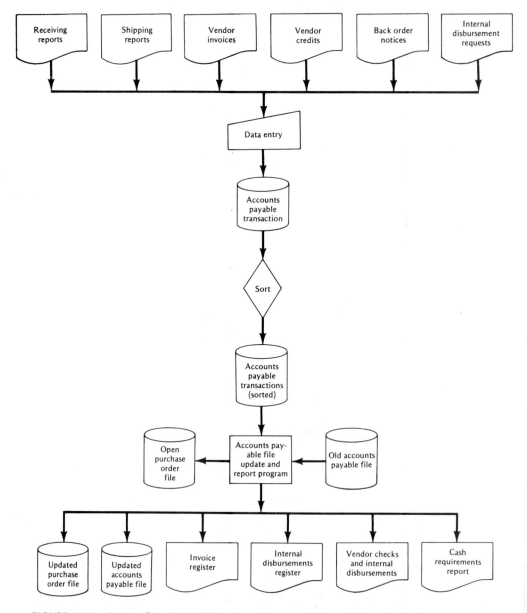

FIGURE 17.7   System flow chart of the accounts payable file update and report program.

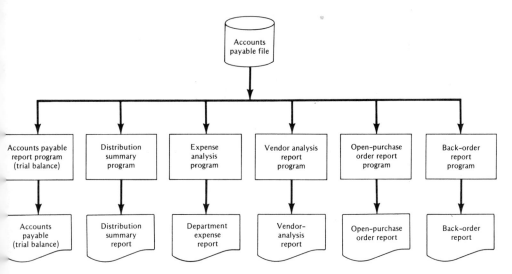

FIGURE 17.8   **System flow chart of reports that are run off the accounts payable file.**

The remainder of the reports generated by the accounts payable system are run off the accounts payable file as shown in Figure 17.8. In general, the concept of developing a program to generate a specific report from the master file is a common practice.

SORTING METHODS

Many data processing applications include a data entry operation for which data values are not entered in order by account number. In these cases, the data must be sorted and the sorting procedure is based on a sort field—usually taken as account number, user number, etc. It is also possible that the sort field may be a name or any other field of characters. The key point is that the sort field is only part of a data record, but it is the part that effectively governs the eventual ordering of the records. For small amounts of data, data can be sorted internally in main storage. For large amounts of data, a file sorting procedure is needed.

Introductory Remark on Data

Throughout this section, lists of numbers will be sorted for simplicity. Numbers can be used because the concepts of sorting are more important than the details of programming. Thus, a series of records, such as:

123	BOLT 3 INCH	50	35	A
151	WRENCH 3 × P	14	6	C
101	BENCH 3 FEET	5	5	A
170	SAW JIG	13	10	B

can be represented as a simple list:

| 123 |
| 151 |
| 101 |
| 170 |

When the list is sorted, as in the diagram below,

| 101 |
| 123 |
| 151 |
| 170 |

the implication is that the complete records are sorted, as in:

101	BENCH 3 FEET	5	5	A
123	BOLT 3 INCH	50	35	A
151	WRENCH 3 × P	14	6	C
170	SAW JIG	13	10	B

Internal Sorting

Three internal sorting methods are introduced: selection sort, bubble sort, and the odd-even transposition sort. Faster sorting methods exist, but the three methods given are particularly appropriate because they are easy to program and aptly demonstrate the concept of sorting. In all cases, a list of n elements is sorted.

In the *selection sort,* the first entry is compared with the second, third, fourth, fifth, and so on, to the nth item. Whenever a value smaller than the first is encountered, it is exchanged with the first item. Thus, at the end of the first pass, the smallest value will be first. The process

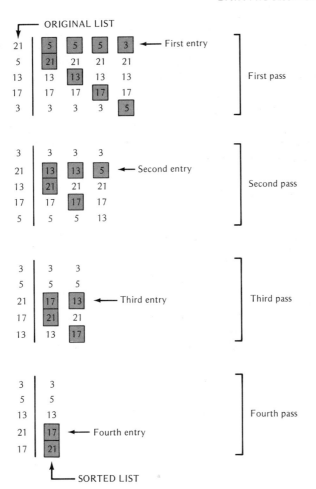

FIGURE 17.9   Example of the selection sort.

is continued in the same manner with the second, third, on up to the *n*th entry. An example of the selection sort is given in Figure 17.9.

In the *bubble sort,* the *n*th entry is compared with the $(n-1)$st entry and the values are exchanged if necessary. Then the $(n-1)$st entry is compared with the $(n-2)$nd entry and the values are exchanged if necessary. The process continues until the second entry is compared with the first entry. Effectively, the smallest value is always "bubbled" to the top. The process is continued and the next smallest value is bubbled into the second position. The loop is repeated until the complete list is sorted, as demonstrated in Figure 17.10.

In the *odd-even transposition sort,* the odd-even numbered entries are compared in one pass and the even-odd numbered entries are compared in the succeeding pass, as follows:

$$\begin{pmatrix} 1 \\ 2 \\ 3 \\ 4 \\ 5 \\ 6 \\ 7 \\ 8 \\ 9 \\ 10 \end{pmatrix}$$

└─succeeding pass

└─one pass

If two successive passes are made through the entries without making an interchange, then the list is sorted. The idea when comparing is to move the smaller entry up—as illustrated in Figure 17.11.

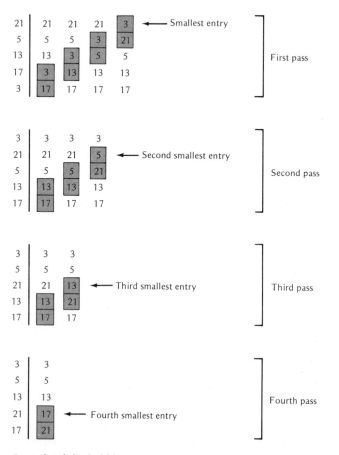

FIGURE 17.10   Example of the bubble so⟩

21	5)	
5	21)	FIRST PASS
13	13)	(odd-even)
17	17)	one exchange
3	3	

5	5	
21	13)	SECOND PASS
13	21)	(even-odd)
17	3)	two exchanges
3	17)	

5	5)	
13	13)	THIRD PASS
21	3)	(odd-even)
3	21)	one exchange
17	17	

5	5	
13	3)	FOURTH PASS
3	13)	(even-odd)
21	17)	two exchanges
17	21)	

5	3)	
3	5)	FIFTH PASS
13	13)	(odd-even)
17	17)	one exchange
21	21	

3	3	
5	5)	SIXTH PASS
13	13)	(even-odd)
17	17)	no exchanges
21	21)	

3	3)	
5	5)	SEVENTH PASS
13	13)	(odd-even)
17	17)	no exchanges
21	21	

FIGURE 17.11   Example of the odd-even transposition sort.

Merge

A *merge* is the process of combining two or more ordered lists or data files so that the combined list or file is also in order. The lists need not contain the same number of entries. Figure 17.12 illustrates a merge operation.

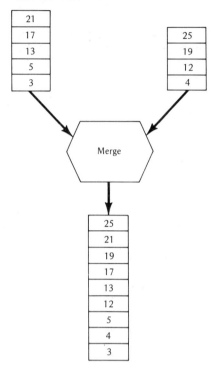

FIGURE 17.12   Example of a merge operation.

External Sort

There are several established methods of performing an external sort. The concept sorting-by-merging technique uses two external files in addition to the file being sorted. An internal storage area is used, and the process works through the following steps:

1. The internal storage area is filled and sorted.
2. The sorted entries are written to one of the unused files.
3. The internal storage area is filled again and sorted.
4. The sorted entries from step 3 are merged with the sorted file and written to the other unused file.
5. The process continues with step 3 until the unsorted file is completely sorted.

Figure 17.13 gives an example of sorting by merging.

In most computer installations, a sorting package is available, and it is rarely the case that a reader has to write a sort program. However, the concepts are ingenious and the student is encouraged to consult

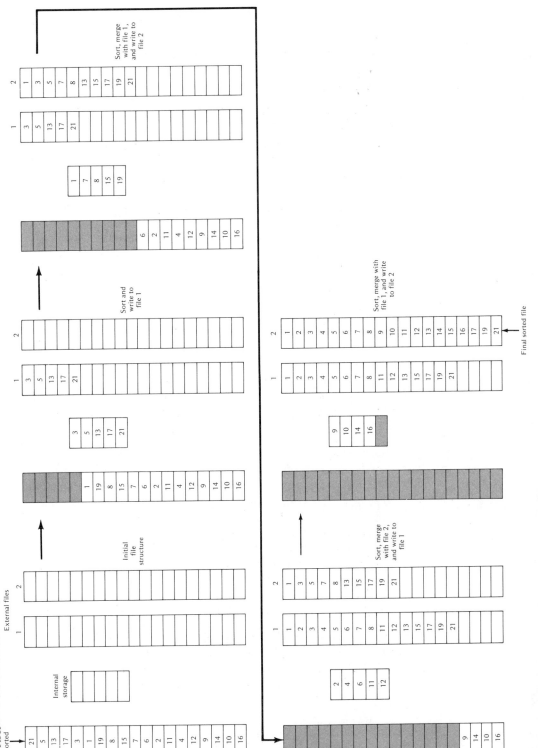

FIGURE 17.13 Example of external sorting by merging.

the reading by Lewis and Smith for a survey of external sorting methods.

Vocabulary   The student should be familiar with the following terms in the context in which they were used in the chapter.

accounts payable system	internal sort
accounts receivable system	merge
bubble sort	odd-even transposition sort
control balancing	payroll
data entry	printing and reporting
editing run	selection sort
external sort	sort run
file update and processing	system flow chart

Exercises   1. Modify the system flow chart for the payroll application in Figure 17.5 to include control balancing.

2. Modify the system flow charts for the accounts payable applications in Figures 17.6 and 17.7 to include editing and control balancing.

3. How can distributed systems be used with payroll applications?

4. Develop algorithms and/or program flow charts for the following:

   a. One internal sorting method
   b. Merge operation
   c. External sorting

5. Using the given information, analyze the three given internal sorting methods. Which would be best (i.e., fastest) for each of the following cases:

   a. The list is probably already sorted.
   b. The list is partially sorted.
   c. The list is in random order.

Related Reading   Lewis, T. G., and Smith, M. Z., *Applying Data Structures.* Boston: Houghton Mifflin, 1976.

Tremblay, J. P., and Sorenson, P. G., *An Introduction to Data Structures with Applications.* New York: McGraw-Hill, 1976.

Sales Inventory System Case Study

FLOW-CHARTING METHODS

Program Flow Chart
System Flow Chart

A HIPO PACKAGE

Visual Table of Contents
Overview Diagrams
Detail Diagrams
Summary

ne of the most common applications of computer technology is the *sales/inventory system,* which provides the following services to an enterprise:

1. Maintains an updated inventory file
2. Validates customer orders
3. Prepares a sales report
4. Prepares a daily inventory report
5. Produces shipping orders and packing slips
6. Generates customer billing invoices and an accounts receivable file
7. Guarantees a specified inventory level by ordering inventory items when the quantity on hand is less than a threshold value and when current inventory is insufficient to satisfy an order (i.e., a back order)

This application is given as an example because most students will be familiar with it. The objective is to give a HIPO description of a hypothetical system of this type and compare it, to a degree, with conventional flow-charting techniques for describing systems.

FLOW-CHARTING METHODS

The conventional methods for describing systems are flow charts, decision tables, and prose descriptions. The flow chart is the most widely used method and comes in two variations: program flow charts and system flow charts. These two types of flow charts will be used here to describe the sales/inventory system and to illustrate the use of flow-charting methods.

Program Flow Chart

A *program flow chart* is a detailed description of the steps involved in the execution of a computer program or a procedural description of the operation of a system. The program or system is organized into meaningful segments, and the flow chart for a segment tells how that segment works.

Figure 18.1 gives a program flow chart for an initial phase of a sales/inventory system. In this phase, a transaction record representing a sales order is analyzed to insure that all of the necessary information is present on the input medium and that the information is valid. The program segment is designed to write the transaction records to an intermediate file and then sort that file by inventory item number, giving a transaction file. A tacit assumption is made that the sales/ inventory system is run on the computer daily. Therefore, the output

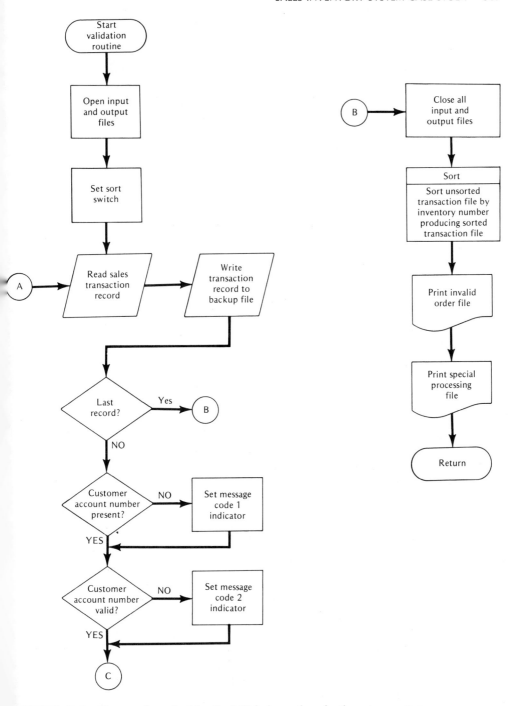

FIGURE 18.1   Program flow chart for the initial phase of a sales/inventory system.

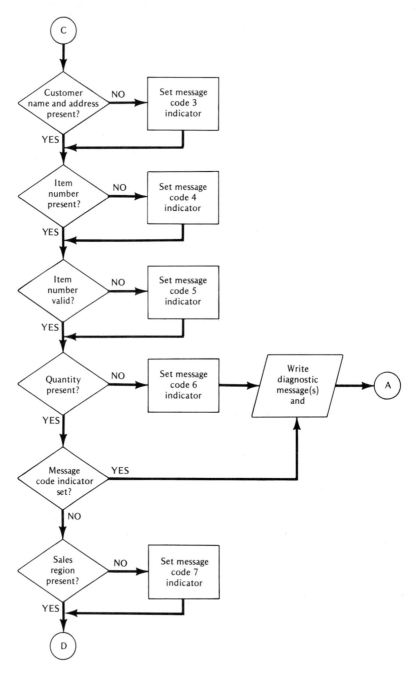

FIGURE 18.1   *(Continued)*

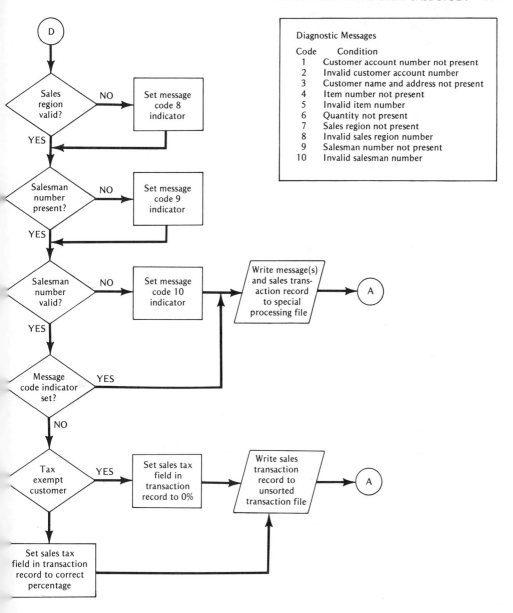

Diagnostic Messages

Code	Condition
1	Customer account number not present
2	Invalid customer account number
3	Customer name and address not present
4	Item number not present
5	Invalid item number
6	Quantity not present
7	Sales region not present
8	Invalid sales region number
9	Salesman number not present
10	Invalid salesman number

FIGURE 18.1   *(Concluded)*

of the analysis-validation segment serves as input to the next segment that generates a daily sales report.

It is evident from Figure 18.1 that the program flow chart involves implementation-dependent thinking. It is also difficult to determine what the segment does from the flow chart because "you can't see the *forest* for the *trees.*" In short, the program flow chart tells how a procedure is performed but is deficient in telling what the procedure is. Because a program flow chart does involve implementation-dependent thinking, however, it is a useful adjunct to a detail diagram in a HIPO package.

System Flow Chart

A *system flow chart* is generally considered to be an input-output diagram of a system. The operation of the system is divided into distinct phases, and the inputs and outputs of each phase are depicted in symbolic form.

Figure 18.2 gives a system flow chart for a sales/inventory system. The diagram would be useful for an operations group because it is possible to tell the exact nature of the inputs and outputs at a glance. Outputs from one phase of the system that serve as input to the next phase are readily apparent from the description. For example, the transaction file produced during the first phase when the inventory transaction is prepared is used during the second phase when the inventory transaction is processed.

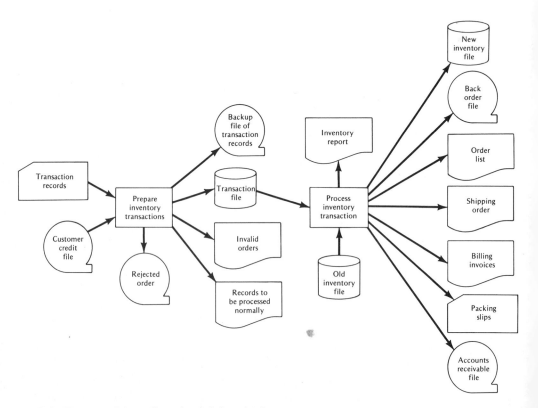

FIGURE 18.2   System flow chart of the sales/inventory system.

It is evident from Figure 18.2 that the system flow chart gives only the inputs and outputs of the system. Again, it is difficult to determine what the system does from the flow chart, since there is no indication of the processing that is performed.

A HIPO PACKAGE

This section gives a HIPO package describing the sales/inventory system. The system, as a whole, was only partially described in the program and system flow charts of the previous section. This is the kind of situation, however, that lends itself to a HIPO description, and the complete system can be documented using the HIPO technique. The student should be able to grasp the essence of the sales/inventory system easily from the HIPO package.

Visual Table of Contents

The visual table of contents of the HIPO package for the sales/inventory system is given in Figure 18.3. From the hierarchy diagram, it is evident that the system is subdivided into two functional components:

1. Preparing sales/inventory transaction records for processing
2. Processing the sales/inventory transaction records and generating associated files and reports

These functions are illustrated in the two rectangular boxes, numbered 2.0 and 3.0, in the second level of the hierarchy diagram. These boxes represent overview diagrams. The overview diagram of the complete system is given at the top level; it contains roughly the same amount of information as the system flow chart. The third (or bottom) level of the hierarchy diagram lists detail diagrams. The number of levels of overview diagrams and of detail diagrams depends upon the application. The top level is always an overview diagram; the bottom level is always a set of detail diagrams.

The legend indicates that a broad solid arrow denotes control flow and that a broad open arrow denotes data movement. The external routine box attached to a broad, solid double-headed arrow denotes the use of a routine or system external to the system being described. Other symbols will be discussed later in the chapter.

The description section groups additional information about each box in the hierarchy diagram, so that the systems analyst need not go to an overview or detail diagram to locate information on a particular function. Although the description section is optional, it serves an important purpose. When it is necessary to locate a specific function

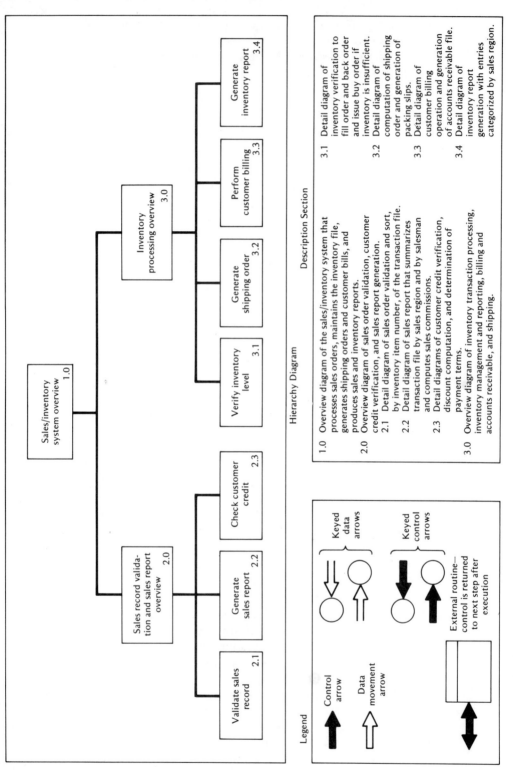

FIGURE 18.3 Visual table of contents of the HIPO package describing the sales/inventory system.

for maintenance or education purposes, that function can be located directly through the hierarchy diagram, eliminating a lengthy search through overview and detail diagrams. Without HIPO, it would be necessary to search through a myriad of system and program flow charts.

Overview Diagrams

In this example, there are two levels of overview diagrams: the top level and the second level. The top level consists of a single overview diagram, given in Figure 18.4, and labeled as box 1.0 in the hierarchy diagram. The inputs and outputs are identified but are not associated with a particular subfunction or with a specific storage medium. The steps in the process block are enclosed in boxes to indicate that they correspond to subfunctions described in turn by an overview or detail diagram. Each box, relating to a subfunction, contains a number in its lower right-hand corner that identifies the corresponding HIPO diagram.

The second-level overview diagrams are given in Figures 18.5 and 18.6. They are logical extensions to the highest-level diagram and possess a similar format. Enclosing the inputs and outputs in a large box indicates that they should be interpreted collectively. (Shading is optional and is used for emphasis.) Again, specific device and medium types are not shown. The question of the level at which to include device types is dependent upon the person developing the HIPO package and upon installation guidelines. The author prefers to leave the device type open until the detail diagram level is reached.

The student will note that as we progress down through the hierarchy diagram the diagrams become more specific about the functions that are performed and that the output blocks and subsequent input blocks reflect intermediate records and files.

Detail Diagrams

The objective of a detail diagram is to relate specific functions to specific inputs and outputs. A detail diagram may also reflect specific device types.

The detail diagram number 2.1 (see the overview diagram in Figure 18.5) that corresponds to the "Validate sales transaction records and generate sorted transaction file" subfunction is given in Figure 18.7. Several new concepts are introduced: a series of steps to be repeated in succession is enclosed in a box and identified with the keyword DO. In this example, the set of steps will be executed for each sales transaction record. Detail diagram number 2.1 depicts the representa-

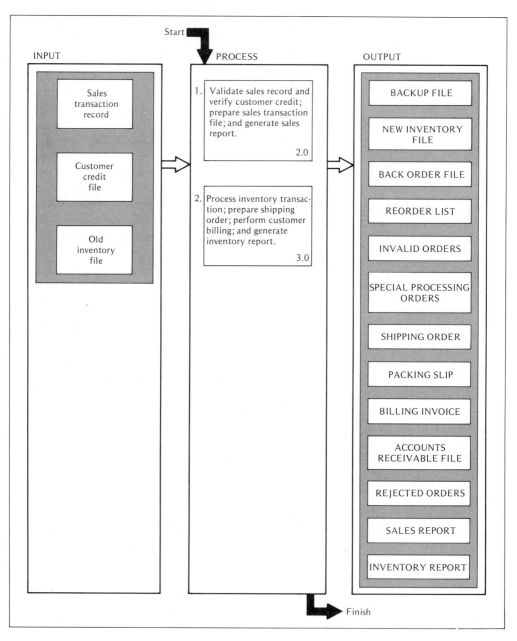

FIGURE 18.4   Overview diagram numbered 1.0 of the sales/inventory system. (This is the highest-level in the HIPO package in Figure 18.3.)

tion of the external routine SORT, used to sort a data file. The double-ended control arrow attached to the external reference box marked SORT indicates that control is returned to the calling program from the SORT routine. The diagram also shows a keyed data movement

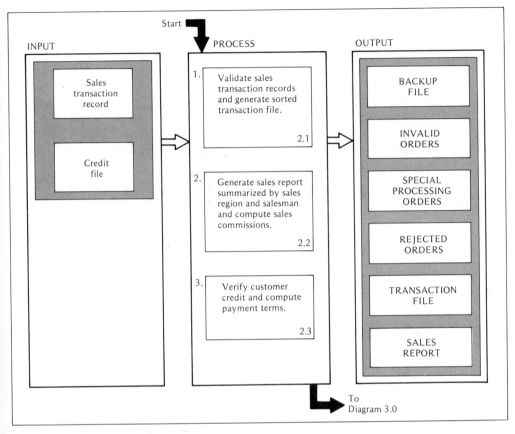

FIGURE 18.5   **Overview diagram numbered 2.0 of the sales/inventory system. (This diagram corresponds to the "sales record validation and sales report" subfunction in Figure 18.3.)**

arrow connector, which is used when a data movement arrow alone would complicate the diagram unnecessarily. (In this case, for example, the invalid order file, written in step 1.B(1) serves as input to step 3.) Inputs and outputs relate to specific steps in the process, and specific types of storage devices and media are indicated. As mentioned earlier, the farther down the hierarchy diagram you go, the closer the diagram comes to representing implementation.

Detail diagram number 2.2, which corresponds to the "generate sales report" subfunction, is given in Figure 18.8. This diagram illustrates two additional concepts: first, since there is no formal means of representing a temporary file, it is denoted by an output symbol drawn with dashed lines; second, step number 2 is composed of two substeps that perform a related function and use the same input. The substeps are enclosed in a box to indicate that they take a common input. The extended description has been omitted from this and subsequent detail diagrams because no new concepts are introduced.

Detail diagram number 2.3 corresponds to the "verify customer

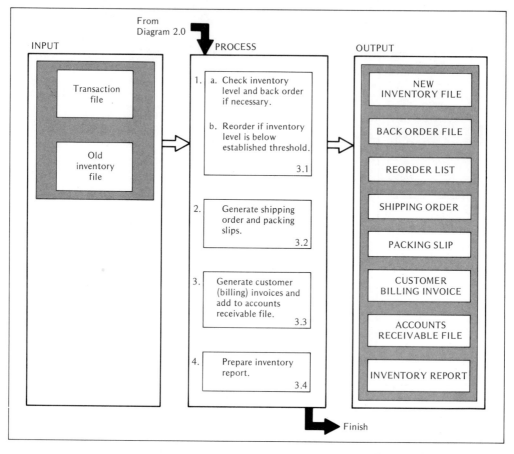

FIGURE 18.6 Overview diagram numbered 3.0 of the sales/inventory system. (This diagram corresponds to the "inventory processing" subfunction in Figure 18.3.)

credit" subfunction and is given in Figure 18.8. The diagram is intended to describe the case in which each transaction record that is read triggers a search of the credit file for that customer's credit record. This technique is contrasted with the DO box used in Figure 18.7, which describes a similar procedure. Since HIPO is intended to communicate, the technique should be selected that best communicates the required information for the case at hand. It should also be noticed in Figure 18.9 that the transaction file appears both as an input and as an output, which means the file is updated. This is the standard convention for denoting a file, record, or field that serves as output as well as input.

Detail diagram number 3.1, corresponding to the "check inventory level" subfunction, is given in Figure 18.10. It demonstrates the case in which two input files serve as input to the same step; the files are sorted and a "match" is made between the transaction file and the old inventory file on the inventory item number. The diagram also shows two output data movement arrows from two distinct steps [i.e.,

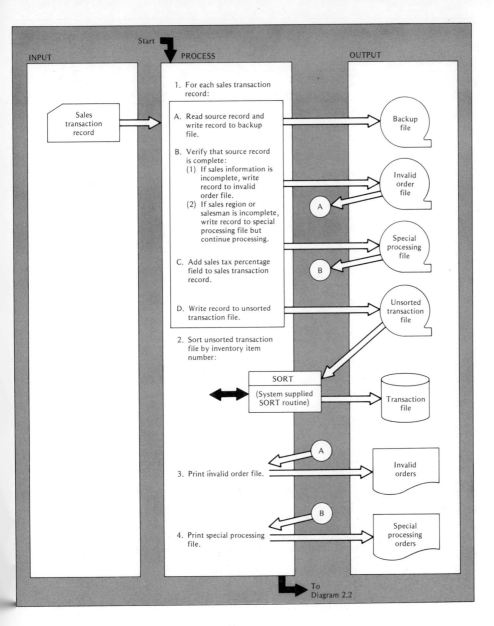

INPUT	PROCESS	OUTPUT

Start

INPUT

Sales transaction record

PROCESS

1. For each sales transaction record:

A. Read source record and write record to backup file.

B. Verify that source record is complete:
   (1) If sales information is incomplete, write record to invalid order file.
   (2) If sales region or salesman is incomplete, write record to special processing file but continue processing.

C. Add sales tax percentage field to sales transaction record.

D. Write record to unsorted transaction file.

2. Sort unsorted transaction file by inventory item number:

SORT

(System supplied SORT routine)

3. Print invalid order file.

4. Print special processing file.

To Diagram 2.2

OUTPUT

Backup file

Invalid order file

Special processing file

Unsorted transaction file

Transaction file

Invalid orders

Special processing orders

Extended Description

Notes	Routine	Label	Flow Chart	Ref.
1. Process sales transaction records, validating various fields, and producing a backup file, invalid order file, special processing file, and unsorted transaction file.	INVALID	BEGIN	VAL1	2.1.1
2. Sort unsorted transaction file, producing transaction file. Use system sort routine.	INVALID	SORT	———	2.1.2
3. Print invalid order file.	INVALID	P1	VAL2	2.1.3
4. Print special processing file.	INVALID	P2	VAL2	2.1.4

FIGURE 18.7   Detail diagram numbered 2.1 of the sales/inventory system. (This diagram corresponds to the "validate sales transaction records and generate sorted transaction file" subfunction in Figure 18.3.)

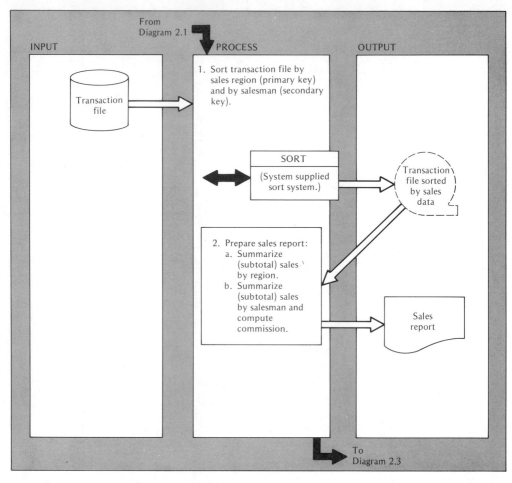

From
Diagram 2.1

INPUT

PROCESS

OUTPUT

Transaction
file

1. Sort transaction file by
   sales region (primary key)
   and by salesman (secondary
   key).

SORT

(System supplied
sort system.)

Transaction
file sorted
by sales
data

2. Prepare sales report:
   a. Summarize
      (subtotal) sales
      by region.
   b. Summarize
      (subtotal) sales
      by salesman and
      compute
      commission.

Sales
report

To
Diagram 2.3

FIGURE 18.8   **Detail diagram number 2.2 of the sales/inventory system with extended description omitted. (This diagram corresponds to the "generate sales report" subfunction in Figure 18.3.)**

Steps 1(c) and 1(d) and also 1(c) and 1(e)] that join a single output symbol. This is called a *multiple output arrow,* which simply means that two or more steps provide output to the same output entry. Diagram number 3.1 also shows a keyed control arrow connector that indicates that control is passed between the specified steps. (In this case, Step 1(c) passes control to Step 1(a).)

Detail diagrams numbers 3.2, 3.3, and 3.4, which complete the HIPO package, are given in Figures 18.11, 18.12, 18.13, respectively. These diagrams further demonstrate how the concepts introduced earlier can be used. Detail diagram 3.4, shown in Figure 18.13, demonstrates a *multiple input arrow,* which indicates that the same input entry is used as input to two or more steps.

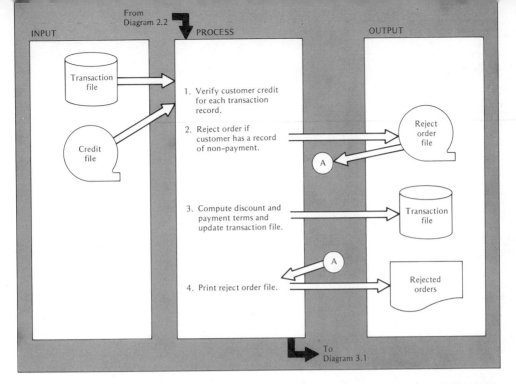

FIGURE 18.9 Detail diagram numbered 2.3 of the sales/inventory system with extended description omitted (this diagram corresponds to the "verify customer credit" subfunction in Figure 18.3).

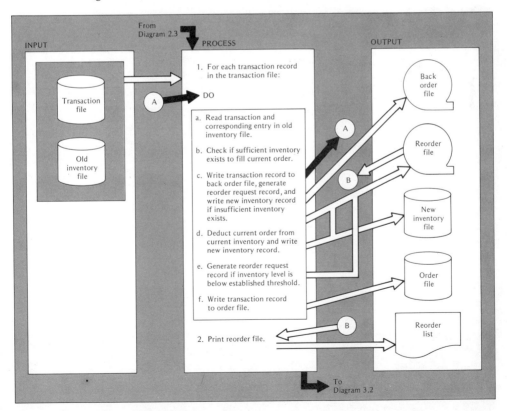

FIGURE 18.10 Detail diagram number 3.1 of the sales/inventory system with extended description omitted (this diagram corresponds to the "check inventory level" subfunction in Figure 18.3).

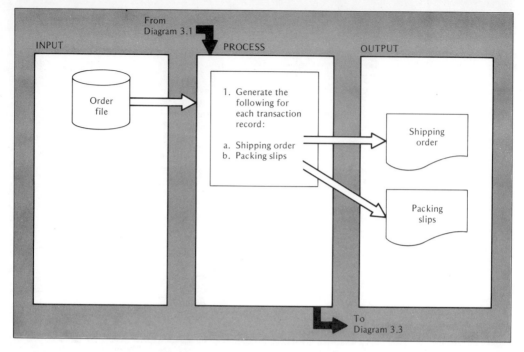

FIGURE 18.11 Detail diagram numbered 3.2 of the sales/inventory system with extended description omitted (this diagram corresponds to the "generate shipping order and packing slips" subfunction in Figure 18.3).

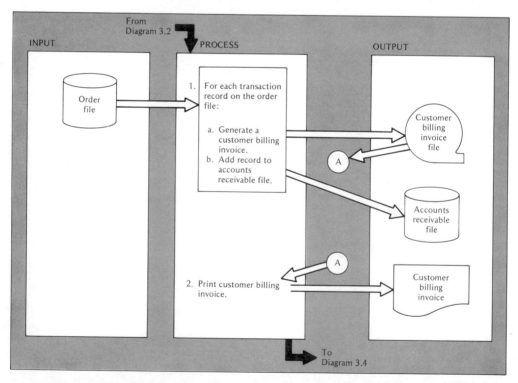

FIGURE 18.12 Detail diagram numbered 3.3 of the sales/inventory system with extended description omitted (this diagram corresponds to the "generate customer invoices . . ." subfunction in Figure 18.3).

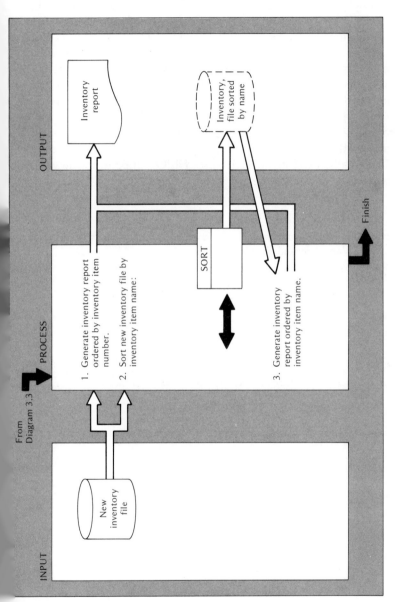

FIGURE 18.13 Detail diagram numbered 3.4 of the sales/inventory system with extended description omitted (this diagram corresponds to the "prepare inventory report" subfunction in Figure 18.3).

Summary

The HIPO package given in this section is intended solely to demonstrate the concepts introduced in Chapter 17. There is no right or wrong way to use HIPO. This is because HIPO is a set of conventions for describing systems, and the degree to which the conventions are adopted will be based on personal preference and installation standards.

There is a natural tendency to regard HIPO as a replacement for flow charts, decision tables, and so forth. This is definitely not the case. The use of HIPO provides a level of system description that is not possible with the older techniques. HIPO does not replace the other techniques; it simply provides a means of presenting the kind of information that would be cumbersome to present with those techniques. Through its extended descriptions, HIPO can point to the various other descriptive techniques.

Related Reading   Katzan, H. *Systems Design and Documentation: An Introduction to the HIPO Method.* New York: Van Nostrand Reinhold, 1976.

Part 6

Topics in Data Processing

File Design Concepts

STORAGE ORGANIZATION FOR FILES

Sequential Organization
Random Organization
Linked Organization
Ring Structures

DATA ORGANIZATION FOR FILES

Entry Sequenced File
Sorted File
Random File

RANDOMIZING TECHNIQUES

Division Method
Digit Analysis Method
Mid-Square Method
Folding Method
Algebraic Coding Method
Storage Management

INVERTED FILES

file is a set of related records, and each file has a set of characteristics that determine how the storage elements in the file are organized and how they can be accessed. When a file is established, the user specifies the file's characteristics and its content. Normally, file input and output operations are provided through the data management facility of an operating system. This chapter covers the technical information needed to effectively design files using the latest concepts in computer technology.

STORAGE ORGANIZATION FOR FILES

The methods of organizing storage for files closely resemble the file organization methods introduced in Chapter 14. Three methods are usually identified: sequential organization, random organization, and linked organization.

Sequential Organization

With *sequential organization,* the records in a file are sequenced by a key field and stored in consecutive order. Sequential organization is not the same as sequential access. A sequentially organized file must be accessed sequentially; however, a file need not be organized sequentially to be accessed sequentially. A case in point is the indexed sequential data set, mentioned previously, which can be accessed either sequentially or directly. One of the major advantages of sequential organization is that the access mechanism is automatically positioned to access the next record. Operational difficulties are encountered with sequential organization when records must be altered, deleted, or inserted. When sequential media are used, the file must be copied to another volume with the modifications being made as required. When direct-access media are used, records can be altered provided that the altered record is not shorter or longer than the original. Performing update operations on files with blocked records is also a problem, since the entire block must be rewritten.

Random Organization

With *random organization,* records are accessed through the physical location of the record or through a mathematical transformation on the key that produces the address where the record is stored. The three methods of accessing files with random organization are:

1. Direct address
2. Dictionary look-up
3. Calculation

With the *direct address* technique, the physical location of the record on direct-access storage is known to the application program and is supplied with a store or retrieve operation. With the *dictionary look-up* technique, a table of record keys is used, as in the indexed sequential access method. The index (or dictionary, as it is frequently called) contains the key and the physical direct-access location of the corresponding record. The primary advantage of the dictionary look-up technique is that the file can be accessed directly or sequentially; however, the time spent in searching the index for a key value may offset some of the advantages of using random organization.

The *calculation* technique involves converting the key to a physical direct-access address that is not necessarily unique. The calculation technique is often referred to as a randomizing technique and is discussed in detail in a later section of this chapter. The direct-address and dictionary look-up methods always provide a unique record address, whereas the calculation method does not. This means that two or more keys can randomize to the same address, so that a randomly organized file must always include the facility for pointer fields and overflow records. The "direct address" in a randomly organized file can be a physical cylinder-head address or relative track number (relative to the beginning of the storage volume) that is translated by the data management system into a cylinder-head address.

Linked Organization

In a file with *linked organization,* the records that comprise the file do not occupy consecutive or random locations but are "chained together" to establish the necessary relationship among records. The records do not necessarily reside in contiguous tracks; however, the tracks are located in extents assigned to the file. The chaining (or linking) of records is achieved through pointer fields that are contained in each record. Thus, the records that comprise a list organized file can be ordered on any field in the record. The only restriction is that a pointer field must exist in each record for each logical ordering in which it participates as a member record. For example, consider a "part inventory" file in which each record contains the following fields:

Part #
Name of part
Engineering drawing #
Warehouse location
Assembly in which the part is used

Figure 19.1 depicts a file in which three lists pass through each record: one list ordered by part #, another list ordered by part name, and the third list ordered by engineering drawing #. In the figure, the

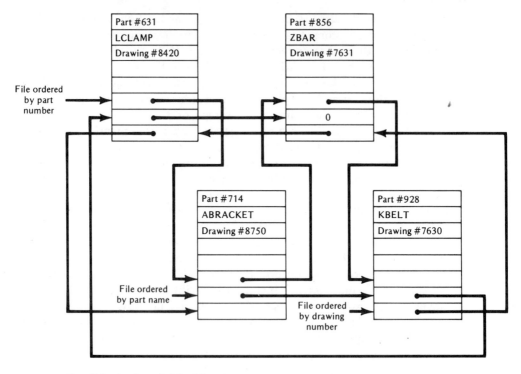

File ordered
by part
number

File ordered
by part name

File ordered
by drawing
number

Key: 0 denotes the end of the list.

FIGURE 19.1   Parts inventory file using linked organization, and ordered in three ways.

pointers are unidirectional for each list. Depending upon the needs of a particular application, they could also be bidirectional pointers. The advantages of linked organization are significant:

1. A record updated as part of one list is automatically updated for all lists in which it participates as a member.
2. Records can be inserted and deleted with a minimum of processing.
3. A record can be accessed directly if its direct address is known.

The disadvantage of linked organization is that file operations, especially searching, are time consuming because of the separate accesses involved.

A file with linked organization must be anchored, and that function is performed by a *master record* (also known as an *owner record* or a *descriptor* record). A master record must exist for each ordering in which the records of the file participate as members. Figure 19.2 gives an example of a linked file in which the method of organizing the storage structure is based on the hierarchical structure of the data.

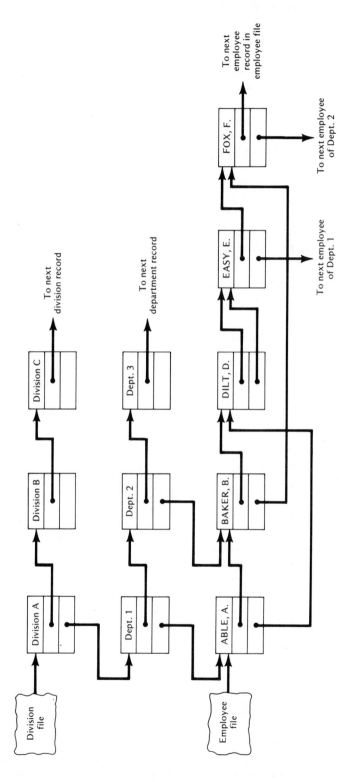

FIGURE 19.2 Linked file organized on the hierarchical structure of the data.

Ring Structures

A *ring structure* is a generalization of linked organization in which the last record in a chain points back to the first record or to the master record. The use of ring structures allows the records in a ring to be processed and to branch off and process logically-related records. Figure 18.3 depicts a policy file implemented using linked organization, in which claim records that belong to a particular policy are represented as a ring structure. Similarly, action records for a particular claim are also represented as a ring structure. Figure 19.3 also shows the flexibility of linked organization with a distinct claim file composed of claim records.

With linked organization and ring structures, the number of chain (or pointer) fields in a record are determined as follows:

1. One chain field for each link organized file in which the record participates, and two chain fields if the ordering is bidirectional.
2. One chain field for each ring structure for which the record serves as a master record.

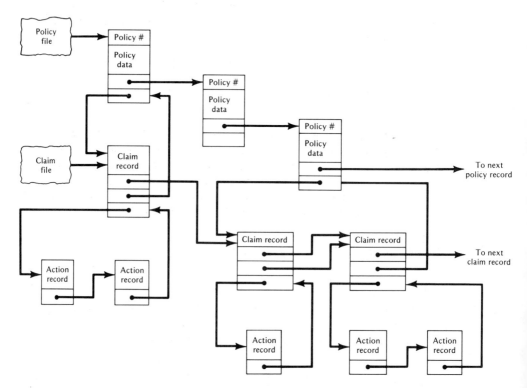

FIGURE 19.3   **Policy and claim files using linked organization with the use of ring structures to associate claim and action records with policy and claim records, respectively.**

3. One chain field for each ring structure of which the record is a member.

Because ring structures have a relatively small number of records and because a ring can be traversed until the appropriate record is reached, record insertion at arbitrary points is less cumbersome than it is with "open ended" list structures.

DATA ORGANIZATION FOR FILES

The way the data records that make up a file are sequenced determines how efficiently a file process can execute and the degree of complexity of the associated computer program. Many file processes can utilize either sorted or unsorted files; however, the use of unsorted files would be unnecessarily time consuming. Three sequencing methods are covered in the following paragraphs: entry sequence, sorted, and random.

Entry Sequenced File

An *entry sequenced file* utilizes sequential or linked organization and is designed to be accessed sequentially. The order of the records in the file depends on the sequence in which they were entered into the system. Most files are originally created as entry sequenced files, for one of the following reasons:

1. The order of records is not significant.
2. The records are entered in a prespecified order.
3. The file must be ordered through an ordering process.

Normally, a linked file exists as an entry sequenced file during its entire life cycle. Even though ordering algorithms have been developed for linked files (and lists, as the case may be), the ordering process is generally considered to be cumbersome and inefficient and is usually not performed. If a file is expected to be ordered, then it will be written as a sequentially organized file.

Sorted File

A *sorted file* is ordered by one or more fields known as sort keys. *Each* record in the file contains a sort key which is used in an ordering relation known as a *collating sequence.*

The collating sequence is governed to a large extent by the bit patterns of the characters involved. The fields are regarded as binary numbers to be ordered from small to large. When more than one field is used in the sort key, then the fields assume a lexicographic relationship and the ordering is determined accordingly.

The use of sorted files permits a search operation to be aborted when a record with a key higher in the collating sequence than the one needed is encountered during the operation. Otherwise, the entire file would have to be searched to determine the existence or nonexistence of a needed record.

Random File

The data records in a file with *random* sequence have no sequential relation to one another. Normally, direct organization is employed with a file of this type; however, an entry sequenced file may also possess a random sequence. Determining the existence or nonexistence of a particular record in a random entry sequence file would require an exhaustive search of the file. For randomly organized data files that are accessed directly, it is usually possible to use the algorithm used to access a record to determine if the record exists. This subject is covered under randomizing techniques.

RANDOMIZING TECHNIQUES

A *randomizing technique* is used with random organization where the address of a record is calculated. For files in which an actual record is expected to exist for each possible key value, the required storage for the file is simply the record size multiplied by the number of possible keys. Access to a record requires only a multiplication of the key value by the record size and the addition of a constant to obtain the record address. This method is known as the *direct multiplication transform*. For files in which the *loading factor*—the ratio of the number of actual records to the number of possible keys—is .5 or less, the direct multiplication transform is wasteful of storage space. Therefore, randomizing techniques are generally regarded as methods for mapping large key spaces into smaller address spaces. This section presents several alternate methods and related concepts. The various transforms are given first and techniques for storage management follow. Numerical keys are assumed; however, alphanumeric keys are easily converted to numeric keys by using binary representation of the characters or by encoding the letters A to Z into the decimal numbers 11 to 36.

Division Method

A frequently used randomization technique is to divide the key by the largest prime number (N) less than the number of available addresses and use the remainder as the record address. This is known as the *division method*. If the storage space can hold 1000 records, then N would be equal to 997 and the transformation of the key 36741 would generate a record address of 849. (The number 36741 divided by 997 gives a quotient of 36 and a remainder of 849.) In actual practice, the addresses generated by the transformed keys normally range between numbers A and B (usually taken to be relative record address locations) where $A < B$. The divisor N is the largest prime number less than $B - A$. The remainder R from the division operation is then added to A to generate the required record address.

Digit Analysis Method

Another method is based on a *digit analysis* of the set of possible keys. The distribution of digits in each position in the key is studied. The positions with the most skewed distribution of digits are eliminated from the key until the number of remaining digits is equal to the desired address length. Thus, if the key size is 6 digits and there are 2000 keys, deleting 3 digits from the key would correspond to a loading factor of .5. For a given file, the same digits are deleted from each key. The criteria for eliminating digits usually involves deleting digit positions in which the distribution of digits has high peaks or has a high standard deviation. If A is the beginning address of an extent assigned to the file, and it is determined from a digit analysis that the 2nd, 3rd, and 6th digits of a six-digit key are to be eliminated, then the key 367415 would correspond to a record address of $A + 341$.

Mid-Square Method

In the *mid-square* method, the key is multiplied by itself, and digits are truncated on both ends until an address of the desired size is obtained. For a storage space of 1000 records (addresses from 0 to 999), the key 367415 would correspond to a record address of $A + 937$. Again, A is the beginning address of the extent assigned to the file and the intermediate calculations are:

$367415 \times 367415 = 134993782225$

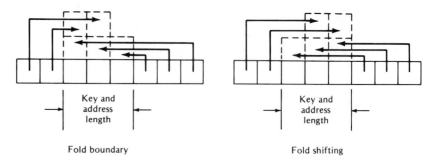

FIGURE 19.4   **Two variations of the folding randomization technique.**

The four leading digits (i.e., 1349) and the five trailing digits (i.e., 82225) are eliminated from the product.

Folding Method

In the *folding method* of randomization, the key is partitioned into fields the same length as the relative address length of the record storage area. Thus, the digits of the key are folded onto themselves and added. Two variations to this method exist: *fold boundary* folds the key at the boundary of the parts as if folding paper; and *fold shifting* shifts over the parts to the further boundary before adding. Both variations are illustrated in Figure 19.4. Using the fold boundary technique, the key 29367415 is transformed into a relative address of 791 for a storage area with 1000 record locations as follows:

$$
\begin{array}{r}
92 \\
514 \\
29\;\boxed{367}\;415 \\
\hline
791 \quad \textit{relative address}
\end{array}
$$

Carries from addition are ignored in the sum that gives the relative address.

Algebraic Coding Method

In *algebraic coding* selected digits of the key are used as coefficients of a polynomial. Thus, a six-digit key of the form $k_1 k_2 k_3 k_4 k_5 k_6$ would generate a relative address for a storage area with 1000 records in the following way:

Key	*Polynomial*
$k_1 k_2 k_3 k_4 k_5 k_6$	$ax^2 + bx + c$

For example, a key of 367415 with a value of 10 for the independent variable x in the polynomial would generate the following relative address:

Key	*Polynomial*	*Relative Address*
3 6 7 4 1 5	$6 \times (10)^2 + 4 \times (10) + 1 =$	641

The respective digits in the key that are used as coefficients are fixed for all records in the file.

Storage Management

The use of randomizing techniques requires an embedded key—a key that exists as a field in the record. To insert a record in a file with random storage organization, a randomization technique is applied to a record key to obtain a record address in the file. If the computed record area is unoccupied, the record is inserted and the operation is complete. It is possible, however, that a previous record may be stored in the record area, since randomization techniques do not guarantee that unique addresses will be generated. Records assigned to the same record area are called *synonyms*. The problem of synonyms can be handled in two ways: (1) an overflow area can be used, or (2) the consecutive spill method can be used. An *overflow area* is a portion of the file set aside for synonyms. When the first synonym record for a given record area occurs, that record is placed in the overflow area and a pointer to it is placed in the primary record area. Successive synonyms for the same record area are chained to previous synonyms in the overflow area. Therefore, when a synonym is generated for the insertion operation, the chain of previous synonyms is traversed to determine that the new record key is unique before it is placed in the overflow area and chained to previous synonyms. For retrieval, the search key must be matched with the record key for the record in the primary record area and for all synonyms in the overflow area.

With the *consecutive spill* method, the storage space is considered to be circular. When a synonym occurs, the insertion process successively searches for vacancies starting from the record's primary address, and places the record in the first vacancy found. If the search for a vacancy returns to the original address, then the storage space is full. For retrieval, the randomization technique generates a primary record address. If the search key and the key of the record in the primary record area agree, the record is retrieved and the operation is complete. Otherwise, the search key is compared with record keys from successive areas until a match is found (indicating success) or a vacancy is encountered (denoting failure).

A variation and a combination of the above techniques is known as the *bucket concept*. With this method, each calculated record address corresponds to a storage area that can hold several records. For a given record, the randomization technique supplies the address of an appropriate bucket. The consecutive spill method is used for records within the bucket and the overflow method is used when the bucket is full. Access time to successive records in a bucket should be shorter than the access time to the bucket itself. Therefore, a disk track is a convenient form for a bucket to take.

The use of randomization techniques requires a certain amount of sophistication in the sense that sequential organization is used with the consecutive spill method and linked organization is used with overflow areas. Randomization is, however, an effective technique for what are known as "70–30 files," in which 70% of the activity concerns only 30% of the file.

INVERTED FILES

A selection operation on unsorted files can be inefficient and, in many cases, an exhaustive search of all of the records in the file may be required. One of the options is to sort the file on the desired key, but then either a duplicate copy of the file is generated or the original ordering is lost. The use of an *inverted file* is a means of achieving the advantages of a sorted duplicate file without processing and storage costs.

Figure 19.5 gives a *matrix representation* of a personnel information file that could be stored sequentially, randomly, or in a form of linked organization. The file is ordered by "employee number," which serves as the identifier field. Suppose that it is necessary to select the records based on one or more of the following attributes:

City
Job
Training
Marital status
Home status
Salary

Clearly, with sequential or linked organization, the entire file would have to be searched. With an *inverted file* structure, however, a list of the attributes on the basis of which a randomly organized file would be searched is predetermined and the identifier fields (or record addresses) of records that possess a particular attribute value are stored (along with that value) as an index file. The inverted file contains

Attribute

Employee Number	Name	S.S. #	City	Age	Job	Training	Marital Status	Home Status	Salary
1234	ROGERS, A. A.	639216034	NEW YORK	42	EXEC	BUS	M	O	37000.00
3198	ADAMS, J. C.	234169132	BOSTON	27	OPER	D.P.	S	R	9134.50
3201	KIRK, B. K.	639417734	NEW YORK	30	PROG	MATH	M	R	14500.00
4226	BART, B. B.	234774420	BOSTON	19	OPER	D.P.	M	R	7350.00
5784	KICK, W. F.	639011234	NEW YORK	54	EXEC	ENG.	M	O	74000.00
5814	FOX, F. C.	639144440	NEW YORK	47	EXEC	BUS	S	R	43500.00
6450	ABEL, Z. L.	513687290	NEWARK	25	PROG	D.P.	S	O	12680.00
7531	THOMS, F. K.	639382227	NEW YORK	28	SALES	BUS	M	R	31500.00

FIGURE 19.5   Matrix representation.

attributes, attribute values, and internal references to records that possess the associated attributes.

An inverted file structure for the personnel information file in Figure 19.5 is given in Figure 19.6. In this case, the file is inverted on all of the attributes and on all the attribute values. If the records of New York residents were needed, for example, the list of identifiers would be retrieved by locating the attribute CITY and the attribute value NEW YORK, to obtain the following list of identifiers:

NEW YORK
   1234
   3201
   5784
   5814
   7531

The required records would then be accessed by either a direct access, dictionary look-up, or randomizing technique. If retrieval is based on multiple attribute values, such as:

Resident of New York,
Single,
Rents home

Attribute	Value	List of Identifiers (or record addresses)
CITY	BOSTON	3198, 4226
CITY	NEWARK	6450
CITY	NEW YORK	1234, 3201, 5784, 5814, 7531
AGE	>30	1234, 5784, 5814
AGE	≤30	3198, 3201, 4226, 6450, 7531
JOB	EXEC	1234, 5784, 5814
JOB	OPER	3198, 4226
JOB	PROG	3201, 6450
JOB	SALES	7531
TRAINING	BUS	1234, 5814, 7531
TRAINING	D.P.	3198, 4226, 6450
TRAINING	ENG	5784
TRAINING	MATH	3201
MARITAL STATUS	M	1234, 3201, 4226, 5784, 7531
MARITAL STATUS	S	3198, 5814, 6450
HOME STATUS	R	3198, 3201, 4226, 5814, 7531
HOME STATUS	O	1234, 5784, 6450
SALARY	>50K	5784
SALARY	>25K and ≤50K	1234, 5814, 7531
SALARY	≤25K	3198, 3201, 4226, 6450

FIGURE 19.6   Inverted file structure for the personnel information file given in Figure 19.5.

then a set operation (such as *intersection*) would be used on the identifier lists as shown below:

$$NEW\ YORK \cap SINGLE \cap RENT = \text{Composite Condition}$$

1234	3198	3198	5814
3201	5814	3201	
5784	6450	4226	
5814		5814	
7531		7531	

In this example, the record with identifier 5814 is the only one that satisfies each of the three conditions stated.

The disadvantage of an inverted file is that it must be updated each time the primary file is updated. Therefore, an alternate method would be to use linked organization and run a chain of pointers through records for a given attribute. This technique increases the number of pointer fields that must accompany each record, but is a viable alternative to the update problem.

Vocabulary   The student should be familiar with the following terms in the context in which they were used in the chapter.

algebraic-coding method	linked organization
bucket concept	loading factor
collating sequence	master record
consecutive spill method	overflow area
descriptor record	primary record area
digit analysis method	random file
direct multiplication transform	randomizing technique
division method	ring structure
entry sequenced file	sequential organization
file	sorted file
folding method	synonym
inverted file	

Exercises   1. Is it possible to sort a linked file? If so, how would it be done?

2. Why does a synonym occur?

3. Develop a flow chart describing the algorithm used in each of the following randomizing techniques: (a) division method, (b) digit analysis method, (c) mid-square method, and (d) folding method.

4. What is a bucket and how is it used?

5. What is a 70–30 file?

6. Develop an algorithm for the consecutive spill method.

Related Reading

Burch, J. G., Jr., and Strater, F. F., Jr. *Information Systems: Theory and Practice.* Santa Barbara: Calif.: Hamilton Publishing, 1974.

Dippel, G., and House, W. C. *Information Systems: Data Processing and Evaluation.* Glenview, Ill.: Scott, Foresman, 1969.

Dodd, G. G. "Elements of data management systems," *Computing Surveys,* vol. 1, no. 2 (June 1969): 117–133.

Katzan, H. *Computer Data Management and Data Base Technology.* New York: Van Nostrand Reinhold, 1975.

Lum, V. Y., Yuen, P. S. T., and Dodd, M. "Key to address transform techniques: A fundamental performance study on large existing formatted files," *Communications of the ACM,* vol. 14, no. 4 (April 1971): 228–239.

Meadow, C. T. *The Analysis of Information Systems.* New York: John Wiley and Sons, 1967.

Data Base Technology

DATA BASE ENVIRONMENT

Conventional Files
Data Management Facilities
Data Base Requirements

DATA INDEPENDENCE AND MAPPING

Entity
Attribute
Value
Representation
Data Mapping
Classification of Data Maps

DATA BASE STRUCTURE

Chained List Structure
Variable Pointer List Structure
Ring Structure

CASE STUDY

DATA BASE MANAGEMENT

data base is a centralized collection of data stored for use in one or more applications. Essentially, this means that the files of an organization are integrated to make better use of the data at a lower storage cost. This chapter presents the basic concepts of data base technology.

DATA BASE ENVIRONMENT

Our interest in data base technology is more than an intellectual excursion into new methods of organizing and accessing data. The modern era in data processing technology has enabled immediate access to integrated informational resources via telecommunications facilities. Inputs to the system are heterogeneous and occur at random intervals. Requests for information from the system are dynamic and time-dependent, so that queries and responses cannot be prepared beforehand. Since files are large, redundant data must be factored out to reduce the time required to access desired information. Information must be current and up-to-date to meet the needs of a modern society. Therefore, an informational change must be reflected immediately in all associated files. Because these requirements are so widely known, it is often forgotten how they evolved and why they constitute a distinct departure from conventional data management techniques.

Conventional Files

A data file has been regarded as a set of related data records; similarly, a record is regarded as a set of related fields. In the absence of data management facilities, however, both file organization and data organization are identical, as illustrated in Figure 20.1. The lack of data management facilities is also characterized by the fact that data organization is reflected in the logic of a program and is "committed" to a single device type. Changes to data organization, device type, or to both require modification of the application program. Moreover, files of this

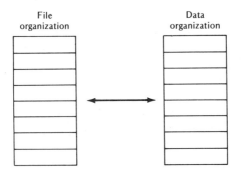

File organization   Data organization

FIGURE 20.1   Without conventional data management facilities, file and data organization are synonymous.

type are normally limited to the set of computer applications for which the data is organized.

Data Management Facilities

When data management facilities are used, a distinction is made between file organization and both data organization and data access. Input and output operations, device control, and direct-access space allocation are managed by data management routines so that data is not bound to a particular set of programs or applications. As Figure 20.2 shows, data can be organized as non-contiguous extents for which several forms of data access are provided. Records can be formatted to achieve operational efficiency. Modern data management facilities greatly extend the file processing capabilities of current systems and are extensive in scope and complexity. However, data management as we know it today is lacking in the following requirement: fast access to large, integrated files that are designed to be updated dynamically in a real time operational environment.

Data Base Requirements

Modern data base environments involve a capability, depicted in Figure 20.3, to define files over the totality of data in the information space.

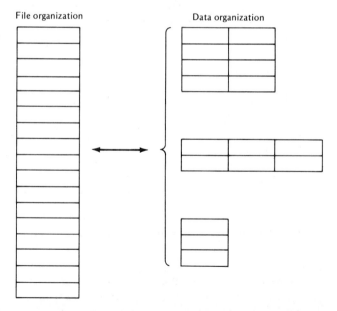

FIGURE 20.2 With data management facilities, file and data organization are distinct, and data is not "committed" to a particular set of programs and applications.

File organization   Data base

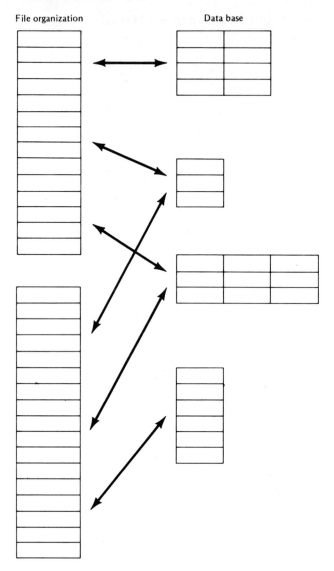

FIGURE 20.3   **In a data base environment, files can be defined over the totality of data in the information space.**

Systems of this type require more than a simple arrangement of data items in storage. File definition involves reference to objects and relationships as they exist in the real world through a complex arrangement of data mappings, structural relationships, and complicated graph structures. One way of characterizing a data base is: *it is the process of taking the knowledge about data that is implicitly built into programs and making it explicitly available to the user in a formal manner at the systems level.*

DATA INDEPENDENCE AND MAPPING

The structural information about data that is customarily built into computer programs is made available to the user in a data base environment as a set of descriptors. (In data base technology terminology, a *schema* is a definition of the data in a data base, and a *subschema* is the definition of that part of the data base that is known to an application program.) Thus, the description of the data in a data base exists independently of the data, so that relationships between data elements can be changed without requiring changes to the application programs that access the data. Data base needs are satisfied by entities, attributes, values, particular methods of representation, and data mapping.

Entity

A person, place, or thing—real or abstract—about which we record data is called an *entity*. Each entity has a set of properties that describe it; different entities have different properties. A collection of similar entities with the same properties is known as an *entity set*. Common examples of entity sets are a set of student records, a set of bank accounts, a set of insurance policies, and a set of automobile licenses. The entities that compose an entity set possess at least one property that distinguishes them from one another; the data value that corresponds to this property is called an *identifier*. A commonly known identifier is a social security number or a student identification number.

Attribute

A property of an entity is called an *attribute*. Typical attributes of a person would be name, age, sex, height, and weight. Similarly, attributes of an employee would be employee number, name, supervisor, job title, and plant location. Attributes of an automobile would be make, body style, age, color, and owner. In a data base environment, attributes can also be entities that possess attributes. For example, the owner attribute of an automobile is a person that has attributes and the job title attribute of an employee has attributes, such as job name, educational requirements, pay range, and career path.

Value

In everyday terminology, a *fact* is a particular value for the attribute of an entity. A typical example is, "Jane has green eyes." In this case, "green" is the value of the eye-color attribute for the entity identified as "Jane." Similarly, in the statement, "The automobile with license number ABC 123 is red," the automobile is the entity, the license number is one attribute, ABC 123 is its value, color is another attribute, and red is its value.

Representation

As a direct result of the method of "data modeling," given above, the concept of information in a data base environment can be reduced to the elements of entity, attribute, and value. An element of information can be represented as a point in a three-dimensional space, as shown in Figure 20.4. The axes correspond to a set of entities, a set of attributes, and a set of values. The three-dimensional space used to represent information is called an *information space*. An attribute/value pair is called a *descriptor*. All of the descriptors of an entity lie in a plane that is parallel to the attribute and value axes and that intersects the entity axes at the correct point.

Another method of representation is with an entity/attribute matrix, such as the one shown in Figure 20.5. Each row of the matrix represents values corresponding to the attributes of an entity. Each column corresponds to values assigned to an attribute for different entities. One attribute set contains unique values, and this attribute set is known as the *identifier*.

When data base information is stored, the attribute names are not also stored, and the attribute values are recognized on the basis of their relative position in the storage space. When more than one data value is being represented, the identifier attribute value is not repeated for each data value. This means that an entity is represented by one entity identifier and one or more attribute values. The entity/attribute matrix is a way of viewing a set of data, which is normally not stored

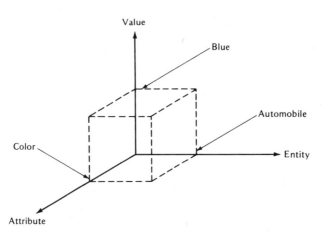

FIGURE 20.4   An element of information can be depicted as a point in a three-dimensional space known as an information space.

Attributes

	A_1	A_2	A_3	...	A_m
E_1	$V_{1,1}$	$V_{1,2}$	$V_{1,3}$	...	$V_{1,m}$
E_2	$V_{2,1}$	$V_{2,2}$	$V_{2,3}$	...	$V_{2,m}$
E_3	$V_{3,1}$	$V_{3,2}$	$V_{3,3}$	...	$V_{3,m}$
Entities •	•				•
•	•				•
•	•				•
E_n	$V_{n,1}$	$V_{n,2}$	$V_{n,3}$	...	$V_{n,m}$

FIGURE 20.5 **Data representation can be conceptualized as an entity/attribute matrix. Each row of the matrix represents values assigned to attributes of an entity.**

as a matrix because of the redundancy of storing the same data value more than once. More efficient storage management is achieved through the use of relations and data mapping.

Data Mapping

It is important to recognize what the process of recording information entails. Recording an item of information establishes a *fact,* which is a relationship between the members of two sets. This relationship is called a *data mapping.* For example, in the following lists the relationship between the student with a student number of 143206319 and a rank of "sophomore (indicated with a connecting line) states that 'The student with student number 143206319 has a rank of sophomore.' " In the example, "student number" and "rank" are attributes; the numbers listed and the names freshman, sophomore, etc. are values of the respective attributes. Data mapping reduces or eliminates the redundancy in a data base. Instead of storing the attribute value for each identifier, it is only stored once and pointers are established linking the identifiers to the associated data values. Because data mappings can be established between records in a data base environment, a considerable amount of storage space can be saved and operational flexibility is increased.

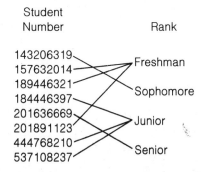

Classification of Data Maps

A data map is classified by whether it is simple or complex. If E represents an identity attribute set and V represents another attribute set, then a mapping is written symbolically as $E{\rightarrow}V$, which is interpreted as a mapping from set E to set V. In a *simple mapping*, each element of E can be related to no more than one element of V. In a *complex mapping*, an element of E can be related to many elements of V. An example of a simple mapping is:

(mapping)
$$Employee \ \# \quad \rightarrow \quad Social \ Security \ \#$$

An example of a complex mapping is:

(mapping)
$$School \ \# \quad \rightarrow \quad Student \ \# \ of \ Students \ in \ School$$

If the set V also represents an identity attribute set, then an inverse mapping can be defined. An example of a simple inverse mapping is:

(inverse)
$$Employee \ \# \quad \leftarrow \quad Social \ Security \ \#$$

This is the same example given above. In this case, both the mapping and the inverse mapping are simple. An example of a complex inverse mapping is:

(inverse)
$$Policy \ \# \quad \leftarrow \quad Billing \ Date$$

In this case, the inverse mapping is complex, as shown, but the original mapping is simple. An example of a complex mapping with a simple inverse mapping is:

(mapping)
$$School \ \# \quad \rightleftarrows \quad Student \ \# \ of \ Students \ in \ School$$
(inverse)

An example of a complex mapping with a complex inverse mapping is:

(mapping)
$$Part \ \# \quad \rightleftarrows \quad Warehouse \ \# \ of \ Warehouse \ Where \ Parts \ are \ Stored$$
(inverse)

DATA BASE STRUCTURE

In a data base system, an item of information is stored as a fact, which is represented as a data mapping. The manner in which a data base is stored is referred to as *data base structure.* Three methods of storage are commonly employed: chained list structure, variable pointer list structure, and ring structure.

Chained List Structure

Chained list structure is analogous to the linked organization presented in Chapter 18. An owner record serves to anchor the list, and records

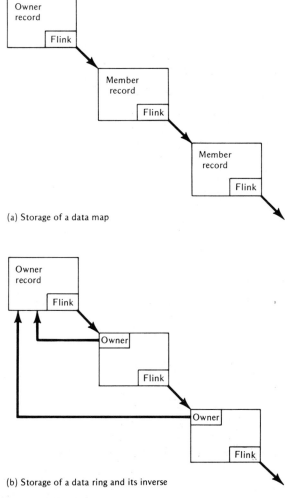

(a) Storage of a data map

(b) Storage of a data ring and its inverse

FIGURE 20.6   Chained list structure.

are linked through pointer fields in each member record. When owner pointers are also given, the inverse mapping can also be represented. A chained list structure is illustrated in Figure 20.6.

Variable Pointer List Structure

In a *variable pointer list structure,* the owner record contains pointers to each of its member records, and if owner pointers are also present, the inverse mapping can be represented. A variable pointer list structure is shown in Figure 20.7. One of the advantages of variable pointer list structure over chained list structure is that if a pointer is destroyed, only one record is lost, rather than the entire list.

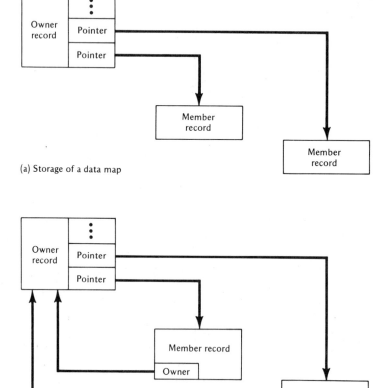

(a) Storage of a data map

(b) Storage of a data map and its inverse

FIGURE 20.7   Variable pointer list structure.

Ring Structure

A *ring structure* is the same as the ring structure presented in Chapter 18, and is depicted in Figure 20.8. A ring structure can be used to represent a data map and its inverse. The inverse is achieved by following the ring until the owner record is reached.

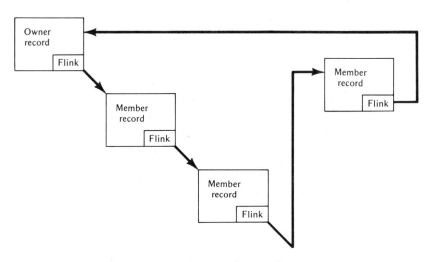

FIGURE 20.8   A ring structure can be used to store a data map and its inverse.

CASE STUDY

A familiar example of a complex data map is the set of project, job, and employee records in an organization. In this example, it is given that: (1) an employee works on one project and is assigned to one job, and (2) employees with different jobs are assigned to the same project. The following assignments are made:

Project	Employees
1	JONES, SMITH, BAKER
2	THOMAS, WORTH
3	STREETER

Job	Employees
A	SMITH, BAKER, STREETER
B	JONES, WORTH
C	THOMAS

The complex data maps are written symbolically as follows:

Project → *Employee*
Job → *Employee*

The implication is that only one copy of each employee record exists and that it participates in two data maps. When a chained list structure is used with the data base, records for employees on the same project are chained together as member records, and the project record serves as the owner record. Similarly, records for employees with the same job are chained together as member records and the job record serves as the owner record. As a result, each employee record includes a pointer field for each of the two list structures in which it participates (see Figure 20.9). When a variable pointer list structure is used with the data base, pointers to member records are stored in the owner record, so that each owner record contains an entry for each of its member records and a member record can only be accessed through its owner record (see Figure 20.10).

DATA BASE MANAGEMENT

The current thinking on data base management is that it should be performed by a combination of human procedures and software facilities. The person involved with data base management is called the *data base administrator* (DBA). Some corporate executives have predicted that in the near future some organizations will have vice-presidents of data base management. The person responsible for software required for data base management is known as the *data base manager* (DBM) and operates under the direction of the data base administrator to establish the structure of the data base and control the manner in which it is used and by whom. The structure of the data base environment is shown in Figure 20.11.

The data base administrator communicates with the data base manager with a language known as the *data description language* (DDL). The data base administrator defines the structure of the data base, assigns names to entities, attributes, records, and files, and specifies the necessary privacy and data security measures that must be taken during access control. In short, the data base administrator defines the *schema*, which describes the data base, and the *subschema*, which describes the part of the data base that an individual user can access.

The user communicates with the data base manager using a *data manipulation language* (DML), which opens and closes files and performs input and output operations. When a user requests access to a file through the data manipulation language, the data base manager uses the description of the file provided by the data base administrator in the data description language (i.e., the schema and subschema) to access

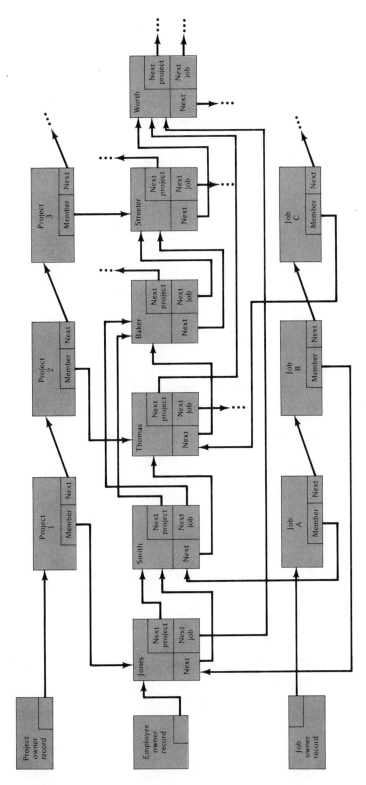

FIGURE 20.9 Chained list structure for a data mapping of the form: *Project → Employee* and *Job → Employee*

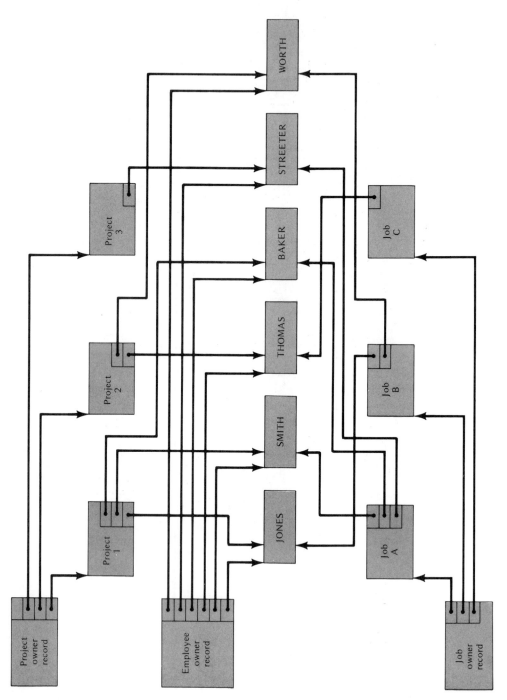

FIGURE 20.10 Variable pointer list structure for a data mapping of the form: *Project → Employee* and *Job → Employee*

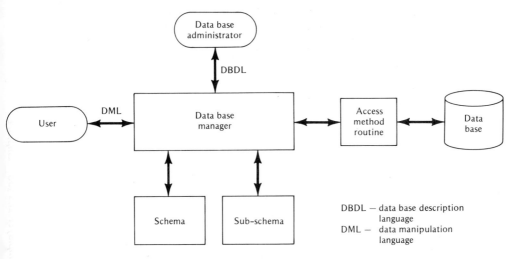

FIGURE 20.11   Structure of the data base environment.

the correct information, perform editing and conversion as required, and provide the requested service.

Vocabulary   The student should be familiar with the following terms in the context in which they were used in the chapter.

attribute	entity set
chained list structure	identifier
complex mapping	information space
data base	inverse mapping
data base administrator	ring structure
data base description language	schema
data base manager	simple mapping
data base manipulation language	subschema
data mapping	value
descriptor	variable pointer list structure
entity	

Exercises   1. How can a ring structure be used to represent an inverted file structure?

2. How does the use of a data base eliminate redundancy?

3. What is the difference between a data base administrator and a data base manager?

4. What is the difference between a schema and a subschema?

5. To what type of file organization, covered in an earlier chapter, is the variable pointer list similar?

6. Represent the file given in matrix representation in Figure 20.5 as a chained list structure.

7. Represent the file given in matrix representation in Figure 20.5 as a variable pointer list structure.

8. Draw a set of data mappings for the following information:

Garment #	Class	Quality Level	Color	Location (Rack #)	Order #
9451	Suit	A	Brown	34	2984
10114	Coat	B	Blue	41	0032
10115	Coat	A	Beige	41	0032
11125	Suit	C	Black	34	6321
12532	Dress	A	White	55	1794
12611	Pants	B	Green	39	2984
13001	Suit	B	Brown	34	3009
15539	Coat	B	Blue	41	0032
16327	Dress	C	Black	55	6321
17199	Dress	C	White	55	6321
18777	Pants	A	White	39	1794
18778	Pants	A	White	39	2984
18779	Pants	A	White	39	0032

9. Represent the data of Exercise 8 as an inverted file stored as a ring structure.

10. Represent the data of Exercise 8 as either a chained list or variable pointer list structure.

Related Reading

Date, C. J. *An Introduction to Database Systems.* Reading, Mass.: Addison-Wesley, 1975.

Katzan, H. *Computer Data Management and Data Base Technology.* New York: Van Nostrand Reinhold, 1975.

Lyon, J. K. *An Introduction to Data Base Design.* New York: John Wiley and Sons, 1971.

Micrographics

OVERVIEW

Steps in the Micrographic Process
Basic Technology of Computer Micrographics
Comparison of Conventional Computer Output and
    Micrographics
Microfilm Technology

MICROGRAPHIC MEDIA

MICROGRAPHIC RECORDING
TECHNOLOGY

Cathode Ray Tube Recording
Light Emitting Diode and Fiberoptic Recording
Electron Beam Recording
Laser Beam Recording

MICROGRAPHIC READERS AND
APPLICATIONS

Retrieval
Applications
Practical Considerations

ne of the most promising areas of data processing technology is *micrographics,* which is defined as the creation and use of all types of microforms and microimages—microfilm, microfiche, and computer output microfilm (COM). Almost everyone is familiar with at least one form of micrographics. The purpose of this chapter is to introduce the technology of modern micrographics and survey several of its most widespread applications.

OVERVIEW

The concept of micrographics has been in existence and in use for many years. Most readers will be familiar with the "microdot" used in spy episodes for concealing secret information. In everyday English, micrographics simply refers to a miniaturized form of a photographed record or document. A familiar example is microfilm used to store reproductions of newspapers, business records, and documents. The primary advantage of the use of microfilm is that the required storage space is reduced and the information remains reasonably accessible.

Steps in the Micrographic Process

The basic steps in the processing (or use) of micrographics are: (1) recording, (2) film developing and printing, (3) storage, and (4) information retrieval. Recording is performed through a photographic process, and the reduction of size is accomplished by the photo-optical recording equipment. The images are then developed and printed on a suitable medium—usually a form of film, because of its optical characteristics. Information is subsequently composed onto film, sheets, or cards and traditional filing techniques can be employed. Because micrographics presents information in a reduced size, special reading devices are required. Typical reading devices are microfilm readers, microfiche viewers, and aperture card readers. Some reading devices also have indexing facilities in order to locate an item of information quickly.

Basic Technology of Computer Micrographics

The basic technology of micrographics is the same, regardless if a computer is used or not. By connecting the computer equipment to the micrographic equipment, however, in either an on-line or off-line mode, the system can produce output at a rate of up to 20 times the rate of printed output.

Figure 21.1 shows the basic technology of micrographic recording in either an off-line or an on-line mode of operation. The off-line mode is slower and less efficient since an output tape, written during

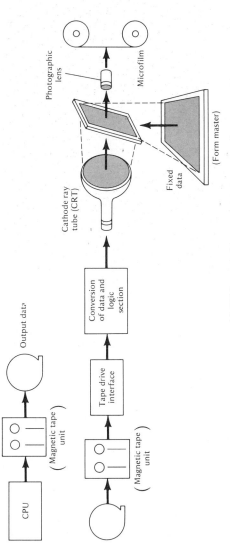

(a) Off-line operation

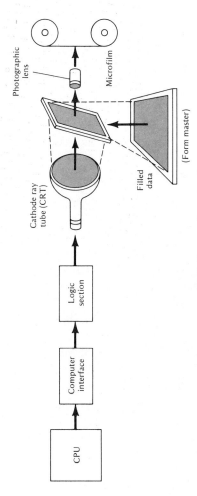

(b) On-line operation

FIGURE 21.1   Basic technology of micrographic recording.

the computer processing part of the cycle, is used as input to the recording part of the cycle. The tape writing and the subsequent tape reading are time consuming operations. This mode of operation has distinct advantages, however, which will be covered later. The on-line mode is fast and efficient since an image generated by the computer at electronic speed is transferred directly to the recording equipment. Micrographic recording is frequently performed through the use of a mini-computer.

Comparison of Conventional Computer Output and Micrographics

In conventional computer output processing the following discrete steps are identified:

1. Computer processing
2. Printed output
3. Decollating
4. Bursting
5. Assembly, binding, and distribution
6. Manual lookup and retrieval
7. Office storage
8. Archival storage

When it is appropriate to use micrographics, the equivalent steps are:

1. Computer processing
2. Micrographic recording
3. Film developing
4. Duplication and distribution
5. Automatic retrieval
6. Office and archival storage

The advantages of using micrographics are clearly inherent in the output rate, the retrieval time, and the storage costs. An overview of computer-output-microfilm workflow is given in Figure 21.2.

Microfilm Technology

Microfilming is performed by passing a document, either automatically or manually, through a microfilming device, such as a rotary microfilmer or a planetary camera. The images are recorded on silver halide original

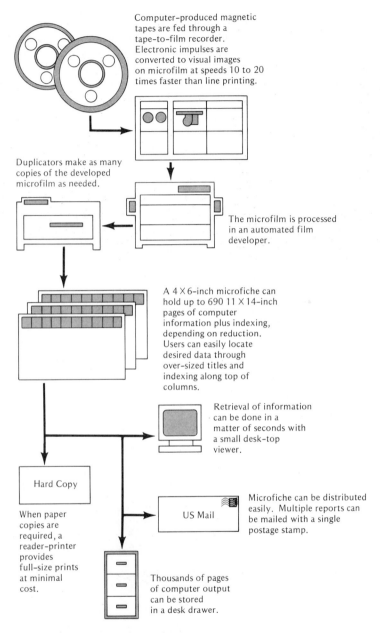

Computer-produced magnetic tapes are fed through a tape-to-film recorder. Electronic impulses are converted to visual images on microfilm at speeds 10 to 20 times faster than line printing.

Duplicators make as many copies of the developed microfilm as needed.

The microfilm is processed in an automated film developer.

A 4 X 6-inch microfiche can hold up to 690 11 X 14-inch pages of computer information plus indexing, depending on reduction. Users can easily locate desired data through over-sized titles and indexing along top of columns.

Retrieval of information can be done in a matter of seconds with a small desk-top viewer.

Hard Copy

When paper copies are required, a reader-printer provides full-size prints at minimal cost.

US Mail

Microfiche can be distributed easily. Multiple reports can be mailed with a single postage stamp.

Thousands of pages of computer output can be stored in a desk drawer.

FIGURE 21.2   Computer-output-microfilm workflow.

film and then developed. Copies of the microimage can then be placed on either silver halide, diazo, or vesicular microfilm.

Silver halide original film contains silver halide crystals bound to the film substrate with a gelatin coating. When exposed to light, the crystals release free silver, producing a negative image. Silver halide film requires a wet chemical bath for developing in a darkroom environment. Although the quality of silver halide microfilm is excellent, the film is easily scratched and is not usually used for computer-output-microfilm files. Because of the negatives, making copies of this type of microfilm requires a separate step.

Diazo microfilm contains azo dyes that produce a positive image when exposed to ammonia vapors and strong light. This type of microfilm has a low cost but is not designed for archival storage.

Vesicular microfilm is durable and permits considerable versatility in printing and copying. With this type of microfilm, either image reversal (positive to negative or negative to positive) or image nonreversal (positive to positive or negative to negative) can be employed. Vesicular microfilm uses a mylar base coated with transparent crystalline particles in a transparent resinous plastic. When exposed to ultraviolet radiation, the crystalline particles change to nitrogen gas. When heat is applied, bubbles that form the image seen by the viewer are created. Figure 21.3 shows several forms of micrographic media.

MICROGRAPHIC MEDIA

The aspect of micrographic technology that is the most readily apparent to the average user is the micrographic media. Several types of media, and variations thereof, are available: microfilm, reels, cartridges, cassettes, microfiche, ultrafiche, microfilm jackets, aperture cards, and micro-opaques.

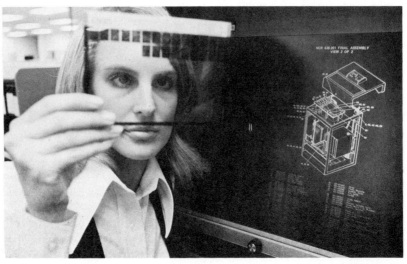

Courtesy of NCR Corporation

FIGURE 21.3   Forms of micrographic media.

Microfilm Reels.   Microfilm reels are similar to ordinary photographic film. They are not particularly useful when high-volume data is generated sequentially and change or updating is not anticipated. Microfilm reels are commonly used with documents, since page indexing facilities are usually available. Sixteen millimeter reels are normally used for documents, bank checks, and correspondence. Thirty-five millimeter reels are normally used for larger source documents, such as drawings, maps, and newspapers. Microfilm reels are usually self-threading.

Microfilm Cartridges.   Microfilm cartridges are similar to reels except that cartridges provide convenient protection from dust and fingerprints. Like most reels, cartridges are self-threading.

Microfilm Cassettes.   A microfilm cassette is a continuous microfilm roll, so that rewinding is not required and a take-up reel is not required in the microfilm cassette viewer. Once a particular frame is located, the cassette can be removed from the viewer without changing the position of the roll.

Microfiche.   A microfiche is a matrix of microimages placed on a sheet of film. Because of the rectangular arrangement of images, update is more feasible than with reels, and viewers are reasonably inexpensive. Microfiche are easily duplicated and are frequently used for disseminating information through the mail. With microfiche, images are normally reduced from 18 to 48 times.

Ultrafiche.   Ultrafiche is similar to microfiche except that the reduction factor is 90 times or greater. Thus, ultrafiche is more efficient than conventional microfiche, although there is the possible cost of a more expensive viewer.

Microfilm Jackets.   A microfilm jacket is a plastic carrier containing one or more sleeves that can accommodate strips of 16-mm or 35-mm film. The plastic jacket provides both protection and a means for visual identification. Micro-images can be read, copied, or printed without removing the film from the plastic carrier.

Aperture Cards.   An aperture card is a computer card with a window for a micro-image or either a 16-mm or 35-mm strip. The punched card can be retrieved and identified using conventional punched card equipment.

Micro-Opaques.   A micro-opaque is an opaque medium on which micro-images, similar to microfiche, are superimposed. Micro-opaques are viewed through the use of reflected light. Both sides of the medium can be used for storing images.

MICROGRAPHIC RECORDING TECHNOLOGY

The basic technology of micrographic recording using a cathode-ray-tube method of image generation was introduced in the overview. The discussion will be supplemented by describing the technologies of light-emitting diode and fiberoptic recording, electron beam recording, and laser beam recording. Figure 21.4 depicts a typical micrographic recording system.

Cathode Ray Tube Recording

A schematic of cathode ray tube recording was given in Figure 21.1. The process works as follows:

1. The cathode ray tube image is generated directly by a computer (on-line mode) or by a data conversion operation from magnetic tape (off-line mode).
2. The image passes through a semi-reflective mirror to a lens and exposes the silver halide original film.
3. The film is advanced.
4. The next image is generated on the face of the cathode ray tube and the process is continued.

Cathode ray tube technology provides a high quality image and is the only recording method that allows a color micrographic recording.

Courtesy of Quantor Corporation

FIGURE 21.4   Typical micrographic recording system.

Light Emitting Diode and Fiberoptic Recording

This technology uses light emitting diodes for image generation and optical fiber bundles as a transport mechanism for transferring infrared light to the lens in the micrographic recording process. The mechanism of light emitting diodes and fiber optics is illustrated in Figure 21.5.

Electron Beam Recording

With electron beam recording, images are displayed directly on the unexposed film by an electron beam. The process, which requires a vacuum chamber, exposes a special type of film through special image generating electronics. The film, which is sensitive to both light and electrons, can be developed through a heating process that does not require a wet chemical process. The mechanism for electron beam recording is depicted in Figure 21.6.

Laser Beam Recording

Laser beam recording is similar in concept to electron beam recording. A laser, controlled by image generating electronics, is used as a light

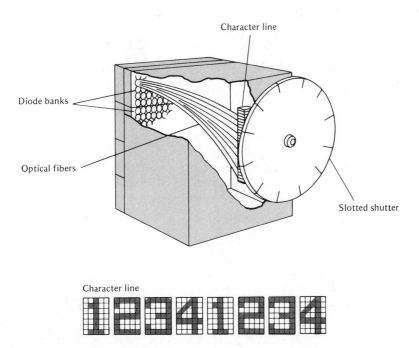

FIGURE 21.5   The mechanism of light emitting diodes and fiber optics as a recording technology.

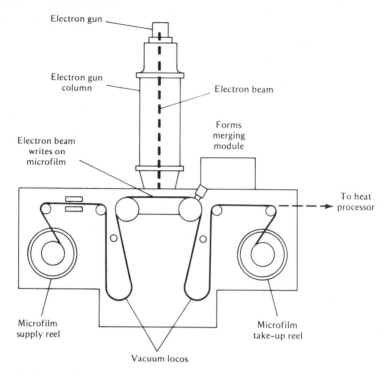

FIGURE 21.6 Mechanism for electron beam recording.

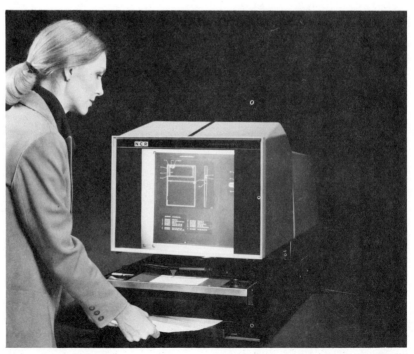

FIGURE 21.7 Micrographic reader/printers.

source to expose either a dry silver halide or vesicular film. The technology requires only dry processing and images can be developed and copied at a rapid rate.

MICROGRAPHIC READERS AND APPLICATIONS

Each application of micrographics and the micrographic media used is associated with a reader/printer and a method of retrieval. Several reader/printers are shown in Figure 21.7.

Retrieval

Micrographic documents are retrieved through the use of indexing techniques that are classified as either microfiche indexing or roll film indexing. Table 21.1 lists microfiche indexing methods with brief descriptions, and Table 21.2 lists roll film indexing methods.

TABLE 21.1   MICROFICHE INDEXING METHODS

Name	Brief Description
Automatic retrieval device	Metal header is placed on the top of each fiche and retrieval is performed through an appropriate reader.
Non-automatic header	Retrieval is performed manually through the header and a fiche index frame located in the lower right hand corner.
Eyeball coding	Information is stored in columns with no index frame. "Eyeball" characters are placed at the bottom of each column and denote the last entry in each column.

Applications

Numerous applications of micrographics have been described in the literature. Some of the most common of these applications are:

1. Parts catalogs
2. Employee personnel records
3. Credit card accounts receivable records
4. Transportation schedules
5. Business correspondence
6. Accounting records
7. Cancelled checks
8. Membership lists
9. Student academic records

10. Claim records for medical insurance
11. Employee benefits records
12. Automobile owner/purchaser records
13. Accounts payable records
14. Tariff information
15. Patent records
16. Criminal information
17. Microfiles of building interiors by fire departments
18. Library material (newspapers, rare volumes, checkout information)
19. Check cashing records for supermarkets
20. Color coordination for interior design
21. Parts lists
22. Patient records
23. Poison records and antidotes
24. Maintenance information by airplane manufacturers
25. Tax records
26. Engineering drawings
27. Circuit diagrams
28. Reference manuals for computers
29. Documents
30. Computer generated reports

TABLE 21.2   ROLL FILM INDEXING METHODS

Name	Brief Description
No coding	Each reel is identified by the information it contains. Desired frames are located through an exhaustive search.
Eyeball	Each frame is encoded with the last entry on each page. Retrieval is performed through an exhaustive search.
Odometer	A particular frame is located through a counter that gives the approximate location of a page. After an approximate location is reached, retrieval is made through a search procedure.
Page counter	Each frame is encoded with a readable marker. A particular page is located by knowing the relative position of that page. Retrieval is performed by locating a page directly.
Codeline	Information is located through coding bars placed on the film.
Microcode	Binary coding bars are placed between frames. Pages are retrieved automatically by entering the desired search parameters.

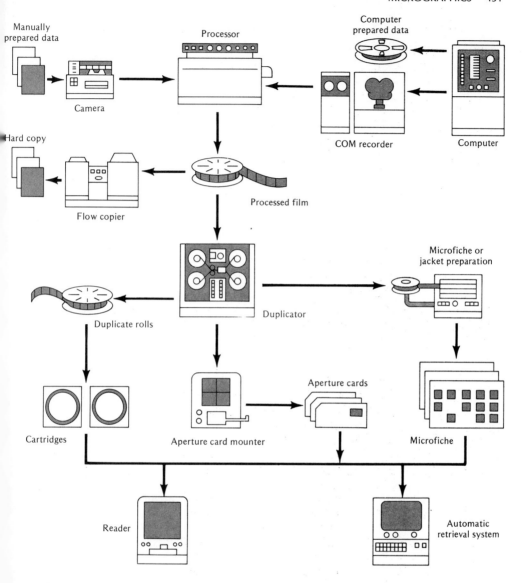

FIGURE 21.8 Typical micrographic system.

Although this is only a small sample of possible applications, it serves to indicate the breadth of the field and its future potential. Figure 21.8 depicts a typical micrographic system that contains many of the concepts presented above.

PRACTICAL CONSIDERATIONS

In May 1977, *Infosystems* magazine published the results of a survey of micrographics users. One of the surprising results was that 31.5%

of respondents indicated that all micrographics were handled by service companies—a good reason for using off-line processing. Only 24% of respondents indicated that all micrographic processing was handled in house.

As far as micrographic systems were concerned, 40.5% of respondents indicated that systems design was performed by the data processing department. This was the highest percentage given for this question. In a related question, 37.3% of respondents replied that the data processing department was in charge of micrographics. Again, this was the highest percentage.

The most frequently used micrographic media was microfiche (at 73.4% of respondents) and 16-mm rolls were a distant second at 39.5%. In the area of film, 84% of respondents used silver halide original film and 66.6% used diazo duplicating film. Again, these were the highest percentages given.

Vocabulary   The student should be familiar with the following terms in the context in which they were used in the chapter.

aperture card
cathode ray tube recording
diazo microfilm
electron beam recording
laser beam recording
light emitting diode and fiber-
    optic recording
microfiche
microfilm cartridge
microfilm cassette

microfilm jacket
microfilm reel
micrographics
micro-opaque
off-line mode
on-line mode
silver halide microfilm
ultrafiche
vesicular microfilm

Exercises   1. Distinguish between the following types of micrographic media:
    a. Microfilm reel
    b. Microfilm cartridge
    c. Microfilm cassette
    d. Microfiche
    e. Ultrafiche
    f. Microfilm jacket
    g. Aperture card
    h. Micro-opaque
2. Describe the steps in the off-line mode and in the on-line mode.
3. For each of the micrographic media above, give a sample application for which it would be most appropriate.

4. Discuss the recording technology that would be appropriate for a computer-output-microfilm system.

5. What recording technology would be best for the off-line mode of operation?

Related Reading

"Micrographics 77. The Best is Yet to Come," *Infosystems* (May 1977): 46–49.

Harmon, Gill. "Reading the Microfilm," *Infosystems* (May 1977): 56–58.

Canning, B. "Micrographics for Small Offices," *The Office* (September 1977): 104–105.

"Microfilm Applications at Michigan Blue Cross," *The Office* (September 1977): 114–118.

"In-House COM Is Profitable for Tektronix," *The Office* (September 1977): 124–128.

"Datsun Saves its Records on Microfilm," *The Office* (September 1977): 140.

"Microfilm Saves $50,000 Yearly for Fling Tiger Line," *The Office* (September 1977): 144–145.

Avedon, D. M. "Micrographics today and in the future," *The Office* (May 1977): 18–19, 31.

Judge, J. C., "Chevron has a high quality micrographics operation," *The Office* (May 1977): 85–87.

"COM's $50,000 annual savings is only a beginning," *The Office* (May 1977): 92–98.

"Micrographics at Pillsbury Company," *The Office* (May 1977): 119.

Computer Networks and Distributed Systems

ur society is becoming increasingly dependent upon computers for routine business activity, and the associated information has emerged as a valuable resource. Timely information distribution and data collection are paramount to efficient and effective business management. Computer networks provide a means of exchanging data and sharing computer resources and have been identified as a powerful national force. This chapter contains an introduction to computer networks and methods for distributing computer processing.

INTRODUCTION

The notion of a network is not new. Typical examples of networks are rail systems, power distribution systems operated by utility companies, and the national telephone service. While computer networks are conceptually similar to other types of networks, they possess one unique characteristic. Unlike most other networks, a computer network can be designed, implemented and used by an independent organization—such as a business, school, or governmental agency.

Definition of a Computer Network

A *computer network* is a collection of computers and terminals connected together by a communications system. This is a very general definition that includes all sorts of on-line systems. However, the term has a more specific meaning in data processing.

A *centralized network* is illustrated by Figure 22.1. Conceptually, it

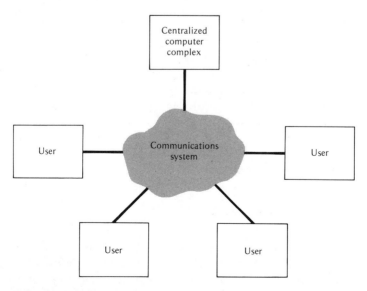

FIGURE 22.1   Centralized computer network.

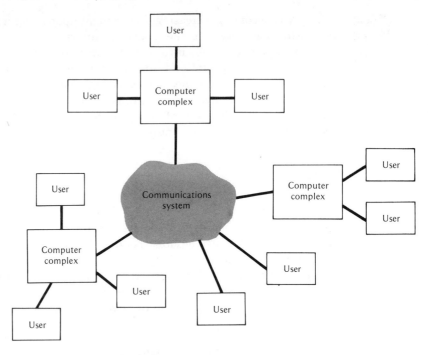

FIGURE 22.2 Distributed computer network.

could represent any time-sharing or remote-terminal inquiry system. A centralized network is characterized by a centralized computer complex, a communications system, and a set of users who can interact with the computer system via local terminal devices.

A *distributed network* is depicted in Figure 22.2. It is characterized by two or more computer complexes that are connected via a communications system. Users may interact with one of the computer complexes via local communications facilities or may be connected to the communications system directly.

When a reference is made to a computer network in a data processing context, a distributed network is usually the intended meaning. A computing system with multiple central processing units is not a distributed network unless the central processing units are connected via a communications system. Thus, a computer system in which multiple central processing units are connected through a shared main storage unit is not a distributed network.

Value Added Network

A private communications system to be used in a computer network is relatively expensive. While such computer networks have existed for many years, in one form or another, their use has been restricted for economic reasons to specialized communities—such as the airline industry, banking institutions, and large corporations.

Network capability is now available to all potential users through a new concept, known as a value added network. A *value added network* is a public network service that builds on existing telecommunications facilities to provide a means of interfacing users' computers and terminals, route messages between locations, and guarantee message integrity. By "pooling resources" in this way, small users can effectively utilize a communications system without having to finance the entire system. The result is that an organization only needs to connect its computers and terminals to a value added network to have the facilities of a complete communications system readily available.

CLASSES OF COMPUTER NETWORKS

A useful classification of computer networks can be based on how a user might view them—whether the user views the networks as a set of computer systems or as a single computer system.

Computer-Communications System

In a *computer-communications system* (see Figure 22.3), the user views the network as a set of separate computer systems. Even though access to the various systems is through a network interface, the user explicitly chooses a specific computer system for service and interacts with that system using local operating conventions.

Network Computer System

In a *network computer system* (see Figure 22.4), the user views the network as one large computer system, even though the network as a whole contains several separate computer systems. The central processor on which a user's program is executed is transparent to the user and only one set of operating conventions need be learned. In this case, the network operating system decides on which computer system a program should be run, based on the resources required.

NETWORK CONFIGURATIONS

The manner in which independent computer systems are connected through a communications system is called the *network topology*. The network topology effectively determines which computer systems can

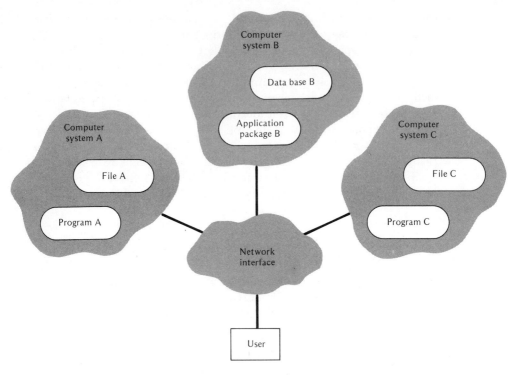

FIGURE 22.3   Computer-communications system.

communicate with each other. Figure 22.5 shows a hypothetical network model.

Centralized Network

The *centralized network* (also known as the *star network*) is characterized by communications channels emanating from a centralized computer system (see Figure 22.6). A centralized network is particularly useful for organizations that require a centralized data base or a centralized processing facility. For example, a centralized network might be used by a large retail store with centralized inventory control. A large bank with many branches might also utilize a centralized network.

Distributed Network

The distributed network is characterized by computer systems that can in the most general case be connected with every other computer system. When each system is connected to every other system, the network is said to possess "full connectivity." In most cases full connec-

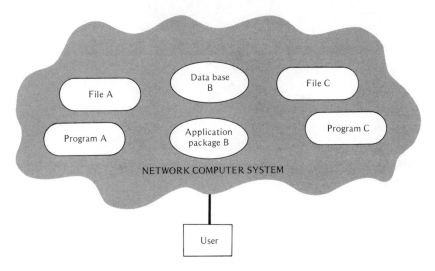

FIGURE 22.4   Network computer system.

tivity is not achieved (see Figure 22.7) and systems are connected on a functional basis. A large manufacturing organization, for example, may utilize a distributed network to connect manufacturing plants that coordinate, in the broadest sense, on a regular basis.

Ring Network

A *ring network* is a special case of a distributed network in which every system is connected to exactly two other systems (see Figure 22.8). A ring network is frequently used by a decentralized organization, in

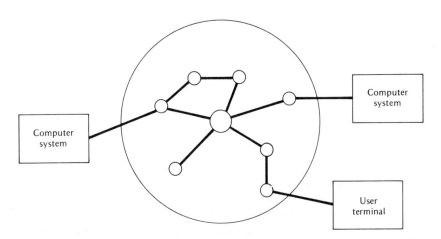

FIGURE 22.5   Hypothetical network model or network topology.

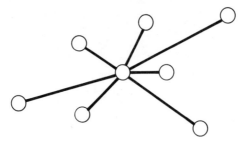

FIGURE 22.6   Topology of a centralized network. (Also known as a star network.)

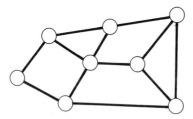

FIGURE 22.7   Topology of a distributed network.

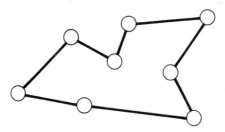

FIGURE 22.8   Topology of a ring network. Each system is connected to two other systems.

which the various locations need to coordinate but not on a regular basis.

Network Composition

Network composition refers to whether the component systems are the same or are different. In a *homogeneous system,* each component computer system is essentially identical. In a *heterogeneous system,* the systems employ different computers. Most computer networks incorporate a combination of centralized, distributed, and ring configurations.

NETWORK DESIGN

The key element in network design is the manner in which the processing is distributed among the computer systems in a network. Three types of networks based on processing are identified: utilitarian, task, and functional. These types of processing distribution generally apply to any of the network configurations discussed above.

Utilitarian Network

In a *utilitarian network,* the work is performed on the same computer system—even though access may have been achieved through the network's communications system. Off-loading may occur for reasons of efficiency, and this means that the work is started on one computer system and finished on another computer system in the network. Figure 22.9 depicts a utilitarian processing environment. In a utilitarian network, systems must be homogeneous in order for off-loading to work.

Task Network

In a *task network,* a single processing job is split between two computer systems (see Figure 22.10). The preassignment of tasks between systems is based on the various computer system configurations and characteristics. For example, a sophisticated network may have separate computer systems with "specializations" for the following types of activity: (1) compilation, (2) execution, and (3) data base retrieval.

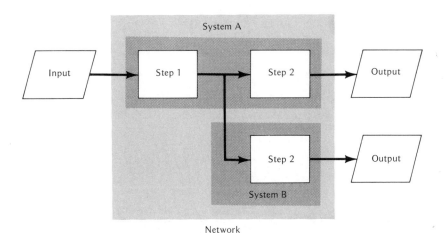

FIGURE 22.9   Utilitarian network for processing distribution.

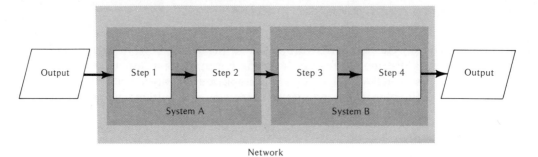

FIGURE 22.10   Task network.

Functional Network

In a *functional network,* a small on-site computer provides access to the network but does not perform a substantial amount of processing. This type of network is illustrated by Figure 22.11. Point-of-sale (POS) devices connected to mini-computers in the offices of retail stores is an example of a functional network.

PACKET-SWITCHING SYSTEMS

The length of data records that are distributed through a computer network may vary depending upon the information contained in them. Depending upon the network configuration employed, this fact may result in a cumbersome data management problem. One method of reconciling the differences in record length is to transfer data between computer systems in packets.

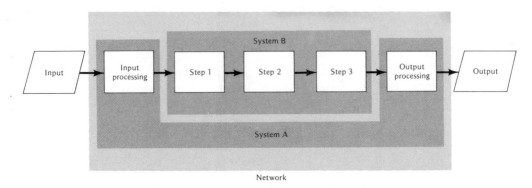

FIGURE 22.11   Functional network.

Packet Concept

A *packet* is a fixed block size—such as eight thousand bits. Essentially, a packet consists of a set of blocked records, and it is the standard unit of transfer over the communications system.

Structure of a Packet-Switching System

A hypothetical packet switching system is conceptualized in Figure 22.12. The network uses a stored-and-forward mini-computer known as an *interface message processor* (IMP). The IMP works in conjunction with its host computer to perform three major functions:

1. It puts packets from the host into the network.
2. It takes packets with the host as destination from the network.
3. It receives and forwards packets from the network for other hosts.

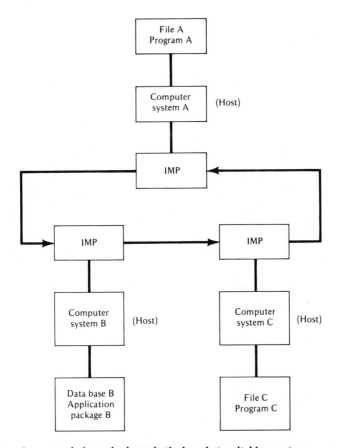

FIGURE 22.12   Conceptual view of a hypothetical packet-switching system.

Because of the structure of the packet switching system, the interface message processors (IMPs) play a key role, so that various kinds of protocols are required to sustain operation.

Operation of a Packet-Switching System

Figure 22.13 contains a schematic of a message as it might exist in a network. The start of header (SOH), start of text (STX), end of transmission block (ETB), and acknowledge (ACK) are control codes. The *header* contains control information including the origin and destination. The text is the set of messages, which must be decomposed by the destination computer system. The acknowledge (ACK) code is issued by the receiving computer to acknowledge receipt of a message.

Figure 22.14 contains a schematic of packet switching between host

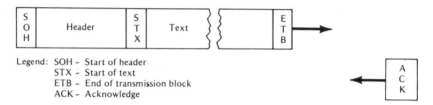

Legend: SOH – Start of header
         STX – Start of text
         ETB – End of transmission block
         ACK – Acknowledge

FIGURE 22.13   Structure of a message in a computer network.

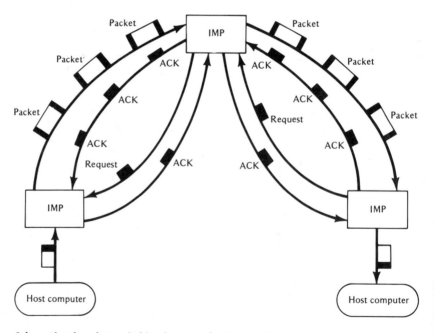

FIGURE 22.14   Schematic of packet switching between host computers.

computers. Each packet is placed in the network and is forwarded to successive IMPs until it arrives at the IMP of its destination. At that point, the messages are transmitted to the host computer via a host-to-IMP protocol.

DISTRIBUTED SYSTEMS

The objective of a distributed computing system is to process information at the most advantageous sites from operational, economic, and geographical points of view. Distributed computing systems use computer networks, but the terms are not synonomous. A computer network takes the job to the processing resource, while a distributed system takes the processing resource to the user.

Definition of a Distributed System

A *distributed system* is a set of independent but interacting computer systems or data bases located at different geographical points. The

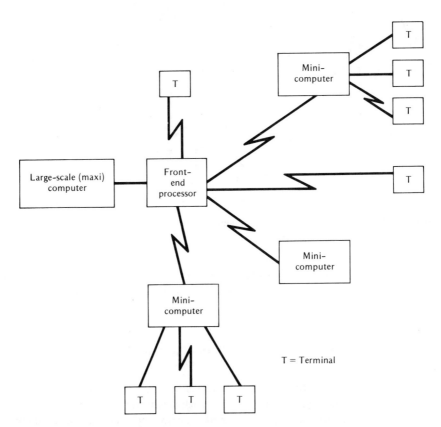

FIGURE 22.15   Centralized maxi-mini distributed System.

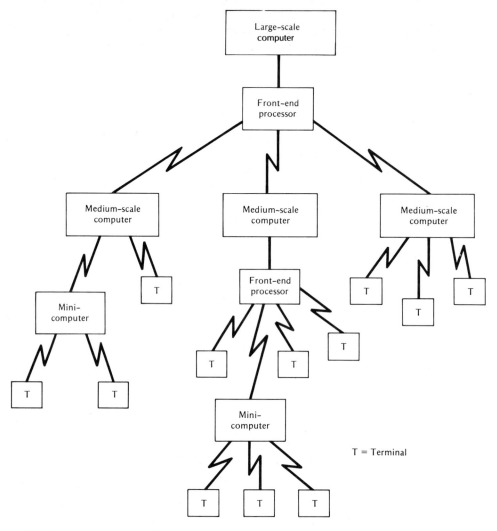

FIGURE 22.16   Multi-tier distributed system.

function of a distributed system is to process some user jobs at the points of user activity, while permitting other jobs to be transmitted to a centralized facility.

Classification of Distributed Systems

Distributed systems are classified according to the scale of computers in the system and the network configuration used. Three major classifications will be described: centralized maxi/mini systems, multi-tier systems, and multi-mini systems.

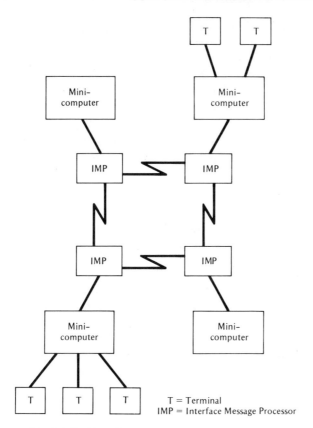

T = Terminal
IMP = Interface Message Processor

FIGURE 22.17   Multi-mini distributed system.

In a *centralized maxi-mini system,* one or more minicomputers are linked to a large-scale (maxi) computer in a centralized network. Depending upon the size of the system, a front-end processor may be used by the large-scale computer for network control. A centralized maxi-mini system (see Figure 22.15) can provide the following functional capabilities:

1. Localized preprocessing of user data
2. Localized data storage
3. Localized application packages
4. Centralized computer processing and data base management

A *multi-tier system* has the same general characteristics as a centralized maxi-mini system, except that more than two sizes of equipment are used (see Figure 22.16). The system forms a hierarchy of computing power that includes large-scale, medium-scale, and mini-computers.

A multi-tier system would be used by an organization with regional offices, such as a large bank or insurance company.

A *multi-mini system* contains mini-computers at points of user activity for local processing. As Figure 22.17 shows, the network is homogeneous, and some tasks are transferred to other host computers for processing because of the availability of special resources or processing requirements. An organization with a high degree of decentralization and dissimilar activities—such as a food distribution service—would benefit from a multi-mini distributed system. In this example, a mini-computer would be located at each distribution depot.

Vocabulary The student should be familiar with the following terms in the context in which they were used in the chapter.

centralized maxi-mini
  distributed system
centralized network
computer-communications
  system
computer network
distributed system
functional network
heterogeneous system
homogeneous system
interface message processor
  (IMP)

multi-mini distributed system
multi-tier distributed system
network computer system
network topology
packet
packet-switching system
ring network
star network
task network
utilitarian network
value-added network

Exercises 1. Distinguish between the following concepts:
  a. Centralized network and distributed network
  b. Computer-communications system and network computer system
  c. Utilitarian network, task network, and functional network
  d. Maxi-mini system, multi-tier system, and multi-mini system
2. Develop an example of each of the following types of networks:
  a. Centralized
  b. Distributed
  c. Ring
3. Develop an example of each of the following types of distributed systems:
  a. Maxi-mini
  b. Multi-tier
  c. Multi-mini
4. What function does an IMP perform?

5. In what way can a computer network increase system availability? (Availability is defined as the time a system can be used divided by the total time).

6. Discuss what type of network would be most appropriate for each of the following organizations: Bank of America, General Motors, International Business Machines, and Exxon.

7. Distinguish between homogeneous and heterogeneous composition.

Related Reading

Abrams, M., Blanc, R. D., and Cotton, I. W. *Computer Networks: A Tutorial.* New York: Institute of Electrical and Electronics Engineers, Inc., 1975.

Blanc, R. D., and Cotton, I. W. *Computer Networking.* New York: IEEE Press, Institute of Electrical and Electronics Engineers, 1976.

Computer Networks: Trends and Applications. Proceedings of the 1974 Symposium, Institute of Electrical and Electronics Engineers, New York, 1974.

Down, P. J., and Taylor, F. E. *Why Distributed Computing?* Manchester, Eng.: NCC Publications, 1976.

23

Issues in Computer Installation Management

COMPUTER ACQUISITION

Factors in Computer Systems Design and Evaluation
Mixed Systems
Computer Operation
Software and Application Packages
Equipment—Purchase, Rent, Lease or Buy Time
Service Bureaus

COMPUTER DATA SECURITY

Computer Security
Spectrum of Data Security
Overview of Data Security Countermeasures
Access Management
Processing Limitations
Auditing and Threat Monitoring
Privacy Transformations
Integrity Management
Level of Authorization and Data File Protection
Management Responsibility
Computer Security Plan

EDP AUDITING AND CONTROL

The Concept of Auditing
Exposure, Cause, and Control

SUMMARY

any people feel that the toughest job in data processing is computer installation management. At first glance, one would assume that computer management is similar to any other kind of management. However, this has not been the case historically. Some of the reasons why computer installation management differs from other kinds of management are:

1. Data processing is a high technology area.
2. The computer field is constantly evolving.
3. The data processing department is subject to many forces from within the organization.
4. Because the data processing department serves as an informational resource, it resides at the focus of many organizational problems.
5. The computer field is relatively young and not enough time has elapsed for effective management techniques to be disseminated.

A realistic explanation would probably combine all five reasons. This chapter covers three topics that are generally regarded as integral parts of effective installation management: computer acquisition, computer data security, and computer auditing and control.

COMPUTER ACQUISITION

There is much more to data processing than a well-designed application and a good programming language. First, the equipment must be selected, configured, and then either purchased or leased. Many factors must be taken into consideration such as characteristics of the equipment, areas of application, requirements, conversion, compatibility, and growth potential—to name only a few. Next, the equipment must be operated: when, how, and by whom is frequently of major significance. Lastly, programs must be either developed or obtained in some way. Often, in fact, the cost of programs exceeds the cost of the equipment itself. No major solution to these problems can be given—perhaps no easy solution exists. The reader, however, should be familiar with the major problem areas of computer acquisition, regardless of whether he or she is a user, COBOL programmer, systems analyst, or data processing manager.

Factors in Computer Systems Design and Evaluation

Although the central processing unit is the most expensive unit in a computer system, its functioning and its selection are usually obscured by the total system configuration and the other units in the system, that is, by the main storage unit and the various input/output devices. If the purpose of the system is to service a real-time need, then the speed of the central processing unit is usually determined by the timing requirements of a physical process. If the computer system is to be used for general-purpose computing, then the amount of main storage, the speed and type of input/output devices, and the overall system organization also affect the effectiveness of the system.

Central Processing Unit.   The selection of a central processing unit for a given application is usually based on five factors:

1. Basic speed of the machine measured in machine cycles per *something*
2. Time required for the execution of critical instructions
3. Appropriateness of the instruction repertoire to the projected workload
4. Functional organization of the central processing unit
5. Other techno-economic factors not necessarily related directly to the functioning of the devices under consideration

These factors are summarized in Table 23.1 along with those for selection of the main storage unit and input/output devices. Appropriate evaluation and analysis techniques are given in Table 23.2. The organization of the central processing unit is particularly significant for reasons other than the raw speed of the circuitry. Two areas are usually candidates for study: (1) dependence upon references to storage and (2) implementation of parallel processes. The dependence upon storage can usually be minimized by providing *multiple arithmetic registers* and by fetching instructions ahead of sequence and holding them in an *instruction stack.* Parallel processes are implemented through multiple execution units for arithmetic operations and by partially executing instructions along the branch and no-branch paths while waiting for the completion of a conditional instruction.

Main Storage.   The main storage unit is important for two reasons:

1. It determines the number of programs that can reside in high-speed storage and the effective size of each
2. It regulates the speed of the central processing unit, since the instructions and operands (i.e., data) are stored there and must be retrieved before execution can take place.

Therefore, the actual size of main storage and the manner in which it is organized is a concern.

With regard to core storage, speed is hampered by the fact that

TABLE 23.1 SYSTEM DESIGN FACTORS

Central Processing Unit	Main Storage Unit	I/O Devices
1. Basic speed (cycles per)	1. Basic speed (accesses per)	1. Data rates
2. Time required for execution of critical instructions	2. Size	2. Access time
3. Instruction repertoire	3. Organization (inter-leaving)	3. Storage capacity
4. Width of data path	4. Width of data path	4. Data organization (serial, direct)
5. Processor organization (parallelism, registers)		5. Data channel capacity
6. Technoeconomic factors		

TABLE 23.2 COMPUTER EVALUATION AND ANALYSIS TECHNIQUES

Technique Used	Area of Widespread Use
1. Cycle time	Measures the speed of main storage or central processing unit. Used mainly as a general indication of system capability.
2. Add time	Used mainly to compare high-performance scientific systems. This measure is usually combined with other evaluation techniques.
3. Instruction times	Compares the relative times for a given set of basic instructions. Frequently used to obtain an overall feeling for the speed of a central processor.
4. Instruction mix	Gives the time required to execute a *set* of instructions, which are representative of a given class of programs. Usually combined with techniques (1), (2), and (3) for evaluating high-performance scientific systems.
5. Kernel problems	Representative programs are coded using the instruction repertoire of the computer being evaluated. Gives a measure of internal computing speed.
6. Benchmark job streams	A means of measuring the throughput of a system. A collection of jobs is run, and the total elapsed time is measured. This technique is affected by I/O performance and the software available with the computer system.
7. Simulation	A complete computer system is simulated by another computer system. Particularly useful during the design phase of computer development.

the storage mechanisms are *destructive* in the sense that once a unit of data is fetched, another unit of data cannot be fetched until the first unit of data is effectively restored. (This operation is performed automatically by the circuitry.) Therefore, it is desirable to have the core storage unit organized into two or more banks so that information can be fetched from one bank while the other is in a restore cycle. The width of the data path from the main storage unit to the processing unit is also relevant. If, for example, the operand for a particular instruction requires eight bytes and the width of the data path is only four bytes, then two storage fetches are required before execution of that instruction can be initiated.

Input/Output.   In spite of the complexity and importance of the processing and storage units, the biggest hindrance to good system design and performance is input and output (I/O). The difficulty is not surprising due to the fact that I/O devices are electromechanical, while the central processing unit and main storage unit are electronic. However, significant advances have been made. In early computers (see Figure 23.1), all data entering or leaving the system had to pass through the central processing unit on their way to or from main storage, so that

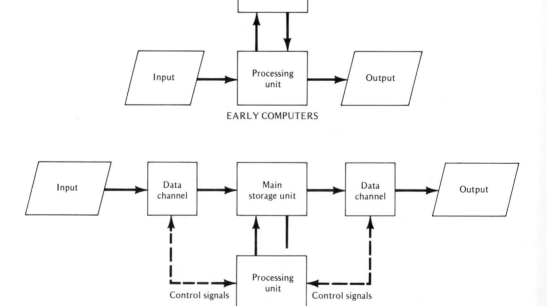

FIGURE 23.1   Input/output and system organization for early (top) and modern (bottom) computers.

the system had to run effectively at I/O speeds. In the modern computer system, the *data channel* (also Figure 23.1)—a small hardware-wired central processing unit used only for the transfer of data—has enabled I/O devices to communicate directly with storage, allowing processing and I/O to overlap to some degree (that is, if provided for in the computer programs). Fortunately, efficient methods of doing input/output are available with most operating systems and programming languages.

Evaluation.   Because of the complexity of modern technology, evaluation of a prospective computer system is indeed an involved process. Factors affecting a decision or sequence of decisions are as often economic and political as they are technical. Nevertheless, various methods have been used to assess the potential effectiveness of computer systems, and they are summarized in Table 23.2. Some techniques measure raw computing speed and are useful for applications requiring high internal speeds, such as particle physics, or for those where the internal performance must be known explicitly to satisfy the needs of a physical process. Other evaluation techniques measure sequences of instructions and even total system throughput—the maximum amount of work that a complete system can do in a given period of time. Simulation, another useful device for evaluating or analyzing performance, relies on another computer to obtain the best results from the simulation effort.

Other factors, which can only be mentioned in passing, influence system evaluation. The problem of *conversion,* or converting an installation's programs to run on the new machine, is a major concern for installations with large investments in programming. Standard programming languages such as BASIC and COBOL are definite assets in this respect. The possibility of *growth* should also be of concern. The capability of adding additional main storage units or I/O devices without changing the central processing unit can solve many problems caused by future increases in data and in new applications.

Mixed Systems

In the 1960s and early 1970s, it was customary to encounter one-vendor installations. This means that the computer system includes units from one vendor only. In recent years, however, some businesses have specialized in particular units, such as CPUs, main storage units, channels, or peripheral devices. Businesses of this type can offer a specific kind of replacement unit—such as a CPU—at a price lower than the principal vendor. The situation was caused in part by a "price umbrella" created by IBM, which is the primary target of replacement units. Other vendors could offer alternative units, which were operationally identical to IBM's units, at a lower price.

Mixed systems create an interesting identity problem, especially when the central processing unit is replaced. In fact, the Control Data Corporation, a major computer manufacturer in its own right, has begun to offer plug-compatible replacement CPUs for IBM systems.

Computer Operation

A question related to computer systems design and evaluation is, "Who operates the computer?" In most cases, an organization acquires a computer system and uses its own personnel to operate it, using either the open-shop or closed-shop philosophy described in Chapter 2. For an initial computer acquisition, computer operators may have to be hired.

Other alternatives, however, exist. An organization can utilize its own management personnel and hire contract operators from a "job shop" company. The advantage of this approach is that the organization is not responsible for training, personnel acquisition, or employee overhead.

Another viable approach is to call in a system management company to manage the organization's computer facility. The package, in this case, may include programmers and programming management but always includes operator personnel and management.

Software and Application Packages

Software generally includes the programs necessary to use the computer. Included in this category are *system control programs* (also known as operating systems, control programs, executive programs, and system monitors), *compilers* and *assemblers* (that are used to translate source programs into machine language programs), and *utility programs* (such as programs to dump core storage and initialize direct-access storage) necessary for maintaining a computer installation. Software is usually available from computer manufacturers without charge or for a slight fee, depending upon whether they have unbundled or not. (*Unbundling* refers to the practice of pricing hardware and software separately.) Software is also available from a software development company on either a lease or proprietary basis, or it can be developed in-house.

Application packages are usually developed by computer manufacturers or software development companies to solve a well-defined class of problems. Included in this category are, to give a few examples, general-purpose programs related to the following topics: sort/merge, matrix algebra, linear programming, differential equations, and report generation. Competition is keen in this category and the prospective user does well to survey what is available.

Equipment—Purchase, Rent, Lease, or Buy Time

The installation that needs computing equipment has two alternatives: install the equipment in-house or buy time, as needed, from another installation. Frequently, an installation will do both, as the workload increases, and then sell time once the new equipment is installed.

In-house equipment can be purchased, rented, or leased from a computer-leasing company. A sophisticated (with respect to the use of computers) user with a substantial programming staff and a workload in excess of two eight-hour shifts per day does well to purchase equipment, if the financial arrangements can be made. Otherwise, renting from a computer manufacturer or leasing from a leasing company is necessary. Computer manufacturers, as a rule, give shift premiums after the first shift to make rental more attractive. The renter can usually expect modern equipment and conversion aids, when required. If an installation needs equipment on a long-term basis, then perhaps the leasing company or an outright purchase is a good alternative. Equipment costs can be reduced considerably with a long-term arrangement, because with purchased or leased equipment the installation must plan on maintenance services generally available from the manufacturer of the equipment.

Computer time is also available from service companies and from installations that have excess time. From both sources, either a block of time is purchased or charges are made on an individual job basis. Individual charges are usually made on the basis of processor time, external storage, and operator time used. When a block of time is purchased, the purchasing group is frequently required to furnish its own operator and storage volumes.

Service Bureaus

Another option that is available in the data processing field is to have a service bureau do the processing. Using payroll applications as an example, all the user organization would supply to the service bureau would be its time sheets. The service bureau provides the programs, operators, and computers and normally returns the paychecks and associated reports in a relatively short period of time. Service bureaus usually offer a variety of applications and provide good service and quick response, because they are specialists.

COMPUTER DATA SECURITY

Because the data processing department serves as an informational resource in many organizations, it can, and has, been a target for violent activity, for unauthorized access to information, and for other computer crimes. The computer has been associated with embezzlement, invasion of privacy, and with related activity such as instructing the computer to initiate an illegal shipment of goods to an unauthorized party.

Computer Security

Data security is part of an overall program of computer security which is a function of an organization's security department. As such, physical protection measures, such as guard service, alarms and locks, closed circuit television, and bugging devices, are an integral part of effective computer security. Also part of computer security are fire protection, catastrophe and disaster control, safes and vaults for removable storage media and paper shredding devices for sensitive listings and reports.

Our concern here is primarily with data security since it is something over which the data processing person has some control.

Spectrum of Data Security

In providing data security, the objective is to restrict the use of information in the computer and on associated storage devices for use by selected individuals. Information is taken to be programs and data in the usual sense. The reason for using diverse data security techniques is to isolate this information from attempts at unauthorized access, which may occur in a variety of forms and in several contexts.

The threats to data security are classified as being accidental or deliberate. Much of this discussion is concerned with deliberate infiltration, although the consequences of an accidental disclosure of sensitive information could be as serious as a case in which unauthorized information was accessed deliberately. *Accidental disclosures* of information could result from hardware failures, software errors as the result of partially debugged or poorly designed programs, or simple operational errors, such as the mounting of the wrong magnetic tape reel or magnetic disk pack. *Deliberate infiltration* is usually performed with one of the following objectives in mind:

1. Gaining access to information in files
2. Discovering the information interests of users
3. Altering or destroying files
4. Obtaining free use of system resources

Not all deliberate infiltration is performed by professional criminals. The knowledgeable student who attempts to gain access to a system just "for the heck of it" is as much a threat to the integrity of a system as his professional counterpart.

Deliberate efforts to gain information are further classified as either passive or active. *Passive infiltration* is akin to eavesdropping or wiretapping and involves the observation of informational traffic at some point in the system. Passive techniques include:

1. Electromagnetic pickup (from the CPU or peripheral input/output devices)
2. Wiretapping (on data communications lines or data bases)
3. Concealed transmitters (to the CPU, peripheral input/output devices, data bases, or data communications lines)

Another passive technique is to inspect periodically the contents of the wastebaskets in or near the computer area and in locations where computer terminals are located. Copies of programs and lists of data are frequently generated during the debugging or checkout process, as well as during everyday operations, and normal security precautions are frequently relaxed in the haste that usually accompanies project completion. The most serious passive threat, however, is in the use of data communications facilities, which are extremely vulnerable to wiretapping and related techniques.

Active infiltration includes the following techniques:

1. Browsing
2. Masquerading
3. Detection and use of "trap doors"
4. Entry and infiltration via an active communications channel
5. Physical means

Browsing involves the use of legitimate access to the system to obtain unauthorized information. *Masquerading* is the practice of obtaining proper identification through improper means (such as wiretapping) and then accessing the system as a legitimate user. *Trap doors* are hardware features, software limitations, or specially planted entry points that provide an unauthorized source with access to the system. Trap doors are frequently uncovered by successively testing the various combinations of system control variables. An *active communications channel* can also be used to gain access to the system. This technique involves the use of a special terminal attached to the communications channels to perform one of the following:

1. Intercept messages between a user and the computer system and then release them, modify them, or return an error message. This technique is referred to as "piggy back."
2. Entry into the system via the communications lines of an inactive

user that is still connected to the computer. This technique is referred to as "between-lines entry."

3. Cancel a user's sign-off signal and then continuing to operate under the user's password and authorization. This technique is a variation of the piggy-back method.

Physical means of entry include access to the system through a position with the computer center, a communications company, or a vendor, the generation and analysis of "core dumps," and the theft of removable storage media. Thus, the possibilities for a compromise of data security are large, especially when valuable information is involved.

Overview of Data Security Countermeasures

The design of an effective security system requires that each of the data security threats mentioned previously be countered by using one or more techniques or operational procedures. Security must be designed into a system and not added as an afterthought. International Business Machines Corporation[1] lists the important factors that influence the design of secure systems:

1. Informational content
2. Environment
3. Communications
4. System facilities

Informational content refers to the sensitivity of programs and data, which may require one of the following: no special data security provisions, normal need-to-know restrictions, or extensive precautions to avoid disclosure. The *environment* refers to users and the methods by which they access the system; users may possess equal or varying levels of authorization and may utilize the computer system in an online or an offline mode. *Communications* refers to the use of data communications facilities, which may be local to the computer, may be a dedicated and private network, or may be a switched network. *System facilities* refers to the services provided by the computer system, which may include, minimally, dedicated functions, interactive problem solving, remote programming support, and a total information system.

Therefore, the choice of an effective countermeasure against a given data security threat involves not only the threat itself but also consideration of one or more of the key factors given above. The following

1. "The Considerations of Data Security in a Computer Environment" (White Plains, N.Y.: IBM Corporation, Form G520–2169), p. 10.

data security countermeasures are considered to be of prime importance and will be described in subsequent sections: access management, processing limitations, auditing and threat monitoring, privacy transformations, integrity management, and level of authorization and data file protection.

Access Management

Access management, frequently referred to as "access control" or "identification," is concerned with preventing unauthorized users from obtaining services from the computer system or gaining access to its files. In a local batch processing environment, access to the system is controlled to some extent by operations personnel who actually enter a given job into the system. In this environment, sensitive files can be protected to a limited degree by a password that is stored with the file or in the system catalog. When an applications program attempts to open the file for input or output, a request is made to the operator to enter the correct password. If the operator cannot enter the correct password, then access to the file is denied.

When the computer is accessed from a remote location using a terminal device, other problems are present. First, the computer operator is usually not involved on the spot to identify a job or a request for data. Second, an unauthorized person can easily masquerade as an authorized person. Third, data communications facilities are frequently used in remote access, and the user must be concerned with the security of both the terminal device and the communications facilities. This type of data security problem is usually solved by providing terminal protection: identifying the terminal, identifying the user, and providing different levels of protection.

Terminal devices can be protected by being placed in a secure location, such as a locked room. This method is frequently used when a "hardwire" connection to the computer is used. When data communications lines are used, the computer can be programmed to respond to terminals with a given address. The address of the terminal accompanies an incoming message, so that a table of terminal addresses can be used to determine the security level of a given terminal. Since it is frequently desirable to switch terminals between addresses for backup purposes, this technique has obvious limitations. Another method for terminal protection is to provide the terminal with the capability of responding to a computer query with a unique tamper-free identification code. The most obvious limitation to terminal protection is that a terminal hardware failure may render the device inoperative, so that computer service is unavailable except through special procedures. To sum up, because terminal protection is cumbersome the practice of identifying the user instead of the terminal has become widespread.

There are three means of identifying a user at a remote terminal in general use:

1. By information the user knows, memorizes, or writes down, such as a password or security code.
2. By a physical artifact such as a badge, card, or key that can be inserted into a reader associated with the terminal device.
3. By a personal physical characteristic, such as a voice print or a fingerprint.

The use of passwords and security codes is the method most frequently used. The user enters his or her name, an identification number, and a password into the system and is granted or denied access. A sign-on procedure might read as follows:

System: ABC SYSTEM GOOD MORNING 1/1/79 10:15 AM PLEASE LOGIN
User: HAMILTON,6714,ALPINE
System: LOGIN ACCEPTED

Usually, the user name, identification code, and password are verified to insure that they have been issued together and are currently active. One of the disadvantages of techniques of this kind is that identification numbers are frequently left exposed for others to see. In fact, program-mers have been known to jot their identification numbers on the wall of the terminal room, just in case the number is forgotten or misplaced, and computer printouts containing user identification numbers are fre-quently found on unused terminals or in wastepaper baskets. In general, user identification numbers and passwords should not be printed. If they are printed, they should be overprinted to avoid curious onlookers. It is also a good practice to change user identification numbers and passwords periodically or when a user feels that his or her identification is known to others. A "new" user identification number or password can be issued to a user on a blank card so that the identification would not be associated with its owner if it were lost. One method of deter-mining a user's identification, however, is to systematically try all possi-ble combinations. Two safeguards are used against this practice. The first safeguard involves disconnecting the infiltrator's data communica-tions line after a given number of incorrect attempts. This can be fol-lowed by sending a message to the computer operator to investigate the situation. The second safeguard involves the use of security codes or procedures to further verify that an authorized user is attempting to access the system. One method is to use a list of security codes; one copy is given to the user and another copy is stored in the computer. Each time the system is accessed, the first unused security code on the list is entered by the user and verified by the computer using the same list. Another method is to ask the user one or two questions, at random, from a pre-specified set of questions. Thus, a casual onlooker probably would not know the answer to a given question—especially if the questions were constructed on an individual basis. Another method is to define a mathematical or logical procedure known only to the user and the computer. The computer generates random data and the user performs a mental manipulation of the data in accordance with the defined procedure. If the user fails to supply the correct answer after several tries, the terminal session is aborted.

The drawbacks to user identification techniques are that users forget numbers, passwords, and codes, and that question-and-answer sessions are frequently tedious and time-consuming. For these reasons, keys and badges have been used with some degree of success. Keys (frequently used with banking systems) and badges (used with airline systems) are designed into the terminal device and provide user identification by turning the key or inserting the badge into the reader unit. Keys and badges have the advantage that they are quick safeguards and that the loss of a key or badge is noticed immediately so that the loss can be reported. The latter point is an advantage over passwords and identification codes that do not have a "loss record." For example, the owner of a password is frequently not even aware of the fact that the password is known to others and security has been compromised. Keys and badges are frequently combined with the use of passwords and identification codes. Thus, a lost or stolen key or badge will be of no use to the holder unless the identity of the owner is known.

Access management through the use of physical characteristics is the least developed and the most costly of the various methods. Both fingerprints and voice prints have been used on an experimental basis; however, neither technique has come into widespread use, for both technical and economic reasons.

Processing Limitations

Some of the most obvious threats to data security can be eliminated by controlling the manner in which work is processed by a computer system. Several methods have been discussed in previous chapters and in the first part of this chapter.

Memory protection features constrain a program to operate in the storage space assigned to it. Zeroing the contents of main storage after a sensitive job has been completed is another simple technique that is frequently useful. When removable storage volumes are used, volume identification and verification at run time is an important consideration. Hardware features for completely "erasing" the contents of magnetic tape or direct-access storage are a useful precaution—when storage media are used on a temporary basis during the processing of sensitive information.

Another data security threat that does not leave a calling card occurs when complete files are copied, since the original copy is left intact and many systems do not monitor the copy operation. This is an activity that requires operational control.

A serious threat to security occurs during program development and testing, because many people are usually involved with a project. Therefore, multiple copies of programs and data are usually available at this time, security constraints are frequently relaxed under pressure to get the job done, and "outsiders" are sometimes called in to provide assistance. To counter security threats during program testing, several types of precautions can be used:

1. Utility programs and testing aids (print routines, trace routines, core dumps, etc.)
2. Dummy test data, when possible.
3. Sign-out and verification procedures for real-life test data, when dummy data cannot be used.
4. Controlled or simulated testing of security routines and tables.
5. Rigid program change and update procedures.
6. Adequate control of manual files when conversion to a computer environment is involved.

Actually, the biggest security problem that results from program testing is that security may be breached at some time during program testing, but an actual violation can take place at a much later time when the system is in normal operation.

Auditing and Threat Monitoring

Auditing and threat monitoring techniques provide an *ex post facto* means of providing data security protection. Attempts to violate the security of the computer system or of data files are recorded for subsequent analysis and possible counteraction. Monitoring can be performed so that it is either known to the infiltrator or transparent to him. When a terminal device is disconnected after several unsuccessful attempts at entering the system, the violator knows what has happened and can respond accordingly. On the other hand, when one user attempts to access another user's files and is denied access, but the system records the attempt, the user is not certain whether or not he or she is being monitored. (The possibility of being monitored is therefore a deterrent in itself.) One approach is to postpone disconnecting a user after several attempts to access another user's files but to report the attempt to the computer operator or security officer for appropriate action.

Monitoring can be performed to varying degrees depending upon the security requirements of the system. This type of activity can range from recording attempts to access certain files to recording all transactions for a given set of users. Violation attempts are sometimes made by accident or by a person who is learning the system, so that in any system, an average number of violation attempts are normally expected. When the number of attempts increases rapidly, however, there is reason to assume that a user or group of users is trying to penetrate the system or some of its data files. On the other hand, if the number of attempts decreases markedly, there might be reason to suspect that a means of illegally accessing the system has been discovered.

Recording the activity within the system or on certain data files is frequently referred to as measurement. Analyzing the security logs of a system is a good means of determining how the efficiency of the system can be improved. Analysis of a heavily used file, for example, may reveal that it is comprised of sensitive and nonsensitive data and that the nonsensitive data are the most widely used. As a result, it might be possible to segment the file so that sensitive and nonsensitive portions can be separated and given different security classifications.

A point to be emphasized is that data security is a dynamic phenomenon that is dependent upon the kind of data stored and the usage patterns of the users that access it. The maintenance and use of security logs is a means of detecting the need for change in data security requirements so that the data security system can be adjusted accordingly.

Privacy Transformations

The term *privacy transformation* refers to the practice of coding information to conceal its contents. This practice has been used for a long time in military and governmental security and is referred to as cryptography. A privacy transformation is a reversible set of logical and arithmetic operations that are performed on the characters of a message to render the message unintelligible.

Privacy transformations are usually associated with data transmission and the storage of files. In data transmission, a message is "scrambled" prior to transmission over telecommunications facilities and then "unscrambled" on the receiving end. The objective is to prevent the disclosure of sensitive information through wiretapping.

In file storage, data files are coded in the CPU prior to being placed on a storage medium. Then, if an intruder gains access to a data file accidentally or deliberately, the information content is not readily discernible, because the key necessary for decoding is not available.

Although most codes and ciphers can theoretically be broken, the objective is to make the cost of uncovering the coded information greater than the value of the information itself. Cryptographic encoding and decoding does require computer time. However, most threats to data security in a normal operating environment are low-level threats that do not require extensive techniques. Thus, relatively unsophisticated techniques can be used without upsetting the balance of CPU and input/output activity.

Integrity Management

The last "general" countermeasure to possible data security threats is *integrity management,* which refers to the integrity of equipment, programs, people, and operating procedures. Physical security measures would also be placed in this category.

First, controls should be established for the modification of hardware and software and the integrity of hardware and software should be verified after the repair or modification process is complete. Storage volumes for programs and data should be kept in locked safes or vaults. When communications channels are used, procedures should be developed for protecting against wiretaps and related techniques, although the process is difficult when common carriers (ordinary telephone lines) are involved.

Personnel security is a knotty problem that extends beyond the computer room. In general, however, outsiders should not be permitted in the computer area, and maintenance and repair personnel should only be permitted with authorization. The loyalty and integrity of computer operations personnel are obviously required; however, the following related topic is of great importance. Security should be designed into a system in such a way that *no one* is allowed to bypass security procedures, security logs, and audit facilities. If the system manager or the computer operator needs to perform a specific function, then appropriate authorization procedures should be designed into the system beforehand. In other words, a "blank check" to access and modify a system or its data is not a desirable facility, regardless of the level of personnel involved.

Standard operating procedures should include provisions for handling cases such as the following:

1. Maintaining logs that record the running of sensitive jobs.
2. Manual and automatic restart and recovery procedures for hardware and software failures.
3. Provisions for the physical transportation of sensitive data, including core dumps and file maps.
4. Restrictions on the use of stand-alone programs that bypass the security controls of the system.

Level of Authorization and Data File Protection

Once a user has gained access to a computer system, the next question is, "What programs can the person use and what files is he or she permitted to access?" Obviously, if users execute their own programs and use their own data files, then the data security system need only restrict use to the users' own information. If, on the other hand, programs and data files are used on a system-wide basis, then different levels of authorization are needed depending upon the functions a given user is allowed to perform.

When programs can be shared on a system-wide basis, each user is normally given a "level of authorization" that determines the programs he or she can use and the degree to which the user can alter or modify programs to satisfy his or her needs. A user's authorization level is usually established when he or she signs on through the password, security or identification code, key, badge, or terminal identification. Authorization is provided through a security table that contains a user's authorization level for various system resources. Before a user is permitted to utilize a given system resource, a resource manager (program) verifies that the user possesses the correct level of authorization. Authorization to use a given resource may be assigned to a given user, such as "only V. BROWN and P. SMITH may use this resource," or to a category of users, such as "all programmers but not trainees," or "all supervisors."

Authorization of this type also applies to data files stored in the system. The protection of data files is more involved, since different levels of access are normally provided and because some fields within a record are more sensitive than others. Typical levels of access to data files are:

1. Read only.
2. Read and modify.
3. Read, modify, but not delete a record.
4. Read, write, but not delete or add a record.

The protection mechanism for data files can be augmented with a *lockword* that accompanies the data file. When the data management system opens a file for a file operation, the lockword is compared with a lockword supplied by the user, either explicitly or through his or her entry in the security table. The lockword is usually a string of characters that may or may not have a mnemonic meaning. The lockword is used in the same way that a password is used. If the user cannot supply the correct lockword, access to the file is denied. Also, as with passwords, it is necessary to guard against repeated attempts to guess the lockword.

Many computer operating systems do not contain explicit security procedures for restricting the use of the system, yet they require protection of sensitive data files. In systems of this type, especially when severe security threats are not involved, the use of lockwords provides adequate protection for data files.

Management Responsibility

Computer security, including data security, is usually regarded as a data processing function, although physical security resources may be obtained through an organization's security office. The first step in security management is to appoint a responsible individual to the job of security manager. This may be a part-time position or a full-time position and may or may not include auditing functions. The systems programming staff is a good source for this position.

Computer security is not a one-man job. A security team should be selected that represents most facets of the data processing organization—operation, programming, applications analysis, and management. Normally, these are not full-time positions, and the members serve on the team only to represent the various points of view within the organization.

The third security management function is the development of a security plan for the approval of senior management. This topic, which is covered in the next section, is necessary for budgeting and organizational support. More importantly, the plan serves to make senior management aware of the role of computer security and its significance to the organization. The final security management function, besides implementation and maintenance, is to assign responsibilities to the various security team members and to develop methods for assessing the effectiveness of the computer security program.

Computer Security Plan

A computer security plan includes the following information:

1. Needs—a complete analysis of the organization's computer security needs.
2. Description—an inspection and description of security procedures and facilities that are currently available.
3. Deficiencies—areas where current facilities do not satisfy needs.
4. Assessment—the costs, technical requirements, and organizational changes necessary to implement the needed security provisions.
5. Implementation—specification of a plan and timetable for implementing the security program.

Some of the factors that would normally be included in the "needs" research are:

1. Physical security
2. Protection and classification of data, programs, and documentation

3. Personnel policies and procedures
4. Internal controls and checks
5. Risk management and insurance
6. Contingency plans
7. Standards and test procedures

Each of these factors is a topic in its own right. The analysis of physical security, for example, involves both threats to physical security (such as fire or flood) and measures used to prevent physical security problems (such as fire safety programs and site selection).

EDP AUDITING AND CONTROL

Because the data processing department is presently involved in almost all organizational functions, it has been necessary to establish control procedures to guarantee the integrity and reliability of information. This practice has led to both internal and external auditing to verify that there is adherence to the established controls.

The Concept of Auditing

Auditing is a process that involves the examination of information by an outside party to ascertain the reliability of that information and the reporting of the results of the examination along with suggestions for improvement. Auditors examine not only computer output but also use the computer to assist in the auditing process. Auditors usually comment freely on the status of the computer installation and how it may relate to the outcome of an audit. Therefore, establishing and adhering to controls that relate to the auditing of data processing functions is a normal and standard data processing activity.

Exposure, Cause, and Control

The primary objective of controls in a data processing environment is to reduce or eliminate exposure, which is informally defined as an adverse business situation. A comprehensive list of exposures is:[2]

Erroneous record keeping
Unacceptable accounting
Business interruption

2. Mair, W. C., Wood, D. R., and K. W. Davis. *Computer Control and Audit.* (Altamonte Springs, Florida: Institute of Internal Auditors, 1976), p. 11.

Erroneous management decisions
Fraud and embezzlement
Statutory sanctions
Excessive costs/deficient revenues
Loss or destruction of assets
Competitive disadvantage

A *cause* is any event that results in one or more exposures, and a *control* is an activity that results in the reduction of exposures.

Controls can be classified in several ways, depending upon the objective of the classification. One such classification, particularly relevant to data processing, divides controls depending upon whether they are preventive, detective, or corrective. A *preventive control* is intended to reduce the frequency of exposure. A *detective control* is intended to detect the occurrence of an exposure after it has occurred. A *corrective control* is intended to eliminate the cause of an exposure. This section introduces seven types of EDP control: pre-installation, organizational, development, operations, processing, documentation, and outside data centers.

Pre-Installation Controls.   Pre-installation controls involve the controls needed to insure that the planning for and acquisition of a computer system and programs proceed on a sound basis. The objectives of pre-installation controls are to insure that the computer is really needed, that the facilities selected are appropriate to the organization's needs, and that an adequate installation plan exists.

Organizational Controls.   Organizational controls are the controls that insure that the organizational structure can support the needed data processing activity. The objectives are to provide effective organizational control over the concentration of resources in the data processing department and to guarantee that the computer resources are used effectively.

Development Controls.   Development controls involve controls over the relationship between the data processing department and user departments, in addition to the planning, design, and programming of new applications. The objectives of development controls are to insure that systems and programs are effectively developed and maintained and that an application is developed only if it will result in benefits to the organization.

Operations Controls.   Operations controls are controls over the operating environment, which includes production runs, physical security, and data security. The objectives of operations controls are to prevent or detect accidental processing errors, fraudulent manipulation of data, and accidental destruction of records.

Processing Controls.   Processing controls are the controls that guarantee that computer-generated information is accurate, complete, and valid. The objective of processing controls is also to insure that audit trails are available.

Documentation Controls.   Documentation controls are intended to insure that computer systems, programming, and operating procedures are clearly understood. The objectives of document controls are to insure that documentation exists and that it adequately covers systems, programs, and instructions for user and data processing personnel.

Outside Data Center Controls.   Outside data center controls are controls over the selection of and internal operation of service bureaus. The objectives of outside data center controls are to insure that the service bureau's facilities are adequate, cost effective, and secure, and that the data processed by them is complete, accurate, authorized, and auditable.

SUMMARY

The three general topics covered in this chapter all affect one another. This may be another important reason that computer installation management is difficult. Since the various factors are interrelated, the manager must be constantly "on top of" many diverse activities.

Vocabulary   The student should be familiar with the following terms in the context in which they were used in the chapter.

access management
add time
auditing
auditing and threat monitoring
benchmark job streams
buy time
cause
computer security
control
cycle time
data security
exposure
instruction mix
instruction times
integrity management

kernel problems
lease
level of authorization and data
  file protection
plug compatible unit
privacy transformations
processing limitations
purchase
rent
replacement
security plan
service bureau
simulation
system management company

Exercises 1. Assume that a check has been lost after it was partially processed in a computerized banking environment. List the exposures that could possibly result.

2. What controls would prevent the situation in Question 1? Be specific.

3. Describe how computer acquisition would probably differ in each of the following cases:
   a. Microcomputer vs. large-scale computer
   b. Small business vs. large corporation
   c. Data processing vs. on-line transaction system
   d. Data processing vs. scientific computing

4. *Research topic.* In your computer installation, the public power system fails regularly, causing a significant number of operational problems, delays, and loss of data. How would you remedy the situation?

5. For each data security countermeasure, prepare a list for the following:
   a. Advantages
   b. Disadvantages
   c. Which threats it is good for
   d. Which threats it would be ineffective for

Related Reading Joslin, E. O. *Computer Selection.* Reading, Mass.: Addison-Wesley, 1968.

Katzan, H. *Computer Data Security.* New York: Van Nostrand Reinhold, 1973.

Mair, W. C., Wood, D. R., and Davis, K. W. *Computer Control and Audit.* Altamonte Springs, Fla.: Institute of Internal Auditors, 1976.

Porter, W. T. *EDP Controls and Auditing.* Belmont, Calif.: Wadsworth Publishing Company, 1974.

Data Entry Case Study— Computers in the Supermarket

ata entry devices were introduced earlier in the book and referred to in subsequent chapters. In selecting a case study on the subject, a decision was made to go with one of the most sophisticated examples— computers in the supermarket. The technology involves the Universal Product Code (UPC) and distributed systems.

INTRODUCTION

Most consumer products these days contain a symbol comprised of a series of vertical lines on the package or label, as shown in Figure 24.1. This symbol is called the Universal Product Code (hereafter denoted by the acronym UPC) and is intended to uniquely identify that product. Most stores do not use the UPC, but the potential savings to consumer and store through its use is estimated by the Super Market Institute to be fairly substantial. At least one consumer activist group

FIGURE 24.1(a)   Example of the use of the Universal Product Code (UPC).

(b)

FIGURE 24.1(b)   Closer look at the Universal Product Code symbol.

has protested against the UPC on the grounds that the consumer is prevented from knowing the price of the item, even though it is attached to the shelf containing the item. However, in a study conducted by an independent research organization, the majority of people surveyed were not bothered by the lack of pricemarks on individual items.

The name associated with the use of UPC in the supermarket is *computer assisted checkout.* From a data processing point of view, it is the technology of computer assisted checkout and its relationship to the total data processing environment that holds the greatest interest.

UNIVERSAL PRODUCT CODE

The Universal Product Code is sponsored by the Uniform Grocery Product Code Council (UGPCC), which is a membership organization of participating companies. In developing the UPC, the Product Code Council prepared guidelines for a suitable code and eventually selected one of the entries submitted by interested organizations.

Guidelines

Although the guidelines have evolved to a minor degree, the original guidelines for the UPC give some indication of how difficult the technical problem was:[1]

1. The code should contain 10 decimal characters.
2. The symbol should be scannable omnidirectionally, i.e., regardless of its orientation with respect to a scanning device.
3. The symbol should be scannable when in motion at a velocity not exceeding 100 inches per second.
4. The scanning reject rate should not exceed 0.01 and the undetected error rate should not exceed 0.0001.
5. The depth of field should be at least one inch.
6. Normal environmental contamination (abrasion, dirt, etc.) should not affect the scanning process significantly.
7. The symbol area should not exceed 1.5 square inches.

The UPC design was further complicated by the fact that the symbol had to be capable of being printed onto thirty different kinds of grocery

1. Savir, D. and G. J. Laurer, "The characteristics and decodability of the Universal Product Code," *IBM Systems Journal,* vol. 14, no. 1 (1975): 18.

packaging materials. In the final design, the symbol also had to be read by a fixed scanner, hand held scanner, and by a cashier.

Selected Symbol

The Universal Product Code (UPC) selected in 1973 was the 10-digit bar code shown in Figure 24.2. The first five digits are the manufacturer's identification, which are assigned by Distribution Codes, Inc. of Washington, D.C., and the remaining five digits are the identification assigned by the manufacturer to a particular product.

Because the UPC is also applicable to non-grocery items, the 10-digit code was prefixed with a number system designator and was suffixed with a check digit. Thus, a UPC would look somewhat as follows:

SMMMMMPPPPPC

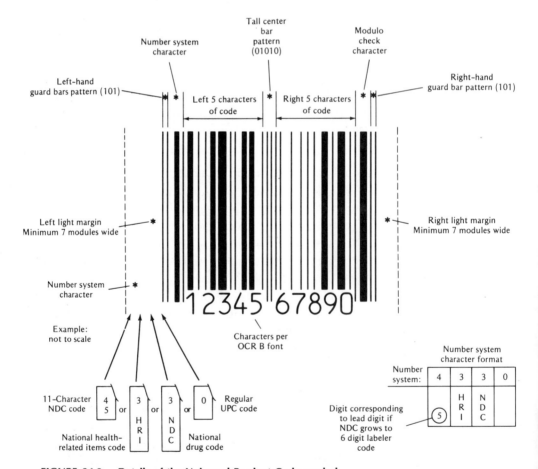

FIGURE 24.2   Details of the Universal Product Code symbol.

	SYMBOL VERSION	NUMBER SYSTEM	
Type	Format	Number System Designator	Use
A	SXXXXX XXXXXC	0	Regular Grocery UPC
		2	Variable Weight
		3	NDC, NHRIC
		5	Coupons
B	SXXXXX XXXXXX	4	Expanded NDC, NHRIC
C	XSXXXXX XXXXXCX	6	Special Version
D	SXXXXX XXXXXCXX . . .	9	General Merchandise
E	XXXXXX	0,1 (implied)	Zero-suppression
	Open	1,7,8	Currently unassigned

Notes: S = Number System Designator
     X = Numeric Digit ID
     C = Check Character

NDC = National Drug Code
NHRIC = National Health Related Items Code

FIGURE 24.3   **Versions of the UPC symbol.**

where S is the number system designator, M is a digit of the manufacturer's identification, P is a digit of the product identification, and C is a check digit. A valid UPC is:

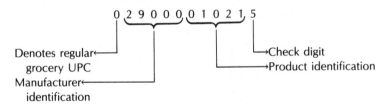

Versions of the UPC symbol are given in Figure 24.3. The length of the code has been increased to 14 digits to accommodate special versions and general merchandise.

Structure of the Symbol

Referring to Figure 24.2, the symbol is structured from left-to-right in the following manner:

Left-hand guard bar pattern
Number system character
Leftmost 5 characters of UPC

Center bar pattern
Rightmost 5 characters of UPC
Check character
Right-hand guard bar pattern

The various patterns are used by the scanner for orientation and validity checking.

The number system designator is printed in the left hand margin and the check digit is printed in the right margin. In Figure 24.1(a), for example, the number system designator is 0 and the check digit is 7.

Symbol Encoding

Each digit in the UPC is encoded as seven bits and the bit patterns are designed so that each digit is composed of two dark bars and two light bars, as illustrated by Figure 24.4. The light and dark bars are of varying widths, depending upon the bit patterns. Each digit has a left-hand and a right-hand version, which permits omnidirectional scanning. Left-hand characters have odd parity (off number of one bits) and right-hand characters have even parity (even number of one bits). A digit to the left of the center bars is called a left-hand character while a digit to the right of the center bars is called a right-hand character. Bit patterns for UPC digits and special characters are summarized in Figure 24.5. The bit pattern for each digit is unique, either left- or right-hand version, when scanning from left to right or right to left.

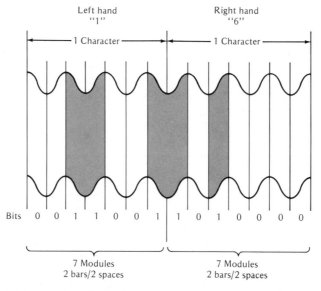

FIGURE 24.4   Digit representation in the UPC.

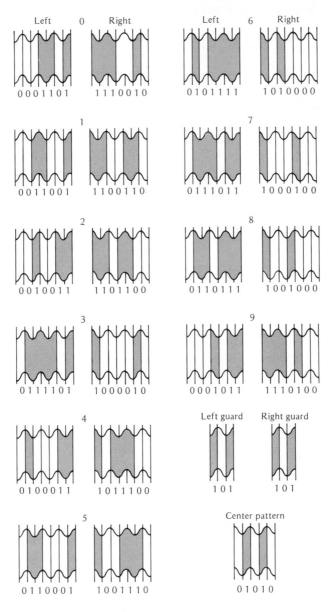

Decimal Value	Left Characters (odd parity – 0)	Right Characters (even parity –E)
0	0001101	1110010
1	0011001	1100110
2	0010011	1101100
3	0111101	1000010
4	0100011	1011100
5	0110001	1001110
6	0101111	1010000
7	0111011	1000100
8	0110111	1001000
9	0001011	1110100

FIGURE 24.5   Bit patterns for UPC characters.

Check Character

The check character is used by the scanning system for error detection. This section describes how the check character is computed. The digit positions in the code are numbered as follows:

0 1 2 3 4 5 6 7 8 9 10
S M M M M M P P P P P

The check digit is computed as follows:

1. Add all even positions.
2. Multiply the results by 3.
3. Add all odd positions.
4. Add the results of steps 2 and 3.
5. Subtract the result from the next highest multiple of 10.
6. The remainder is the check digit.

An example is computed as follows:

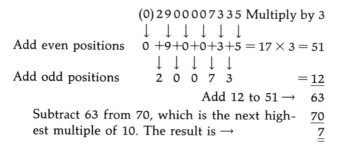

Thus, the check digit for this example is 7, which is confirmed by the symbol in Figure 24.1(a).

Small Products

Some products, such as a pack of chewing gum, are so small that the entire symbol cannot be printed. This requirement resulted in an abbreviated version of the symbol in which zeroes are suppressed. This form of the symbol is given as type E in Figure 24.3. An example of the abbreviated code is given in Figure 24.6.

SCANNING DEVICES

The equipment necessary for scanning UPC symbols varies depending upon the retail concern and the UPC scanning equipment vendor. Figure

FIGURE 24.6   Abbreviated version of the UPC for small products.

24.7 gives a sample configuration. The following three units constitute a minimum viable system: UPC scanner, electronic cash register, and minicomputer. Auxiliary computer equipment that is needed for a "total" data processing configuration is covered in a later section.

Scanning Operation

To use a UPC scanner, the cashier moves a product over a postcard-sized window in the top of the checkout counter. The UPC symbol must face the window, but any orientation is satisfactory.

When an item is passed over the window, a light beam is broken. This action causes scanner electronics to turn on a laser beam that effectively looks for a UPC symbol. When a complete UPC symbol

Courtesy of IBM Corporation

FIGURE 24.7   Sample configuration of a supermarket system.

is stored in the scanner's buffer, the scanner signals an interrupt condition that is picked up by the minicomputer during a polling operation. The minicomputer reads the UPC, looks up the price and identity in a table, and sends the information retrieved to the electronic cash register for tabulation. The cash register tape normally lists the price of the item and its identity.

Other Devices

A variation to the fixed-window scanner is a hand-held wand, which looks like a light pen. The wand works in exactly the same manner, except that it is moved across the UPC symbol.

Some supermarket systems also include scales that weigh and price items at the checkout counter, and similar scales that weigh, price, and generate UPC labels are additionally available for use in the meat and produce departments.

SYSTEMS CONCEPTS

The design of a supermarket data entry system involves several interesting systems concepts. The minicomputer employed to service scanners can be used additionally for inventory control and as a backup for "sister" stores. In either case, the minicomputer usually includes file storage, a display device for entering, changing, and deleting codes, and a printer for generating reports. In some cases, a backup computer is available as a standby in the event of failure of the primary system.

Another option in the case of failure is to utilize a computer in a "sister" store via telecommunications facilities. In any case, backup facilities must be anticipated in a total systems design. One of the options that was first considered for supermarket systems was to use a central computer for all stores in a region. Using phone lines in a real-time environment has been known to cause problems, and this option, except under special conditions, is usually not selected.

DATA PROCESSING CONCEPTS

From a data processing point of view, the primary advantage of computer assisted checkout is inventory control. Every item sold is immediately deducted from the inventory so that automatic reordering can be implemented if desired. Computer assisted checkout also provides a means of tracking an item so that sales orders and delivery dates can be adjusted accordingly. Thus, warehouse space can be used in an optimum manner.

Through the use of a minicomputer, the cash register tape is both day, date, and time stamped. The day, date, and time information can be used, if recorded by the inventory control system, by store management to schedule stock and service personnel to provide better service when business is heavy. An effective inventory control system can also help identify buying patterns so that coupons and sale items can be scheduled to maximize store revenue.

Vocabulary   The student should be familiar with the following terms in the context in which they were used in the chapter.

check character	scanner
computer assisted checkout	Uniform Grocery Product Code
Distribution Codes, Inc.	Council
minicomputer	universal product code
number system character	

Exercises   Prepare a brief report or essay on the following topics:

1. Operator fatigue
2. Multiple item pricing
3. Check cashing and electronics funds transfer systems (EFTS)
4. Over-rings and under-rings
5. Taxable items
6. Faster checkout
7. Shopper awareness of price changes
8. Work-force adjustment
9. Who pays for the system?
10. Store managers raising prices during periods of peak demand

Related Reading   *IBM Systems Journal,* vol. 14, no. 1 (1975).

McEnroe, P. V., Huth, H. T., Moore, E. A., and Morris, W. W. "Overview of the Supermarket System and the Retail Store System."

Savir, D. and Laurer, G. J. "The characteristics and decodability of the Universal Product Code."

Antonelli, D. C., "The role of the operator in the Supermarket and Retail Store Systems."

Metz, W. C., and Savir, D. "Store performance studies for the Supermarket System."

Berk, M. A., Dunbar, C. W., and Hobson, G. C. "Design and performance considerations for the Retail Store System."

Hippert, R. O., Palounek, L. R., Provetero, J., and Skatrud, R. O. "Reliability, availability, and serviceability design considerations for the Supermarket and Retail Store Systems."

Automated Offices

ntil recently, the stronghold of computers in modern organizations has been in the areas of accounting, finance, science, and engineering. In the last few years, however, one of the areas of greatest potential growth has been in the office. The subject of office automation is commonly associated with "data entry type" terminals and with word processing. Recent research into the topic, however, has shown that other possibilities in this area are substantial and that many new concepts should be forthcoming. This chapter gives a brief introduction to the expected future of office automation.

INTRODUCTION

In the present context, the term *automated office* refers to the use of a computer in an office environment to facilitate normal operating procedures. The impact of automated offices, however, can be very great depending upon the extent to which organizational structures are affected.

Some of the basic issues that have been raised with regard to automated offices emphasize that increased technology does not translate directly into increased office productivity. Even getting started with an automated office may be somewhat of a problem since routine changes to normal office functions almost always have to be justified. Another consideration is that doing what is being done now—producing letters and reports—but at a faster rate may not be desirable from an organizational point of view. Thus, the overall gain from an automated office may lie in the prospect of reorganizing everyday office functions so that less paper is produced. Perhaps the most significant consideration is the fact that office work is not as well structured as accounting, scientific, and engineering work, where computers are regularly used, so that the concept of an automated office may be considerably more difficult to implement.

Automated Office Functions

Office functions have been divided into six general classes for purposes of delineation and description. The classes are: communications, information storage and retrieval, data analysis, decision making, personal assistant, and linkage to corporate data bases. The area of communications is the most widely developed; however, research has been done in each of the other areas.

Communications refers to the process of exchanging information in which people are involved, as compared to direct computer-to-computer communication. Facilities have been designed or considered for the following types of communication: messages, text and graphics, and conferences. Word processing, electronic mail, and computer conferencing would fall into this category.

Information storage and retrieval refers to electronic filing systems, indexing, and the interplay between computer and micrographic techniques.

Data analysis refers to the availability of computational facilities for analyzing non-numeric data, such as newspapers, magazines, and reports. This capability would be analogous to statistical packages and forecasting models that are presently available for numeric data.

Decision making refers to computational aids in areas such as budget planning, budget analysis, resource deployment, and strategic planning.

Personal assistant refers to the use of a computer for routine tasks such as scheduling meetings, providing daily reminders, establishing priorities, and storing frequently used information. In this context a personal assistant is a computer program that is roughly analogous to a person's alter ego. Usually implemented through a time-sharing system, the ultimate development of the concept of a personal assistant envisions that two individual's personal assistants communicate to perform routine tasks—such as to schedule a meeting, in the same manner that a secretary would.

Linkage to corporate data base refers to a facility with which an executive can reference the corporate data base—possibly for budgeting or planning—through the use of an easy-to-use query language or a data-entry system. In the latter case, the executive would be provided computer assistance in entering management budgeting and planning data.

While only a few of the above functions are currently available, except as isolated cases, it is important to recognize the direction in which the industry is heading. The following sections give a brief introduction to word processing, electronic mail, and teleconferencing.

WORD PROCESSING

The term *word processing* is used to refer to any process that involves textual information, such as copiers, typesetters, and automatic typewriters. As a data processing function, *word processing* refers to a text editing system wherein a document, such as a letter or report, is typed and recorded on a magnetic recording media. Through editing functions, portions of text can be rearranged, inserted, deleted, or replaced. Draft copies can be run off, and when the final version is prepared, it can then be typed or printed in the desired form.

History

Word processing was introduced in 1964 when IBM added magnetic tape storage and playback to an electric typewriter. The system is known as MTST, for Magnetic Tape Selectric Typewriter. Since then, magnetic cards, tape cassettes, and semiconductor (i.e., transistor) memories have been used.

Modern Systems

Modern word processing systems use a micro or minicomputer that permits extensive storage, editing, and filing facilities. Textual information is entered, edited, and reviewed through a CRT/keyboard device and small disks, called diskettes, are utilized for storage. Letters and reports are printed, using a character-by-character printer or a line printer, at speeds up to 500 lines per minute. In today's world, word processing systems are commonplace, and much competition exists among word processing system vendors.

ELECTRONIC MAIL

Modern methods for transmitting messages at high speeds over telecommunications facilities are referred to as *electronic mail*. Historically, this definition has included telegram, mailgram, TWX/Telex, and facsimile transceivers. In fact, in some cases facsimile transmission can be combined with word processing systems. The above methods of electronic mail are expected to be used for some time into the future because of the ongoing need to achieve rapid communication.

Computer-based electronic mail systems were introduced in the early 1970s through the use of time-sharing services. The basic idea is that one user of the service could place a message to another user in a special system repository, which was accessible by the second user. The primary advantage of electronic mail is that the people engaged in communications can be in remote locations and need not be available for communication at the same time. Electronic mail systems can be implemented through computer networks and have been used to tie the following types of media together: data, video, voice, facsimile, micrographics, and optical character recognition.

TELECONFERENCING

The term *teleconferencing* refers to the use of computers and telecommunications equipment for conducting an on-line conference among people at remote locations. Initially, teleconferencing was used for technological forecasting; however, its greatest benefit may eventually be related to the concept of "working in the home."

Delphi Method

The *Delphi Method* is a technological forecasting technique in which the computer or another means is used to obtain a consensus among a panel of experts. The experts can be together in a meeting room or can be in remote locations. In the latter case, communication is achieved by mail service, telephone, telegraph, or through the use of a computer. The computerized method is naturally of interest to data processing people.

In the computer-based version of the Delphi Method, the expert has access to a remote job entry station or terminal device that is connected via telecommunications facilities to a central computer. The process of forecasting is managed by a specially written computer program that performs the following functions:

1. Requests a judgment from the experts. (A typical question might be, "What will be the state of transportation technology in the year 2000?) Supporting evidence from the experts may also be requested.
2. Tabulates responses by the experts and constructs a summary and a profile of responses.
3. Informs the experts by the computer, via communications facilities, of the summary and profile and asks them to evaluate their previous responses.
4. The experts respond with an adjusted opinion.
5. The sequence continues with step 2.

The process of making judgments, tabulating them, and requesting adjusted opinions continues until a concensus is reached. The computer is particularly useful for the Delphi Method because it can be programmed to be objective and can tabulate forecasts faster than its human counterpart.

Computer Conferencing

The concept of computer conferencing is currently in the research and development stage, but it holds great promise for working meetings in which reports are developed and analyzed. As in the computer-based Delphi Method, the participants are in remote locations and are connected to a "meeting chairman" via data communications facilities. The participants communicate with each other and with the chairman through remote job entry stations or terminal devices.

One of the major benefits that is projected for computer conferencing is that certain classes of employees can work at home for selected periods. Overall, this method would tend to reduce transportation problems, especially in commuter areas, and allow the employee more time for leisure activity by eliminating travel time. The use of computer conferencing would also reduce the amount of intercity traveling that is done by employees of certain organizations.

Business Satellites

One of the major disadvantages of teleconferencing in particular and telecommunications in general is the high cost of public data communications facilities. As a means of reducing line costs, several organizations have engaged in the development of business satellite systems that reduce communication costs by bouncing microwave signals off earth satellites. Large corporations would have their own transmitter/receivers, while smaller organizations would probably pool resources. The use of business satellites would increase the amount of telecommunications traffic and our dependence upon telecommunications.

Business satellites would reduce costs and improve performance. A facsimile transmission currently takes about 6 minutes per page and costs a few dollars. With a business satellite, it would take about 8 seconds and cost approximately 15 cents.

Vocabulary   The student should be familiar with the following terms in the context in which they were used in the chapter.

automated office
business satellite
"communications" function
computer conferencing
"data analysis" function
"decision making" function
Delphi Method
electronic mail

"information storage and
  retrieval" function
"linkage to corporate data
  base" function
"personal assistant" function
teleconferencing
word processing

Exercises   1. Using the concepts and facilities explained in the chapter, devise the functional design and layout of an automated office.

2. The notion of an automated office is of great interest to office layout designers and to office furniture designers. How might these two areas evolve as the direct result of the automated office?

Related Reading   Burns, J. C. "The evolving market for word processing and typesetting systems." *Proceedings of the 1976 National Computer Conference,* AFIPS, vol. 45: 617–623.

Caswell, S. A. "Word processing meets DP." *Computer Decisions,* vol. 9, no. 2 (February, 1977): 52–56.

Miller, F. W. "Electronic mail comes of age," *Infosystems,* vol. 24, no. 11 (November, 1977): 56–64.

Morgan, H. L. "Office automation project—a research prospective," *Proceedings of the 1976 National Computer Conference,* AFIPS, vol. 45: 605–610.

A

ost programmers recognize that the process of constructing a computer program is a creative act and that once a program is suitably encoded, it is as much a contribution to the world of knowledge as a poem, a mathematical formula, or an artist's sketch. In fact, computer programming is usually regarded as an art rather than a science. A computer program written in a programming language becomes a body of knowledge when a description of that language is available that can be used to distinguish between a syntactically valid program and a syntactically invalid program and to determine the meaning of the program. A language that describes another language is called a *metalanguage,* and most programming languages utilize a set of syntactical conventions of this kind.

The most frequent use of a metalanguage is to describe a statement in a programming language in a way that allows the reader to construct a valid instance of a particular statement. Thus, the metalanguage should utilize a notation outside of the programming language being described by a user of the language described.

The metalanguage used in this book employs seven rules and appropriate symbols, given as follows:

1. A *notation variable* names a constituent of a programming language. It takes one of two forms: (1) Lower-case letters, digits, and hyphens—beginning with a letter. For example:
   constant
   arithmetic-variable
   date-name-1
   or (2) Two or more words separated by hyphens where one word consists of lower-case letters and the others consist of upper-case letters. For example:
   DATA-statement
   MAT-READ-statement
   MOVE-statement
   A notation variable represents information that must be supplied by the user and is defined formally or informally in preceding or adjacent text.

2. A *notation constant* stands for itself and is represented by capital letters or by special characters. A notation constant must be written as shown. For example:
   GOSUB statement-number
   NEXT arithmetic-variable
   PROCEDURE DIVISION.
   In this statement, the words GOSUB, NEXT, and PROCEDURE DIVISION are notation constants and must be written as indicated.

3. A *syntactical unit* is a notation variable, a notation constant, or a collection of notation variables, notation constants, and notation symbols enclosed in braces and brackets.

4. The *vertical bar* | is read "or" and indicates that a choice must be made between the item to the left of the bar and the item to the right of the bar. For example:

    character-reference | arithmetic-reference
    &PI | * E | * SQE2

5. A set of *braces* { } is used for grouping or to indicate that a choice is to be made among the syntactical units contained in the braces. For example:

    { + | − }
    {integer-constant | fixed-point constant}

    Alternately, the syntactical units may be stacked vertically within the braces. For example:

    $$\begin{Bmatrix} \text{identifier-1} \\ \text{literal} \end{Bmatrix}$$

6. A set of *brackets* [ ] represents an option and indicates that the enclosed syntactical units can be omitted. For example:

    [+ | −]
    alphabetic-character [numeric-character]

    Alternately, the optional syntactical units may be stacked vertically within the brackets. For example:

    $$\begin{bmatrix} \text{RIGHT} \\ \text{LEFT} \end{bmatrix}$$

7. The *ellipsis* (a series of three periods) indicates that the preceding syntactical unit may be repeated one or more times. For example:

    DATA constant[,constant] . . .

    $$\text{MOVE} \begin{Bmatrix} \text{identifier-1} \\ \text{literal} \end{Bmatrix} \text{TO identifier-2[identifier-3] . . .}$$

The syntactical conventions can be further illustrated by giving some examples from the BASIC and COBOL languages. The *FOR statement* in BASIC has the form:

FOR arithmetic-variable=arithmetic-expression TO
    arithmetic-expression [STEP arithmetic-expression]

An example of this FOR statement is:

FOR I=J TO M/2 STEP 2

The *IF statement* in COBOL has the form:

$$\text{IF condition} \begin{Bmatrix} \text{statement-1} \\ \text{NEXT SENTENCE} \end{Bmatrix} \left[\text{ELSE} \begin{Bmatrix} \text{statement-2} \\ \text{NEXT SENTENCE} \end{Bmatrix} \right].$$

An example of the IF statement is:

IF AGE > 40 MOVE 'EKG TEST' TO CREMK ELSE ALL 1 TO LCOUNT.

Number Systems

APPENDIX B   NUMBER SYSTEMS

omputers are designed to process data in two principal forms: numeric and nonnumeric (or descriptive). A numeric data item is 123; a nonnumeric data item is "TEA FOR TWO." Even though the two data items are usually stored in the computer in a similar manner, the difference between the two is substantial. The number 123 means more than the characters "1," "2," and "3" written next to each other. The form of the number 123 implies the Arabic number system, so that 123 can be interpreted as:

$$1 \times 10^2 + 2 \times 10^1 + 3 \times 10^0$$

where 10^2 means 10×10, 10^3 means $10 \times 10 \times 10$, 10^n means $\underbrace{10 \times 10 \times \ldots \times 10,}_{n \text{ tens}}$ and $10^0 = 1$. The Arabic system is frequently referred to as the *positional number system.* We all know the Arabic system but usually take it for granted in everyday arithmetic. A nonnumeric data item means just what is written. Thus, "TEA FOR TWO" means just that and no more. Related to the subject of data are the ways that it is used, the manner in which it is organized, and the manner in which it is stored and referenced. This necessarily requires that variables, operators, expressions, and arrays be covered. A basic knowledge of number systems, conversion, and data representation is needed in data processing. Once these concepts are known, however, they are usually subordinated to a more intensive study of systems, languages, and applications.

BASIC CONCEPTS

When discussing number systems, two items are of importance: the radix and the radix point. The *radix* is the base to which a number is taken. Normally, we deal with base-10 numbers in everyday affairs. Most computers use base-2 numbers. Most people say that we use base-10 because we have 10 fingers and toes; base-2 is frequently used in computers because two states, on and off, are easily implemented. This will be discussed later. The *radix point* (for example, the decimal point) tells where the integer (or whole) portion of a number ends and where the fraction starts. More specifically, the radix point implicitly gives the magnitude of each numeral in the number. For example, the number 215 means:

$$2 \times 10^2 + 1 \times 10^1 + 5 \times 10^0$$

while the number 21.5 means:

$$2 \times 10^1 + 1 \times 10^0 + 5 \times 10^{-1}$$

The decimal number system is normally used by people for calculations using calculators or manual processes. The three number systems that are widely used in computer systems are binary, octal, and hexadecimal. The *binary system* is a base-2 system; the *octal system* is a base-8 system; and the *hexadecimal system* is a base-16 system.

Every number system has a set of symbols that represents the numerals of that number system. The decimal system has the ten symbols: 0, 1, 2, 3, 4, 5, 6, 7, 8, and 9. Accordingly, a base-n system uses n symbols. The rules of arithmetic are the same for all number systems, but different arithmetic tables are used. For example, the following *addition table* is used for the decimal system:

+	0	1	2	3	4	5	6	7	8	9
0	0	1	2	3	4	5	6	7	8	9
1	1	2	3	4	5	6	7	8	9	0*
2	2	3	4	5	6	7	8	9	0*	1*
3	3	4	5	6	7	8	9	0*	1*	2*
4	4	5	6	7	8	9	0*	1*	2*	3*
5	5	6	7	8	9	0*	1*	2*	3*	4*
6	6	7	8	9	0*	1*	2*	3*	4*	5*
7	7	8	9	0*	1*	2*	3*	4*	5*	6*
8	8	9	0*	1*	2*	3*	4*	5*	6*	7*
9	9	0*	1*	2*	3*	4*	5*	6*	7*	8*

The asterisk denotes a carry of 1 into the next place.

BINARY SYSTEM

The binary number system is a base-2 system that uses the symbols 0 and 1. The binary number 101, for example, is evaluated in the decimal system as:

$$(101)_2 = 1 \times 2^2 + 0 \times 2^1 + 1 \times 2^0$$
$$= 1 \times 2 \times 2 + 0 \times 2 + 1 \times 1$$
$$= 4 + 0 + 1$$
$$= (5)_{10}$$

(Remember, our own calculating is done to the base 10.) In the preceding example, the subscript denotes the base. Thus, $(101)_2$ means "the number 101 to the base 2," and $(5)_{10}$ means "the number 5 to the base 10." When dealing with different number systems, it is important to state the base, since a number can be interpreted in more than one base.

The use of a binary point is demonstrated in the following decimal expansion for the binary number 1011.1:

$$(1011.1)_2 = 1 \times 2^3 + 0 \times 2^2 + 1 \times 2^1 + 1 \times 2^0 + 1 \times 2^{-1}$$
$$= 1 \times 8 + 0 \times 4 + 1 \times 2 + 1 \times 1 + 1 \times \tfrac{1}{2}$$
$$= 8 + 0 + 2 + 1 + \tfrac{1}{2}$$
$$= (11\tfrac{1}{2})_{10} = (11.5)_{10}$$

Recall that a negative exponent means "take the reciprocal." Thus, 10^{-1} means $\frac{1}{10}^1$, 2^{-4} means $\frac{1}{2}^4$, and m^{-n} means $\frac{1}{m}^n$.

The addition table for binary addition is:

```
+ | 0 1
--+------
0 | 0 1
1 | 1 0*
```

The asterisk denotes a carry of 1 into the next place. Thus,

```
  101                  1011
+ 10                 + 101
-----      (Carry)     111
  111      (Sum)     10000
```

OCTAL SYSTEM

The octal number system is a base-8 system that uses the symbols 0, 1, 2, 3, 4, 5, 6, and 7. The octal number 375 is evaluated in the decimal system as follows:

$$(375)_8 = 3 \times 8^2 + 7 \times 8^1 + 5 \times 8^0$$
$$= 3 \times 64 + 7 \times 8 + 5 \times 1$$
$$= 192 + 56 + 5$$
$$= (253)_{10}$$

The octal system uses an *octal point,* as in the following example:

$$(24.5)_8 = 2 \times 8^1 + 4 \times 8^0 + 5 \times 8^{-1}$$
$$= 2 \times 8 + 4 \times 1 + 5 \times \frac{1}{8}$$
$$= 16 + 4 + \frac{5}{8}$$
$$= (20\frac{5}{8})_{10} = (20.625)_{10}$$

The addition table for octal addition is:

```
+ | 0  1  2  3  4  5  6  7
--+-------------------------
0 | 0  1  2  3  4  5  6  7
1 | 1  2  3  4  5  6  7  0*
2 | 2  3  4  5  6  7  0* 1*
3 | 3  4  5  6  7  0* 1* 2*
4 | 4  5  6  7  0* 1* 2* 3*
5 | 5  6  7  0* 1* 2* 3* 4*
6 | 6  7  0* 1* 2* 3* 4* 5*
7 | 7  0* 1* 2* 3* 4* 5* 6*
```

The asterisk denotes a carry of 1 into the next position. Thus,

425		136	
+ 31		+ 45	
	(Carry)	11	
456	(Sum)	203	

The identity $2^3 = 8$ gives a clue to a useful relationship between binary and octal numbers. The identity implies that an octal numeral can be represented "exactly" by three binary digits (or bits, as they are called), as demonstrated in the following table:

Decimal	Octal	Binary	Decimal	Octal	Binary
0	0	000	5	5	101
1	1	001	6	6	110
2	2	010	7	7	111
3	3	011	8	10	1000
4	4	100	9	11	1001

As a result, a long sequence of binary digits can be written more conveniently as octal digits by replacing each sequence of three binary digits by an equivalent octal digit from the preceding table. Thus, a series of bits such as:

101001011010111001

is expressed simply as 513271 in octal. The forms are equivalent, as suggested in the following additions:

Binary	Octal	Decimal
010011 =	23 =	19
+ 011101 =	+ 35 =	+ 29
110000	60	48

HEXADECIMAL SYSTEM

The hexadecimal number system is a base-16 system that uses the symbols 0, 1, 2, 3, 4, 5, 6, 7, 8, 9, A, B, C, D, E, and F. The various symbols have the following decimal equivalents:

Hexadecimal Symbol	Decimal Equivalent
0	0
1	1
2	2
3	3
4	4
5	5

Hexadecimal Symbol	Decimal Equivalent
6	6
7	7
8	8
9	9
A	10
B	11
C	12
D	13
E	14
F	15

The hexadecimal number 2B7, for example, is evaluated in decimal as

$$(2B7)_{16} = 2 \times 16^2 + B \times 16^1 + 7 \times 16^0$$
$$= 2 \times 256 + 11 \times 16 + 7 \times 1$$
$$= 512 + 176 + 7$$
$$= (695)_{10}$$

Use of a hexadecimal radix point is seen in the following example:

$$(1A.C)_{16} = 1 \times 16^1 + A \times 16^0 + C \times 16^{-1}$$
$$= 1 \times 16 + 10 \times 1 + 12 \times \frac{1}{16}$$
$$= 16 + 10 + \frac{3}{4}$$
$$= (26.75)_{10}$$

Examples of hexadecimal addition are:

```
  6A2              A6C
+ 4B                47
           (Carry)   1
  6ED      (Sum)   AB3
```

A useful relationship also exists between binary and hexadecimal numbers, since $2^4 = 16$. A hexadecimal numeral can be represented "exactly" by four binary digits, or bits, as demonstrated in the following table:

Decimal	Hexadecimal	Binary
0	0	0000
1	1	0001
2	2	0010
3	3	0011
4	4	0100
5	5	0101
6	6	0110

Decimal	Hexadecimal	Binary
7	7	0111
8	8	1000
9	9	1001
10	A	1010
11	B	1011
12	C	1100
13	D	1101
14	E	1110
15	F	1111

As a result, a long sequence of binary digits can be written more conveniently as hexadecimal digits by replacing each sequence of four binary digits by an equivalent hexadecimal digit from the preceding table. Thus, a series of bits such as

```
1000101100010110111000101100 1101
```

is expressed more simply as 8B16E2CD in hexadecimal. The forms are equivalent, as illustrated by the following additions:

Binary	Hexadecimal	Decimal
00100011	23	35
+ 01001101	+ 4D	+ 77
01110000	70	112

CONVERSION BETWEEN DIFFERENT NUMBER SYSTEMS

The method given previously for converting numbers from binary, octal, and hexadecimal to decimal is known as literal expansion. *Literal expansion* of a base-r number consists of the evaluation of the following mathematical identity:

$$(A_{n-1}A_{n-2} \cdots A_1 A_0 A_{-1} A_{-2} \cdots A_{-m})_r$$
$$= A_{n-1} r^{n-1} + A_{n-2} r^{n-2} + \cdots + A_1 r^1 + A_0 r^0 + A_{-1} r^{-1}$$
$$+ A_{-2} r^{-2} + \cdots + A_{-m} r^{-m}$$

in the number system *into* which the conversion is being made. The method works well for conversions *into* decimal, since we are familiar with decimal calculations. However, the following conversion from decimal to hexadecimal—

$$(286)_{10} = 2 \times A^2 + 8 \times A^1 + 6 \times A^0$$
$$= 2 \times 64 + 8 \times A + 6$$
$$= C8 + 50 + 6$$
$$= (11E)_{16}$$

—where the calculations are performed using hexadecimal arithmetic, shows the inconvenience and confusion that can result from performing calculations in a base other than decimal.

Conversion to Decimal. Literal expansion is the most straightforward method of converting numbers from other bases to base 10, as demonstrated in the following examples:

Binary-to-decimal

$$(11101010.1)_2 = 1 \times 2^7 + 1 \times 2^6 + 1 \times 2^5 + 0 \times 2^4 + 1 \times 2^3 + 0 \times 2^2$$
$$+ 1 \times 2^1 + 0 \times 2^0 + 1 \times 2^{-1}$$
$$= 128 + 64 + 32 + 8 + 2 + 0.5$$
$$= (234.5)_{10}$$

Octal-to-decimal

$$(352.4)_8 = 3 \times 8^2 + 5 \times 8^1 + 2 \times 8^0 + 4 \times 8^{-1}$$
$$= 192 + 40 + 2 + 0.5$$
$$= (234.5)_{10}$$

Hexadecimal-to-decimal

$$(EA.8)_{16} = E \times 16^1 + A \times 16^0 + 8 \times 16^{-1}$$
$$= 14 \times 16 + 10 \times 1 + 8 \times \frac{1}{16}$$
$$= 224 + 10 + 0.5$$
$$= (234.5)_{10}$$

The integer and fractional parts can be converted separately, and there is a "short-cut" method for evaluating the integer part. Consider the decimal expansion of $(352)_8$:

$$3 \times 8^2 + 5 \times 8^1 + 2 \times 8^0$$

This expression can be rewritten as follows:

$$(8 (8 \times 3 + 5))) + 2$$

This is called "nested multiplication." This process is summarized as follows:

1. Multiply the leftmost digit by the radix n and add it to the next digit, progressing to the right.
2. Multiply this sum by the radix n and add it to the next digit.
3. Repeat this process until the rightmost digit has been added.
4. The resulting sum is the decimal equivalent of the given base-n number.

For example, $(1101010)_2$ is evaluated as

$$(2 (2 (2 (2 (2 (2 \times 1) + 1) + 0) + 1) + 0) + 1) + 0 = 234$$

Conversion from Decimal.   Conversion from decimal to any base is most frequently performed by treating the integer and fractional parts separately. As an example, the decimal integer 7361 is converted to octal by successively dividing the number by 8 until a quotient of 0 is obtained. The successive remainders form the equivalent octal number beginning with the rightmost digit:

$$
\left.
\begin{array}{rl}
0 & \text{r.1} \\
8\overline{)1} & \text{r.6} \\
8\overline{)14} & \text{r.3} \\
8\overline{)115} & \text{r.0} \\
8\overline{)920} & \text{r.1} \\
8\overline{)7361} &
\end{array}
\right\} \quad 16301
$$

Remainders

Thus, $(7361)_{10} = (16301)_8$. The process is summarized as follows:

1. Repeatedly divide the decimal integer by the radix n of the target base, saving the remainders until a quotient of 0 is obtained.
2. The equivalent base-n number is formed from the remainders, where the first remainder is the rightmost digit and the last remainder is the leftmost digit.

The following examples depict the process for binary and hexadecimal integer conversions:

$$
\left.
\begin{array}{rl}
0 & \text{r.1} \\
2\overline{)1} & \text{r.0} \\
2\overline{)2} & \text{r.0} \\
2\overline{)4} & \text{r.1} \\
2\overline{)9} & \text{r.0} \\
2\overline{)18} & \text{r.1} \\
2\overline{)37} &
\end{array}
\right\} \quad 100101
\qquad
\left.
\begin{array}{rl}
0 & \text{r.2} \\
16\overline{)2} & \text{r.0} \\
16\overline{)32} & \text{r.4} \\
16\overline{)516} & \text{r.13} \\
16\overline{)8269} &
\end{array}
\right\} \quad 204D
$$

$$(37)_{10} = (100101)_2 \qquad\qquad (8269)_{10} = (204D)_{16}$$

The conversion of a fraction from decimal to another number system is essentially the inverse of integer conversion. Whereas an integer is converted by a process of successive divisions, the fraction is converted by a process of successive multiplications. The decimal fraction 0.8125 is converted to a binary fraction by successively multiplying the fraction by 2; the integer parts of the products are the successive digits of the binary fraction starting with the most significant digit. After the first multiplication, the integer part is ignored in the next multiplication; the process continues until the fraction has been reduced to zero or the required number of binary places is generated. For example,

Decimal Fraction	Product	Integer Part
$0.8125 \times 2 = 1.625$		1 (most significant digit)
$0.625 \times 2 = 1.250$		1
$0.250 \times 2 = 0.5$		0
$0.5 \times 2 = 1.0$		1 (least significant digit)

Thus, $(0.8125)_{10} = (0.1101)_2$. The process is summarized as follows:

1. Repeatedly multiply the decimal fraction by the radix n of the target base, saving the integer parts of the products as the digits of the target fraction.
2. The multiplication is repeated using only the fractional result of the previous multiplication.
3. The first integer obtained is the most significant digit (i.e., leftmost) of the fraction, and so forth.
4. The process is continued until a zero fraction or the desired accuracy is generated.

The following examples depict the process for octal and hexadecimal fraction conversions:

Decimal Fraction	Product	Integer Part
$0.8125 \times 8 = 6.5$		6 (most significant digit)
$0.5 \times 8 = 4.0$		4 (least significant digit)

$(0.8125)_{10} = (0.64)_8$

Decimal Fraction	Product	Integer Part	Hexadecimal Digit
$0.8125 \times 16 = 13.0$		13	D

$(0.8125)_{10} = (0.D)_{16}$

Decimal Fraction	Product	Integer Part	Hexadecimal Digit
$0.78125 \times 16 = 12.5$		12	C (most significant digit)
$0.5 \times 16 = 8.0$		8	8 (least significant digit)

$(0.78125)_{10} = (0.C8)_{16}$

Number conversions are usually lengthy and tedious when dealing with actual computer numbers, so self-explanatory tables are fre-

quently used to lessen the chore. In general, however, a basic understanding of the process is all that is needed in computer science.

COMPLEMENTS AND SUBTRACTION

One of the topics that is conspicuous by its absence thus far is subtraction. As the inverse operation to addition, the concept of subtraction
is well understood. Binary subtraction is presented as an example. Binary addition takes the form:

$$0 + 0 = 0$$
$$0 + 1 = 1$$
$$1 + 0 = 1$$
$$1 + 1 = 10$$

Its inverse operation, binary subtraction, takes the form:

$$0 - 0 = 0$$
$$1 - 0 = 1$$
$$1 - 1 = 0$$
$$10 - 1 = 1$$

The case $0 - 1$ is handled by borrowing from the next position, similar
to the manner in which borrowing is done in decimal subtraction.
The following example of binary subtraction requires no borrowing:

Binary Form		Decimal Equivalent
	No Borrowing	111
10101		2̶1̶
− 100		− 4
10001		17

The following example does depict borrowing:

Binary Form		Decimal Equivalent
010010	Borrowing	
1̶0̶1̶0̶1		21
− 1010		− 10
1011		11

Similar conventions are used for octal and hexadecimal subtraction.
   Another method for representing negative numbers and for performing subtraction is to use complement arithmetic. Consider, for
example, the expression:

$$684 - 435 = 249$$

The subtraction operation can also be expressed by using the ten's complement of the subtrahend, as follows:

$$684 + (1000 - 435) - 1000 = 249$$

The term $(1000 - 435)$ is referred to as the *ten's complement* of 435, which evaluates to

$$\begin{array}{r} 1000 \\ - 435 \\ \hline 565 \end{array}$$

The ten's complement of a number can be developed by inspection. (Each digit is subtracted from 9 and a 1 is added to the low-order digit.) The difference is then computed by adding the complement of the subtrahend to the minuend:[1]

$$\begin{array}{r} 684 \\ 565 \\ \hline 1249 \end{array}$$

Lastly, the 1000 is subtracted by dropping the high-order 1. Later, we will see that when fixed-length arithmetic registers are used, the high-order digit is dropped automatically.

The *complement* of a number N (or more specifically, a *radix complement*) is defined as follows:

Complement of $N = b^n - N$

where b is the radix (or base) and n is the number of digits in N. Actually, $b^n - 1$ is the largest possible number. Thus, the ten's complement of 435 is 565 and the two's complement of 1010 is 0110.

In the computer, numbers are stored in "fixed-length" storage locations or are held in fixed-length arithmetic registers during arithmetic calculations. Although computers vary, the left-most digit of a "computer" number is used to represent the arithmetic sign. Thus, the following 16-digit binary word:

| 0000000000000101 |

represents the value +5 in decimal, where the high-order (i.e., the leftmost digit) represents the plus sign. Similarly, a 1 bit is used to represent a minus sign. Negative numbers are generally represented in two ways. In the first method, the value is stored in true form

1. The terminology is: MINUEND-SUBTRAHEND=DIFFERENCE.

with a negative-sign bit, as in the following binary representation of −5:

| 1000000000000101 |

The second method involves storing a number in complement form, so that the binary representation of −5 is

| 1111111111111011 |

The second method has several distinct advantages. First, it is relatively simple to find the two's complement of a binary number. It is performed as follows: 1. Convert all 0's to 1's. 2. Convert all 1's to 0's. 3. Add 1 to the result.[2] For example,

Binary number	0000101100101011
Bits inverted	1111010011010100
Add 1	+1
Two's complement	1111010011010101

The two's complement is easily implemented in computer circuitry. The second advantage is that arithmetic operations can be executed in a straightforward manner without regard to the sign of the operands. For addition, numbers are simply added as follows:

	Binary	*Decimal*
	0000000000000101	(5)
+	0000000000001101	+(13)
	0000000000010010	18 (result)
	1111111111111011	(−5)
+	0000000000001101	+(13)
1	0000000000001000	8 (result)

└─ discarded

| | 0000000000000101 | (5) |
| + | 1111111111110011 | +(−13) |

2. The process of converting all 1s to 0s and all 0s to 1s is referred to as the *one's complement.*

Binary	Decimal
1111111111111000	−8 (result)

Binary	Decimal
1111111111111011	(−5)
+ 1111111111110011	+(−13)

| 1111111111101110 | −18 (result) |

The simplicity of the above technique should be compared with the conventional method, listed below:

1. If the numbers to be added have like signs, add the magnitude of the numbers and give the sum the common sign.
2. If the numbers to be added have unlike signs, compute the difference of the numbers and give it the sign of the number with the largest magnitude.

Complement arithmetic has similar advantages for subtraction. It is performed by taking the two's complement of the subtrahend and adding it to the minuend, as demonstrated in the following examples:

Binary	Decimal
0000000000001101	13
− 0000000000000101	−5

becomes

| 0000000000001101 | (13) |
| + 1111111111111011 | +(−5) |

| 0000000000001000 | 8 (result) |

| 0000000000000101 | (5) |
| − 1111111111111011 | −(13) |

becomes

| 0000000000000101 | (5) |
| + 1111111111110011 | +(−13) |

Binary	Decimal
1111111111111000	−8 (result)
0000000000000101	(5)
− 1111111111110011	−(−13)

becomes

Binary	Decimal
0000000000000101	(5)
+ 0000000000001101	+(13)

Binary	Decimal
0000000000010010	18 (result)
1111111111111011	(−5)
− 1111111111110011	−(−13)

becomes

Binary	Decimal
1111111111111011	(−5)
+ 0000000000001101	+(13)

Binary	Decimal
0000000000001000	8 (result)

The above technique is very similar to the conventional manual method of inverting the subtrahend and adding it to the minuend.

The primary advantage of complement arithmetic for a computer lies in the simplicity of the arithmetic unit—it uses the adder for both addition and subtraction. When complement arithmetic is used in a computer as described above, negative numbers are normally stored in two's complement form.

Virtual
Storage

APPENDIX C   VIRTUAL STORAGE

ne of the fundamental operating system requirements implied by the multiprogramming and time-sharing modes of operation is that several user jobs must reside in main storage at the same time. The allocation of main storage to jobs is regarded as a management function in an operating system and the techniques used are known as *storage management.* Earlier, the concept of swapping was discussed, which is one means of managing main storage. Three methods will be covered in this section: partition allocation, region allocation, and virtual storage. The topics of partition and region allocation serve as lead-ins to the main subject—*virtual storage,* an advanced storage management technique. This presentation is not exhaustive, since other methods have and will be developed. The methods covered here, however, are the most widely used and are necessary to an understanding of the terminology frequently encountered in data processing.

ENVIRONMENT FOR STORAGE MANAGEMENT

Before multiprogramming and time-sharing concepts were established, jobs were executed serially by the operating system. Normal delays in the execution of a job simply caused the central processing unit to wait. Main storage organization in a serially operating environment is depicted in Figure C.1. It should be noted that main storage is not fully utilized, so that serial operation results in the inefficient use of the two most costly components of a computer system: the central processing unit and main storage. This problem, as we know, can be alleviated through multiprogramming.

   With multiprogramming, the upper limit on the number of active jobs is usually determined by the design of the computer and/or the operating system. Although some multiprogramming systems permit

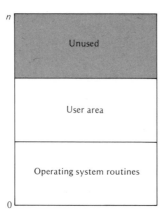

FIGURE C.1   **Main storage organization in an operating environment in which jobs are executed serially. The central processing unit must wait when normal delays in program execution occur. Also, main storage is not fully utilized.**

the movement of programs on a dynamic basis between main storage and an external storage medium in a manner similar to swapping, programs are resident in most systems for the duration of execution. Thus, the level of multiprogramming is partially determined by the size of main storage and the size of individual programs.

With time-sharing, the main objective is to service many users, and the size of main storage does not in general determine the number of active users the system can sustain. The size of main storage *does*, however, determine the efficiency and response time of the system. In time-sharing, therefore, programs are expected to be moved between main storage and an external storage medium on a dynamic basis.

Of the three methods covered here, both partition allocation and region allocation are used in "static" multiprogramming environments. The third method, virtual storage, is used for both multiprogramming and time-sharing.

PARTITION ALLOCATION

With the *partition method* of storage management, main storage is partitioned into fixed-sized areas. The size of each partition is established by the computer operator when the computer is started through operator commands to the system. A typical partitioned storage organization is depicted in Figure C.2.

The user must specify the amount of main storage required (usually

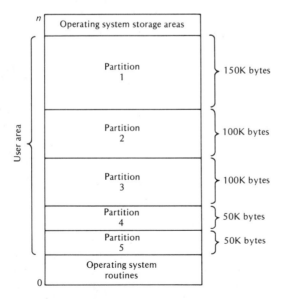

FIGURE C.2   Partitioned storage organization. The size of partitions is established by the computer operator when the computer is started up using operating system facilities.

with the JOB card) when a job is submitted. Using this information, routines of the operating system can assign the job to the smallest partition in which the programs of the job can be placed. (The concept is similar to the placement of different-sized books in a bookcase with different-sized shelves. Books are placed on shelves so as to obtain the best utilization of the bookcase.[1]) Once a job is assigned to a partition, it must execute in that partition until the job is completed.

The major advantage of partition allocation is that the assignment of a job to a partition is straightforward and efficient. The disadvantages are almost obvious. First, the number of active jobs is limited by the number of partitions, even if the jobs are small in size. Second, most jobs will not fit exactly in a partition, and thus some main storage space is left unused. Last, big jobs that fit into only the largest partition must be executed serially, even if there are no small jobs in the system.

Partition allocation is frequently used when one or more jobs must be resident for long periods of time, as in the case of an on-line information system. A partition is allocated to jobs of this type. The job is initiated, as any other job, and it stays resident by virtue of the fact that it does not terminate.

REGION ALLOCATION

The disadvantages of partition allocation are partially eliminated by an alternate method known as *region allocation*. As in partition allocation, each job with region allocation also specifies its main storage requirements through the JOB card. When storage requirements are not stated, a default value is assigned. As suggested in Figure C.3, as many jobs are loaded into the user area of main storage as possible. Each job is given the requested amount of storage and is constrained to execute in that region. (In a logical sense, "fences" are established in the user area of main storage.) Jobs are selected for execution on the basis of internal priority; if insufficient "available" storage is available for that job, then it must wait. When a job completes execution, the main storage space assigned to it is freed for use by other jobs. Main storage does become fragmented after several jobs terminate and new jobs are initiated. However, region allocation is more efficient than partition allocation because there is never a partially used partition.

VIRTUAL STORAGE

Virtual storage is a storage management technique that allows an addressing capability that exceeds the physical main storage capacity of the computer—hence the name "virtual storage," which implies storage

---

1. Some parking lots have special areas for compact cars for similar reasons.

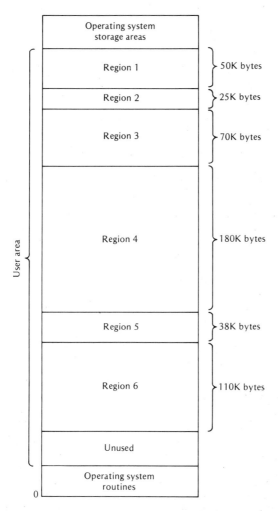

FIGURE C.3   **The region allocation method of storage management. Main storage is assigned to jobs dynamically, based on actual requirements.**

that does not exist. Virtual storage is "mapped" into a combination of real main storage and external storage, such as magnetic drum or disk. The basic idea behind a virtual storage system is that virtual storage, real main storage, and external storage are divided into fixed-size units of storage called *pages*. Typical page sizes are 2048 bytes and 4096 bytes. Only needed pages of a program, including data and storage areas, must be in real main storage for the program to execute. A *needed page* is defined as the page in which the program is actually executing or a page that contains an operand used by an instruction. Usually, several pages are needed to sustain execution, but this number is considerably less than the complete program. As a result, the amount of main storage can be "overcommitted"; when a particular page is needed, it can be retrieved from external storage on a demand basis. When a virtual storage system operates, pages are constantly moved between main storage and the external storage device, because new pages are constantly needed and old pages must be displaced to make room for new pages. The process of moving pages in and out of main storage is referred to as *paging* and is depicted in Figure C.4. The external device used to hold pages when they are not in use is called the *paging device.* Under heavily loaded conditions, even the primary paging device becomes saturated, and infrequently used pages are migrated to a secondary paging device. *Page migration* is performed by a system management routine when the amount of available space on the primary paging device goes below a certain threshold. Pages are migrated by reading them into main storage and then writing them out to the secondary paging device. Virtual storage is implemented through a combination of hardware facilities and software support.

The key concept behind the implementation of virtual storage is a mapping between the virtual address space and the physical address space, as shown in Figure C.5. Programs and data occupy contiguous page locations in virtual storage, but need not occupy contiguous page locations in real main storage. The reason is that each effective address used during computer processing is translated prior to the referencing of main storage. Each program address must be translated; however, because complete pages are used, only the locations of pages need be adjusted and byte addresses within a page are the same in virtual storage as they are in main storage. A simplification of the translation of virtual addresses to real addresses is illustrated in Figure C.6. The

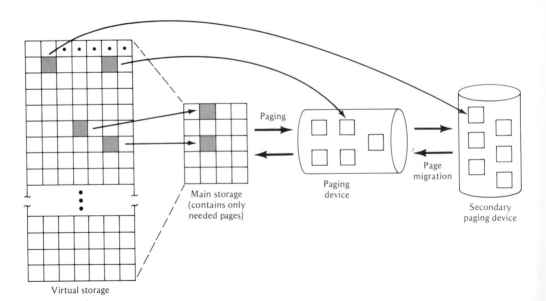

Paging

Main storage
(contains only
needed pages)

Paging
device

Page
migration

Secondary
paging device

Virtual storage

FIGURE C.4   Conceptual view of the paging process.

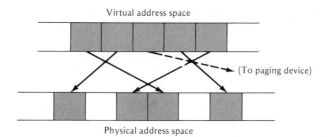

Virtual address space

(To paging device)

Physical address space

FIGURE C.5   **The mapping of addresses from the virtual address space to a physical address space is the key concept behind the implementation of a virtual storage system.**

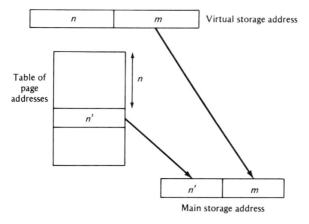

FIGURE C.6   **Simplification of the process of translating virtual storage addresses, using a page table.**

high-order bits of a virtual address are displacements in a page table containing the main storage addresses of pages. The low-order bits are unchanged because they denote storage addresses within a page. Thus, translation essentially consists of a table lookup. Page tables are constructed and maintained by software. In order to facilitate page table management and translation, the virtual storage address space is divided into segments, and segments are divided into pages. The segmented effective virtual address, shown in Figure C.7, allows a hierarchical set of lookup tables.

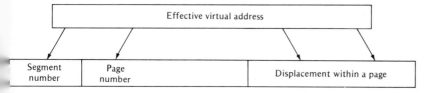

FIGURE C.7   **The effective virtual address is segmented to allow a hierarchical set of lookup tables.**

The process of translating virtual addresses to main storage addresses is called *dynamic address translation* and uses the following hardware features and software concepts:

1. A *table register* that contains the address of the segment table
2. A *segment table* that contains the origin (i.e., addresses) of the page tables
3. A *page table* for each segment
4. An *associative memory* to speed up translation (also known as a *lookaside buffer*)
5. A hardware feature known as the dynamic address translation *(DAT) box* that physically performs the address translation using the above tables

The *dynamic address translation* procedure operates as follows:

1. The table register is used to locate the segment table.
2. The segment field of the virtual storage address is added to the origin of the segment table to locate the page table for that virtual storage segment.
3. The page field of the virtual storage address is added to the origin of the page table (Step 2) to determine the real address of the page in main storage or to indicate that the page is not in main storage but resides on the paging device.
4. If the referenced page is in main storage, then the address in the page table becomes the high-order portion of the main storage address as indicated above. If the referenced page is not in main storage, then an interruption is generated so that the page can be "paged in" by the operating system.

Figure C.8 gives a conceptual view of a page table entry. The control bits indicate whether the main storage address found in the page table

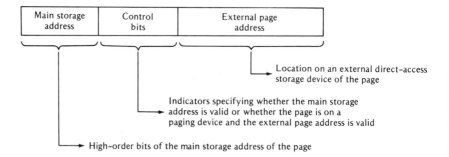

FIGURE C.8   Conceptual view of a page table entry.

entry is valid. During dynamic address translation, the control bits are inspected by the DAT box so that an interruption can be generated if necessary.

When a paging interruption is received by the operating system, it locates the page through the external page address found in the appropriate page table entry. When the page is paged in, the high-order bits of the main storage location where the page was placed replace the main storage address field of the page table entry, and the control bits are set to indicate that the page is in main storage. When a page is paged out because its space is needed in main storage, the process is reversed:

1. The page is written to the paging device.
2. The external location of the page replaces the external page address of the page table entry.
3. The control bits are set to indicate that the page is not in main storage.

Dynamic address translation is performed automatically by the hardware using the DAT box for each reference to main storage. The segment and page tables are built and maintained by the operating system. Segment and page tables are held in main storage, so that each main storage reference by the executing program effectively re-quires three references: segment table, page table, and the actual refer-ence itself. This is a high price to pay, from a performance point of view, for virtual storage capability. Most systems that employ virtual storage, therefore, augment the dynamic address translation process with a small associative memory that contains the virtual storage and main storage addresses of the most recent storage references. When a virtual storage address is to be translated, the segment and page fields of the virtual address are compared with the first part of *all* associative registers in parallel. If an equal match exists, then the second part of the matched associative register becomes the page address di-rectly and the main storage accesses of segment and page tables required during dynamic address translation need not be made. Since the cur-rently used instructions and data tend to cluster in a program, the use of an associative register speeds up the dynamic address process considerably. The process of dynamic address translation is shown in Figure C.9, and an example of address translation is given in Figure C.10.

Virtual storage is used in two primary ways in operating system technology. In multiprogramming systems, virtual storage is used to overcommit main storage that has been allocated as partitions or re-gions. This type of system is illustrated in Figure C.11. In systems of this type, a single virtual storage is used and one set of segment and

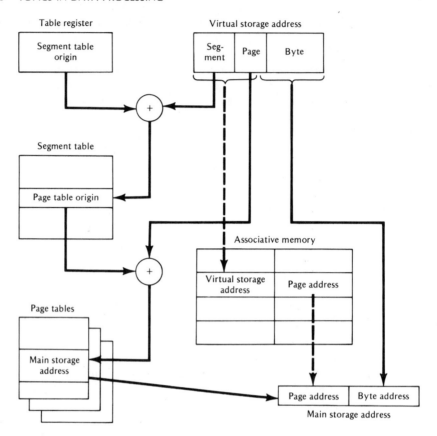

FIGURE C.9   Dynamic address translation.

page tables exists for the entire system. In time-sharing systems that utilize virtual storage, a complete virtual storage is assigned to each job, and each job has its own set of segment and page tables. Prior to giving control of the central processing unit to a job, the job's segment and page tables are brought into main storage by a system management routine, and the table register is set to point to the segment table. A system that employs multiple virtual storage is depicted in Figure C.12.

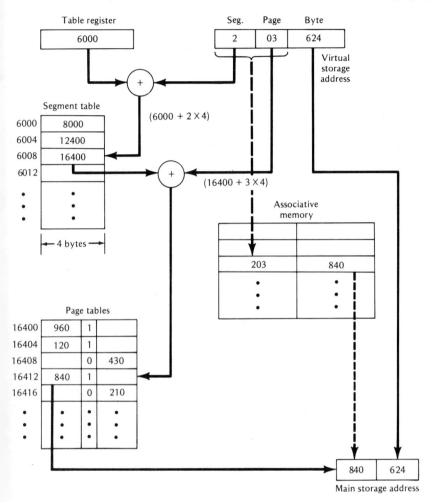

FIGURE C.10   Example of dynamic address translation.

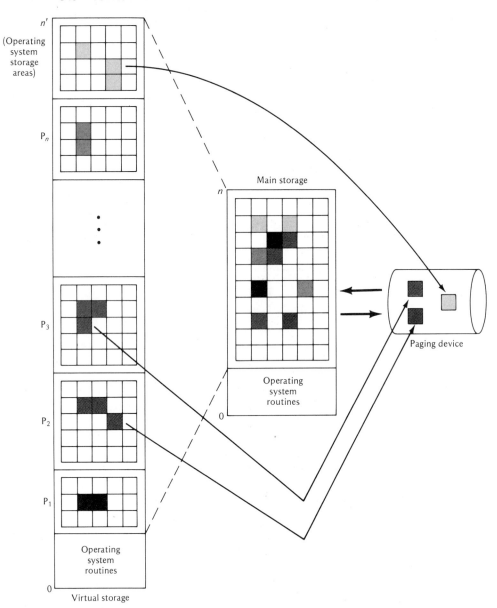

FIGURE C.11 The use of virtual storage permits main storage to be overcommitted in a multiprogramming system in which storage is allocated as partitions or regions.

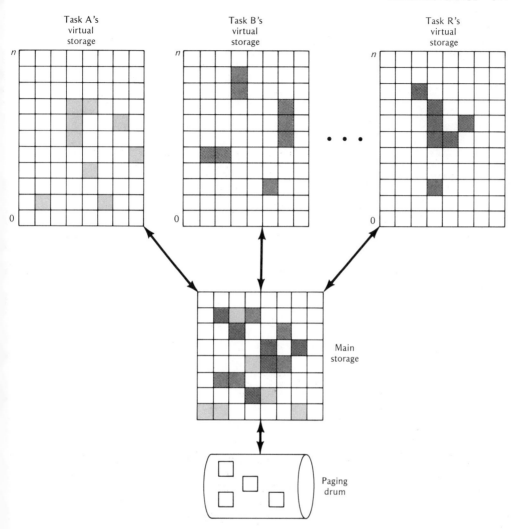

FIGURE C.12   **Virtual storage in a time-sharing system in which each task is assigned a complete virtual storage.**

Extended Glossary of Data Processing*

access generally the obtaining of data. A few examples: random-devices, such as disc and drum; serial-devices, such as magnetic tape.

access arm the mechanical device in a disc storage unit that holds one or more reading and writing heads.

access methods the technique and/or program code for moving data between main storage and I/O devices. By concentrating this code in common subroutines, the task of producing a program is simplified. Individual access methods are based upon a variety of data and/or file structures.

access time the time interval between when data are called for or requested to be stored in a storage device and when delivery or storage is completed, i.e., the read/write time.

accounting the interpretation, and organized method of recording all the transactions affecting the financial condition of a given business. In data processing, proper accounting for total data processing resources (personnel, equipment, facilities, and funds) requires:

- Identification of resources expended on information systems broken out by such items as equipment, telecommunications, manpower, and travel.
- Monitoring of actual expenses against planned figures on a periodic basis for both development and operations.
- Identification of expense transfers between locations and functions.
- Resource accounting by functional users to identify expenses in support of functional information requirements.
- Accurate measurement of expenses against plans.

accounting machine a keyboard-controlled machine that automatically produces accounting records or tabulations, usually on continuous forms.

accounts payable a liability representing amounts owed for merchandise or services purchased on open account or short term credit.

accounts receivable money due a business enterprise for merchandise sold on open account.

accumulator a register or storage location that forms the result of an arithmetic or logic operation.

accuracy the degree of freedom from error, frequently confused with precision. Accuracy refers to the degree of closeness to a "correct" value; precision refers to the degree of preciseness of a measurement. A mathematical algorithm may give a result to 10 decimal places (high precision), but be reliable (accurate) to only five places, if it is poorly designed.

acoustic coupler a data communications device that converts electrical data signals to/from tones for transmission over a telephone line using a conventional telephone headset.

---

* The glossary contains terms commonly used in data processing that were specially selected for this book from a comprehensive glossary containing over 1300 definitions, © 1976 DATAPRO RESEARCH CORPORATION, DELRAN, NEW JERSEY 08075. Reprinted with permission.

acronym   a word formed from the first letter (or letters) of the words in a phrase or name.

add-subtract time   the time required to perform addition or subtraction, not including the time required to fetch the operands from storage and put the result back into storage.

address   a computer system location that can be referred to in a program. It can refer to a main memory location, a terminal, a peripheral device, a cursor location, or any other physical item in a computer system.

address space   the complete range of addresses that is available to a programmer.

address translation   the process of changing the address of an item of data or an instruction to the address in main storage at which it is to be loaded or relocated. In virtual storage systems, the process of changing the address of an item of data or an instruction from its virtual storage address to its real storage address. See also dynamic address translation.

ADP (Automatic Data Processing)   see data processing.

algebraic language   an algorithmic language whose statements are structured to resemble the structure of algebraic expressions, e.g., algol, FORTRAN.

algol   a programming language designed for the concise, efficient expression of arithmetic and logical processes and the control of these processes. Taken from algorithmic language.

algorithm   a specific set of defined rules of processes for the solution of a problem in a finite number of steps. Contrast with heuristic.

allocate   to assign a resource for use in performing a specific task.

alphabetic character   a letter or other symbol, excluding digits.

alphameric characters   in programming, usually the characters A through Z, digits 0 through 9, and #, $, and @.

alphanumeric   see alphameric.

alternate route   in communications networks, a secondary path used to reach a destination if the primary path is unavailable.

ALU   arithmetic and logic unit. See arithmetic unit.

American Standard Code for Information Interchange   see ASCII.

analysis   the methodical study of a problem, and the separation of the problem into smaller related units for further detailed investigation.

analyst   a person who analyzes and defines problems and develops algorithms and procedures for their solution.

application-oriented language   a problem-oriented language whose statements contain or resemble the terminology of the user, e.g., a report program generator.

application package   a commercially available applications program. In most cases the routines in the application packages are necessarily written in a generalized way and will need to be modified to meet each user's own specific needs.

application program   a program written for or by a user that applies to his own work that tells the computer how to do specific jobs, e.g., payroll, inventory control. These programs do the productive work that serves the company, and usually represent the single biggest user investment in data processing.

application system   a collection of programs and documentation relevant to applications.

arithmetic and logic unit   see arithmetic unit.

arithmetic unit   the section of the CPU in a computing system that contains the circuits that do arithmetic operations and perform logical comparisons.

array   a named, ordered collection of data elements, all of which have identical attributes. An array has dimensions and its individual elements are referred to by subscripts. An array can also be an ordered collection of identical structures (PL/1 and FORTRAN).

ASCII   American (National) Standard Code for Information Interchange, X3.4–1968. This is a seven-bit-plus parity code established by the American National Standards Institute (formerly American Standards Association) to achieve compatibility between data services. Consists of 96 displayed characters (64 without lower case) and 32 non-displayed control characters.

Also called USASCII in an attempt to follow several name changes of the USA standards body; the last name change to ANSI was not followed. Although adopted in the early 1960's and, for a while, strongly supported by the U.S. government, the code has had limited usage outside of teleprinters and display terminals by vendors other than IBM (who has supported the code to some degree). Possibly, the code has survived because of the large Teletype teleprinter user base. Originally, it was a seven-level code. Later, an eighth bit was added, which could be fixed or represent character parity. Now, parity is a standard part of the code.

assemble the process of preparing a machine language program from a symbolic language program by substituting absolute operation codes and addresses for symbolic operation codes and addresses on a one-for-one basis.

assembler a computer program that converts symbolically coded computer source programs into object level, executable code. The assembler was the first major step in the automation of software development. It permitted symbolic (i.e., named) references to storage locations, rather than requiring the use of numbers, and eliminated the necessity of programming in binary or other machine language—a tedious and frustrating task at best. The development of macro capability, in which subroutines can be conveniently addressed symbolically, improved the programmer's lot still further.

assembler language a source language that includes symbolic machine language statements in which there is a one-to-one correspondence with computer instructions. This language lies midway between high level language and machine language (perhaps closer to the latter). Programmers use "assemblers" to make more efficient use of the computer. Mnemonics are used by the programmer.

assembly program a computer program that takes nonmachine-language instructions prepared by a programmer and converts them into a form that may be used by the computer.

associative storage a storage arrangement in which storage locations are identified by their contents, not by names or positions. Synonymous with content-addressed storage.

auditing computer management audit procedures are needed for development and operational projects to help ensure effective and efficient use of information systems resources. In setting up auditing procedures, the following requirements should be considered:

- audit teams should be made up of personnel with greater experience and technical range than those assigned to the projects under audit
- audits should be conducted by personnel other than those responsible for development, implementation and operation of the projects under audit
- audit findings should be reviewed by the appropriate levels of management to ensure resolution
- audit reporting should provide for periodic status meetings, immediate action reports, and a formal final report.

Audits of development projects cover:

- project plans and controls
- financial and internal controls
- mission status and goals
- user relationships
- interorganizational requirements
- security of data
- fallback capability
- hardware planning
- morale of personnel.

Audits of operational projects cover:

- data processing operations
- programming support
- data integrity, control and management
- total resource utilization
- user relationships and requirement
- security of data
- physical working conditions
- training of personnel.

Automatic Data Processing (ADP) see data processing.

automatic programming the process of using a computer to perform some stages of the work involved in preparing a computer program.

auxiliary equipment equipment not under direct control of the central processing unit. Synonymous with ancillary equipment.

auxiliary operation an operation performed by equipment offline or not under continuous control of the central processor.

auxiliary storage supplementary data storage other than main storage; for example, storage on magnetic tape or direct access devices. Synonymous with external storage, secondary storage. Contrast with main storage.

availability the degree to which a system or resource is ready when needed to process data.

available time time consisting of idle time and operating time. Synonymous with up-time. Excludes maintenance time. Operating time consists of development time, production time, and makeup time.

background in multiprogramming, the environment in which low-priority programs are executed. Under IBM's TSO extension of the operating system, the environment in which jobs are executed. One job step at a time is assigned to a region of main storage and remains in main storage to completion. Contrast with foreground.

background job a low-priority job, usually a batched or noninteractive job. Contrast with foreground job.

background processing the execution under automatic operating system control of lower-priority computer programs when higher-priority programs are not using the system resources. Contrast with foreground processing.

background program in multiprogramming, the program with the lowest priority. Background programs execute from batched or stacked job input. Under IBM's TSO extension of the operating system, a program executed in a region of main storage that is not swapped. Contrast with foreground program.

back up the advance provision of facilities, logical or physical, to speed the process of restart and recovery following failure. Such facilities might include duplicated files of transactions, periodic dumping of core or backing storage contents, duplicated processors, storage devices, terminals or telecommunications hardware and the switches to effect a changeover.

backup copy a copy of a file or data set that is kept for reference in case the original file or data set is destroyed.

BAL basic assembly language of the IBM 360 and IBM 370.

BASIC (Beginner's All-purpose Instruction Code) a common algebra-like high-level time-sharing computer programming language. It is easily learned and used for problem solving by engineers, scientists and others who may not be professional programmers. The language is similar to FORTRAN II and was developed by Dartmouth College for a General Electric 225 computer system. It is now common on almost all computer systems.

batched job a job that is grouped with other jobs as part of an input stream to a computing system.

batch mode application programs run on the computer one at a time. For example, financial transactions may be accumulated for a week, then fed into the computer in a batch to update the general ledger files and produce accounting reports. Batch processing computer systems generally do not require immediate updating of files. In batch processing, data is gathered up to a cutoff time and then processed. The user receives the output after a period usually measured in hours or days. Contrast this with on-line processing.

batch processing a technique in which a number of similar data or transactions are collected over a period of time and aggregated (batched) for sequential processing as a group during a machine run.

benchmark a point of reference from which measurements can be made. Involves the use of typical problems for comparisons of hardware performance. Used in determining which computer can best serve a particular purpose.

benchmark problem a problem used to evaluate the performance of computers relative to each other. A flowchart is often written out that is coded for execution on various systems. The problem-solving ability of different systems can thus be compared under as nearly equal circumstances as possible for an overall set of conditions.

binary a numbering system using only the two symbols 0 and 1 which is especially well adapted to computer use since 0 and 1 can be represented as on and off or negative charges and positive charges. The binary digits appear in strings of 0's and 1's. Most computers do their calculations in binary.

Binary Coded Decimal (BCD) a numbering system used in many computers where the basic binary system is used to represent decimal numbers.

binary digit (bit) in the binary notation either of the characters 0 or 1. "Bit" is the commonly used abbreviation for binary digit. The basic unit of information with which the computer works. The bit can take the form of a magnetized spot, an electronic impulse, a positively charged magnetic core, etc. A number of bits together are used to represent a character in the computer. (cf. byte, word).

bit transfer rate the number of bits transferred per unit time, usually expressed in bits per second (bps).

block a group of characters, bytes, or words communicated as a unit. See also, packet.

block diagram a diagram in which a system or computer program is represented by annotated boxes and interconnecting lines to show the basic function and the functional relationship between the parts. See flowchart.

blocking combining two or more records into one block.

blocking factor the number of logical records combined into one physical record or block. If the blocking factor were 4, there would then be four logical records in one (physical) block.

block length a measure of the size of a block, usually specified in units such as records, words, computer words, or characters.

bpi bits per inch.

bps bits per second. In serial data transmission, the instantaneous bit speed with which a device or channel transmits a character.

branch see conditional transfer.

bubble memories tiny cylinders of magnetization whose axes lie perpendicular to the plane of the single-crystal sheet that contains them. Magnetic bubbles arise when two magnetic fields are applied perpendicular to the sheet. A constant field strengthens and fattens the regions of the sheet whose magnetization lies along it. A pulsed field then breaks the strengthened regions into isolated bubbles, which are free to move within the plane of the sheet. Because the presence or absence of bubbles can represent digital information, and because other external fields can manipulate this information, magnetic-bubble devices will likely find uses in future data-storage systems.

bucket some addressing and indexing techniques provide as their output the address of a stored record. Others are less precise and provide the address of an area where a group of records is stored. We will refer to an area holding a group of records which are addressed jointly as a bucket. The bucket could be a physical record, a track, or a cell, but often it is a grouping determined by an addressing technique such as hashing and not necessarily related to the hardware.

buffer a high-speed area of storage that is temporarily reserved for use in performing the input/output operation, into which data is read or from which data is written. Used to accumulate data into blocks of sufficient size to be handled efficiently by a processor or terminal. Synonymous with I/O area.

business data processing see data processing. Synonym for administrative data processing.

byte a sequence of bits operated upon as a unit and usually shorter than a computer word. The representation of a character. Often, a sequence of eight adjacent binary digits that are operated upon as a unit and that constitute the smallest addressable unit in the system.

central processor (central processing unit) see CPU.

centralized data processing   data processing performed at a single, central location on data obtained from several geographical locations or managerial levels. Decentralized data processing involves processing at various managerial levels or geographical points throughout the organization.

chaining   a system of storing records in which each record belongs to a list or group of records and has a linking field for tracing the chain.

channel   in data communications, a path for electrical transmission between two or more points. Also called a circuit, facility, line, link or path. Within a computer, the device along which data flows between the input-output units of a computer and the CPU. Devices attached to the CPU communicate electronically with it via these channels.

character   an individual letter, numeral, or special character. In computers, characters are made up of a number of bits. Synonymous with byte.

character printer   a device that prints a single character at a time. Contrast with line printer.

character recognition   see magnetic ink character recognition.

checkpoint/restart facility   a facility for restarting execution of a program, at some point other than the beginning, after the program was terminated due to a program or system failure. A restart can begin at a checkpoint or from the beginning of a job step, and uses checkpoint records to reinitialize the system. In teleprocessing, a facility that records the status of the teleprocessing network at designated intervals or following certain events. Following system failure, the system can be restarted and continue without loss of messages.

circuit   in communications the complete electrical path providing one or two-way communication between two points comprising associated go and return channels. Compare: channel.

circuit switching   a method of communications, where an electrical connection between calling and called stations is established on demand for exclusive use of the circuit until the connection is re-

leased. See also: packet switching, store and forward, message switching.

closed shop   the operation of a computer facility in which programming is performed by a group of specialists rather than by the problem originators. The operation may also be described as closed shop if full-time trained operators, rather than user/programmers, serve as the operators. Contrast with open shop.

COBOL   COmmon Business Oriented Language. A data processing language that makes use of English language statements. It is especially adapted to business and commercial problems.

CODASYL   COnference On DAta SYstems Languages. The conference which developed COBOL.

code   to write a program. Also, the conventions specifying how data can be represented in a particular system.

coder   a person whose primary duty is to write (but not design) computer programs.

coding   the writing of a list of instructions which will cause a computer to perform specified operations.

collate   to compare and merge two or more similarly ordered sets of items into one ordered set.

collating sequence   an ordering assigned to a set of items, such that any two sets in that assigned order can be collated.

COM   records information onto microfilm or microfiche; stands for Computer Output Microfilm. Normal printed output of a computer reduced to one of several available microforms by a special output device that takes the place of the line-printer. The COM device allows high-quality output at speeds of 5000 or more lines per minute. Computer magnetic tape files are fed directly into a recording device for rapid preparation of the data, normally output to a printer, into extensively reduced film images. Viewers are used at strategic locations for rapid dissemination of information. The system has the advantage of rapid access to vital business data, and reducing storage space.

common carrier   a government-regulated private company that furnishes the general public with telecommunications service facilities; for example, a telephone or telegraph company.

communication transmission of intelligence between points of origin and reception without alteration of sequence or structure of the information content. See also data communication.

communication line any medium, such as a wire or a telephone circuit, that connects a remote station with a computer for the purpose of transmitting/receiving information.

compilation time the time during which a source language is compiled (translated) into a machine language object program as opposed to the time during which the program is actually being run (execution time).

compile to prepare a machine language program from a high-level, symbolic language program by generating more than one machine instruction for each symbolic statement, as well as performing the function of an assembler.

compilers programs that accept instructions in high-level language and convert each instruction into a multitude of machine language instructions, from which the computer can run the jobs. Also called language processors. If users program in a compiler language, the compiler will, for all practical purposes, become the computer; users could program for years and never know or care how many registers the computer has, or what the instruction set is; they need not be aware that the compiler has a host computer. But, if users want to make full use of all of the ranges, flexibilities and capabilities of a computer, they will program in assembly language.

computer a device capable of solving problems or manipulating data by accepting data, performing prescribed operations on the data, and supplying the results of these operations. Various types of computers are: analog computer, digital computer calculator.

computer assisted instruction (CAI) a data processing application in which a computing system is used to assist in the instruction of students. The application usually involves a dialog between the student and a computer program which informs him of his mistakes as he makes them.

computing system a central processing unit, with main storage, input/output channels, control units, direct access storage devices, and input/output devices connected to it.

concentrator a device which matches a larger number of input channels with a fewer number of output channels. The input channels are usually low-speed, asynchronous, and the output channel(s) is high-speed, synchronous. The low-speed channels may have the capability to be polled by a computer and may in turn poll terminals.

conditional transfer an instruction that may cause a departure from the sequence of instructions being followed depending upon the result of an operation, the contents of a register, or the setting of an indicator.

conditioning conditioning applies to voice grade lines. The better conditioned a line is, the less distortion is found and errors are less. Conditioning provides specified minimum values of line characteristics, and ranges from C1 to the best, C4. The common carrier will often recommend no conditioning for lines transmitting at 1200 Baud, C1 conditioning is recommended for 2400 Baud, C2 for 4800 Baud, and C4 for speeds above 4800 Baud.

configuration a group of machines which are interconnected and are programmed to operate as a system.

connect time a measure of system usage by a user, usually the time interval during which the user terminal was on line during a session. See also: CPU time.

console that part of a computer used for communication between the operator or maintenance engineer and the computer. A CRT terminal overcomes most of the disadvantages of a typewriter console. Its display rate is very fast—thousands of characters per second. It is quiet. Its output is flexible, easily modified and rearranged. Pointing facilities, such as light pens, allow users to easily designate symbols or vectors of interest.

contention a condition on a communications channel or in a peripheral device when two or more stations try to transmit at the same time, or access to a resource is simultaneously required by two or more users.

continuous form paper that is used on printers and accounting machines. Can represent checks or any type of pre-printed forms as long as the small holes are on the outer edges of the form. Holes are used by equipment to advance the paper line by line.

control cards see job control language.

control unit intermediary device between peripheral devices and channel. May be part of the I/O device or actual hardware.

conversational pertaining to a program or a system that carries on a dialog with a terminal user, alternately accepting input and then responding to the input quickly enough for the user to maintain his train of thought. See also interactive.

conversational mode communication between a terminal and a computer in which each entry from the terminal elicits a response from the computer and vice versa.

conversational remote job entry an IBM operating system facility for entering job control language statements from a remote terminal, and causing the scheduling and execution of the jobs described in the statements. The terminal user is prompted for missing operands or corrections. Abbreviated CRJE.

conversion the process of changing from one method of data processing to another or from one computer system to another. The so-called "controlled transition" from an old system to a new one. It involves careful planning for the various steps that have to be taken, and equally careful supervision of their execution. Also applies to the representation of data.

core memory core memory is the computer's internal information storehouse. Known as "real" memory as opposed to "Virtual Storage (VS)." Core memory is fast and expensive, but getting cheaper. Information in core memory is located by "addresses." Physically, core memory is made up of tiny doughnut-shaped pieces of magnetizable mate-

rial that can be in either an on or off state and can represent either a binary 1 (on) or binary 0 (off).

counter a device (e.g., a register) used to represent the number of occurrences of an event.

CPU (central processing unit) the heart of the general purpose computer that controls the interpretation and execution of instructions. Does not include interface, main memory or peripherals. It also controls input and output units and auxiliary attachments. Synonymous with mainframe.

CPU time the amount of time devoted by the central processing unit to the execution of instructions. Synonymous with CPU busy time. See also connect time.

CRJE an IBM designation meaning Conversational Remote Job Entry, and referring to a conversational language employed by a terminal user in submitting jobs to a central site and controlling their processing from a remote terminal station.

cross-assembler program refers to a program run on one computer but which was "built" or prepared on another computer. Small computers, especially, microcomputers generally do not have enough memory or are not equipped with the necessary peripheral devices to support many utility programs. In such a situation, another, larger computer is used to perform the assembly or compilation, and the programs used are called cross-assemblers or cross-compilers. For example, a microcomputer program might be cross-assembled on a time-sharing system or a large mainframe. Punched tape output from the time-sharing terminal or large mainframe would then be loaded into the microcomputer.

CRT display device a television-like picture tube used in visual display terminals on which images are produced on a cathode ray tube. The CRT enables batches or blocks of information in memory to be instantly accessed, read and displayed on a screen. In an on-line or real-time data processing system, the device permits instant or impromptu display of any desired information. It eliminates the necessity for printing the same information where the display, in temporary form, serves the application need.

cylinder an access mechanism may have many reading heads, each of which can read one track. A cylinder refers to that group of tracks which can be read without moving the access mechanism.

DAA see: data access arrangement.

DASD direct access storage device. See direct access.

DAT see dynamic address translation.

data 1) a general term that is used to denote any or all facts, numbers, letters, symbols, etc. which can be processed or produced by a computer, 2) implying source data or raw data as contrasted with information which is then defined to mean the knowledge obtained by the processing of data.

data bank a comprehensive collection of libraries of data. For example, one line of an invoice may form an item, a complete invoice may form a record, a complete set of such records may form a file, the collection of inventory control files may form a library, and the libraries used by an organization are known as its data bank. Synonymous with data base.

data base a nonredundant collection of interrelated data items processable by one or more applications:
- Nonredundant means that individual data elements appear only once (or at least less frequently than in normal file organizations) in the data base.
- Interrelated means that the files are constructed with an ordered and planned relationship that allows data elements to be tied together, even though they may not necessarily be in the same physical record.
- Processable by one or more applications means simply that data is shared and used by several different subsystems.

Development of a data base has some obvious benefits. By consolidating files, the user can obtain better control of data and reduce storage space and processing time. Equally important are the resultant data synchronization and timeliness. Use of a single information source makes processing more accurate because all subsystems refer to the same data.

A data base system helps overcome some of the complexities of data management by managing data centrally. It can provide additional data relationships while minimizing storage redundancy.

While the data are stored together with as little redundancy as possible to serve one or more applications in an optimal fashion; some measure of redundancy exists in many data bases in order to give improved access times or simpler addressing methods. Some records are duplicated to provide the capability to recover from accidental loss of data. There is a trade-off between nonredundancy and other desirable criteria, and so it would be better to use the phrase controlled redundancy or minimal redundancy.

data base administrator the custodian of the corporation's data—or that part of it which his system relates to. He controls the overall structure of the data. Note that being custodian of the data is quite separate from being its owner. A bank manager is the custodian of what is in his bank vault but not its owner. A department or an individual may own the data. The data administrator is responsible for safekeeping and controlling the data. The data may be used by any persons who are given authority to use it.

Note further that controlling the data does not mean that the data administrator knows the content of records. He knows that the PAYROLL record contains a SALARY data item, but he does not know the value recorded in this data item; indeed, he is specifically locked out of that data item so that he cannot read it. However, if the SALARY data item must be expanded from six digits to seven digits, only the data administrator can accomplish this change.

data base management system this establishes and employs rules about file organization and processing (e.g., a personnel record file) and establishes relationships between files and "records" in each file.

This subject is broad and complex. Many systems exist and others are evolving steadily. Adopting a given system locks you into a major commitment of dollars and computer resources.

data capture   in point-of-sale systems, "data capture" refers to functions performed by a terminal or computer in capturing information relative to a sale. The information captured is stored in a data base; it can then be accessed for providing audit trails, printing statements for customers, and other purposes.

data center   this is an abbreviated term applied to a computer equipped, central location. The center processes data and converts it to a desired form such as reports or other types of management information records.

data collection   the act of bringing data from one or more points to a central point.

data communication   the transmission and reception of data, often including operations such as coding, decoding and validation. Much data communication is carried over ordinary telephone lines, but often it requires specially conditioned leased lines where, in effect, several telephone lines are linked "side by side" to provide the required wide carrier bandwidth which carry a heavy and broad flow of information traffic. This is in contrast to voice-grade communication for which narrower carrier bandwidths are sufficient.

data communication equipment   the equipment that provides the functions required to establish, maintain, and terminate a connection, the signal conversion, and coding required for communication between data terminal equipment and data circuit. The data communication equipment may or may not be an integral part of a computer; e.g., a modem.

data conversion   the process of changing data from one form of representation to another.

data division   one of the four main component parts of a COBOL program. The data division describes the files to be used in the program and the records contained within the files. It also describes any internal working-storage records that will be needed.

data entry device   see key data entry device.

data file   a collection of related data records

organized in a specific manner. For example, a payroll file (one record for each employee, showing his rate of pay, deductions, etc.) or an inventory file (one record for each inventory item, showing the cost, selling price, number in stock, etc.). Data files are currently being replaced in information system design by a data base. Data files were developed to satisfy the particular needs of individual functions or departments. Operation of such systems may result in redundancy, inaccuracy and untimeliness of information. Therefore, an important potential benefit from the design of an information systems network is the collection of similar and related data into a data base, which can then supply this data to computer applications as needed. By capturing data once and making it available to all with a need to know, the data base satisfies the requirement of Business Systems Planning for data independence and organizational flexibility. This design overcomes many of the inherent problems of multiple files. See also data set.

data independence   often quoted as being one of the main attributes of a data base. It implies that the data and the application programs which use them are independent so that either may be changed without changing the other. In particular, the application programmer is insulated from the effects of changes made to the data, their organization, or the physical devices on which they are stored. In reality, just as the data are rarely completely nonredundant, so they are rarely completely independent.

data integrity   a performance measure based on the rate of undetected errors. See also integrity.

data item   a data item is the smallest unit of named data. It may consist of any number of bits or bytes.
A data item is often referred to as a field or data element. In COBOL it is called an elementary item.

data management   a major function of operating systems that involves organizing, cataloging, locating, storing, retrieving, and maintaining data.

data management system   assigns responsibility for data input and integrity, within the organization, to establish and maintain the data bases. Also provides necessary procedures and programs to collect, organize and maintain the data required by the information systems.

data manipulation language (DML)   the interface between the application program and the data-base management system, referred to as the data manipulation language, is embedded in a host language such as COBOL. It is desirable that it should have a syntax compatible with the host language because the application program has host language and data manipulation language statements intimately mixed. In fact it should appear to the programmer as though he were using a single language. There should be no enter or exit requirements from one language to the other.

data rate   the rate at which a channel carries data, measured in bits per second (bit/s).

data security   see security.

data set   in data organization and storage, a collection of records with logical relationships. See also data base. In data communications, see modem.

data set organization   in data organization and storage, the arrangement of information in a data set. For example, sequential organization or partitioned organization.

data sharing   the ability of users or computer processes at several nodes to access data at a single node.

data storage   the preservation of data in various data media for direct use by the system.

data transmission   the sending of data from one part of a system to another part. See also data communication.

DB/DC systems   data base/data communications systems.

debug   checking the logic of a program to isolate and remove the mistakes from a computer program or other software. Synonymous with troubleshoot.

decimal   numeric representation having a selection, choice, or condition in which there are ten possibilities.

decimal digit   one of the characters 0 through 9.

decision table   a matrix of contingencies that are to be considered with the actions to be taken. Sometimes used in place of flowcharts for program documentation.

decollate   to separate the copies of a multipart paper stock after printing.

delimiter   in data communications, a character that separates and organizes elements of data.

demand paging   in System/370 virtual storage systems, transfer of a page from external page storage to real storage at the time it is needed for execution.

demodulation   see modem.

destructive read   a computer memory read process that also erases the data in the source.

detail file   see transaction file.

development time   the time used for debugging new routines or hardware. Considered part of the operating time.

device independence   the ability to request I/O operations without regard for the characteristics of specific types of input/output devices. See also symbolic I/O assignment.

diagnostic   when the computer malfunctions, diagnostic programs or routines are brought into play to facilitate maintenance by identifying the problem and what piece of equipment is the culprit. Diagnostics are messages that are outputted from the compiler or assembler indicating possible errors in the source program.

dial-up line   a communications circuit that is established by a switched circuit connection.

digit   a character used to designate a quantity. The decimal system uses the digits 0–9; binary system: 0–1; hexadecimal system: 0–F. See also binary digit.

digital computer   a computer that solves problems by operating on discrete data representing variables by performing arithmetic and logical processes from a stored program on these data. Contrast analog computer.

digital data   information represented by a code consisting of a sequence of discrete elements.

direct-access storage device (DASD)   refers

to a basic type of storage medium which allows information to be accessed by positioning the medium or accessing mechanism directly to the information required, thus permitting direct addressing of data locations. The time required for such access is independent of the location of the data most recently accessed. Synonymous with random access. File organizations can be sequential, direct or indexed sequential. Contrast with serial or sequential access.

disc storage   see disk storage.

disk pack   a removable direct access storage media containing magnetic disks on which data is stored. Disk packs are mounted on a disk storage drive, such as the IBM 2311 Disk Storage Drive.

disk storage   stores information by magnetic recording on continuously rotating platters. Handles huge amounts of storage "on-line." Storage is "random access," meaning the recording arms hop around fast to any "address" (location) on any "track" on any disk to "read" or "write" (record) information. Much slower than core, but much less expensive for a given amount of information.

display   the representation of data in visible form, i.e., cathode ray tube, lights or indicators on the console of a computer, or a printed report.

distributed network   a network configuration in which all node pairs are connected either directly, or through redundant paths through intermediate nodes.

distributed processing   distributed-intelligence systems differ from multiprocessing systems in the way that tasks are handled. Although both systems use multiple processors, the tasks assigned to a distributed system remain fixed. By contrast, in a multiprocessing environment, a continuous stream of assignments is fed to a single node and allowed to be distributed according to complex resource allocation algorithms across the entire network.

distributed systems   refers to various arrangements of computers within an organization in which the organization's computer complex has many separate computing facilities all working in a cooperative manner, rather than the conventional single computer at a single location. Versatility of a computer system is often increased if small computers in geographically dispersed branches are used for simple tasks and a powerful central computer is available for larger tasks. Frequently an organization's central files are stored at the central computing facility, with the geographically dispersed smaller computers calling on the central files when they need them. Such an arrangement lessens the load on the central computer and reduces both the volume and cost of data transmission.

division   one of the four major portions of a COBOL program: the identification division, which names the program, the environment division, which indicates the machine equipment and equipment features to be used in the program, the data division, which defines the nature and characteristics of data to be processed, and the procedure division, which consists of statements directing the processing of data in a specified manner at execution time.

document   a medium and the data recorded on it for human use, e.g., a report sheet, a book. By extension, any record that has permanence and that can be read by man or machine.

documentation   the process of collecting and organizing documents or the information recorded in documents. Usually refers to development of material specifying inputs, operations and outputs to a computer program. Consists of information that describes an application (what it does, for whom, when, what data files it uses, etc.) This information is needed to understand what services are currently available.

documentation aids   these aids help automate the documentation process, and include flowcharts, programs, etc.

double precision   pertaining to the use of two computer words to represent a number.

down time   the period during which a computer is malfunctioning or not operating correctly because of mechanical or electronic failure, as opposed to available time, idle time, or stand-by time, during which the computer is functional.

drum storage   a direct access storage device

that records data magnetically on a rotating cylinder. A type of addressable auxiliary storage associated with some computers.

dump   to transfer all of the information contained in a record into another storage medium. For example, a disc record could be dumped onto tape. Usually, however, dump refers to copying from an internal storage device to an external storage device for a specific purpose such as to allow other use of the storage, as a safeguard against faults or errors or in connection with debugging. Also referred to as core dump, tape dump, or disk dump.

duplex   simultaneous two-way independent transmission in both directions. Also referred to as full-duplex.

dynamic address translation   in System/370 virtual storage systems, the change of a virtual storage address to a real storage address during execution of an instruction. See also address translation. A hardware feature that performs the translation. Abbreviated DAT.

EBCDIC (extended binary coded decimal interchange code) includes all 51 COBOL characters. The code provides for 256 different bit patterns. This 8-bit code is one of the top basic codes used in the IBM System. The other is an extended version of the USASCII code, called 8 bit USASCII (USASCII-8) used especially by IBM.

edit   the insertion of constant characters such as page numbers and decimal points into computer output to make it more recognizable and meaningful. Editing may include the modification or the addition of data, the deletion of unwanted data, format, code conversion, and the application of standard processes such as zero suppression.

EFTS   Electronic Funds Transfer Systems describes various computerized electronic communications systems which transfer financial information from one point to another. Although EFTS encompasses many diverse electronic automation projects, it is most frequently used to describe five types of systems: 1) "Paperless" clearing of checks between banks. This is accomplished locally and regionally by automated clearinghouses, and nationally by the Fed Wire and Bank Wire, 2) Centralized, checkless payrolls. This is accomplished by electronically debiting a business firm's account and crediting the bank accounts of the firm's employees, via magnetic tape rather than checks, 3) Centralized payment of recurring bills (utilities, mortgage, etc.) via payment authorization systems, 4) Point-of-sale systems. These are retail services that include check and credit authorization and overnight or immediate transfer of funds from customer accounts to merchant accounts, 5) Automated teller devices—unmanned banking stations. What makes these applications a part of EFTS is the use of computer technology to expedite the transfer of money without associated paper payment instruments.

emulation   the use of programming techniques and special machine features to permit a computing system to execute programs written for another system. This form of imitation is primarily done via hardware. Emulation is generally used to minimize the impact of conversion from one computer system to another, and is used to continue the use of production programs—as opposed to "simulation" which is used to study the operational characteristics of another (possibly theoretical) system.

emulator   when changing from one computer to a "new generation" computer, existing programs frequently won't run on the new machine. To save the cost of reprogramming, the manufacturer provides software and hardware to accept old programs and translates them to the new computer's machine language. Many programs for computers, two and three generations old, are running on present computers in emulation mode . . . very inefficiently and at excessive hardware/software cost. See also emulation.

encoding   this usually denotes inscribing or imprinting MICR characters on checks, deposits, and other documents, to be processed by an MICR (Magnetic Ink Character Recognition) sorter/reader.

environment division   one of the four main component parts of a COBOL program.

The environment division describes the computers upon which the source program is compiled and those on which the object program is executed, and provides a linkage between the logical concept of files and their records, and the physical aspects of the devices on which files are stored.

error a difference between a computed value and the theoretically correct value.

execute to carry out an instruction or perform a routine.

execution time for a computer system, the time at which an object program actually performs the instructions coded in the procedure division, using the actual data provided. For the arithmetic and logic unit portion of the CPU, the time during which an instruction is decoded and performed. See also instruction. Abbreviated E-time.

extent an extent is a collection of physical records which are contiguous in secondary storage.
How many records are in an extent depends on the physical size of the volume and the user's request for space allocation. Associated records are not necessarily stored contiguously; this depends on the storage organization.

feedback the return of part of the output of a machine, process, or system, to the computer as input from another phase especially for self-correcting or control purposes. Actual performance can thus be compared with planned performance.

field a group of characters that collectively mean something—a customer number, a telephone number, your weight, are fields.

file an organized, named collection of records treated as a unit, or the storage device on which these records are kept.

file maintenance the activity of keeping a file up to date by adding, changing, or deleting data.

file organization is concerned with the view of the data as perceived by the application programmers. The programmer may, for example, view the files as a master record with subordinate detail records. he describes his view of the files in his application program.

floppy disks these small flexible disks (about the size of 45 rpm phonograph records) are used for small random access requirements in controllers and CPU's and as a compact substitute for punched cards. A typical floppy disk provides capacity for about 300,000 data bytes. Floppies were originally developed for low cost, low capacity data storage, and relatively low data transfer rates.

flow-chart a systems analysis or programming tool to graphically present a procedure in which symbols are used to designate the logic of how a problem is solved. A flowchart represents the path of data through a problem solution. It defines the major phases of the processing as well as the various data media used. Flowcharts also enable the designer to conceptualize the procedure necessary and to visualize each step and item on a program. A completed flowchart is often a necessity to the achievement of accurate final code. A program is coded by writing down the successive steps which will cause the computer to perform the necessary logical operation for solving the problem as presented by the flowchart. Synonymous with block diagram.

foreground job a high-priority job, usually a real-time job. A teleprocessing or graphic display job that has an indefinite running time during which communication is established with one or more users at local or remote terminals. Contrast with background job.

foreground processing high-priority processing, usually for real-time activities, automatically given precedence, by means of interrupts, over lower priority "background" processing.

FORTRAN FORmula TRANslating system. A common language primarily used to express computer programs by arithmetic formulas. It is especially adapted to mathematical, scientific, and engineering problems.

front end processor a dedicated communications computer at the "front end" of a host computer. It may perform line control, message handling, code conversion, error control and applications functions such as control and operation of special-purpose terminals.

full duplex   see duplex.

function   in business, a job. In mathematics, an algebraic expression describing the relation between two or more variables.

general purpose computer   a computer designed to solve a large variety of problems, e.g., a stored program computer which may be adapted to any of a very large class of applications. Usable by most commercial installations.

general purpose operating system   an operating system designed to handle a wide variety of computing system applications.

generator   a computer program that constructs other programs to perform a particular type of operation—e.g., a report program generator.

GIGO (Garbage In-Garbage Out)   a term used to describe the data into and out of a computer system—that is, if the input data is bad (garbage in) then the output data will also be bad (garbage out).

grandfather cycle   the period during which magnetic tape records are retained before reusing so that records can be reconstructed in the event of loss of information stored on a magnetic tape.

half duplex   a circuit designed for transmission alternately in either direction but not both directions simultaneously. Contrast with duplex.

hardware   refers to physical computer equipment, for example, mechanical, magnetic, electrical, or electronic devices. Contrasts to software.

head   a device that reads, writes or erases data on a storage medium, e.g., a small electromagnet or the set of perforating, reading or marking devices used for punching, reading or printing on paper tape.

header   the initial portion of a message containing any information, control codes, and so on that are not part of the text (e.g., routine, priority, message type, destination addressee, and time of origination.)

header record   a record containing common, constant, or identifying information for a group of records which follow.

heuristic   pertaining to exploratory methods of problem solving in which solutions are arrived at by an interactive self-learning method.

hexadecimal   pertaining to a number system with a base of 16; valid digits range from 0 through F, where F represents the highest units position (15). Synonymous with hex.

hierarchical (computer) network   a computer network, in which processing and control functions are performed at several levels by computers specially suited in capability for the functions performed.

high-level languages   these are the ones you are most likely to hear about, such as COBOL (for business applications), FORTRAN (for mathematical work), PL/1, and BASIC (a simple, easy to use language). These languages were originally intended to be "machine independent," but it has not worked out that way, and variations are common. High level languages allow the programmer to express operations in a less direct form that is closer to the normal human language representation of the procedures the computer is to perform. Such languages are usually problem-oriented or procedure-oriented programming languages as distinguished from machine-oriented and/or mnemonic languages.

Hollerith code   an alphanumeric punched card code invented by Dr. Herman Hollerith in 1889, in which the top three positions in a column are called "zone" punches (12, 11, and 0, or Y, X, and 0, from the top downward), and are combined with the remaining punches, or digit punches (1 through 9) to represent alphabetic, numeric, and special characters.

host computer   the primary or controlling computer in a multiple computer network operation. This computer normally provides high level services such as computation, data base access, or special programs or programming languages for other computers in the network. A computer used to prepare programs for use on another computer or on another data processing system; for example, a computer used to compile, link edit, or test programs to be used on another system.

identification division   one of the four main component parts of a COBOL program. The identification division identifies the source program and the object program and, in addition, may include such documentation as the author's name, the installation where written, date written, etc.

implementation   in information systems, implementation is from the bottom up. The systems must be able to relate the existing data and applications to those needed to support the business processes and the organizations responsible and involved with the processes.

indexed sequential organization   a file organization used on direct access storage devices in which records are arranged in logical sequence by key. Indexes to these keys permit direct access to individual records.

information   the meaning derived from data which has been arranged and displayed in such a way that it can be related to that which is previously known (cf. data).

information bits   in telecommunications, those bits which are generated by the data source and which are not used for error control by the data transmission system.

information retrieval   a complete system application for cataloging vast amounts of stored data so that any part or all of this data can be called out at any time.

input   the data to be processed. Also the transfer of data to be processed from keyboard or an external storage device to an internal storage device.

input device   a device such as a card reader, CRT, teletypewriter, etc. which converts data from the form in which it has been received into electronic signals that can be interpreted by the computer.

input media   punched cards, punched tape, or MICR encoded documents are typical input media. The word input used alone often includes the medium or media. Any process which transfers data from an external source to an internal storage is designated as input.

input/output   a general term for the equipment used to communicate with a computer, commonly called I/O. The data involved in such communication.

input/output control system (IOCS)   a set of programs used in an operating system. It handles all input and output work such as opening files, closing files, backspacing tape, moving tape forward when a bad spot is encountered, etc. IOCS is used on all secondary storage devices. The programmer's source instructions (macro instructions) call in the IOCS instructions.

inquiry   a request for information from storage, for example, a request for the number of available airline seats, or a machine statement to initiate a search of library documents.

inquiry station   a terminal frequently with a typewriter keyboard where inquiries can be entered directly into the computer. The inquiry terminal can be geographically remote from the computer or at the computer console.

installation   a particular computing system, in terms of the work it does and the people who manage it, operate it, apply it to problems, service it, and use the results it produces.

instruction   a statement to the computer that specifies an operation to be performed by the system and the values or locations of all operands. An instruction is usually made up of an operation code and one or more operands.

integer   a numeric data item or literal that does not include any character positions to the right of the decimal point, actual or assumed, i.e., a whole number.

integrated circuit   a combination of the interconnected circuit elements inseparably associated on or within a continuous substrate.

integrity   preservation of data or programs for their intended purpose.
The resistance of a system to breakdown; automatic backup in which the system detects a potential failure and automatically uses alternatives to the failing component. An example would be a duplicated reference file employed so that the copy would be used if input errors were detected on the primary ver-

sion. Another example would be a permanently connected switch to provide two data paths to a storage device.

intelligent terminal
- Has some data processing ability built in.
- Communicates with CPU as necessary to obtain information and get big jobs done.
- Generally fast devices.

The intelligent terminal has flexible design for simplified user interface including custom keyboards, modularity to meet a variety of user requirements including control of other terminals and buffering capability to simplify the communications interface and the impact on host computer software. In other words, more and more of the communication functions can be done inside the terminal rather than at the host computer site.

interactive   pertaining to an application in which each entry elicits a response, as in an inquiry system or an airline reservation system. An interactive system may also be conversational, implying continuous dialog between the user and the system.

interface   a shared boundary defined by common physical interconnection characteristics, signal characteristics, and meanings of interchanged signals.

internal sort   a sorting technique that creates sequences of records or keys. Usually, it is a prelude to a merge phase in which the sequences created are reduced to one by an external merge.

interpreter   a computer program that translates and executes each source language statement before translating and executing the next one. Also known as incremental compiler. In EAM equipment, a machine used for printing data on cards.

interpreting   printing on paper tape or punched cards, with the meaning of the holes punched in the same tape or cards.

interrupt   a break in the normal flow of a computer routine such that the flow can be resumed from that point at a later time. An interrupt is usually caused by a signal from an external source. The availability of an interrupt feature relieves the computer of the need for time-consuming scanning to sense special conditions.

inverted file   in information retrieval, a method of organizing a cross-index file in which a keyword identifies a record; the items, numbers, or documents pertinent to that keyword are indicated. A file whose sequence has been reversed.

I/O channel   a piece of equipment forming part of the input-output system of a computer. Under the control of I/O commands the "channel" transfer blocks of data between the main store and peripherals.

item   a group of related characters treated as a unit. (A record is a group of related items, and a file is a group of related records.)

job   refers to a unit of work for the computing system from the standpoint of installation accounting and/or operating system control. A job consists of one or more job steps or programs. Usually includes all necessary computer programs, linkages, files and instructions to the operating system.

job control language (JCL)   a programming language used to code job control statements. These statements supply information to the operating system and the operators about the program; e.g., name of user, how much memory is required, estimated run time, priority, tapes required, other programs, etc. The JCL for modern operating systems is often quite complex and there are probably nearly as many user-prepared jobs which fail to execute due to JCL errors as failures due to compiler language errors.

K   two raised to the tenth power = 1024.

key data entry devices   the equipment used to prepare data so that the computer can accept it, including old-faithful keypunches (card punches) plus the newer key-to-tape and key-to-disk units.

keypunch   a keyboard operated device that punches holes into a card to represent data.

keyword   one of the significant and informative words in a title or document that describe the content of that document.

label   one or more characters used to identify a program statement or a data item.

language   a set of rules and conventions used to convey information.

language processor   see processor program.

laser   a device which transmits an extremely narrow and coherent beam of electromagnetic energy in the visible light spectrum.

latency   the time between an address interpretation and the start of the actual transfer. Latency includes the delay associated with access to storage devices.

light pen   a tool for terminal operators. This optional device can cause the computer to change or modify the display on the cathode-ray tube. The pen's response is transmitted to the computer which, in turn, relates the computer action to the section of the image being displayed. In this way, the operator can delete or add text, maintain tighter control over the program and choose alternative courses of action.

line printer   the computer output peripheral that prints an entire line of characters as a unit. This principle is largely responsible for the high printing speed.

list   a data structure in which each item of data can contain pointers to other items. Any data structure can be represented in this way, which allows the structure to be independent of the storage of the items.
Also means to print data. An 80–80 list means to print exactly as the data are contained on the card. Refer also to detail printing and group printing.

listing   a printout, usually prepared by a language translator, that lists the source language statements of a program.

load   in computer operations, the amount of scheduled work, usually expressed in terms of hours of work. In programming, to feed data or programs into the computer.

load sharing   the distribution of a given work load among a number of computers on a network.

loop   in programming, a sequence of computer instructions that repeats itself until a predetermined count or other test is satisfied.

machine instruction   an instruction that a particular machine can recognize and execute.

machine language   the final language all digital computers must use is binary. All other programming languages must be compiled or translated ultimately into binary code before entering the processor. Binary language is used directly by a machine, and is machine language.

magnetic bubble memory   an emerging new technology with storage densities of 10 million bits per square inch, and with realized densities of up to one billion bits/square inch conceivable.

magnetic core   a tiny doughnut-shaped piece of magnetic material that is used to store data in "main" memory.

magnetic disk   a flat circular plate with a magnetic surface on which data can be stored in the form of magnetized spots. These data are arranged in circular tracks around the disks and are accessible to reading and writing heads on an arm which can be moved to the desired track as the disk rotates.

magnetic drum   stores information in the form of magnetized spots on a continuously rotating cylinder. A magnetic reading and writing head is associated with each track so that the desired track can be selected by electrical switching. Provides faster access to information than disks do.

magnetic ink character recognition (MICR)   machine reading recognition of characters printed with magnetic ink. The MICR code consists of a set of 10 numeric symbols and four special symbols standardized as Font E-13B developed for the American Bankers Association. The special symbols are: amount, dash, transit numbers, and on us.

magnetic storage   any storage device that stores data, using magnetic properties such as magnetic cores, tapes, and films.

magnetic tape   flexible plastic tape, often 0.5 in. wide with 7 or 9 channels or horizontal rows, that extends the length on the tape. One side is uniformly coated with magnetic material on which data is stored. It is used for registering television images, sound or computer data. Magnetic tape is a "sequential" medium with a very low cost per bit, used for archival storage, sorts, etc. Magnetic tape is being suspended as a storage medium in on-line systems where immediate access is required.

main memory the primary storage facilities forming an integral physical part of the computer and directly controlled by the computer. In such internal facilities all data are automatically accessible to the computer. Contrast with external storage.

main program a program unit not containing a FUNCTION, SUBROUTINE, or BLOCK DATA statement and containing at least one executable statement. A main program is required for program execution.

main storage the general purpose program-addressable storage of a computer from which instructions may be executed and from which data can be loaded directly into registers.

management information system (MIS) a data processing system that is designed to furnish management and supervisory personnel with current information to aid in the performance of management functions. Data is recorded and processed for operational purposes, problems are isolated and referred to upper management for decision making and information is fed back to reflect progress in achieving major objectives.

manual input data entered manually by the operator or programmer to modify, continue, or resume processing of a computer program. Also entries which are manually recorded by the operator of an accounting machine, teller machine, etc.

mass storage massive amounts of on-line, secondary storage, readily accessible to the CPU of a computer providing lower cost for a given amount of information stored than main memory. Includes devices such as magnetic disk, drum, data cells, etc.

master file a main reference file of information used in a computer system. It provides information to be used by the program and can be updated and maintained to reflect the results of the processing operation.

media media can be classified as source, input and output. Checks are an example of source media. Input media can be punched tape or cards and magnetic tape. Output media can be punched tape, cards or magnetic tape.

medium (plural; media) the material on which data is recorded; for example, paper tape, cards, or magnetic tape.

memory memories accept and hold binary numbers and must be capable of storing data as well as programs. Memory must allow rapid access to information. Various types are: disc, drum, semiconductor, magnetic core, charge-coupled devices, bubble domain, etc.

memory dump a listing of the contents of a storage device, or selected parts of it.

merge an operation combining two or more files of data into one in a predetermined sequence.

message a sequence of characters used to convey information or data. In data communication, messages are usually in an agreed format with a 'heading,' which controls the destiny of the message and 'text' which consists of the data being carried.

message switching a method of receiving messages over communications networks, transmitting it to an intermediate point, storing it until the proper outgoing line and station are available and then transmitting it again towards its destination. The destination of each message is indicated by an address integral to the message.

microcomputer a complete tiny computing system, consisting of hardware and software, that usually sells for less than $500 and whose main processing blocks are made of semiconductor integrated circuits. In function and structure it is somewhat similar to a minicomputer, with the main difference being price, size, speed of execution, and computing power. The hardware of a microcomputer consists of the microprocessing unit (MPU) which is usually assembled on a PC board with memory and auxiliary circuits. Power supplies, control console, and cabinet are separate. Microprocessors fill the needs of low cost applications, such as electronic games, small-intersection traffic-control signals, simple industrial systems, appliances, vending machines, and of more complex control functions, such as editing typewriters, measurement systems, accounting machines, etc.

microfiche   a rectangular transparency approximately 4" × 6" containing multiple rows of greatly reduced page images of reports, catalogs, rate books, etc. Data reductions range from 13 up to several hundred times smaller than the originals. Uses are consistent with those of microfilm. Multiple copies are easily made to distribute pertinent data to various levels of operations. See "COM—Computer Output Microform."

microfilm   a roll of photographic film, small in size, but the record shown when the film is developed and projected onto a screen produces a legible copy of the item or form photographed. See "COM—Computer Output Microform."

microprocessors   most microprocessor systems are prototypes of the product development cycle. Microprocessors have almost no supporting software. The user is not only responsible for generating this support software, but also for defining the computer's instruction set, designing the supporting circuitry and· testing the resulting computer subsystem.

microsecond   one-millionth of a second.

minicomputer   a small programmable general purpose computer typically used for dedicated applications. Minicomputer often refers only to the mainframe, which typically sells for less than $25,000. Usually it is a parallel binary system with 8, 12, 16, 18, 24 or 36-bit word length incorporating semiconductor or magnetic core memory offering from 4K words to 64K words of storage and a cycle time of 0.2 to 8 microseconds or less. A bare minicomputer (one without cabinet, console and power supplies) consisting of a single PC card can sell for less than $1,000 in OEM quantities. Minicomputers are used nearly everywhere large computers were used in the past but with much lower prices. Minicomputer prices decay at the rate of 20 to 30% per year. As minicomputer prices have dropped, performance has increased and is likely to continue increasing as faster memories and logic evolve, thereby broadening the

applications base for the already ubiquitous minicomputer.

mnemonic   the assisting of human memory. Thus a mnemonic term is often an abbreviation designed to help programmers remember instructions, e.g. ART for arithmetic operation of MPY for multiply.

mode   the most common or frequent value in a group of values.

model   an approximate mathematical representation that simulates the behavior of a process, device or concept so that an increased understanding of the system is attained.

modem   contraction of Modulator-DEModulator. A device which modulates and demodulates signals transmitted over communication facilities. A modem is also known as a data set.

module   a program unit that is discrete and identifiable with respect to compiling, combining with other units, and loading.

multi-drop line   a communication system configuration using a single channel or line to serve multiple terminals. Use of this type of line normally requires some kind of polling mechanism, addressing each terminal with a unique ID. Also called multipoint line.

multiplexing   the division of a transmission facility into two or more channels either by splitting the frequency band transmitted by the channel into narrower bands, each of which is used to constitute a distinct channel (frequency-division multiplexing), or by allotting this common channel to several different information channels, one at a time (time-division multiplexing).

multiprocessing system   a computing system employing two or more interconnected processing units each having access to a common, jointly-addressable memory, to execute programs simultaneously. Also, loosely refers to parallel processing.

multiprogramming   since the CPU is usually the fastest component in the computer system, multiprogramming attempts to balance the CPU's speed with the slower peripherals by allowing several computer programs to run on the computer system at the same time. The goal is to make more efficient use of the system, by keeping more parts of it busy more of the time. The difficulty is that this increases greatly the complexity and cost of the Operating System and the overall computer system operation. This interleaving of the execution of two or more programs results in time-sharing of machine components.

nanosecond (ns, nsec) one-thousand-millionth (billionth) of a second. (10^{-9} second).

networking hooking geographically separated computers together over transmission lines. This allows computers to ship data to each other or ship jobs around (either in case of overload or because one of the computers has the necessary computer programs or data to do a particular job). In teleprocessing, a number of communication lines connecting a computer with remote terminals. In general communication applications, the interconnection of multiple communication channels, multiple terminals and/or computers (nodes). See also, multiprocessing.

node any station, terminal, terminal installation, communications computer, or communications computer installation in a computer network.

non-switched line a communications link which is permanently installed between two points.

numeric character a character that belongs to one of the set of digits 0 through 9.

object code absolute language output from a compiler or assembler which is itself executable machine code or is fully compiled and is ready to be loaded into the computer. The programmer writer, the source program, and a processor program translates it into object code.

OCR (optical character recognition) refers to light-sensitive recognition by machines of printed or written characters printed by an output device, such as cash register or adding machine, on a listing tape that serves as direct input to a computer system. This permits capturing input data at the entry source, bypassing additional processing operations. Contrast with MICR.

OEM (original equipment manufacturer) the OEM manufactures a product for assembly into a final system or larger subassembly by another manufacturer. Often OEMs make computer peripherals that are integrated into a complete system by a mainframe vendor.

off-line pertaining to equipment or devices not under direct control of the central processing unit. For example, the computer might generate a magnetic tape which would then be used to generate a report off-line while the computer was doing another job. May also be used to describe terminal equipment which is not connected to a transmission line.

on-line processing a general data processing term concerning access to computers, in which the input data enters the computer directly from the point of origin or in which output data is transmitted directly to where it is used. The process usually requires random access storage. In on-line processing, a user has direct and immediate access to the computer system via terminal devices. Information and instructions are entered via a terminal, processing by the computer is begun virtually immediately, and a response is received as soon as possible, often within seconds, for processing transactions are entered into the computer directly as they occur. Examples: stockbroker getting information on current stock price, credit card checking, factory terminals for production control information. Contrast with batch processing.

open shop a computer facility in which programming is performed by the user rather than by a group of computer programmers. The computer operation itself may be described as open shop if the user/programmer also serves as the operator, rather than a full time trained operator.

operand the part of a computer instruction that tells the computer where the data to be processed is stored.

operating system software that controls the operation of a data processing system and that may provide the following services:
- Determine what jobs are running and what parts of the computer system

are working on each job at any given time

- Impose standards and procedures on machine operation
- Take care of countless little details lumped together as "housekeeping."
- Invoke standard troubleshooting actions in cases of malfunction. They're usually very complex, gobbling up big quantities of core and disk storage. Sometimes called Supervisor, Executive, Monitor, Master Control Program, depending on the computer manufacturer.

operating time   that part of available time during which the hardware is operating. It includes development time, production time and makeup time. Contrast with idle time.

operation code   that part of a computer instruction that tells it what function (such as addition) to perform.

operator console   the device which enables the operator to communicate with the computer, i.e., it is used to enter data or information, to request and display stored data, to actuate various preprogrammed command routines, etc.

output device   a computer peripheral such as a card punch that converts electrical signals into the form used by the output device, such as holes punched into cards, etc.

output media   reports, documents and punched cards or tape are typical examples of output media. Output is a process of transferring data from internal memory to external storage or display. (Also into control signals for process control systems.)

overhead   nonproductive effort, taking place when the Operating System and the programs are performing administrative tasks, but no production work is getting done. In worst cases, overhead may eat up more machine time than data processing does. In general business, costs which cannot be directly related to individual products or services. These costs such as light, heat, supervision, and maintenance, are grouped in several pools (department overhead, factory overhead, general overhead) and distributed to units of product or service, by some standard method such as direct labor hours, direct labor dollars, direct materials dollars.

packet transmission   a packet-switching network is able to store and forward short standardized packets of messages very rapidly, typically within a fraction of a second. This is made possible by the use of very high-speed switching computers in which messages (packets) are stored in fast-access core memory exclusively, rather than on slower disk drives such as are used in conventional message switching systems. Packet switching, instead of structuring charges on the duration of the transmission or on the geographic distance between source and destination, enables charges to be based upon the quantity of data sent. As a result, users may process data with little concern for the geographic locations of computers and terminals.

page   in virtual storage systems, a fixed-length block of instructions, data, or both, that can be transferred between real storage and external page storage; typically about 4K bytes. A program will be divided into pages in order to minimize the total amount of main memory storage allocated to the program at any one time. The pages will normally be stored on a fast direct access store and can be moved into main memory by an operating system or hardware whenever the instructions of that subdivision need to be performed.

paging   in virtual storage systems, the process of transferring pages between real storage and external page storage. If a page is not transferred from auxiliary storage until it is actually needed, then paging is said to be done by demand. Look-ahead schemes have been implemented with some success.

paging rate   in virtual storage systems, the average number of page-ins and page-outs per unit of time.

paragraph   a set of one or more COBOL sentences, making up a logical processing entity, and preceded by a paragraph name or a paragraph header.

parity bit   used to check that data has been transmitted accurately; a receiving device counts the 'on' bits of every arriving byte; if odd parity is specified, an error condition will be flagged any time an even number of 'on' bits are detected.

password a unique word or string of characters that a program, computer operator, or user must supply to meet security requirements, before gaining access to data. In systems with time sharing, a one-to-eight-character symbol that the user may be required to supply at the time he logs on the system. The password is confidential, as opposed to the user identification.

performance together with facility, one of the two major factors on which the total productivity of a system depends. Performance is largely determined by a combination of three other factors: throughput, response time, and availability.

peripheral equipment usually called simple "peripherals." These are external (to the CPU) devices performing a wide variety of input, output and other tasks. "On-line" peripherals are connected electronically to the CPU. Others are "off-line" (not connected). Examples are card punches, card readers, magnetic tape and high speed printers.

physical record a basic unit of data which is read or written by a single input/output command to the computer. It is those data which are recorded between gaps on tape or address markers on disk. One physical record often contains multiple logical records, or segments. On most systems the length of a physical record is determined by the system programmer, on some devices it is of fixed length.

picosecond one trillionth of a second. One thousandth of a nanosecond.

PL/1 a high-level programming language, designed for use in a wide range of commercial and scientific computer applications which has features of FORTRAN and COBOL plus others.

polling a centrally controlled method of calling a number of points to permit them to transmit information in which each of the terminals sharing a communications line is periodically interrogated to determine whether it requires servicing. The multiplexer or control station sends a poll which, in effect asks

the terminal selected, "do you have anything to transmit?"

POS systems supermarkets and department stores are currently using point-of-sale (POS) systems, in which the cash register is actually a special-purpose computer terminal that can monitor and record transactions directly in the store's data files, inventory control, perform checks on credit card validity and handle many other marketing data functions. The supermarket industry's adoption of a universal product code system, under which most items sold in supermarkets are marked with machine-readable labels, is also spurring new POS applications. All POS functions could be integrated in a single EFT system. In such an integrated system, communications between banks and retail terminals would be handled by special switching and processing centers. Compatibility and standardization of POS/EFTS are important.

printer an output device that produces "printouts." Very slow compared to the CPU's electronic speed.

problem-oriented language a source language suited to describing procedural steps that is designed for convenience of program specification in a general problem area rather than for easy conversion to machine instruction code. The components of such a language may bear little resemblance to machine instructions. POLs are generally machine independent (Fortran, BASIC, COBOL, PL/1, etc.).

problem program any program that is executed when the central processing unit is in the problem state; that is, any program that does not contain privileged instructions. This includes language translators and service programs, as well as programs written by a user.

procedure division one of the four main component parts of a COBOL program. The procedure division contains instructions for solving a problem. The procedure division may contain imperative statements, conditional statements, paragraphs, procedures, and sections.

program a set of instructions arranged for directing a digital computer to perform a desired operation or operations. Also to prepare a program.

program library   a collection of programs and routines.

programmer   a person involved in designing, writing and testing computer programs. Depending upon the philosophy of the particular institution, programming can include substantial amounts of analysis, etc.

programming   preparing a list of instructions for the computer to use in the solution of a problem.

programming languages   the major kinds of programming languages are as follows: 1) Assembly or symbolic machine languages-one-to-one equivalence with computer instructions, but with symbols and mnemonics as aid to programming, 2) macroassembly languages which are the same as assembly or symbolic machine languages but permitting macroinstructions used for coding convenience, 3) procedure-oriented languages for expressing methods in the same way as expressed by algorithmic languages and 4) problem-oriented languages for expressing problems.
Procedure-oriented languages may be further divided into: (a) algebraic languages (numerical computation), (b) string-manipulating languages (text manipulation), (c) simulation languages (such as GPSS, DYNAMO) and (d) multipurpose languages (such as PL/1).

punched card   one of the oldest forms of mechanized data storage—a paper card in which numbers, letters, and special characters are represented by the holes punched in the card.

punched card equipment   conventional data processing machines operated by control panel rather than from a stored program. Feeds punched card information into computer (each card is a unit record), punches cards from information fed out by CPU and may include some sorting and collating (interleaving) ability.

RAM (Random-Access-Memory)   read and write from or to any memory location at high speed. There is no difference in the time required to operate to or from any address. Core memories are RAMs,

however the term is usually used with respect to semiconductor memories.

random access   pertaining to a storage device where data or blocks of data can be read in any particular order (e.g., disk). Random access devices do not have to be read from the beginning to find a specific address as is necessary with paper tape and magnetic tape. See direct access storage.

reading   the transferring of input data into the computer system.

read only memory (ROM)   information is permanently stored, and can be read from any location at high speed, but can never be altered. Users have to be sure that their program is right before they enable it into a ROM. On most computers once enabled, the program gives no flexibilities. Because programming ROMs is expensive, relatively short programs are usually enabled in a ROM.

real storage   in virtual storage systems, the storage of a computing system from which the central processing unit can directly obtain instructions and data, and to which it can directly return results. Same as processor storage.

real-time   the processing of transactions as they occur rather than batching them. Pertaining to an application in which response to input is fast enough to affect subsequent inputs and/or guide the process, such as a process control system or a computer assisted instruction system. On-line processing is used for real-time systems; however, not all on-line processing is real-time. An on-line system may be shared by many users so that response time is not always immediate.

record   a collection of related items of data (fields) treated as a unit.

redundancy   a repetition of information; or the insertion of information which is not new. Example: the use of check bits and check characters in data communication is a form of redundancy, hence the terms: cyclic redundancy, longitudinal redundancy, vertical redundancy.

register   a special section of main memory where data is held while it is being worked on.

relocatable addresses   the addresses used in

a program that can be positioned at almost any place in primary storage are relocatable addresses. Usually, however, once the program is link edited, the addresses used are absolute for the remainder of that processing run. Some programs are self-relocating—they can be located at any storage position at any particular time. Addresses are assigned by the use of base address and displacement or paging.

remote access pertaining to communication with a computer by terminal stations that are distant from that computer.

remote batch a method of entering jobs into the computer from a remote terminal in a conversational mode, for processing later in a batch processing mode. In this mode, a plant or office geographically distant from the central computer can load in a batch of transactions, transmit them to the computer and get back the results by mail or directly transmitted to a printer or other output device at the remote site.

remote job entry (RJE) allows various systems to share the resources of a batch oriented computer by giving the user access to centrally located data files and access to the power necessary to process those files. Allows input of a batch job by a card reader at a remote site and receipt of the output via a line printer or card punch at a remote site.

report program generator (RPG) a processing program that can be used to generate object programs that produce reports. RPG has powerful and relatively simple input/output file manipulation (including table look-up), but is relatively limited in algorithmic capabilities.

rerun a repeat of a machine run, usually because of a correction, an interrupt, or a false start.

response time the amount of time elapsed between generation of an inquiry at a data communications terminal and receipt of a response at that same terminal. Response time, thus defined, includes: transmission time to the computer, processing time at the computer, including access time to obtain any file records needed to answer the inquiry, and transmission time back to the terminal.

ring network a computer network where each computer is connected to adjacent computers.

running time the time during which a machine is actually producing. For example, the running time would include execution, but would not include set up, maintenance, waiting for the operator.

satellite computer a processor connected locally or remotely to a larger central processor, and performing certain processing tasks—sometimes independent of the central processor, sometimes subordinate to the central processor.

security the general subject of making sure the computerized data and program files of the company can't be accessed, obtained or modified by unauthorized personnel, and can't be fouled up by the computer or its programs. Security is implemented by special software, special hardware and the computer's operating procedure.

seek to position the access mechanism of a direct access device at a specified location.

seek time the time that is needed to position the access mechanism of a direct access storage device at a specified position. See also access time.

selector channel a channel designed to operate with only one I/O device at a time. Once the I/O device is selected, a complete record is transferred one byte at a time. Contrast with block multiplexer channel, multiplexer channel.

sequential in numeric sequence, normally in ascending order.

sequential access a term used to describe files such as magnetic tape which must be searched serially from the beginning to find any desired record.

sequential data set a data set whose records are organized on the basis of their successive physical positions, such as on magnetic tape. Contrast with direct data set.

sequential storage secondary storage where data are arranged in ascending or descending order, usually by item number. This type of storage is usually associated with magnetic tape. Sequential storage usually is processed in a batch.

simulation the use of programming techniques alone to duplicate the operation of one computing system on another computing system. In computer programming, the technique of setting up a routine for one computer to make it operate as nearly as possible like some other computer. Contrast with emulation.

software the term software was coined to contrast with the "iron" or hardware of a computer system. Software is the programs (stored sets of instructions) which govern the operation of a computer system and make the hardware run. Software is a key determining factor in getting more computer power per dollar. The processor programs library routines, manuals and other service programs supplied by a computer manufacturer to facilitate the use of a computer. In addition, it may refer to other programs specially developed to fit the user's needs. All the documents associated with a computer.

solid-state device any element that can control current without moving parts, heated filaments, or vacuum gaps. All semiconductors are solid-state devices, although not all solid-state devices (e.g., transformers) are semiconductors.

sort a processing run or operation to distribute data in numerical, alphabetic, or alphanumeric groups according to a given standard or rule. A key consisting of a prescribed, uniform string of characters can be used as a means of making workable size groups from a large volume of records.

source deck stack of program cards ready to feed to compilers.

source document an original record of some type which is to be converted into machine readable form.

source program a computer program written in symbolic language which will be converted into an absolute language object program using a processor program.

special character a character that is neither numeric nor alphabetic. Special characters in COBOL include the space ( ), the period (.), as well as the following:
$$+-*/=\$,;")($$

spooling the reading and writing of input and output streams on auxiliary storage devices, concurrently with job execution, in a format convenient for later processing or output operations. Synonymous with concurrent peripheral operations. By placing the output to slow devices into queues on mass storage devices to await transmission, more efficient use of the system is allowed, since programs using low-speed devices can run to completion quickly and make room for others.

star network a computer network with peripheral nodes all connected to one or more computers at a centrally located facility. See also centralized network.

statement in programming, an expression or generalized instruction in a source language.

storage a computer oriented medium in which data is retained. Primary (main) storage—internal storage area where the data and program instructions are retained for active use in the system—normally core storage. Auxiliary or external storage is for less active data. These may include magnetic tape, disk, or drum.

storage capacity the amount of data that can be contained in a storage device or main memory. 1K = 1024 bytes. If the storage capacity of a computer is 16K, the capacity is 16,384 characters.

storage fragmentation a phenomenon observed in systems using dynamic allocation of core storage which permit variability in the amount allocated. Smaller areas of core tend to become frequent as requests are met by allocation of larger spaces. The number of separate spaces which fail to meet requests increases, giving rise to an increasing list of spaces available and an increasing time to service requests. Curable by reorganizing core. Preventable by allowing only a few fixed sizes of buffer in core requests.

storage protection methods of preventing access to storage. Synonymous with memory protection.

string a connected sequence of characters of bits that is treated as a single data item.

subroutine subroutines are program segments which perform a specific function. A major reason for using subroutines is that they reduce programming and debugging labor when a specific function is required to be executed at more than one point in a program. By creating the required function as a subroutine, the statements associated with that function may be coded once and executed at many different points in a program.

swapping in systems with time sharing, a process that writes a job's main storage image to auxiliary storage, and reads another job's main storage image into main storage.

switched line typically a telephone line that is connected to the switched telephone network.

symbolic language a language used in programming which is convenient for the programmer because it uses mnemonic terms that are easy to remember. Once the program has been written in symbolic language, it must be converted to absolute language using a "processor program."

symbolic name a data field identifier. It is synonymous with symbolic address. The programmer creates symbolic names; the computer changes these symbolic names into storage addresses. FORTRAN and BASIC call the symbolic name a variable while other languages refer to it as a symbolic name.

system programmer a programmer who plans, generates, maintains, extends, and controls the use of an operating system with the aim of improving the overall productivity of an installation. Also, a programmer who designs programming systems and other applications.

systems analyst defines the applications problem, determines system specifications, recommends equipment changes, and designs data processing procedures. Devises data verification methods. Prepares block diagrams and record layouts from which the programmer prepares flow-charts. May assist in or supervise the preparation of flow-charts.

systems test the running of the whole system against test data. A complete simulation of the actual running system for purposes of testing out the adequacy of the system.

tape drive a peripheral unit that writes data on a reel of magnetic tape. Storage is sequential in that access requires moving along the length of tape to the desired record position. Tape storage is less expensive than disk storage and access is slower.

telecommunications data transmission between a computing system and remotely located devices via a unit that performs the necessary format conversion and controls the rate of transmission.

telepak a leased channel offering of telephone companies and Western Union providing specific-size bundles of voice-grade, telegraph-grade, subvoice-grade, and broadband channels between two points; also, just the broadband channels. Mileage charges are constant for each mile rather than regressive as in conventional single-leased lines.

teleprocessing the processing of data that is received from or sent to remote locations by way of telecommunication lines. Such systems are essential to hook up remote terminals or connect geographically separated computers. See also telecommunications.

terminal a device equipped with a keyboard and some kind of display that is connected to a computer system for the input and/or output of data. A terminal may be as simple as a telephone; as complex as a small computer. Terminals are generally used for on-line systems.

text editing refers to specific flexible editing facilities which have been designed into a computer program to permit the original keyboarding of textual copy without regard for the eventual format or medium for publication. Once the copy has been placed in computer storage, it can be edited and justified easily and quickly into any required column width and for any specified type font, merely by specifying the format required.

time-sharing a method of operation in which the resources of a computer facility are shared by several users via terminals for different purposes at (apparently) the same time. Although the computer actually services each user in sequence, the high speed of the computer makes it appear that the users are all handled simultaneously. The user and the computer usually communicate by way of a higher level, easy-to-learn computer language.

time slice   an interval of time on the central processing unit allocated for use in performing a task. Once the interval has expired, CPU time is allocated to another task; thus a task cannot monopolize CPU time beyond a fixed limit. IN systems with time sharing, a segment of time allocated to a terminal job.

track   a track on a direct-access device contains that data which can be read by a single reading head without changing its position. It may refer to the track on a drum or disk which rotates under a reading head.

turnaround time   the elapsed time between submission of a job to a computing center and the return of results. In communications, the actual time required to reverse the direction of transmission from send to receive or vice versa when using a half-duplex circuit. For most communications facilities, there will be time required by line propagation and line effects, modem timing, and machine reaction. A typical time is 200 milliseconds on a half-duplex telephone connection.

turnkey system   a system in which the manufacturer takes full responsibility for complete system design and installation, and supplies all necessary hardware, software, and documentation elements.

unbundled   the services, programs, training, etc. sold independently of the computer hardware by the computer hardware manufacturer. Thus, a computer manufacturer who does include all products and services in a single price is said to be "bundled."

unit record   a card containing one complete record; a punched card.

update   to modify a master file with current transaction information according to a specified procedure.

up time   the time during which a piece of equipment is either operating or available for operation as opposed to down time when no productive work can be accomplished.

user   anyone who requires the services of a computing system.

utility program   specialized program per-

forming a frequently required everyday task. Examples include: sorting, report generation, file updating, file dump, and backup (maintaining backup files in case a master working file is destroyed). Those programs are usually supplied by the manufacturer of the equipment.

variable   a quantity which can assume any of a given set of values.

variable-length record   a record having a length independent of the length of other records with which it is logically or physically associated.

virtual address   in virtual storage systems, an address that refers to virtual storage and must, therefore, be translated into a real storage address when it is used.

virtual storage   addressable space that appears to the user as real storage, from which instructions and data are mapped into real storage locations. The size of virtual storage is limited by the addressing scheme of the computing system (or virtual machine) and by the amount of auxiliary storage available, rather than by the actual number of real storage locations. This procedure leaves the programmer free to address total storage without concern as to whether primary or secondary storage is actually being addressed, and effectively includes the large, inexpensive capacity of secondary storage in the system. Optimally, the computer should be able to operate either with or without virtual storage without major software modification. Benefits of virtual storage operation are enhanced when it is implemented by hardware which carries out the data swapping algorithms.

voice-grade channel   typically a telephone circuit normally used for speech communication, and accommodating frequencies from 300 to 3,000 Hz. Up to 10,000 Hz can be transmitted.

volume   a recording medium that is mounted and demounted as a unit, for example, a reel of magnetic tape, a disk pack, a data cell.

WATS (Wide Area Telephone Service)   a service provided by telephone companies which permits a customer, by use of an access line, to make calls to telephones in a specific zone on a dial basis for a flat monthly charge. Monthly charges are based on the size of the area in which the calls are placed, not on the number or length of calls. Under the WATS arrangement, the U.S. is divided into six zones to be called on a fulltime or measured-time basis.

wait state   the condition of a central processing unit when all operations are suspended.

word   a group of characters occupying one storage location in a computer. It is treated by the computer circuits as an entity, by the control unit as an instruction, and by the arithmetic unit as a quantity.

word processing   the transformation of ideas and information into a readable form of communication through the management of procedures, equipment and personnel.

write   to record data in a storage device, a data medium, or an output display.

zero suppression   the elimination of nonsignificant zeros in a numeral.

INDEX